MASTERING
LOTUS 1-2-3

A Problem-Solving Approach/Release 2.2

MASTERING LOTUS 1-2-3

A Problem-Solving Approach/Release 2.2

JAMES GIPS
Boston College

WILEY

JOHN WILEY & SONS, INC.

New York ■ Chichester ■ Brisbane ■ Toronto ■ Singapore

Cover: *Hans Holbein the Younger, Portrait of Erasmus of Rotterdam. Paris, Louvre. Scala/Art Resource, New York.*

ACQUISITIONS EDITOR	Joe Dougherty	MANUFACTURING MANAGER	Lorraine Fumoso
PRODUCTION MANAGER	Joe Ford	COPY EDITOR	Marjorie Shustak
DESIGN SUPERVISOR	Ann Marie Renzi	DIGITAL PRODUCTION SUPERVISOR	Ann Louise Stevens
PRODUCTION SUPERVISOR	Gay Nichols		

CREDITS

The data in Exercise 15-2 are excerpted from *Datamation* (June 1990), © 1990 by Cahners/Ziff Publishing Associates, L.P.

The data in Exercise 15-4 are from *The 100: A Ranking of the Most Influential Persons in History.* Copyright © 1978 by Hart Publishing Company, Inc. Published by arrangement with Carol Publishing Group. A Citadel Press Book.

The real estate spreadsheet in Figure 1-3, and later, is from an example used by Lotus. The material in Appendixes A, B, C, E, H, and I is based on the Lotus 1-2-3 Help system. Copyright © 1990 Lotus Development Corporation. Used with permission.

Lotus®, 1-2-3®, Symphony®, and Visicalc® are registered trademarks of Lotus Development Corporation.

Allways™ is a trademark of Lotus Development Corporation.

Apple II® and Apple III® are registered trademarks of Apple Computer Inc.

Compaq® is a registered trademark of Compaq Computer Corporation.

dBASE II®, dBASE III®, and dBASE III Plus® are registered trademarks of Ashton-Tate Corporation.

Epson® is a registered trademark of Seiko Epson Corporation.

Excel™ is a trademark of Microsoft Corporation.

IBM®, IBM PC®, IBM PS/1®, IBM PS/2®, and OS/2® are registered trademarks of International Business Machines, Inc.

Paradox® and Quattro® are registered trademarks of Borland International.

Q&A® is a registered trademark of Symantec Corporation.

SuperCalc® is a registered trademark of Software Associates Inc.

UNIX System V™ is a trademark of AT&T Bell Labs.

VAX™ is a trademark of Digital Equipment Corporation.

Microsoft Works® is a registered trademark of Microsoft Corporation.

Library of Congress Cataloging-in-Publication Data

Gips, James, 1946-
  Mastering Lotus 1-2-3 release 2.2: problem-solving approach/James Gips.

    p. cm.
    Includes index.
    ISBN 0-471-53995-3 (paper)
    1. Lotus 1-2-3 (Computer program) 2. Business—Computer programs. 3. Electronic spreadsheets. I. Title.

HF5548.4.L67G57   1991   90-29066
650′.0285′5369—dc20   CIP

Printed in the United States of America

10 9 8 7 6 5 4 3

TO AMY AND JONATHAN

PREFACE

Lotus® 1-2-3® is both useful and fun. Millions of people have purchased Lotus 1-2-3 to run on their personal computers, and many of them use the program every day to solve all kinds of problems. Lotus 1-2-3 is fun to learn and fun to use. The program is rich and well-designed and has many capabilities. There is a real sense of satisfaction in mastering the fundamentals of the program and then in mastering more and more of its features. As you become increasingly capable in Lotus 1-2-3, you can use the program to solve a wider variety of problems and increasingly difficult problems.

The purpose of this book is to help you master Lotus 1-2-3.

This book has grown out of my teaching thousands of people to use the computer over the past fifteen years, both in colleges and in industry. I love teaching. I love seeing people walk in knowing little or nothing about using the computer and perhaps being a bit fearful, then watching the lights turn on in their minds as they become increasingly capable, and then seeing them leave brimming with confidence in their newly gained abilities.

Over the years I have been fortunate to be able to teach people to use Lotus 1-2-3 and other similar programs many times. I believe I have learned from this process and have been able to refine my presentations—to see what works and what doesn't, to see where people have problems and where people gain valuable insights and skills. I hope this is reflected in this text book.

My general approach to teaching Lotus 1-2-3 is to explain and demonstrate the program at a keystroke level, but also at a conceptual level. I like to show how a capability of Lotus 1-2-3 can be used to solve a problem, and along the way make sure that people understand the basic concept involved. But then, after an hour of listening and watching and asking, it is important for people to try to use that aspect of the program on their own to solve increasingly challenging problems.

This book is structured the same way. In the body of each chapter, we discuss new capabilities in Lotus 1-2-3 and use them to solve problems. We cover the keystrokes involved and the concepts that underlie the keystrokes. We look at the pitfalls and some of the unexpected applications, and I try to answer the questions that I think might arise. At the end of each chapter is a set of exercises. Some of the exercises take you step-by-step through the keystrokes. Some of the exercises are paper and pencil exercises that help you ensure that you understand the ideas in the chapter. Some of the exercises simply present you with a problem that can be solved using the capabilities and features just covered. This is where the real learning and integration takes place. It is in the exercises, in the problem solving, that the real mastery of Lotus 1-2-3 develops. An old proverb says, "I hear and I forget. I see and I remember. I do and I understand."

Overall, the book is divided into two parts. In Part I, we proceed through the *fundamentals* of Lotus 1-2-3. Here the material is presented sequentially and the instructor or reader is encouraged to go through the material in the order presented. In Part II, we cover various *features* of Lotus 1-2-3. Here the instructor or reader can select the chapters of interest. The Appendixes are meant to be a rich source of reference material on Lotus 1-2-3.

A brief note about the cover. The cover shows a portrait of Erasmus that was painted by Hans Holbein the Younger in 1523 and is on display in the Louvre Museum in Paris. Erasmus (1466?–1536) was a Dutch priest and scholar. He is said to have been the last person to have mastered all of human knowledge, to know all that was known at his time. All of human knowledge! If Erasmus could master all of human knowledge, surely we can master Lotus 1-2-3.

Mastering Lotus 1-2-3 is both useful and fun. Let's get started!

JAMES GIPS

ACKNOWLDGEMENTS

This book is based on classes and seminars I have given at several institutions and I would like to acknowledge them here. My home is Boston College, where I teach undergraduates and graduate students about computers. For four summers I taught "Computing in a Business Environment" at Harvard University. I have taught in the Master of Science in Management program at the Arthur D. Little Management Education Institute and in their shorter executive education programs. Over the past ten years I have taught managers and executives at many organizations, including Arthur D. Little, Chase Manhattan Bank, Digital Equipment, McGraw-Hill, and State Street Bank, at locations from New York to Manila.

Harvey Deitel inspired and encouraged me to develop this book. Pete Olivieri of Boston College got me started in teaching about personal computers and electronic spreadsheets. Ed Ridolfi at McGraw-Hill and Ken Hoadley and Steve Hurley at Arthur D. Little have been firm supporters of my efforts. David Helmstadter of Houghton Mifflin gave me key advice and encouragement at a critical juncture for this project. Thanks!

This book was written mainly during a sabbatical from Boston College. I am grateful for the university's continuing support.

I have benefitted from the suggestions of reviewers at various stages of this project. I would like to thank Gary Armstrong of Shippensburg University, Jim Davies of DeAnza College, Wallace J. Growney of Susquehanna University, Priscilla McGill of Rogue Community College, Marilyn Meyer of Fresno City College, John W. Miller of Pennsylvania College of Technology, Pandu Tadikamalla of University of Pittsburgh, and James Teng of University of Pittsburgh for their insightful and encouraging reviews.

Any book is a team effort. I would like to thank Joe Dougherty, Bill Oldsey, Steve Kraham, Carolyn Henderson, Will Pesce, Bonnie Lieberman, Mike Donahue, Paul Constantine, Cary Weinberger, Ann Marie Renzi, David Levy, Marjorie Shustak, Sally Ann Bailey, Laura Nichols, Ann Louise Stevens, Joe Ford, and Gay Nichols (listed in chronological order) and all of the other people at John Wiley & Sons, Inc., for their efforts. No doubt there were many more people involved before the book saw the light of day. I especially would like to thank Joe Dougherty, the editor for this project, for all of his help and good advice.

Pat, my wife, and Jonathan and Amy, our children, have borne the many hours I have spent sitting before my computer screen with encouragement and good humor. I am grateful.

I would like to be able to acknowledge *your* contribution in the next edition of this book. If you have any suggestions or modifications or additions or exercises or any comments whatsoever, please write me at Carroll School of Management, Fulton Hall 423, Boston College, Chestnut Hill, Mass., 02167. I hope to hear from you and hope you enjoy and benefit from this book.

JAMES GIPS

■ CONTENTS

PART II: FEATURES

FUNDAMENTALS

INTRODUCTION

WHAT IS LOTUS 1-2-3 ?

Lotus 1-2-3 is a best-selling computer program published by Lotus Development Corporation of Cambridge, Massachusetts. The program has been put to a wide variety of uses. It is especially useful for tasks requiring numerical calculations, that is, problems that would be done by hand using paper, pencil, and calculator. There are several versions of Lotus 1-2-3. This book is about Lotus 1-2-3 Release 2.2, the most popular version, which runs on IBM® Personal Computers®, IBM PS/1® and PS/2® computers, Compaq® computers, Epson® computers, and other compatible computers.

WHAT DOES "1-2-3" MEAN ?

The primary meaning conveyed by "1-2-3" is that the program has three functions:
(1) **electronic spreadsheet**, (2) **business graphics**, and (3) **data management**.

The most important and most common use of the program is as an electronic spreadsheet. In an electronic spreadsheet program, the main memory of the computer is divided into rows and columns. The computer is used to perform mainly numeric computations. An example of the use of Lotus 1-2-3 as an electronic spreadsheet is shown in Figure 1-1. Here, one enters in the Net Sales and different Operating Expenses for each of the quarters. The computer calculates the Year To Date totals in column F, the Total Operating Expenses figures in row 17, and the Operating Income figures in row 19.

In business graphics, the computer automatically draws bar charts, line charts, pie charts, and other types of charts used in business. Lotus 1-2-3 draws these charts based on numbers in the spreadsheet. For example the bar chart in Figure 1-2 can be drawn automatically from the numbers shown in the spreadsheet in Figure 1-1.

In data management, the computer is used to deal with large amounts of information. Figure 1-3 shows Lotus 1-2-3 being used for data management. Each row corresponds to a different house for sale. Lotus 1-2-3 could be instructed to find all the houses with more than three bedrooms that are heated with oil. Or the program could be instructed to rearrange the rows so they are in order by price.

	A	B	C	D	E	F
			INCOME STATEMENT 1990			
			Widgets Unlimited			
5		Q1	Q2	Q3	Q4	YTD
7	Net Sales	$65,400	$68,900	$58,600	$73,445	$266,345
10	Operating Expenses:					
11	Payroll	9,120	10,667	10,230	11,878	41,895
12	Utilities	2,133	2,471	2,490	1,751	8,845
13	Rent	1,900	1,900	1,900	1,900	7,600
14	Ads	2,040	2,584	2,176	3,468	10,268
15	COG Sold	24,924	26,014	21,882	30,041	102,861
17	Tot Op Exp	40,117	43,636	38,678	49,038	171,469
19	Operating Income	$25,283	$25,264	$19,922	$24,407	$94,876

FIGURE 1-1 A sample Lotus 1-2-3 worksheet.

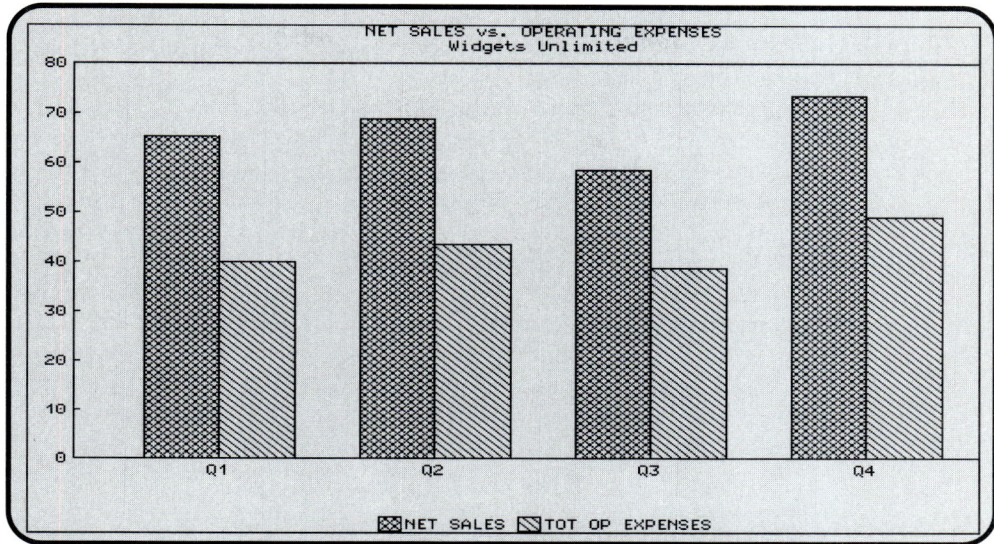

FIGURE 1-2 A graph drawn by Lotus 1-2-3 based on the worksheet in Figure 1-1.

FIGURE 1-3 Part of a real estate data base in Lotus 1-2-3.

Thus, Lotus 1-2-3 was one of the first **integrated software** programs. Integrated software is a program that has more than one function. As we have seen, Lotus 1-2-3 has three: electronic spreadsheet, business graphics, and data management.

A second, perhaps subconscious, message conveyed by the name "1-2-3" is the phrase "Easy as 1-2-3." Lotus 1-2-3 is relatively easy to learn and easy to use. In the "bad old days" of computers, before the advent of personal computers and electronic spreadsheets, people who wanted to use the computer to solve some numerical or financial problem usually had to write a special-purpose computer program, in a language like BASIC or Fortran. It is *much* easier to use Lotus 1-2-3 to solve a problem than it is to write a special-purpose computer program. A problem that requires 1 hour to solve using Lotus 1-2-3 might require 10 hours or more to solve by writing a traditional program. Still, the program is not quite "Easy as 1-2-3." If it were, there would be no reason for this book and no reason for you to "learn" to use the program. You would simply start up the program, and it would be immediately obvious what you should do. There are important concepts and key techniques to learn about 1-2-3 in order to use it effectively. The purpose of this book is to show you how to use this very important and useful program.

A LITTLE HISTORY

The idea of an electronic spreadsheet was invented by Dan Bricklin when he was an MBA student at the Harvard Business School.

> Sitting there in the spring of 1978, I came up with the idea of the electronic spreadsheet. With all those other classmates to contend with the professor, there's lots of time for daydreaming, especially if you sit in the front row and the professor looks out above you. I invariably made simple addition mistakes in my homework. I wanted to do what the professor did on his blackboard: he would erase one number and Louis in the back of the room would give him all the calculations that he had done all night to recalculate everything. I wanted to keep the calculations and just erase one number on my paper and have everything recalculated. (Dan Bricklin, "VisiCalc and Software Arts: Genesis To Exodus," *The Computer Museum Report*, Summer, 1986, p. 8.)

Dan Bricklin and a friend, Bob Frankston, wrote the first electronic spreadsheet program, for the Apple II®, and called it VisiCalc® ("Visible Calculator"). VisiCalc was published by a small company called Personal Software in 1979. VisiCalc became wildly popular, the best-selling computer software of its day. Personal Software changed its name to VisiCorp and brought out related software, including VisiPlot and VisiTrend, which were written by Mitch Kapor. Mitch Kapor became a product manager for the company, but then left to form Lotus Development Corp. Lotus brought out 1-2-3 for the IBM PC in 1983. The developers of VisiCalc thought that the Apple III®, the ill-fated successor to the very popular Apple II, was the computer of the future and targeted their advanced version of VisiCalc for the Apple III. Bricklin and Frankston also became involved in a messy lawsuit with VisiCorp. Lotus wisely concentrated on the IBM Personal Computer from the beginning.

Lotus 1-2-3 became the best-selling applications computer program of all time. Its spreadsheet portion is a direct descendant of VisiCalc, which is published no more. Lotus brought out Release 2 of 1-2-3 in 1985 to take advantage of the increasing use of built-in hard disks and the increased speed and memory of personal computers. Release 2.01 was brought out shortly afterward to correct some minor problems in Release 2. In 1989 Lotus brought out two new versions of 1-2-3. Release 2.2 was an evolutionary product that added many nice features to Release 2.01. Release 3 was a major new product that allowed for three-dimensional spreadsheets instead of the traditional two-dimensional spreadsheets. However, Release 3 and the subsequent Release 3.1 require a more powerful computer with more memory than does Release 2.2. Lotus has developed versions of 1-2-3 for other computers and operating system environments, including UNIX System V™, VAX™ minicomputers, IBM mainframe computers, and a graphical version for the personal computer running under OS/2®. Release 2.2 is the core version of Lotus 1-2-3 and the standard spreadsheet for industry and universities. This book focuses on Release 2.2 of Lotus 1-2-3.

Lotus has over 70% of the spreadsheet market. Competitors of 1-2-3 include SuperCalc®, Works®, Quattro®, and Excel™. In addition to 1-2-3, Lotus publishes a similar product called Symphony®, which has word processor and communications capabilities. All spreadsheet programs are reasonably similar. Some rival spreadsheet programs are almost identical to 1-2-3. Once you learn 1-2-3, it is a straightforward matter to learn to use any other spreadsheet program.

WHY LEARN TO USE 1-2-3 ?

Lotus 1-2-3 is widely used for many problems. Many of its most devoted users work with accounting and financial problems, for example, budgets, cash flow projections, sales reports, balance sheets, and expense accounts. Some of these applications tabulate past results. For example, we were budgeted to spend so much in each of these different categories. So far this year we have spent this much in each of these areas. How much do we have left in our budget?

Other applications look to the future. For example, we hope to sell so many copies of this proposed product at such and such a price. Our expenses for the product are expected to be so much. How much money will we make? If certain expenses are 25% more than expected, how will this affect our profits? What if we sell only so many copies? What if we lower our price and increase our advertising budget? This is known as using Lotus 1-2-3 to perform "**What if**" analysis. "What if" analysis is an area where spreadsheet programs excel. Indeed, if you return to the quote by Dan Bricklin, the inventor of electronic spreadsheets, "What if" analysis is the specific type of application for which electronic spreadsheets were developed.

Lotus 1-2-3 is used for nonfinancial problems as well. It is used for alphabetizing lists, drawing graphs, and performing engineering calculations.

Many people have purchased personal computers just so they could run Lotus 1-2-3. I hope you will soon see why.

CREATING SIMPLE SPREADSHEETS

THE BASIC IDEA

An electronic spreadsheet program can be likened to an electronic piece of paper with a built-in pencil, eraser, and calculator.

A simple Lotus 1-2-3 spreadsheet is shown in Figure 2-1. This spreadsheet was set up to give price quotes for potential customers. There are three products: widgets, grommits, and connectors. Widgets cost 1.19 each. Grommits cost 2.49 each. Connectors cost 0.69 each. A 6% sales tax is added to each order.

In Lotus 1-2-3 the screen is divided into **columns** and **rows**. The columns have letter names (A, B, C, ...). The rows have numbers for names (1, 2, 3, ...). The intersection of each row and column is called a **cell**. Each cell has a name. Cell E7 is in column E and row 7. (See Figure 2-2.) That is, the name of each cell is the letter name of its column followed by the number name of its row.

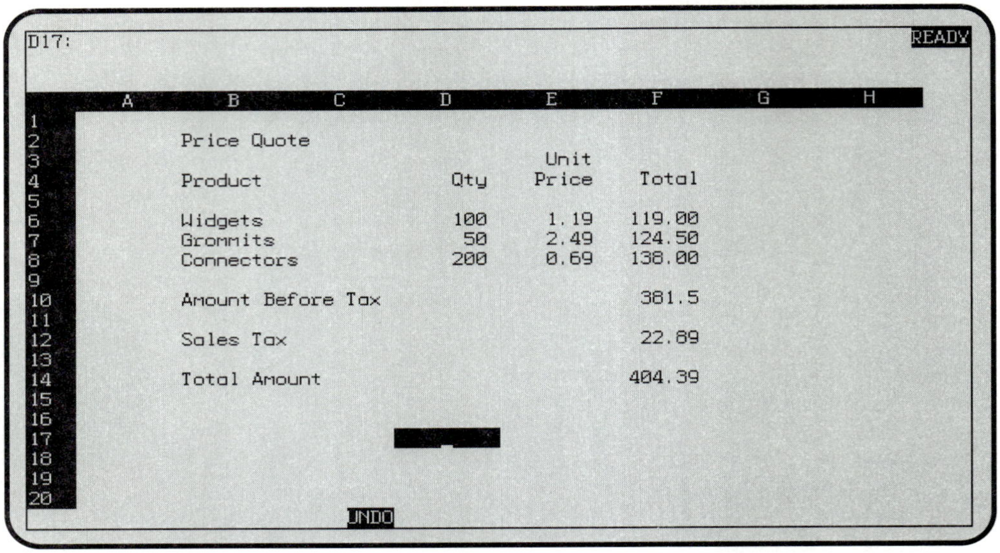

FIGURE 2-1 A simple spreadsheet for giving a price quote.

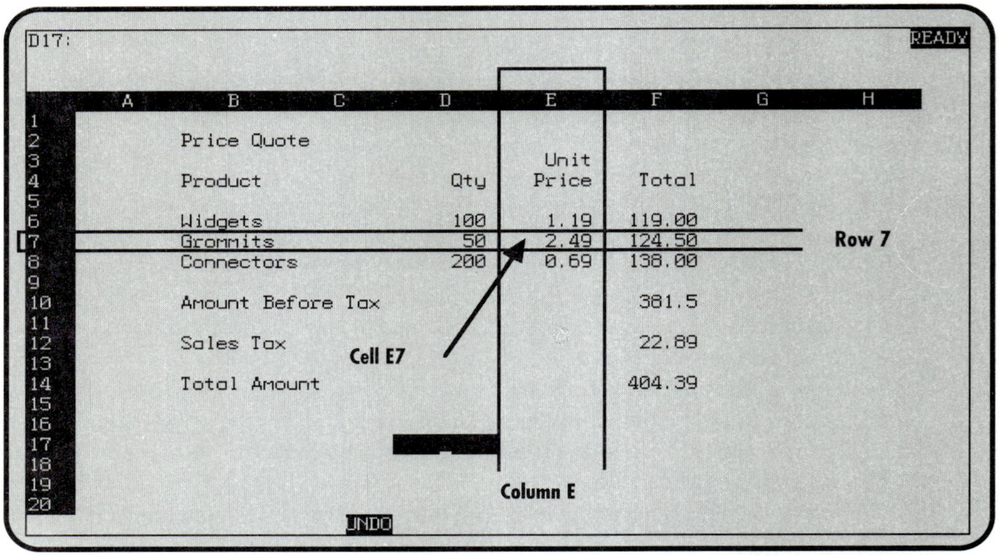

FIGURE 2-2 Cell E7 is in column E and row 7.

Each cell can be **blank**, or it can contain a **label**, a **number**, or a **formula**. A "label" is what Lotus calls text. A label can be a word or phrase. Cells F4 and B7 in the spreadsheet in Figure 2-1 are labels, as they contain words. Cells D6 and E7 contain numbers.

The key to electronic spreadsheets is the formulas. Cells in column F contain formulas. The formula in cell F6 is

$$+D6*E6$$

The initial plus sign indicates that this is a formula. In Lotus 1-2-3, the asterisk means multiplication. This formula tells Lotus 1-2-3 that the number that is displayed in cell F6 is the number in D6 multiplied by the number in cell E6. The formula has been typed into the cell, but the computer normally displays the result of evaluating the formula in the cell. That is, the computer displays 119.00, the result of the multiplication, in the cell.

The formulas in the spreadsheet are shown in Figure 2-3. Here the actual formulas are displayed in the cells, rather than the values that result from calculating the formulas. The formula in cell F7 is

$$+D7*E7$$

so the value in cell F7 is the result of multiplying the number in D7 times the number in E7.

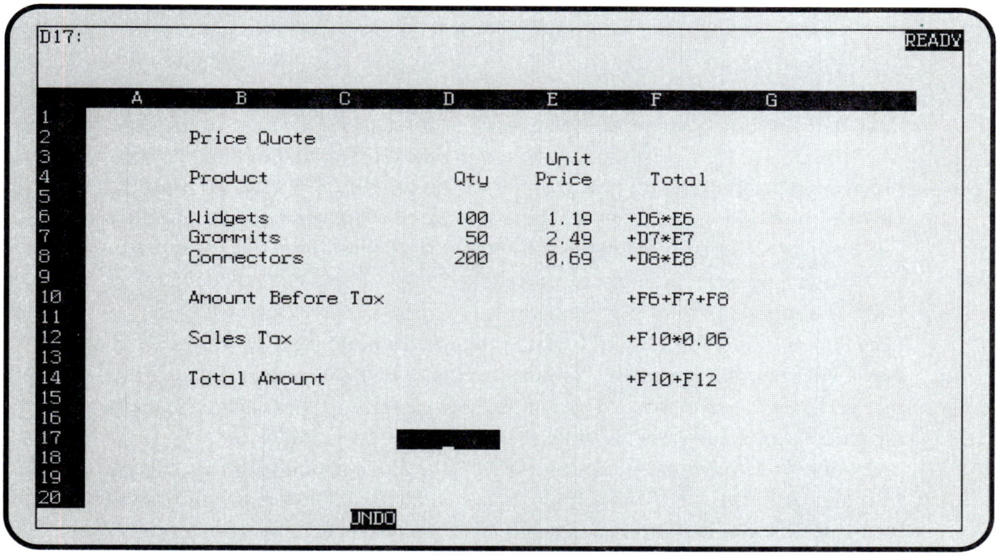

FIGURE 2-3 The spreadsheet with the underlying formulas displayed rather than the values that result from evaluating the formulas.

Similarly, the formula in cell F8 is

+D8*E8

Cell F10 contains the total for the order before sales tax. This value is calculated by the computer by adding the values in F6, F7, and F8. The formula is

+F6+F7+F8

The sales tax is 6% of the Amount Before Tax. The formula for the sales tax in cell F12 is

+F10*0.06

Finally, the Total Amount is the sum of the Amount Before Tax and the Sales Tax. This formula, in cell F14, is

+F10+F12

SO WHAT?

Here we have spent over $1000 for a computer and the Lotus 1-2-3 software. Plus, we have to take the time to learn to use the computer and Lotus 1-2-3. Wouldn't it just be easier and faster to do this by hand? You could do the same "spreadsheet" with paper and pencil. For $10 you could buy a calculator to do the arithmetic. Why bother with a computer?

In using a computer, the benefit usually is not realized the first time you perform some action. The benefit is in the repetition, especially in the ability to make changes. If you have used a word processing program, you know that the major benefit of word processing is the ability to make changes or revisions without retyping the entire manuscript. Similarly, the payoff of a Lotus 1-2-3 spreadsheet is in the third or the tenth or the hundredth time you use the spreadsheet.

What happens with our price quote spreadsheet? The potential customer says, "Oh, no. I don't want 50 widgets. I want 500 widgets." If you are using paper and pencil, you must erase the numbers in F7, F10, F12, and F14 and then recalculate the new amounts. The next person you speak with has new quantities to order. You would have to do the calculations all over again for that person's order. If you give out hundreds of price quotes each day, you would have to redo the calculations hundreds of times.

Watch what happens on the computer. We change the number in cell D7 from 50 to 500. The formulas in cells F7, F10, F12, and F14 are recalculated *automatically* by the computer, and the results of these calculations automatically appear in the cells. (See Figure 2-4.) Similarly, we change the price for Widgets from 1.19 to 0.98 by changing the number in cell E6 from 1.19 to 0.98. As soon as we make the change, the formulas in cells F6, F10, F12, and F14 automatically are recalculated by Lotus 1-2-3.

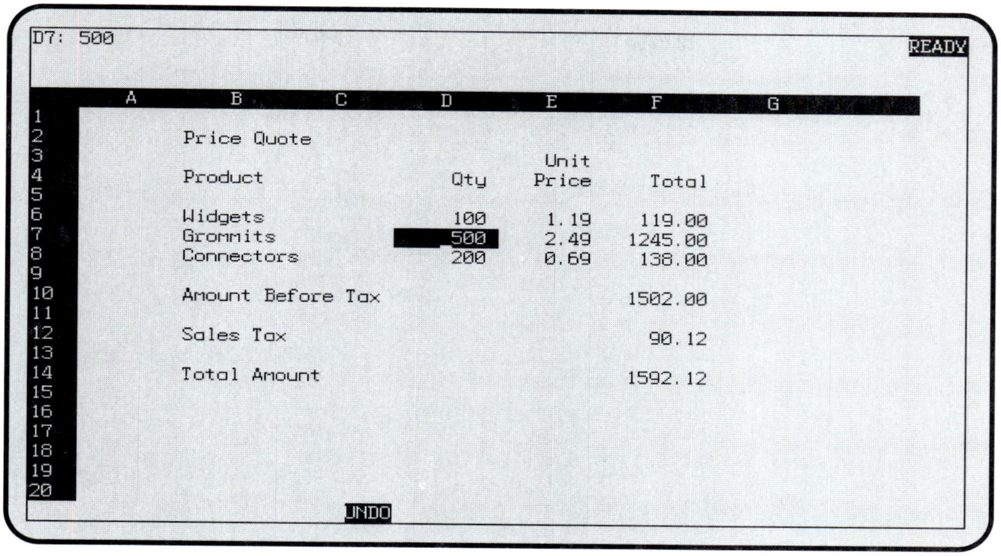

FIGURE 2-4 When we change the number in D7 from 50 to 500, the formulas in F7, F10, F12, and F14 are automatically recalculated.

The key to electronic spreadsheets is in the automatic recalculation of the formulas. Text, numbers, and formulas are entered into the spreadsheet. Whenever any number is changed, the relevant formulas are recalculated by the computer automatically. The lightning-fast speed of the computer allows the recalculation to be done almost instantaneously.

Lotus 1-2-3 has been described as an electronic piece of paper with a built-in pencil, eraser, and calculator. You enter in the spreadsheet, including the formulas. The computer performs all the calculations automatically.

Now we will take a look at the process of actually using Lotus 1-2-3 on the computer.

GETTING STARTED ON THE COMPUTER

How Lotus 1-2-3 should be started up depends on how your computer is set up. On computers without a built-in hard disk, at the prompt of A> you would insert the Lotus System disk in drive A, type LOTUS, and press the Enter key. On computers where the Lotus 1-2-3 program has been installed on a hard disk, at the C> prompt you would type LOTUS and press the Enter key. On computers that have a master menu system, you would select Lotus 1-2-3 from the master menu.

After you start up the Lotus program, the computer copies the Lotus 1-2-3 Access System program from the disk and displays the Lotus 1-2-3 Access System screen, as in Figure 2-5. Press the Enter key once. The program identification screen shows briefly, displaying the name of the

```
1-2-3  PrintGraph  Translate  Install  Exit
Use 1-2-3

                        1-2-3 Access System
                       Copyright  1986, 1989
                    Lotus Development Corporation
                        All Rights Reserved
                           Release 2.2

The Access system lets you choose 1-2-3, PrintGraph, the Translate utility,
and the Install program, from the menu at the top of this screen.   If
you're using a two-diskette system, the Access system may prompt you to
change disks.   Follow the instructions below to start a program.

o  Use → or ← to move the menu pointer (the highlighted rectangle
   at the top of the screen) to the program you want to use.

o  Press ENTER to start the program.

You can also start a program by typing the first character of its name.

Press HELP (F1) for more information.
```

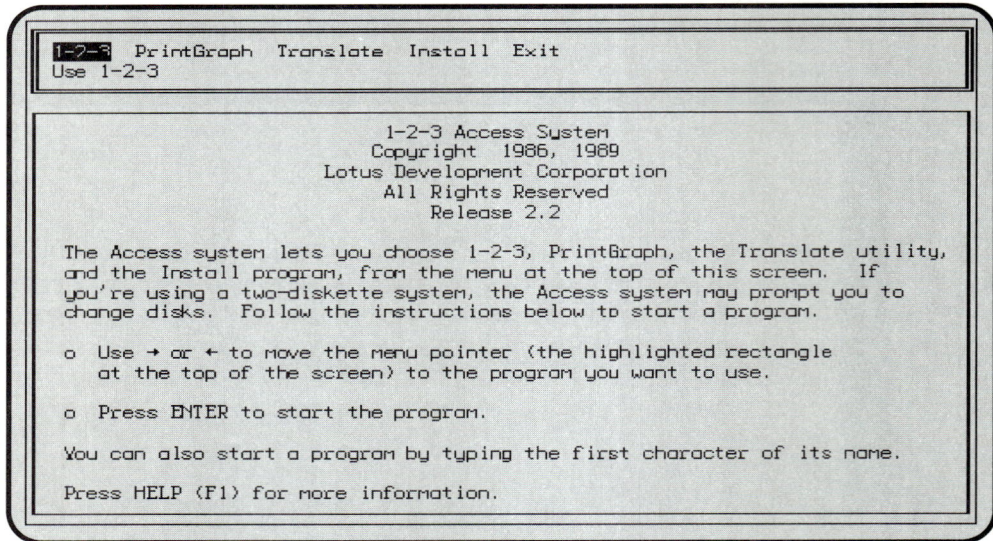

FIGURE 2-5 When you first start up Lotus 1-2-3, normally you see the 1-2-3 Access System screen.
Press the Enter key to proceed.

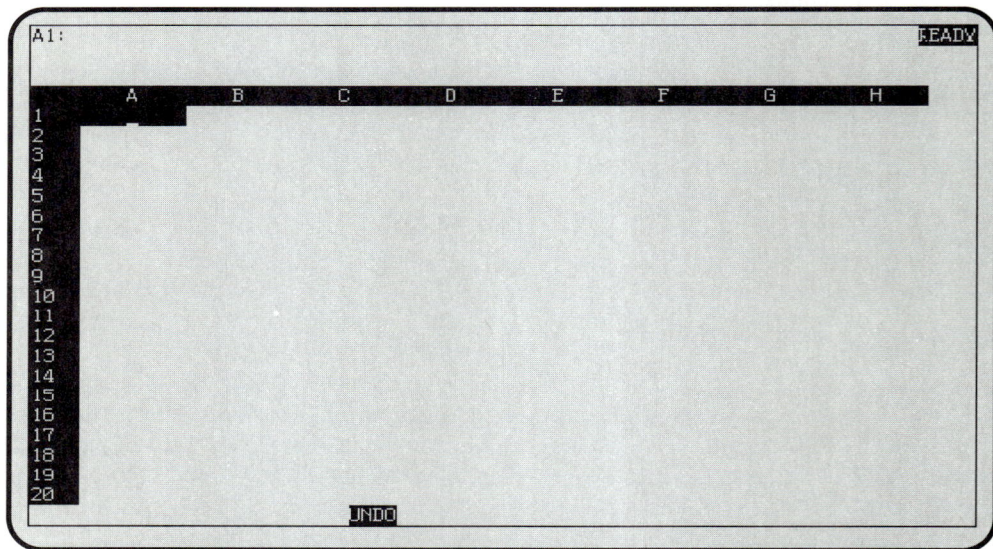

```
A1:                                                              READY

        A        B        C        D        E        F        G        H
  1
  2
  3
  4
  5
  6
  7
  8
  9
 10
 11
 12
 13
 14
 15
 16
 17
 18
 19
 20
                              UNDO
```

FIGURE 2-6 The blank Lotus 1-2-3 worksheet.

owner of the program. The name of the owner was entered into the system when the program was "installed" before it was used the first time. The computer then copies the rest of the 1-2-3 program from the disk and displays a blank worksheet, as in Figure 2-6.

In the top right corner of the screen is the **mode indicator**. The mode indicator shows the current status of Lotus 1-2-3. If the mode indicator is "READY" then the computer is ready and waiting for you to type. Other possible words that might appear as the mode indicator are given in Appendix A.

Notice that right now cell A1 is different from the other cells. All the other cells are one color. Cell A1 is the opposite color. Cell A1 also contains a blinking underline, called the **cursor**. The word "cursor" comes from the Latin and means "runner." The cursor runs around the screen and indicates into which cell you are typing.

The easiest way to move the cursor around the screen is by using the **arrow keys**. Before discussing how to move the cursor around the screen, let's look at the keyboard.

THE KEYBOARD

Personal computer keyboards have three basic types of keys: **function keys**, **typewriter keys**, and **cursor control/numeric keys**.

The function keys are labeled F1, F2, and so on. Function keys are program-specific keys that have no universal meaning. The meaning of the function keys varies from program to program. For example, function key F5 may mean "delete this paragraph" in a word processing program and "move the cursor to a certain cell" in Lotus 1-2-3. On the keyboard, the function keys are located either on the very left of the keyboard, as in Figure 2-7a, or on the top of the keyboard, as in Figure 2-7b. Some keyboards have 10 function keys; others have 12 function keys. Lotus 1-2-3 uses only function keys F1 through F10.

Note that typing function key F5 is completely different from typing the key F followed by the key 5. If you wish to type function key F5, be sure to press the key labeled F5 rather than the F key followed by the 5 key, or the computer will not understand what you mean.

The typewriter keys are similar to the keys on a typewriter, but with some differences.

The **Shift key** is marked with a thick up arrow (see Figure 2-7). As on a typewriter, the Shift key does nothing when typed by itself. If you hold the Shift key down while you type a letter, you will type a capital letter rather than a lowercase letter. Most non-letter keys are imprinted with two symbols. If you just press one of these keys by itself, you will type the lower symbol on the key. If you hold the Shift key down while pressing the key, you will type the upper symbol on the key. For example, holding the Shift key down and pressing the 4 key above the E and R keys will result in your typing a $, the upper symbol on the key.

The **Caps Lock key** only affects the letter keys on the personal computer keyboard. This differs from the way the Caps Lock key works on a typewriter. If you press the Caps Lock key once, then all letters that you type will come out in capitals. If you press the Caps Lock key again, then the letters normally will appear in lowercase. Lotus 1-2-3 indicates to you whether the Caps Lock is on. If the Caps Lock is on, then the word CAPS appears in the lower right of the screen. (See Figure 2-8.)

Escape key   **Tab key**   **Backspace key** **Enter key**   **Arrow keys**

FIGURE 2-7a The original PC keyboard.

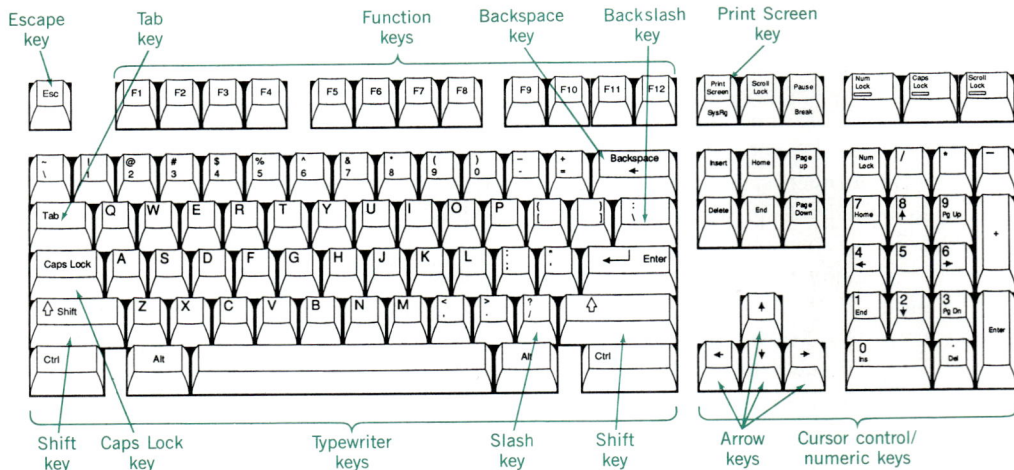

Function keys   Shift key   Backslash key   Typewriter keys   Slash key   Caps Lock key   Shift key   PrtSc key   Cursor control/ numeric keys

Escape key   **Tab key**   **Function keys**   **Backspace key**   **Backslash key**   **Print Screen key**

Shift key   Caps Lock key   Typewriter keys   Slash key   Shift key   Arrow keys   Cursor control/ numeric keys

FIGURE 2-7b The enhanced keyboard.

   Note that it does not matter whether you use lowercase letters or capital letters in Lotus 1-2-3. Some people just put the Caps Lock key on at the beginning and then type everything in capital letters.

   If the Caps Lock is on, then using the Shift key will give you lowercase letters. This feature of personal computers also differs from the way a typewriter works.

The **cursor control/numeric keys** generally appear on the right side of the keyboard. Included here are keys that control the movement of the cursor and a **numeric keypad** for the rapid entry of numbers. On most keyboards, the numeric keypad keys contain other symbols, for example, arrows, beneath them. If you want to use the numeric keypad, press the Num Lock key once first. This tells the computer that when you press a key in the numeric keypad you mean to type the number on the top of the key rather than the symbol below it on the key. The Num Lock key is very similar to the Caps Lock key. If the Num Lock key is on, then the word NUM appears on the bottom right of the Lotus 1-2-3 screen, as in Figure 2-8. Most people just use the keys in the top row of the typewriter part of the keyboard for entering numbers.

MOVING THE CURSOR

The **arrow keys** move the cursor one cell at a time. Press the right arrow and the cursor moves one cell to the right. Press the down arrow and the cursor moves down one cell. The current address of the cursor is indicated in the top left corner of the screen.

If the cursor is in a cell in row 1 and you press the up arrow, the computer will beep at you, as an error message. The cursor cannot move up one cell, as it is at the top of the spreadsheet. Similarly, if the cursor is in a cell in column A and you press the left arrow, the computer will beep at you. Column A is the leftmost column in the spreadsheet.

What happens if the cursor is in row 20 and you press the down arrow? The cursor moves to row 21. The screen displays rows 2 through 21. Row 1 moves off the top of the screen.

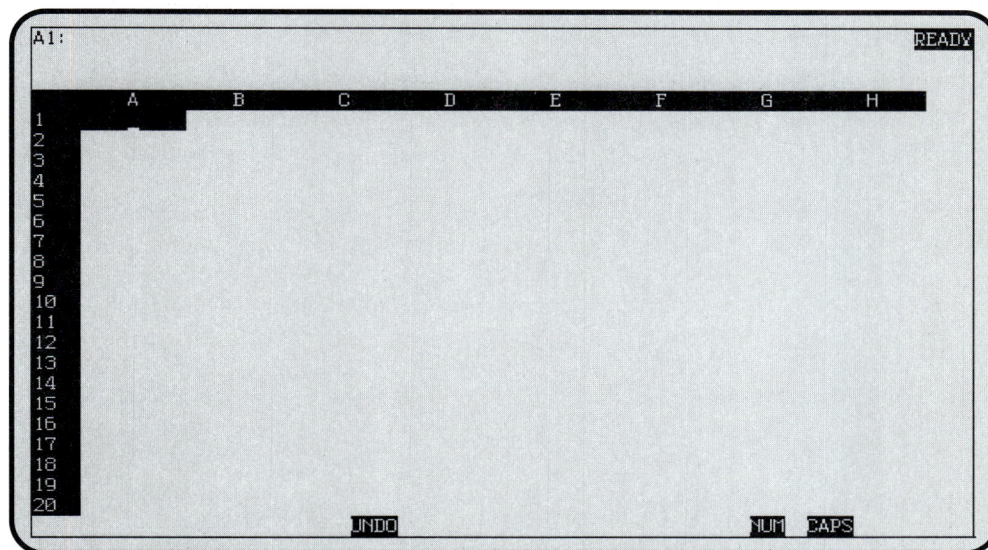

FIGURE 2-8 Lotus 1-2-3 indicates whether the Caps Lock key and the Num Lock key are depressed.

THE SIZE OF THE SPREADSHEET

The screen is actually a window onto a much larger worksheet. When you start up Lotus 1-2-3 you see 8 columns (A through H) and 20 rows (1 through 20). The actual Lotus 1-2-3 worksheet contains 256 columns and 8192 rows! The columns are named A through Z and then AA through AZ and then BA through BZ and so on until IV. The rows are named 1 through 8192. (See Figure 2-9.) Some quick calculations show that to display all the cells in the worksheet at the same size they usually appear would require a screen 20 feet wide and 360 feet high! Your computer screen would have to be as high as a 30-story building to display the entire worksheet!

The screen is best thought of as a window that displays a small portion of the entire worksheet. This "window" follows the cursor around so that the cursor always is displayed on the screen. If the cursor is in the rightmost column of the screen and you press the right arrow key, the window moves moves to the right along with the cursor so the cursor still is displayed.

LARGER CURSOR MOVEMENTS

The arrow keys move the cursor one cell at a time. There are several other ways to move the cursor around the spreadsheet.

The **PgDn** (Page Down) key moves the cursor down one screen at a time. That is, if the cursor is in cell B3 and you press the PgDn key, the cursor will move down to cell B23. (Remember, there are 20 rows displayed in the screen.) Similarly, the **PgUp** key moves the cursor up 20 rows each time.

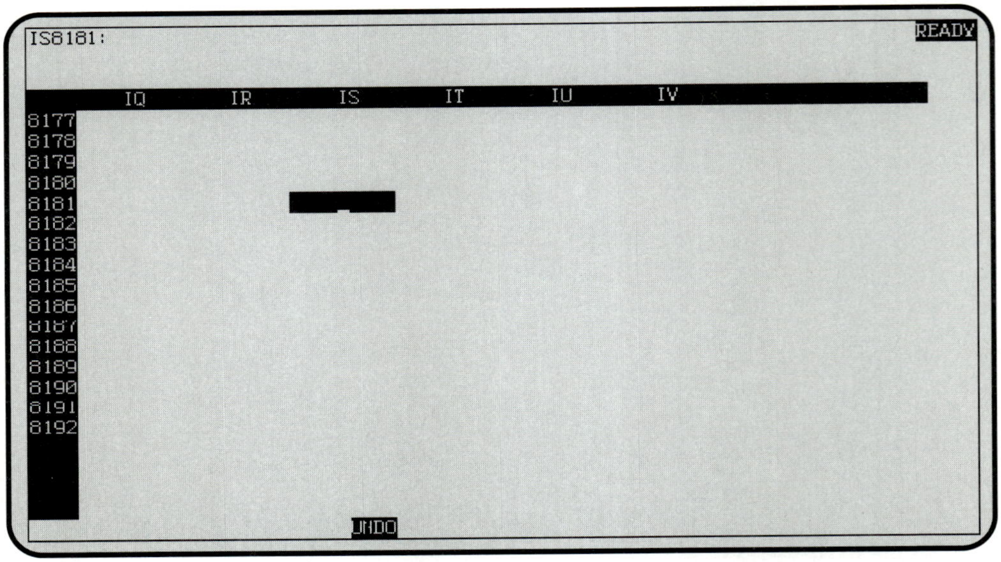

FIGURE 2-9 The bottom right corner of the worksheet.

The **Tab** key moves the cursor right one screen at a time. Pressing **Shift-Tab** (that is, holding down the Shift key and pressing the Tab key) moves the cursor left one screen at a time. If we have just started up and the cursor is in A1, pressing the Tab key will move the cursor to cell I1.

Suppose we start up Lotus 1-2-3 and we want to move the cursor to cell X4001. Using the arrow keys, we would have to press the down arrow key 4000 times and the right arrow 23 times. Using the PgDn key and the Tab key still would require over 200 key presses.

Lotus 1-2-3 provides an even faster way of making large cursor movements. Function key **F5** sometimes is called the **GoTo** key. If we press function key F5, the computer will instruct us to "Enter the address to go to:". This will appear on the second line of the screen, above the worksheet. If we type X4001, as in Figure 2-10, and then press the Enter key, the computer will move the cursor directly to cell X4001, as in Figure 2-11.

How can we move the cursor back to cell A1? We could use the up arrow key or the PgUp key. We also could us function key F5 again. An even faster way is to press the key labeled **Home**. (See Figure 2-7.) The Home key always moves the cursor back to cell A1, the cell in the top left corner of the spreadsheet.

Thus we have looked at several ways of moving the cursor: the arrow keys move the cursor one cell at a time; PgDn, PgUp, Tab, and Shift-Tab move the cursor one screen at a time; F5 moves the cursor to a cell that you specify; the Home key moves the cursor back to A1.

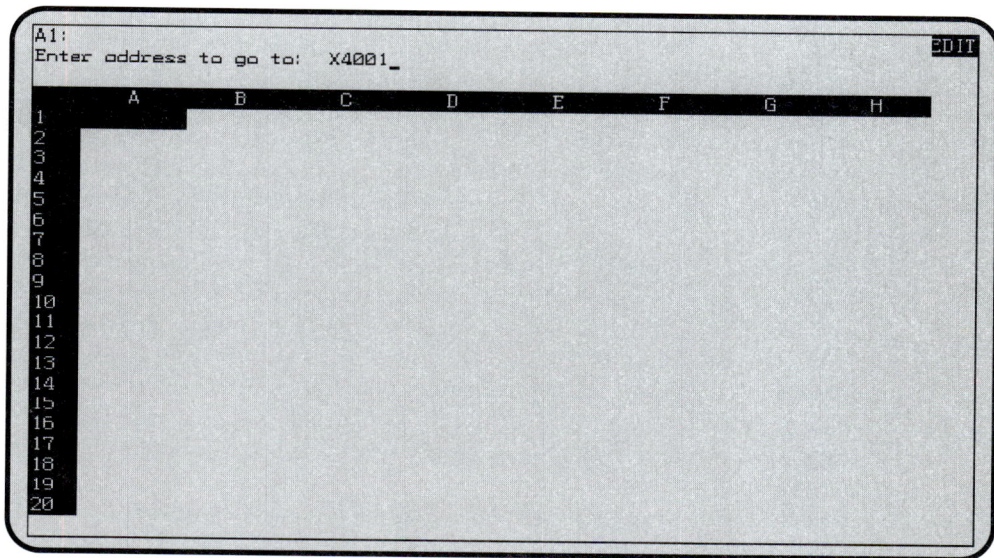

FIGURE 2-10 Using function key F5, the GoTo key.

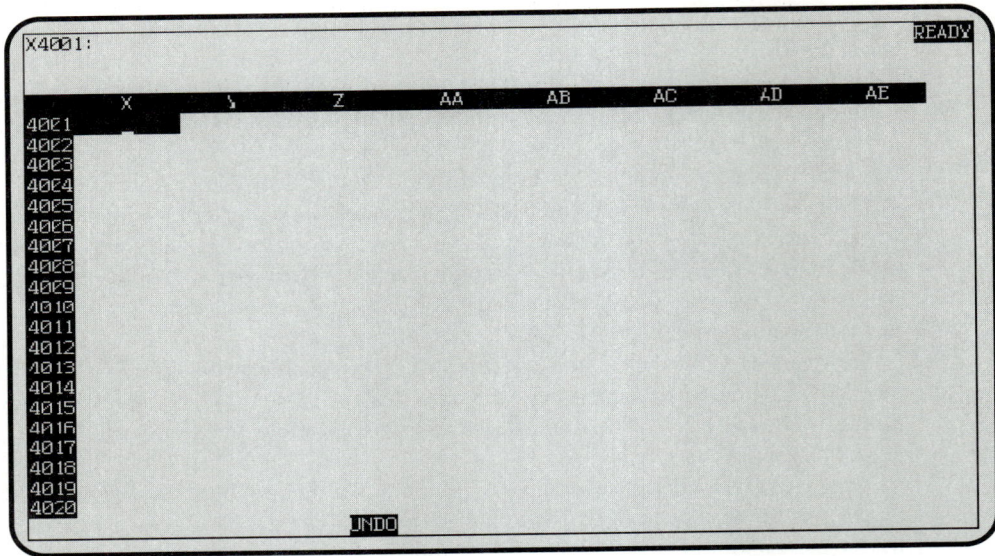

FIGURE 2-11 The result of going to X4001.

ENTERING INFORMATION INTO CELLS

Suppose we want to enter the Price Quote spreadsheet from the previous chapter into the computer. We start with a blank spreadsheet, move the cursor to cell B4, and type the word `Product`. Notice that it appears on the second line of the screen, above the spreadsheet (Figure 2-12). Now press the Enter key. The word is "entered" into the cell (Figure 2-13). Move the cursor down to cell B6 by pressing the down arrow key twice. Type the word `Widgets`, and so on.

How does Lotus 1-2-3 know which entries are labels and which entries are formulas or numbers? The program looks at the first keystroke, at the first character that we type into a cell. From that first keystroke Lotus 1-2-3 decides whether the entry in the cell will be a label or a value. (A **value** is a formula or a number.) If the first character we type is a letter or a space or an apostrophe (') or a quote (") or a caret (^) or a backslash (\ ), then the computer displays the word "LABEL" as the mode indicator in the top right corner of the screen and treats the cell entry as text to be displayed. If the first character we type is a digit from 0 to 9 or a plus sign (+) or a minus sign (-) or an at sign (@) or a period (.) or a left parentheses (( )or a dollar sign ($) then the computer displays the word "VALUE" as the mode indicator in the top right corner of the screen and treats the cell entry as a formula to be evaluated or as a number that can be used in arithmetic in other cells.

This is an important point, a common source of errors for the beginner. Be careful how you begin each cell entry. Do not begin a number by typing a few spaces. This looks like it will adjust the position of the number in the cell. However, by beginning the cell entry with a space, you are telling the computer that the entry is a label, that the entry is to be treated as text. If in another

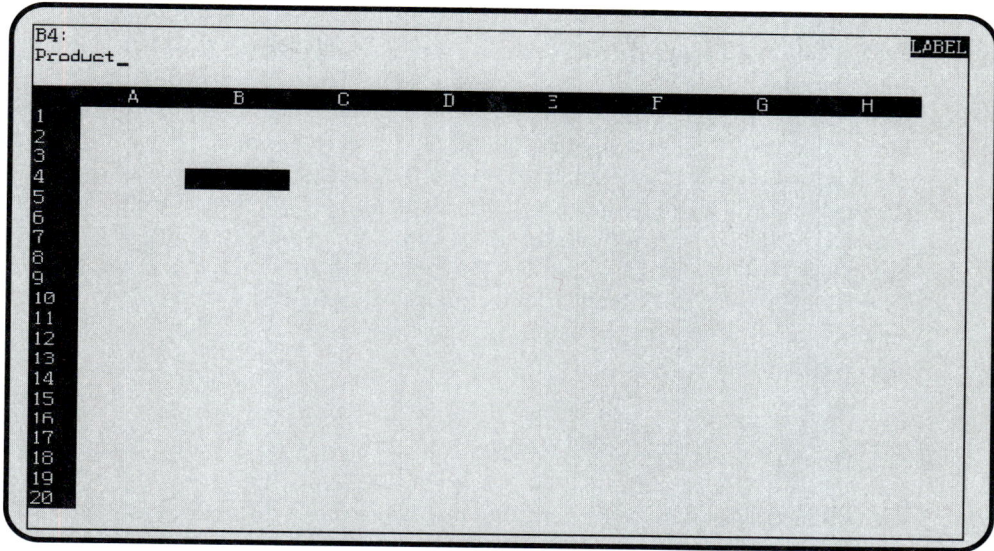

FIGURE 2-12 We moved the cursor to cell B4 and typed the word Product but have not yet pressed the Enter key. Notice that the mode indicator in the top right of the screen says LABEL.

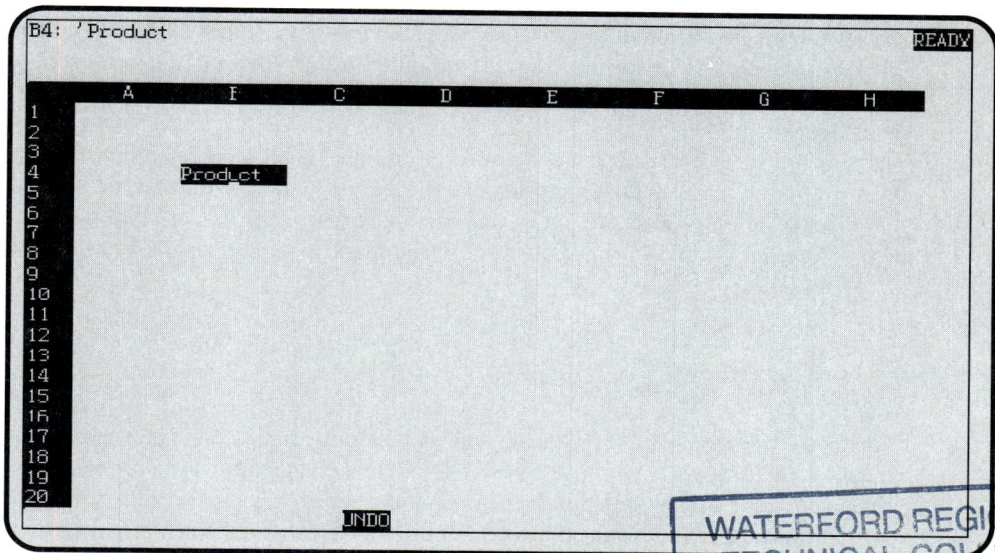

FIGURE 2-13 The screen after pressing the Enter key to enter the word Product into cell B4.

cell you try to add the number in that cell, it will not work. You cannot do arithmetic on labels, only on values. Similarly, be sure to begin a formula with a plus sign or left parenthesis or other valid character. If you type C7*D7 into a cell, the computer will take this to be the text C7*D7 rather than a formula because it begins with a C, a letter. The computer will not evaluate the formula. Rather, it will simply display C7*D7 in the cell as text.

Sometimes we want a cell entry that looks like a formula to be treated as text. For example, suppose we have a spreadsheet to help calculate the payroll, and we need to enter each employee's Social Security number into a cell. If we simply type 123-45-6789 into a cell, Lotus 1-2-3 will treat it is a formula. In the cell we will see -6711, the result of subtracting 45 from 123 and then 6789 from that number. If we type a space and then 123-45-6789 or a quote and then 123-45-6789, the computer will treat the cell entry as a label and the entry will be displayed as typed.

CORRECTING TYPING ERRORS

It is common to make typing errors. The best way to correct a typing error depends on when the error is discovered.

If you realize that you have made a mistake before what you have typed has been entered into the cell, then you can correct the error by pressing the **Backspace** key. The Backspace key is located on the top right of the typewriter portion of the keyboard and often is indicated with a long left arrow. The Backspace key erases the most recently typed character.

When typing into a cell, the **Esc** key ("Escape" key) will erase the entire entry. The Escape key is located on the top left of the keyboard. Here the Escape key acts as a "superbackspace" key, erasing all the characters you have just typed for the cell rather than just the most recent one. The Escape key will not erase an entry that already has been entered into a cell. In general, if you are in trouble in Lotus 1-2-3, pressing the Escape key a few times will usually get you out of trouble.

If you realize that you have made a mistake in a label or formula or number that already has been entered into a cell, then simply move the cursor to the cell and retype the entry.

To erase the entry in a cell, put the cursor on the cell and type /RE followed by the Enter key. Here you are invoking a Lotus 1-2-3 command. We will explain exactly what these keystrokes mean in Chapter 3.

UNDO

Have you ever done or said something and wished immediately that you could undo it or take it back? Lotus provides that capability in 1-2-3 Release 2.2. Perhaps you have noticed the word **UNDO** at the bottom of many of the Lotus 1-2-3 screens that appear in the figures. When the word UNDO appears it means that you can undo your most recent action in Lotus 1-2-3. To undo the action you type **Alt-F4**. That is, hold your finger down on one of the keys labeled Alt, next to the space bar, and while holding down the Alt key, press function key F4.

The word UNDO can appear on the screen only when the program is in Ready mode. If you type Alt-F4, Lotus 1-2-3 will return the spreadsheet to the way it was the previous time it was in Ready mode.

The Undo feature requires some extra memory. It is possible to disable the Undo feature. If this has been done on your Lotus 1-2-3 program, then the word UNDO will not appear on your screen.

SIMPLE FORMULAS

The key part of Lotus 1-2-3 is the formulas. As discussed, formulas must begin with a digit or with one of the following characters: + - ($. @.

Examples of formulas include

$$3+4*5$$

$$+C4/5+7$$

$$(D3+G5)*(H7-(5+D6)/8)$$

Formulas can contain numbers, cell addresses (like C4 or H7), arithmetic operators, and parentheses. The arithmetic operators include

+	addition
-	subtraction
*	multiplication
/	division
^	exponentiation

For example, 2^3 means 2 to the third power, which is 8.

EVALUATING FORMULAS

What would be the result of evaluating the formula 3+4*5? Is it 35? Is it 23? The correct answer depends on whether the computer performs the addition first or the multiplication first, on the "order of precedence" of the operators. Generally, multiplication is done before addition. Thus, the value of the formula 3+4*5 would be 23. If we want the addition to be performed first, we would type (3+4)*5. The parentheses tell the computer to perform the operation inside, in this case the addition, first. The value of (3+4)*5 would be 35.

What would be the value of the formula 6-5-1 ? Is it 0? Is it 2? The correct answer depends on which subtraction the computer performs first. That is, it depends on whether 6-5-1 is the same as (6-5)-1 or whether it is the same as 6-(5-1). Lotus 1-2-3 performs the left subtraction before the right subtraction so to the computer 6-5-1 is the same as (6-5)-1, which evaluates to 0.

Now we can state the general rules that Lotus 1-2-3 follows when evaluating simple formulas:

1. Evaluate anything in parentheses first.
2. Evaluate the arithmetic operators in the following order:
   (a) exponentiation
   (b) multiplication or division
   (c) addition or subtraction
3. In case of tie, evaluate the operators from left to right.

The complete order of precedence for operators in Lotus 1-2-3 is given in Appendix D.

YOU TRY EVALUATING A FORMULA

What would be the result of evaluating the formula 23+((5+9)*3)/7-5? This problem uses each of the three general rules just given. Try it before reading further. Write down your answer.

The computer first would add 5+9 to get 14. Then it would multiply the 14 times 3, which is 42. It would divide the 42 by 7 to get 6. Then it would add 23 and 6 to obtain 29. Finally, it would take the 29 and subtract 5 to obtain the final answer of 24.

ENTERING FORMULAS

When entering formulas it is very important that you do *not* include any spaces within your formula. If you do, the computer will beep at you, the word "EDIT" will appear as the mode indicator in the top right of the screen, and the computer will display your mistaken entry in the second line of the screen. (See Figure 2-14.) At this point, press the Escape key to erase the entire formula and then retype the formula without spaces.

Lotus 1-2-3 is very fussy about what you type. For example, you may not include commas in large numbers. If you are entering the number 5 million, you would type 5000000 rather than 5,000,000. Similarly, do not include $ signs in numbers that represent monetary amounts. We will discuss how to format cells so that dollar signs and commas appear in numbers in Chapter 5.

USING CELL ADDRESSES IN FORMULAS

Consider again the Price Quote worksheet. Suppose that in cell F6 instead of the formula +D6*E6 we had put 100*1.19 . (See Figure 2-15.) Would this formula have worked? It might first appear that this new formula would work fine. After all, the result of evaluating this new formula would be the same as evaluating the original formula, namely, 119. But what would happen if we then changed the number in cell D6 from 100 to 300? The result of evaluating

```
F6:                                                                    EDIT
+D6 * E6

          A         B         C         D         E         F         G
1
2                Price Quote
3                                              Unit
4                Product              Qty      Price     Total
5
6                Widgets              100      1.19   ███████████
7                Grommits              50      2.49
8                Connectors           200      0.69
9
10               Amount Before Tax
11
12               Sales Tax
13
14               Total Amount
15
16
17
18
19
20
```

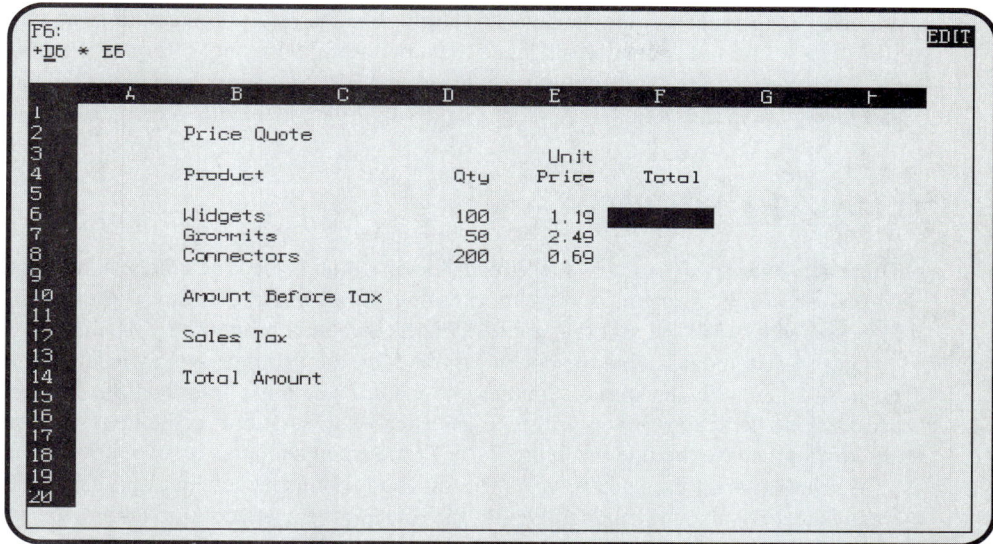

FIGURE 2-14 Trying to put spaces in your formulas lands you in Edit mode.

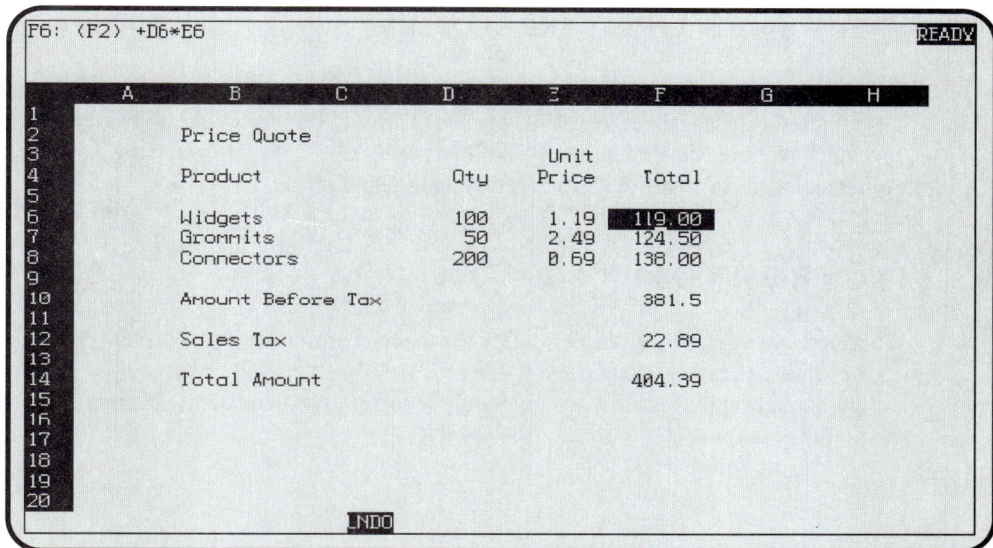

```
F6: (F2) +D6*E6                                                        READY

          A         B         C         D         E         F         G         H
1
2                Price Quote
3                                              Unit
4                Product              Qty      Price     Total
5
6                Widgets              100      1.19   ██119.00██
7                Grommits              50      2.49     124.50
8                Connectors           200      0.69     138.00
9
10               Amount Before Tax                       381.5
11
12               Sales Tax                               22.89
13
14               Total Amount                           404.39
15
16
17
18
19
20                              ▐UNDO▌
```

FIGURE 2-15 The formula in F6 is +D6*E6. Would the formula 100*1.19 work for cell F6? No! If we change the number in D6 the value in F6 would not change.

the original formula would change accordingly. But the result of evaluating the new formula 100*1.19 would not change at all, since the new formula does not refer to the numbers in the cells. It is very important that you use cell addresses in your formulas rather than the numbers that (now) are in the cells.

PRINTING THE SCREEN

There are several ways to print the spreadsheet in Lotus 1-2-3. The quickest, but least elegant, way is to simply print the screen by pressing the **PrintScreen** key. When you press the PrintScreen key, all the text that appears on the screen is printed on your printer.

On some keyboards, like the one in Figure 2-7a, the PrintScreen key is labeled **PrtSc** and it shares a key with an asterisk. On these keyboards you must hold the Shift key down while pressing the PrtSc key or you will type the asterisk, the symbol on the lower part of the key. On keyboards like the one in Figure 2-7b, PrintScreen occupies its own key.

When you print the screen, you print all the text on the screen. You print not only the spreadsheet but also the mode indicator, the row numbers and column letters, the current cell address, and everything else that appears on the screen. There are two much better methods of printing spreadsheets—the Print command and the Allways add-in program. The Print command is far superior to the PrintScreen key. The Allways program is far superior to the Print command. The Print command and the Allways program are covered in later chapters.

ERASING THE ENTIRE SPREADSHEET

Suppose you just have completed one of the computer exercise problems that follow. You have constructed a spreadsheet, tested it, printed it. Now you would like to erase the spreadsheet and start over on a new exercise. To do this, type /WEY. Again, you have issued a command to Lotus 1-2-3. We will discuss commands in Chapter 3.

EXITING FROM LOTUS 1-2-3

The correct way of exiting from 1-2-3 is to type the commands /QYYE. This returns you back to the Disk Operating System.

On some computers it is possible simply to remove your disks, if any, and turn off the computer.

PAPER AND PENCIL EXERCISES

2-1   Consider the following spreadsheet

	A	B	C	D
1				
2				
3	86	-4	-8	fun
4	-47	5	26	37
5	2.3	7	Lotus	198
6	computer	18	4.6	3
7	56	102		-19
8				

What would be the result of evaluating each of the following formulas? Write out your answers on paper. Do not use the computer.

(a) +B6+1

(b) +B5+2*D6

(c) +C3*(D6+B3)-6*C4+A7

(d) +256/C3/2/B3

(e) +B4^2+B3^3

2-2   Salespeople make a base salary of $10,000 per year plus a commission of 3% of sales. The following spreadsheet has been created for our four salespeople.

	A	B	C	D	E	F	G
1							
2		SALESPEOPLE					
3							TOTAL
4		NAME	SALES	SALARY	COMMISSION		EARNINGS
5							
6		ADAMS	795000	10000	23850		33850
7		BAKER	243000	10000	7290		17290
8		CAREY	4700	10000	141		10141
9		DUNN	2400300	10000	72009		82009
10							
11		TOTAL	3443000	40000	103290		143290
12							

Columns E and G and Row 11 contain *formulas*.

(a) Cell E6 gives Adams's Commission. What is the formula in E6?

(b) Cell E7 gives Baker's Commission. What is the formula in E7?

(c) Cell G7 gives Baker's Total Earnings. What is the formula in G7?

(d) Cell E11 Gives the Total Commission. What is the formula in E11?

(e) Cell G11 gives the Total Total Earnings. What is the formula in G11?

(f) Give an alternative formula for G11.

COMPUTER EXERCISES

2-3 Start up Lotus 1-2-3. You should first see the Lotus 1-2-3 Access System screen, as in Figure 2-1. Press the Enter key. Now you should see a blank Lotus 1-2-3 spreadsheet.

(a) Use the arrow keys to move the cursor right and left and down and up.
     Move the cursor to cell F12 using the arrow keys.
     Move the cursor to cell K23 using the arrow keys.
     In cell K23 type the word HELLO and press the Enter key.

(b) Press the Home key to return the cursor to A1.

(c) Enter your name in cell D4.
     Type EXERCISE 2-3 in cell D5.
     Type the date in cell D6.
     (You should type your name, the exercise number, and the date at the top of each spreadsheet you do for homework.)

(d) Type the number 140 in cell B2.
     Type the number 233 in cell B3.
     Type the formula +B2+B3 in cell B5. (The number 373 should appear now in B5.)

(e) Change the number in B2 to 56. (The total in B5 should change automatically to 289.)

(f) Change the number in cell B3 to 375.6. (The total in B5 should change again.)

(g) In cell D10 type ABC and then press the Backspace key. Do you see the effect of the Backspace key? Press the Backspace key twice more.

(h) Put the cursor on cell B5.
     Print the screen by pressing the PrintScreen key (or by holding down the Shift key and pressing the PrtSc key if your keyboard is like the one in Figure 2-7a).

(i) Erase the worksheet by typing /WEY.

2-4 Put your name in cell F2. Put EXERCISE 2-4 in cell F3. Put the date in F4.

(a) Enter the following worksheet exactly as shown.

	B	C	D
3		UNITED GROMMITS	
4		May 1991	
5			
6			
7	GROMMITS		34
8	WIDGETS		27
9	CONNECTORS		63
10			
11	TOTAL SALES		+D7+D8+D9
12			
13	COST OF GOODS SOLD		55
14			
15	GROSS MARGIN		+D11-D13
16			
17	SELLING EXPENSES		42
18			
19	NET PROFIT		+D15-D17

(b) Change the number in D8 to 31. The numbers in D11, D15, and D19 should change automatically.

(c) Change the number in D13 to 83. The numbers in D15 and D19 should change.

(d) Obtain a printout of the screen.

(e) Erase the worksheet by typing /WEY.

2-5 Enter the spreadsheet of Exercise 2-2 into the computer. Remember that columns E and G and row 11 contain *formulas*. Do not use commas or dollar signs when entering the numbers. Change Carey's Sales to 615000. Do all the other numbers change appropriately?

2-6 Joggers often are curious about how fast they run. Create a spreadsheet like the one given that allows you to enter two numbers: a distance in miles and the number of minutes required to run the distance. The spreadsheet then should calculate two quantities: the average number of minutes per mile and the average miles per hour for the run. Try the spreadsheet on the following runs: 1 mile in 4 minutes, 3.5 miles in 42 minutes, 26.21875 miles in 129.7 minutes by changing the numbers in E4 and E5.

```
       A        B        C        D        E
1
2                   JOGGER'S CALCULATOR
3
4      NUMBER OF MILES RUN:                  4.5
5      TIME IN MINUTES:                      36
6
7      AVERAGE MINUTES PER MILE:             8
8      AVERAGE MILES PER HOUR:               7.5
9
10
```

2-7   Create a well-labeled spreadsheet that allows you to enter two numbers: the number of feet and inches in a person's height. The spreadsheet then should calculate the person's height in centimeters. Try your spreadsheet on the following heights: 5 feet, 2 inches; 6 feet, 0 inches; 7 feet, 4.5 inches.

2-8   The Widget Division factory purchases 25,000 couplers per year for use in its widget manufacturing process. The Director of Purchasing figures that it costs $20.00 (in personnel and computer time) for the company to process an order to purchase couplers. It costs the company $4.00 per year to carry a coupler in inventory (including space allocation, breakage, theft, insurance). As the new Assistant to the Director of Purchasing your job is to calculate how many couplers should be ordered at one time. If you order 100 couplers at a time, then orders will be arriving almost daily, so you will have low carrying costs, but you will have to pay for 250 purchases per year. If you order 100,000 couplers at a time, then you will have low purchase costs but very high inventory carrying costs.

The Economic Order Quantity (EOQ) is the amount that should be ordered at one time to minimize carrying and ordering costs. The EOQ is calculated by

$$\sqrt{\frac{2DO}{C}}$$

where D is the annual demand, O is the cost for processing an order, and C is the annual carrying cost for a unit in inventory.

(a) Create a spreadsheet for determining the Economic Order Quantity. You should have an appropriate heading at the top. You should have separate well-labeled cells for the annual demand, order cost, and annual unit carrying cost. Your spreadsheet should work for any quantities entered. (Note that the square root of a quantity can be calculated by raising the quantity to the 0.5 power.) How many couplers should be purchased at a time? Try your spreadsheet on the numbers in the first paragraph. Remember not to enter dollar signs and commas with your numbers. Print the spreadsheet.

(b) Suppose the demand for widgets increases dramatically, and now we need to purchase 100,000 couplers per year. How many should be purchased at a time? Print the spreadsheet.

2-9 We would like to create a spreadsheet that will allow us to compare what we were supposed to sell in each region (our "quota") with what we actually sold.

(a) Enter the following worksheet with appropriate *formulas* in the blank cells in the bottom row and right column. Just as a check, the number calculated for AMOUNT OVER QUOTA for AFRICA should be 3.3.

```
SALES IN $ MILLIONS

                                               AMOUNT OVER
REGION                  QUOTA      ACTUAL          QUOTA

AFRICA                    24        27.3
ANTARCTICA                 3        89.4
ASIA                      20        33.5
EUROPE                    32        31.2
LATIN AMERICA             17        11.8
NORTH AMERICA             25        46.1

TOTAL
```

(b) Change the ASIA ACTUAL sales to 56.7 and the LATIN AMERICA ACTUAL sales to 15.1. The numbers in the TOTAL row and AMOUNT OVER QUOTA column should change automatically.

(c) Add formulas in a new column that calculate PERCENT OVER QUOTA for each of the regions and for the TOTAL. The PERCENT OVER QUOTA calculated for AFRICA should be 13.75. For EUROPE it should be -2.5.

2-10 Create a spreadsheet to calculate the Break-Even Point for a product. Allow the user to enter three values: a unit Selling Price, the percentage of the selling price required for the Variable Cost of each unit, and the total Fixed Cost. The spreadsheet should be well-labeled and should contain formulas to calculate automatically two values: the Break-Even Point in units sold and the Break-Even Point in dollar volume sold. The spreadsheet also may calculate some intermediate values, if you wish. Do not type dollar signs or commas when entering the values into your spreadsheet. Print your spreadsheet with the following sets of input values: (a) Selling Price 200, Variable Cost Percent 60, Fixed Cost 40000, (b) Selling Price 250, Variable Cost Percent 50,

Fixed Cost 50000. Write out by hand on your printout the formulas that appear in each cell.

ISSUING

COMMANDS

C
H
A
P
T
E
R

3

There are three aspects to learning to master Lotus 1-2-3. The first part is learning how to construct spreadsheets, how to construct formulas, and how to interpret formulas. The second is learning the Lotus 1-2-3 commands. The third is learning to create and use macros. In this chapter we will begin our discussion of Lotus 1-2-3 commands.

Lotus 1-2-3 has over 400 commands. Commands allow you to save your work on disk, to display numbers with dollar signs and commas, to rearrange the rows in your spreadsheet in some order, and to draw graphs.

Commands can be issued whenever the mode indicator on the top right of the screen says READY. To tell the computer you would like to issue a command, you type a slash key /. Note that there is a slash key and a backslash key on the keyboard. The slash key is located under the question mark. The slash key is used both to issue a command and within a formula to indicate division.

COMMAND MENUS

When you type the slash key to issue a command, several changes happen on the screen. (See Figure 3-1.) On the top line, the mode indicator changes to **MENU**. The second line shows the **main command menu**. This is the choice of commands that you can issue. You can issue the **Worksheet** command or the **Range** command or the **Copy** command and so on.

There are two ways to issue a command. First, you can simply type the first letter of the command. For example, if you wanted to issue the Worksheet command, you would type a W. Commands in a menu always have different starting letters so there is no confusion when you type a letter.

The second way to issue a command is to use the arrow keys or the space bar to move the **menu pointer** to the command you wish to issue and then press the Enter key. The menu pointer also is called the **highlighter**. As you can see in Figure 3-1, after you press the slash key the Worksheet command is highlighted initially. Pressing the right arrow key or the space bar once will cause the Range command, the next command to the right, to be highlighted. Pressing the Enter key tells Lotus that you wish to issue the command that currently is highlighted.

SUBMENUS

Suppose you wish to erase the current worksheet on the screen and start over. You type the slash key. The main command menu appears on the screen. Next you type a W to issue the Worksheet

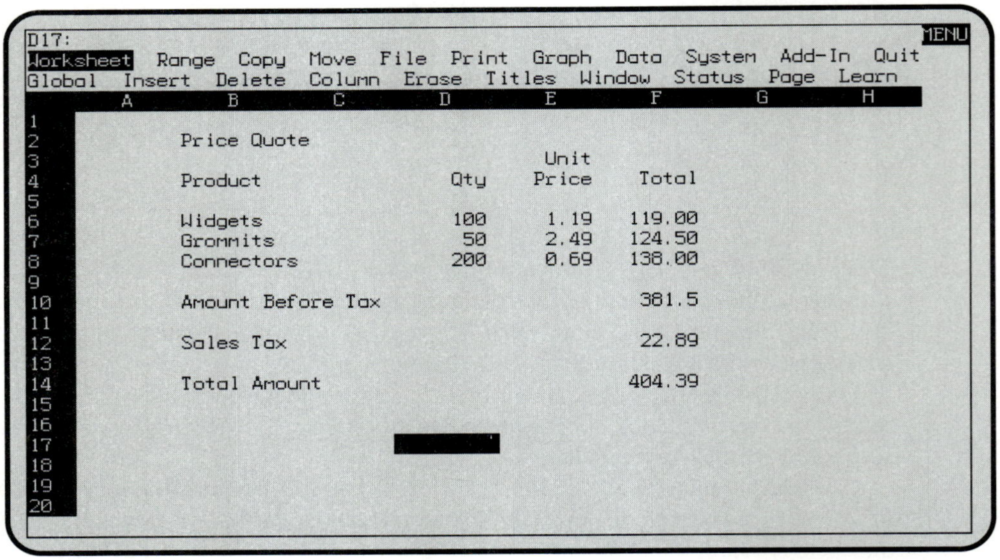

FIGURE 3-1 The main command menu appears after you type the slash key /.

command. Now you are confronted with the screen in Figure 3-2. This is the **submenu** for the Worksheet command. Lotus in effect is saying, "OK you want to change the worksheet somehow. What do you want to do: Insert a row? Delete a row? Change the width of the columns? Erase the worksheet? ..." There are many possibilities. You wish to erase the worksheet, so you now type E for Erase. Finally, you are confronted with the choice in Figure 3-3. Lotus is saying, "This is a serious action. Are you sure you want to erase the worksheet? Type N for No if you don't want to erase it. Type Y for Yes if you really do." You type Y and the worksheet is erased.

In the exercises Chapter 2, you were instructed to erase the current worksheet by typing /WEY. Now we can see that what you were doing was issuing commands to Lotus 1-2-3. In particular, you were telling Lotus 1-2-3 / Worksheet Erase Yes.

Incidentally, if you have just erased the worksheet and you change your mind *right away* and the Undo feature is enabled (the UNDO indicator appears on the bottom of the screen), you can revert back to the worksheet you just erased by typing Alt-F4.

THE COMMAND TREE

When you type the slash key, you are confronted with the main command menu of Figure 3-1. Select one of the commands in the menu and you are confronted with another menu. You continue selecting commands until you have fully specified the action you would like performed.

The choices of commands can be represented as a **command tree** as in Figure 3-4. Here the initial slash that you type is at the bottom of the tree. The first layer of branches represent the

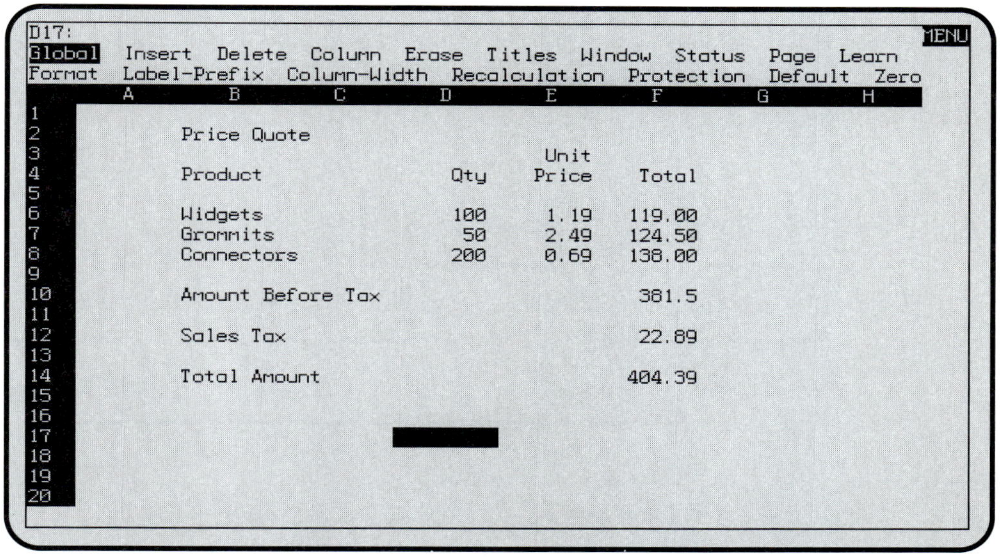

FIGURE 3-2 Typing a W brings you to the sub-menu for the Worksheet command.

```
D17:                                                                    MENU
No  Yes
Do not erase the worksheet; return to READY mode
        A        B          C        D       E        F        G        H
1
2               Price Quote
3                                            Unit
4               Product              Qty     Price    Total
5
6               Widgets              100     1.19     119.00
7               Grommits             50      2.49     124.50
8               Connectors           200     0.69     138.00
9
10              Amount Before Tax                     381.5
11
12              Sales Tax                             22.89
13
14              Total Amount                          404.39
15
16
17
18
19
20
```

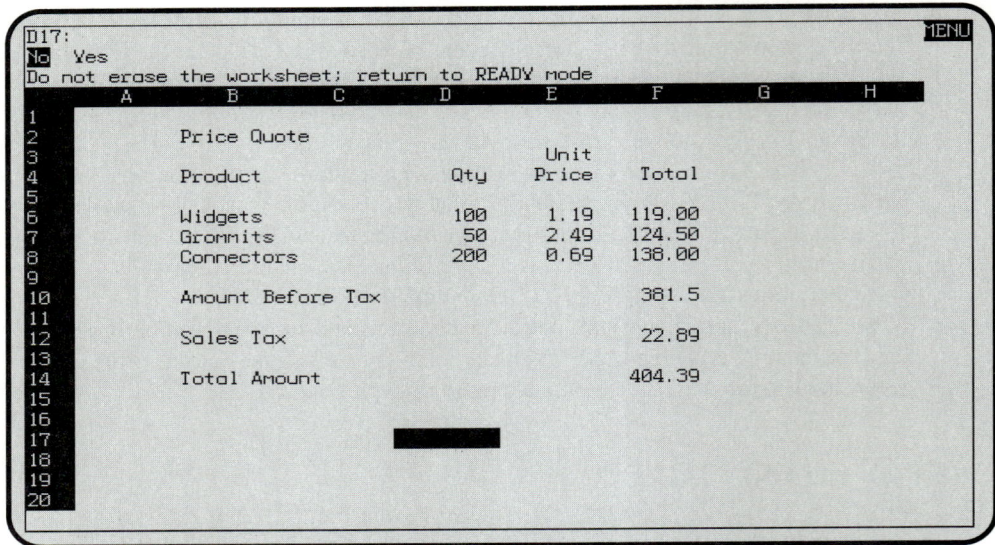

FIGURE 3-3 Are you sure you want to erase this worksheet? Type N (for No) or Y (for Yes).

FIGURE 3-4 A very small portion of the Lotus 1-2-3 command tree. See Appendix G for the complete tree.

choices in the main command menu. Each of those commands leads to further choices. You instruct the computer to perform some action by selecting a first branch and continuing to select branches until you reach the "leaves" of the tree. Some of the paths are three branches long. Others are six or more.

The complete command tree for Lotus 1-2-3 is given in Appendix G. By convention, the command tree is drawn upside down with the root of the tree at the top of the page and the leaves of the tree at the bottom. That is, the initial commands are given at the top of the page and you keep moving down the page as you make choices by issuing subcommands. As you can see, the Lotus 1-2-3 command tree has over 400 branches; there are over 400 commands.

Issuing commands is like ordering dinner in a restaurant. You are given the initial menu. You tell the waitress that you would like the chicken. "That comes with soup or salad. Which would you like?" "I'll take the salad." "We have French, Italian, or house dressing. What kind of dressing would you like on your salad?" And so on. You select from the initial menu and then continue to select from the "submenus" until you have ordered your dinner.

When you type the slash key, the main command menu appears on the second line of the screen. On the line below it Lotus 1-2-3 displays further information about the highlighted selection. In Figure 3-5 the Copy command is highlighted. The line beneath says "Copy a cell or range of cells" as an explanation for the action that would be taken if you select Copy. When the Worksheet command is highlighted, as in Figure 3-1, the line below the command menu says "Global Insert Delete...". This also is an explanation of the Worksheet command, but of a different kind. This line is telling you that if you select Worksheet now, then your next

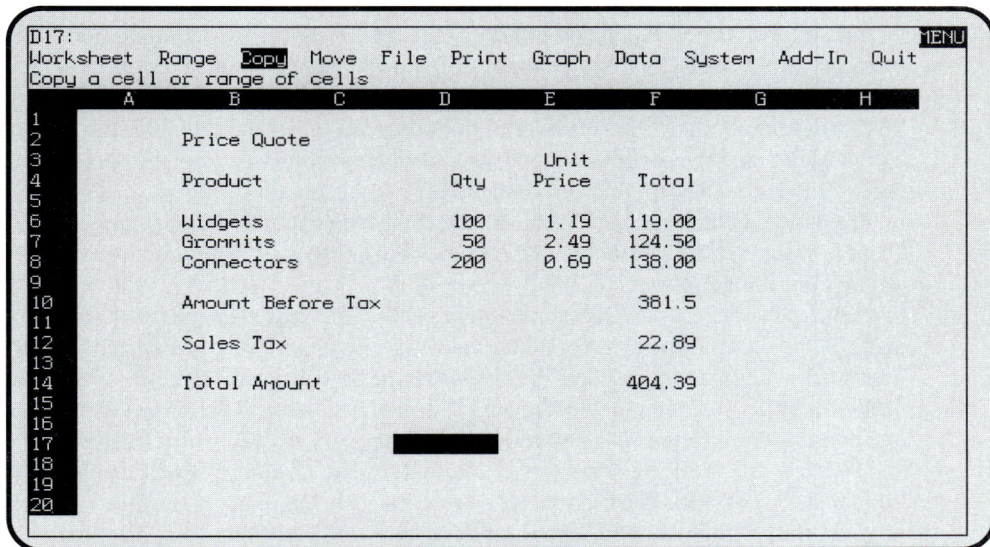

FIGURE 3-5 The Copy command is highlighted in the menu. The line below provides an explanation for the highlighted command.

choice will be "Global Insert Delete...". In other words, when the Worksheet command is highlighted, the next line shows the Worksheet submenu. When the Range command is highlighted, the next line shows the Range submenu.

THE ESCAPE KEY

It is not unusual to select the wrong command and then find yourself on the wrong branch of the command tree. You wanted to erase the worksheet but by mistake you typed /G instead of /W. Now you are confronted with the Graph submenu instead of the Worksheet submenu. How do you recover? The Backspace key does not work for commands. You cannot use Alt-F4 (Undo) because you are not in Ready mode. The answer is to press the Escape key. The Escape key undoes the last menu item that you selected. That is, if you are in the command tree and you press the Escape key, you move one branch down the tree. If you continue to press the Escape key, you eventually will back your way out of the command menu system and into READY mode.

Indeed, the Escape key is the general "get out of trouble" key. If Lotus 1-2-3 is beeping at you or flashing ERROR at you and you don't know what is going on, just press the Escape key a few times and you'll probably get out of trouble.

USING THE DISK

When you enter your spreadsheet into the computer, the information is saved in the primary memory (also called RAM, or Random Access Memory) of the computer. The primary memory is temporary, working memory. If you start a new spreadsheet or if you lose electric power or if you quit out of Lotus 1-2-3 or if you turn off the computer, then the spreadsheet that is in primary memory will be erased. For the computer to remember the spreadsheet, the spreadsheet must be saved on disk. It is *your* responsibility to save the spreadsheet on disk; Lotus 1-2-3 does not do this automatically.

If you would like to access the disk, select the **File** command in the main command menu. That is, typing /F tells Lotus 1-2-3 that you would like to use the disk. There are several choices in the File submenu.

To save the current worksheet on the disk, select /File Save. The computer will ask you for the name of the file you wish to save. Here you would enter a name of up to eight characters. You may use letters or digits. Do not use spaces or periods in the file name. However, you may use underscores (Shift-Hyphen). You should select a name that will make sense to you three weeks from now. For the homework exercises I suggest you use something like EXER3_4 for Exercise 3-4.

To retrieve a file on the disk, select / File Retrieve. Lotus 1-2-3 will then show you on the second line a list of the worksheet files now on the disk. You can use the arrow keys or spacebar to move the highlighter to the name of the file you would like to retrieve and then select that file by pressing the Enter key. Or you can simply type the name of the worksheet you would like to retrieve. Be warned! Retrieving a file from the disk erases the entire current worksheet. If you have been working on a spreadsheet, be sure to save it on the disk before retrieving another one.

To see a complete list of the worksheet files on the disk, select / File List Worksheet.

Sometimes you retrieve a worksheet from the disk, make changes in it, and tell Lotus 1-2-3 to save the worksheet back on the disk using the same name. If you instruct Lotus 1-2-3 to save a worksheet and one with the same name already exists on the disk, Lotus 1-2-3 asks you if you are sure, if you want to Replace the worksheet on the disk, Cancel the command, or Backup the existing file. This is done just to make sure that you don't accidentally select a name you used six months ago and inadvertently lose the important spreadsheet stored under that name on the disk. If you select Replace, the worksheet on the disk will be erased and the worksheet you are working on now will replace it on the disk.

As you may know, on the computer, files have a second name, called the **file extension**. Lotus 1-2-3 Release 2.2 automatically uses the extension .WK1. Thus if you save a worksheet under the name BUDG93, the full name of the file on the disk will be BUDG93.WK1. The "WK" stands for "Worksheet."

Files can be saved on various disks and disk drives. If you have one floppy disk drive, it usually is designated **A:**. A second floppy disk drive is **B:**. If you have a built-in hard disk it is usually designated **C:**. You also can specify a directory on the disk in which to save the worksheet. Thus if you instruct Lotus 1-2-3 to save your worksheet in C:\LOTUS\BUDG92, then your worksheet will be saved as BUDG92.WK1 in the LOTUS directory of your hard disk C.

Lotus 1-2-3 has a **default disk drive and directory**. This is the disk drive and directory it assumes you want to use if you do not specify one. When you select / File Retrieve or / File

```
D17:                                                                  EDIT
Enter name of file to save: C:\LOTUS\BOOK\CH3\_

         A        B        C        D        E        F        G        H
 1
 2            Price Quote
 3                                            Unit
 4            Product              Qty       Price     Total
 5
 6            Widgets              100        1.19     119.00
 7            Grommits              50        2.49     124.50
 8            Connectors           200        0.69     138.00
 9
10            Amount Before Tax                        381.5
11
12            Sales Tax                                22.89
13
14            Total Amount                            404.39
15
16
17
18
19
20
```

FIGURE 3-6 The default directory currently is \LOTUS\BOOK\CH3 on drive C. To save the worksheet in a different disk or directory first press the Escape key.

Save, the computer displays this default disk drive and directory, as in Figure 3-6. If you want to override these, just press the Backspace key or the Escape key one or more times and then type the disk or directory you would like to use. To change the disk or directory for future file retrieves and saves during this session with Lotus 1-2-3, use the command / File Directory. If you are working on a computer that has a built-in hard disk and that is used by other people as well— for example, if you are working on a computer in a college laboratory—then you should be sure to save your worksheet on your own floppy disk.

It is surprisingly easy and common to lose files that are saved on disks. Floppy disks can be misplaced or fall in a puddle. Hard disks can "crash." Files can be erased by mistake. I strongly advise you to buy an extra floppy disk and routinely keep at least two disk copies of all your work. Floppy disks are quite inexpensive. The $2 for an extra disk and the extra 20 seconds to save a copy on the second disk are an exceedingly good investment. Personally, I will not leave the computer without having copies of my work on two disks. Forewarned is forearmed. To save the file on a second floppy disk, simply remove the first floppy disk, insert the second disk, and select / File Save and the file name again.

ERASING A CELL

The correct way to erase a cell is to put the cursor on the cell, type / RE, and then press the Enter key. Here you invoke the command / Range Erase. Pressing the Enter key confirms that the cell you wish to erase is the cell with the cursor.

Warning! Some people get into the bad habit of "erasing" a cell by putting the cursor on the cell and then entering a space into the cell. This looks like it erases the cell, but it does not. The cell appears blank but actually contains the label consisting of a space. This can have unintended harmful effects, for example when using the @AVG or @COUNT functions described in Chapter 4.

HELP!

Lotus 1-2-3 has over 400 commands, 92 built-in functions, and many, many sundry features. No one could remember all the features and details of operating Lotus 1-2-3. Our brains hold only so much. Each time I learn another command, I seem to forget the telephone number of a friend.

Lotus 1-2-3 has a **Help** feature to assist us. If you press function key **F1**, you will activate the Help system. The Help system is "context sensitive" so that Lotus attempts to provide Help for what you are doing when you press F1.

If you are in Ready mode and press function key F1, Lotus 1-2-3 will display the 1-2-3 Help Index, shown in Figure 3-7. Note that one of the entries in the index is highlighted. You can move the highlighter around in the usual way using the arrow keys. When the topic you wish to learn more about is highlighted, press the Enter key. Lotus 1-2-3 will then display a Help screen on the topic indicated. You can continue browsing through the Help system by highlighting another topic and pressing the Enter key. When your question is answered or you give up in despair, press the Escape key to return to where you were before calling for Help.

```
D17:                                                              HELP

1-2-3 Help Index

About 1-2-3 Help          Linking Files          1-2-3 Main Menu
Cell Formats              Macro Basics           /Add-In
Cell/Range References     Macro Command Index    /Copy
Column Widths             Macro Key Names        /Data
Control Panel             Mode Indicators        /File
Entering Data             Operators              /Graph
Error Message Index       Range Basics           /Move
Formulas                  Recalculation          /Print
@Function Index           Specifying Ranges      /Quit
Function Keys             Status Indicators      /Range
Keyboard Index            Task Index             /System
Learn Feature             Undo Feature           /Worksheet

To select a topic, press a pointer-movement key to highlight the topic and then
press ENTER.  To return to a previous Help screen, press BACKSPACE.  To leave
Help and return to the worksheet, press ESC.
```

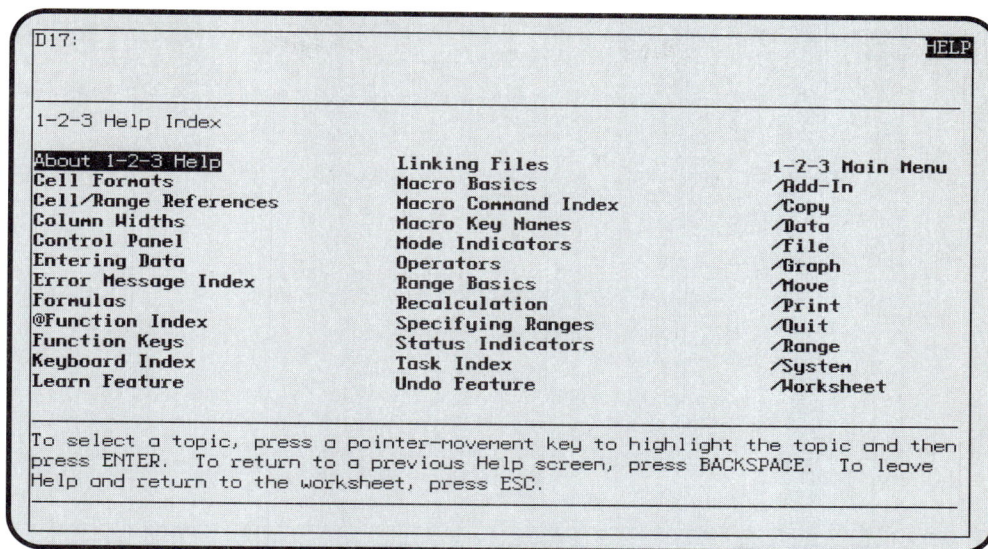

FIGURE 3-7 The Help Index. If Lotus 1-2-3 is in READY mode and you press F1, the Help key, Lotus 1-2-3 will enter the Help system and display the Help Index.

If you are in the middle of entering a command when you press F1, Lotus 1-2-3 will display a Help screen for the command. For example, if you select / File Retrieve and then press F1 to obtain Help, Lotus 1-2-3 will display the screen in Figure 3-8. To find out more about file names, move the highlighter to File Names in the bottom right corner and press the Enter key. The Help system is very convenient and useful.

TOP LEVEL COMMANDS

When you type a slash to enter the command system you are confronted with the main command menu shown in Figure 3-1. There are 11 different top-level commands from which to choose. The basic effects of each of the top level commands are as follows:

Worksheet	Invoke commands that affect the worksheet as a whole. (For example, /WEY erases the entire worksheet.)
Range	Invoke commands that affect a range, or rectangular portion, of the worksheet. (For example, /RE enter erases a single cell.)
Copy	Make one or more copies of a cell or range of cells.
Move	Move a cell or range of cells in the worksheet.
File	Use the disk. (For example, /FS saves the current spreadsheet on the disk.)
Print	Use the printer.

```
D17:                                                                    HELP
Name of file to retrieve: C:\LOTUS\BOOK\CH3\
───────────────────────────────────────────────────────────────────────────
/File Retrieve -- Reads a file on disk into memory, replacing
the worksheet that was current when you selected /File Retrieve.

CAUTION  /File Retrieve replaces the worksheet.  If you want to save it,
use /File Save before you retrieve another file.


1. Select /File Retrieve.
2. Specify the name of a file you want to retrieve.
3. If the file is password-protected, type the password and press ENTER.

   NOTE  Although 1-2-3 Release 2.2 can read data from files created with
   1-2-3 Release 1A (.WKS) and Symphony (.WRK and .WR1), it cannot save
   files in those formats.  When 1-2-3 reads a file with a .WKS, .WRK, or
   .WR1 extension, it beeps, converts the file to .WK1 format with the same
   file name, and displays a message indicating that the file and extension
   were converted.
───────────────────────────────────────────────────────────────────────────
Continued                     Using Menus of Names           File Names
File Commands                                                Help Index
```

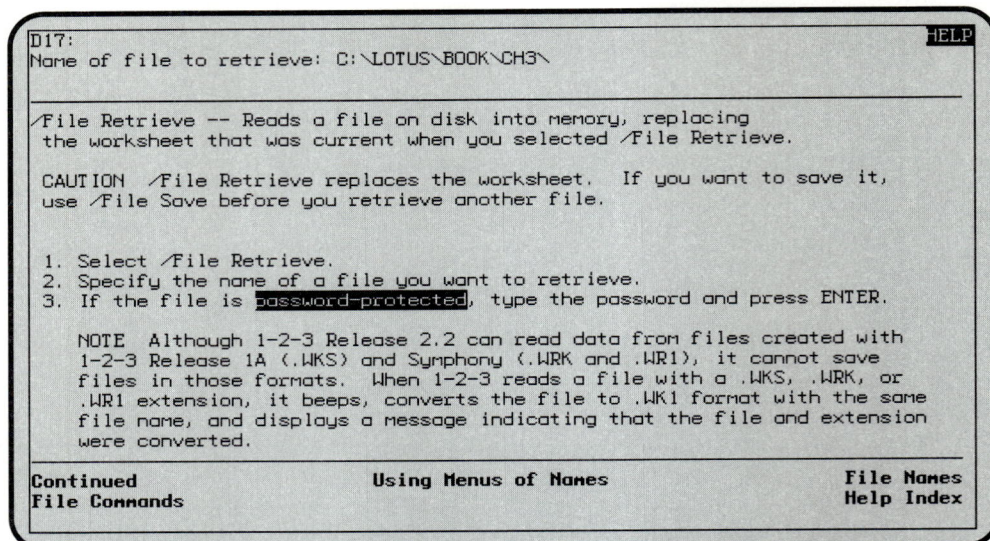

FIGURE 3-8 The Help screen for / File Retrieve. If you have selected / File Retrieve and then press F1, the Help key, this is the first screen you will see.

Graph	Draw a graph.
Data	Use the data mangement capabilities of Lotus 1-2-3.
System	Temporarily exit Lotus 1-2-3 to the Disk Operating System to issue a DOS command.
Add-In	Use an Add-In program, for example Allways. An **add-in program** is a separate program that was designed to work closely with Lotus 1-2-3 and enhance the capabilities of Lotus 1-2-3.
Quit	Exit Lotus 1-2-3

COMPUTER EXERCISE

3-1 This exercise is designed to give you practice entering commands and using the Help system of Lotus 1-2-3. You will need a formatted disk for this exercise.

(a) Press the Caps Lock key once. The word CAPS should appear at the bottom of the screen.

(b) Enter the following spreadsheet, which converts a temperature from Centigrade to Fahrenheit.

Cell	Contents
B3:	SPREADSHEET TO CONVERT TEMPERATURES
F3:	*Your name*
F4:	*Today's date*
F5:	EXERCISE 3-1
B5:	HELLO
B7:	ENTER THE TEMPERATURE IN CENTIGRADE:
G7:	10
B9:	EQUIVALENT TEMPERATURE IN FAHRENHEIT:
G9:	(1.8*G7)+32

Cell G9 should show 50, the Fahrenheit equivalent of 10 degrees Centigrade.

(c) Move the cursor to G7. Enter the number 20. The number in G9 should change to 68.

(d) Move the cursor to cell B5. Press the slash key. The main menu choices should appear on the screen. Type R for Range and E for Erase. Press the Enter key. The word HELLO should be erased.

(e) Insert your disk in the disk drive. Select / File Save by typing /FS . The message at the top of the screen should look like

```
Enter name of file to save: A:\*.wk1
```

If the computer waits a while and then beeps at you and the word ERROR appears at the top right of the screen, your disk is in the wrong disk drive or, possibly, you have inserted the disk incorrectly. Press the Escape key twice to clear the error message. Remove the disk. Place your thumb on the label. Insert the disk in the indicated drive. Select / File Save again.

Type EXER3_1 for the name of the file to save. The symbol between the 3 and the 1 is an underscore, a Shift-Hyphen, or Shift-Dash. Press the Enter key. The red light should go on next to the disk drive. Your spreadsheet is being saved on the disk.

(f)   To be sure the spreadsheet was saved, select / File List Worksheet. You should see EXER3_1 listed on the screen along with any other worksheet files saved on the disk. If EXER3_1 is not there, repeat step (e) and then try again.

(g)   Print the spreadsheet by pressing the PrintScreen key (or Shift-PrtSc if required on your keyboard).

(h)   Erase the current spreadsheet by selecting / Worksheet Erase Yes. You now should be confronted with a blank worksheet on the screen.

(i)   Retrieve the worksheet from the disk by selecting / File Retrieve and then typing EXER3_1 and pressing Enter. The temperature worksheet should return.

(j)   Press the slash key. Now activate the Help system by pressing function key F1. Move the highlighter down to the entry for File Commands by pressing the down arrow key four times. Press the Enter key to see the first Help screen on the File commands.

(k)   Print the Help screen for the File Commands by pressing PrintScreen.

(l)   Explore the Help system by moving the highlighter to different entries and pressing the Enter key.

(m)   When finished with the Help system, press the Escape key to return to the spreadsheet. Press the Escape key again to exit from the menu system.

(n)   Exit Lotus 1-2-3 by selecting / Quit Yes . You now should see the Lotus 1-2-3 Access System screen. Select Exit to return to DOS. Remove your disks and turn off the computer.

4

SIMPLE FUNCTIONS AND THE COPY COMMAND

In the first three chapters we have seen how to create and use simple spreadsheets. The basic idea is that the memory is organized into a two-dimensional worksheet made up of rows and columns. The intersection of each row and column is called a cell. Initially all the cells are blank. We can fill each of the cells with labels (text), numbers, or formulas. The key to Lotus 1-2-3 is in the formulas. Whenever any cell is changed, all the relevant formulas are recalculated. We can save and manipulate worksheets by using the Lotus 1-2-3 commands. To invoke a command, press the slash key and then select from the sequence of menus.

In this chapter we begin to explore how to construct larger, more realistic spreadsheets. There are two important tools for doing this: built-in functions and the Copy command. In many ways this is the pivotal chapter of the book. Once you understand how to use built-in functions and the Copy command, you are well on your way to mastering Lotus 1-2-3.

BUILT-IN FUNCTIONS SAVE YOU TYPING

Figure 4-1 is a spreadsheet showing the monthly sales by region for the first half of the year. The total sales for Africa is in cell H7. What would be the formula in this cell ? Clearly, it could be

$$+B7+C7+D7+E7+F7+G7$$

What if we would like to analyze sales for 60 months? Our formula would have 60 terms. Or, suppose we had 400 regions and would like to find the total sales for January? The formula would have 400 cell addresses and 400 plus signs. We need a shorter way of specifying formulas like this.

The best way to add up a list of numbers is to use the **built-in function** @SUM as follows:

$$@SUM(B7..G7)$$

This formula, which would appear in H7, tells Lotus 1-2-3 that the number that should appear in the cell is the result of adding all the numbers from B7 through G7. Similarly, the formula in cell B14 could be

$$@SUM(B7..B12)$$

```
H7:                                                              READY

              A          B        C        D        E        F        G        H
   1
   2
   3                        SALES SUMMARY BY REGION
   4
   5                     JAN      FEB      MAR      APR      MAY      JUN    TOTAL
   6
   7   AFRICA          4.6      3.4      4.2      5.4      3.9      4.9  ████████
   8   ANTARCTICA      1.1      0.8      0.7      1.3      0.9      1.3
   9   ASIA           43.2     46.4     45.4     47.8     47.1     46.3
  10   EUROPE         32.5     33.7     34.1     33.8     33.5     35.2
  11   LATIN AMERICA  14.7     13.8     13.4     17.5     15.2     18.9
  12   NORTH AMERICA  39.5     41.3     40.8     42.4     38.7     43.5
  13
  14   TOTAL
  15
  16
  17
  18
  19
  20
                              UNDO
```

FIGURE 4-1 What formula should be entered in cell H7?

If we had 400 regions, we could add up all the sales for January with the formula

@SUM(B7..B406)

Clearly, typing this formula is easier than typing out 400 cell addresses and 400 plus signs. Built-in functions can save lots of typing. They help make large spreadsheets easy to construct.

THE VARIETY OF FUNCTIONS

There are 92 built-in functions in Lotus 1-2-3 Release 2.2. Each of the built-in function names begins with an @ (Shift-2), which identifies the name as a built-in function. We will discuss 5 of the more common functions here. Other functions will be discussed later in the book. A complete list of the built-in functions is provided in Appendix E.

The most frequently used function by far is @SUM. Other common functions include

@AVG	Calculates the average or arithmetic mean of a list of values.
@COUNT	Counts the number of nonblank cells in a list.
@MAX	Finds the largest value in a list.
@MIN	Finds the smallest value in a list.

Thus, for the spreadsheet for Figure 4-1, @AVG(B7..G7) would find the average monthly sales for Africa. The result of evaluating the formula would be 4.4. The formula @MAX(B7..G7) would find the highest monthly sales for Africa, namely, 5.4. The formula @COUNT(B7..G7) would count the number of sales figures for Africa, namely, 6. Note that @COUNT determines how many nonblank cells there are rather than how many cells contain numbers. Thus, @COUNT(B5..B12) would evaluate to 7, as the label in B5 would contribute to the count but the blank cell in B6 would not.

The @AVG function really is just the @SUM function divided by the @COUNT function. The formula @AVG(B7..G7) is the same as @SUM(B7..G7)/@COUNT(B7..G7). This is important for understanding how missing values are treated in the @AVG function. If the number in F7, the May sales for Africa, were missing and the cell were blank, the average would be computed by adding the numbers and dividing by 5 rather than 6. Incidentally, if one of the cells in the range of a function is a label, Lotus 1-2-3 Release 2.2 considers the cell to contain a 0 in performing the calculations.

Built-in functions not only save typing. They also provide a wide variety of calculations. Some of these calculations are impossible to specify using the normal arithmetic operators. For example, there is no formula using addition, subtraction, multiplication, and division for calculating the largest number in a list. @SUM saves typing. @MAX provides a completely new capability.

ARGUMENTS AND RANGES

The inputs to a function are placed inside the parentheses and are called **arguments**. Multiple arguments in a function are separated by commas. For example, the formula @SUM(C6,3,4*B2) instructs Lotus 1-2-3 to add up the number in cell C6, the number 3, and the result of multiplying 4 times the number in B2. The @SUM function here has three arguments: C6, 3, and 4*B2. The functions @SUM, @AVG, @COUNT, @MAX, and @MIN can have any number of arguments.

The most useful type of argument for these functions is a **range**. The argument in @SUM(B7..G7) is B7..G7 , which is a range.

Ranges are very important in Lotus 1-2-3. Ranges commonly are used both in formulas and in commands. A range always specifies a rectangular portion of a spreadsheet. A range consists of a cell address followed by two periods followed by another cell address. The first cell address gives one corner of the range. The second address indicates the diagonally opposite corner of the range. Usually, the first address is the top left corner of the range; the second address is the bottom right corner of the range.

The range B7..G7 is a 1-by-6 cell horizontal rectangle. The range B7..B12 is a 6-by-1 vertical rectangle. The range B7..G12 would contain 36 cells in a rectangle 6 cells across from column B through G and 6 cells down from row 7 through row 12.

What should be the formula in cell H14 in the spreadsheet in Figure 4-1? This is the grand total of the sales for the six months. There are three choices. The formula could be

@SUM(H7..H12)

This would calculate the grand total by adding up the product totals. The formula in H14 could be

@SUM(B14..G14)

This would calculate the grand total by adding up the monthly totals. The third possibility is for the formula in H14 to be

@SUM(B7..G12)

This would calculate the grand total by adding up the original 36 monthly sales numbers. All three formulas would give the same answer.

How many numbers would be added up in the following formula ?

@SUM(23,C12,B4..B7,47,C2..E5)

There are five arguments:

1. The number 23—1 number

2. The cell C12—1 number
3. The range B4..B7—4 numbers
4. The number 47—1 number
5. The range C2..E5—12 numbers

Thus this formula instructs the computer to add 19 numbers.

POINTING

A convenient way to specify cell addresses in formulas is to **point** to them instead of typing them. Pointing is a special feature of Lotus 1-2-3 that is commonly used but takes some practice on the computer. The idea of pointing is to use the arrow keys to point to the address that you would like to include in a formula. Pointing is especially useful when specifying a range, because when you point to a range, Lotus 1-2-3 highlights the range on the screen.

To illustrate, consider the spreadsheet in Figure 4-2. We are in the process of entering the formula for cell H7. We have typed @SUM(and now are about to enter the range. Instead of typing the first address of the range, we press the left arrow key. Now the screen changes to Figure 4-3. The mode indicator in the top right of the screen changes to POINT. The address of the cell we are pointing to appears in the formula. We press the left arrow key five more times. We now are pointing to cell B7, as in Figure 4-4. Cell B7 is the leftmost cell in the range,

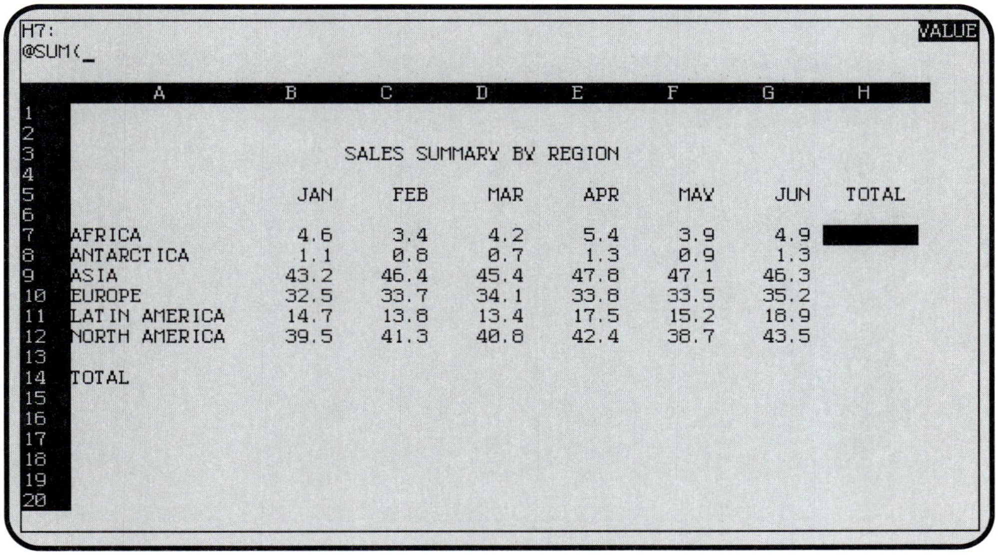

FIGURE 4-2 Entering the formula into H7 before we begin pointing.

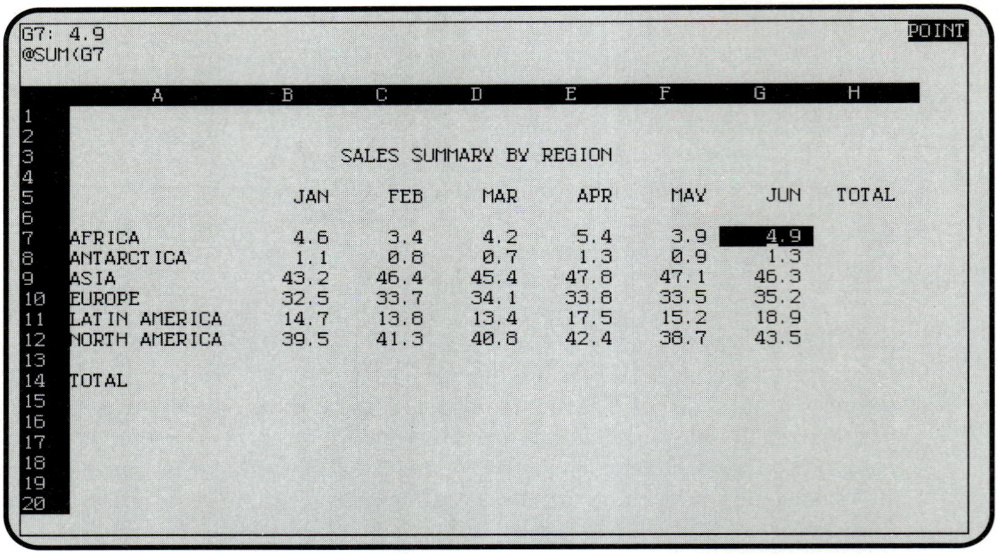

```
G7:  4.9                                                           POINT
@SUM(G7

           A          B        C        D        E        F        G        H
 1
 2
 3                            SALES SUMMARY BY REGION
 4
 5                   JAN      FEB      MAR      APR      MAY      JUN    TOTAL
 6
 7    AFRICA          4.6      3.4      4.2      5.4      3.9      4.9
 8    ANTARCTICA      1.1      0.8      0.7      1.3      0.9      1.3
 9    ASIA           43.2     46.4     45.4     47.8     47.1     46.3
10    EUROPE         32.5     33.7     34.1     33.8     33.5     35.2
11    LATIN AMERICA  14.7     13.8     13.4     17.5     15.2     18.9
12    NORTH AMERICA  39.5     41.3     40.8     42.4     38.7     43.5
13
14    TOTAL
15
16
17
18
19
20
```

FIGURE 4-3 The screen after we press the left arrow and begin to point to the range to be summed.

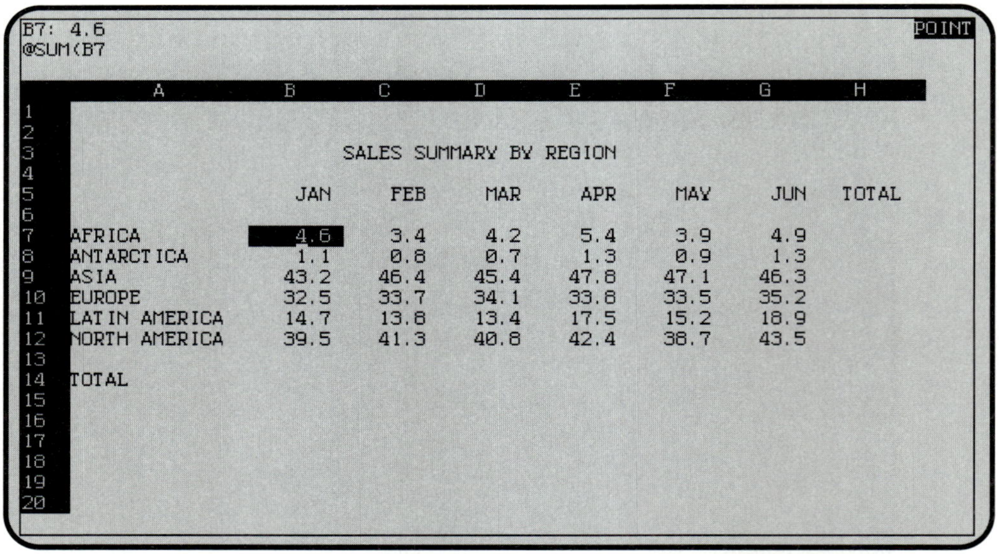

```
B7:  4.6                                                           POINT
@SUM(B7

           A          B        C        D        E        F        G        H
 1
 2
 3                            SALES SUMMARY BY REGION
 4
 5                   JAN      FEB      MAR      APR      MAY      JUN    TOTAL
 6
 7    AFRICA          4.6      3.4      4.2      5.4      3.9      4.9
 8    ANTARCTICA      1.1      0.8      0.7      1.3      0.9      1.3
 9    ASIA           43.2     46.4     45.4     47.8     47.1     46.3
10    EUROPE         32.5     33.7     34.1     33.8     33.5     35.2
11    LATIN AMERICA  14.7     13.8     13.4     17.5     15.2     18.9
12    NORTH AMERICA  39.5     41.3     40.8     42.4     38.7     43.5
13
14    TOTAL
15
16
17
18
19
20
```

FIGURE 4-4 After pressing the left arrow key five more times we are pointing to B7, the leftmost cell of the range to be summed. Now we continue the formula by typing a period.

the cell we would like to specify here. We proceed with the formula by typing two periods. This "anchors" the range. Now we begin to specify the opposite cell in the range by pressing the right arrow key. We press the right arrow key four more times and arrive at cell G7, our destination. The screen is shown in Figure 4-5. As we have been pointing, Lotus 1-2-3 has been highlighting the range we are specifying. We now type the right parenthesis and Enter key to complete the formula. Many people find this graphic approach to specifying ranges more convenient than typing.

The basic idea here is to type the formula, but whenever we are about to type a cell address, we point to it using the arrow keys instead. In the example, the actual keystrokes were as follows:

$$@SUM\ (\leftarrow\ \leftarrow\ \leftarrow\ \leftarrow\ \leftarrow\ \leftarrow\ .\ .\ \rightarrow\ \rightarrow\ \rightarrow\ \rightarrow\ \rightarrow)\quad \text{Enter}$$

The final formula for cell H7 is shown in Figure 4-6.

Pointing can be used in Lotus 1-2-3 in commands as well as in formulas. Any time you are about to type an address, you can point to it instead.

A COMMON ERROR: CIRCULAR REFERENCE

A common error that people make when entering a formula is to include the address of the cell in the formula itself. An example is shown in Figure 4-7. The formula in H7 should be

```
G7: 4.9                                                                    POINT
@SUM(B7..G7

                 A         B        C         D        E        F        G        H
 1
 2
 3                           SALES SUMMARY BY REGION
 4
 5                      JAN       FEB      MAR       APR      MAY      JUN    TOTAL
 6
 7    AFRICA           4.6       3.4      4.2       5.4      3.9      4.9
 8    ANTARCTICA       1.1       0.8      0.7       1.3      0.9      1.3
 9    ASIA            43.2      46.4     45.4      47.8     47.1     46.3
10    EUROPE          32.5      33.7     34.1      33.8     33.5     35.2
11    LATIN AMERICA   14.7      13.8     13.4      17.5     15.2     18.9
12    NORTH AMERICA   39.5      41.3     40.8      42.4     38.7     43.5
13
14    TOTAL
15
16
17
18
19
20
```

FIGURE 4-5 As we point to the opposite side of the range, Lotus 1-2-3 highlights the range we are specifying.

```
H7:  @SUM(B7..G7)                                                        READY

        A        B        C        D        E        F        G    H
 1
 2
 3                    SALES SUMMARY BY REGION
 4
 5                 JAN      FEB      MAR      APR      MAY      JUN    TOTAL
 6
 7   AFRICA        4.6      3.4      4.2      5.4      3.9      4.9    26.4
 8   ANTARCTICA    1.1      0.8      0.7      1.3      0.9      1.3
 9   ASIA         43.2     46.4     45.4     47.8     47.1     46.3
10   EUROPE       32.5     33.7     34.1     33.8     33.5     35.2
11   LATIN AMERICA 14.7    13.8     13.4     17.5     15.2     18.9
12   NORTH AMERICA 39.5    41.3     40.8     42.4     38.7     43.5
13
14   TOTAL
15
16
17
18
19
20
                        UNDO
```

FIGURE 4-6 The final formula in cell H7. The next step is to copy the formula down column H.

@SUM(B7..G7). By mistake in H7 we have entered the formula @SUM(B7..H7). This could have occurred, for example, if we were pointing to the range and pressed the right arrow once too often. The formula @SUM(B7..H7) instructs the computer that the value to be shown in H7 is the sum of the numbers from B7 through H7. That is, the computer needs to know the value in H7 in order to calculate the value in H7.

A formula that depends on its own value has a **circular reference**. A spreadsheet that contains a circular reference often gives unexpected answers. Lotus 1-2-3 indicates when a circular reference is present in the current spreadsheet by displaying the status indicator CIRC at the bottom of the spreadsheet, as in Figure 4-7. (For a list of all possible status indicators and their meanings, see Appendix B.)

If formulas are yielding unexpected answers, you should check to see if the word CIRC is displayed at the bottom of the screen. If you have a circular reference in your spreadsheet but you do not know which cell contains the circular reference, you can find out by selecting / Worksheet Status. To correct a formula with a circular reference, you can simply move the cursor to the cell and reenter the formula.

NESTED FUNCTIONS

The arguments of a function can include other functions. A function inside another function results in a **nested function**. An example of a nested function is

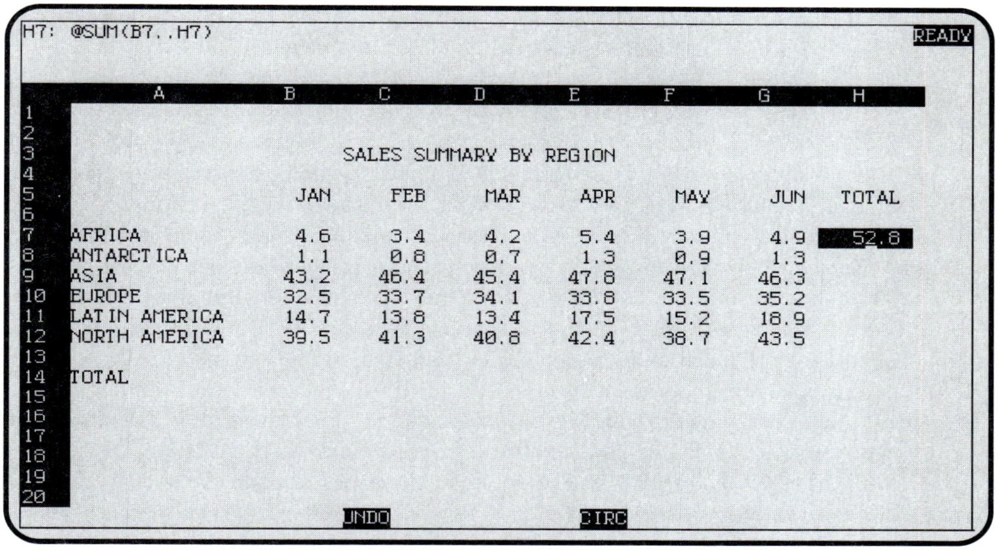

FIGURE 4-7 A mistake has been made. A circular reference occurs because cell H7 contains a formula that refers to itself. Lotus 1-2-3 signals that a circular reference has occurred by displaying CIRC at the bottom of the screen.

$$@MAX(@SUM(C7..C10),@SUM(D7..D10),@SUM(E7..E10))$$

Here the @MAX function has three arguments. Each of the arguments is an @SUM function. The computer would add up C7 through C10. Then it would add up D7 through D10. Then it would add up E7 through E10. The value calculated by the whole formula would be the largest of these three totals. This is the number that would appear in the cell.

THE COPY COMMAND

Built-in functions with ranges provide an important tool for constructing large spreadsheets. They allow us to enter a formula that adds up 400 numbers by entering @SUM and two addresses. The Copy command allows us to make multiple copies of the formula, so we do not have to type it over and over again into a column of cells or row of cells.

Return to our example of tabulating the monthly sales by region. In Figure 4-6 the final formula in cell H7 is shown. We now would like to enter the formulas to total each of the other regions. The formulas for these cells would be as follows:

H7:   @SUM(B7..G7)
H8:   @SUM(B8..G8)

H9:   @SUM(B9..G9)
H10:   @SUM(B10..G10)
H11:   @SUM(B11..G11)
H12:   @SUM(B12..G12)

We could type each of these formulas, though it would be tedious. But suppose we had 400 regions? We would have to type the @SUM formula 400 times. A better solution than typing each of the formulas is to type the first formula and then use the Copy command.

Once we have entered the formula in cell H7, we can use the Copy command to tell Lotus 1-2-3 to copy the formula down the column into the other cells. But notice that we do not want Lotus 1-2-3 to make an exact copy of the formula in cell H7. If it did make an exact copy, then each of the cells from H8 through H12 would contain the formula @SUM(B7..G7), and the number that appeared in each of the cells would be the total for Africa. Rather, Lotus 1-2-3 has an "intelligent" copy command. As Lotus 1-2-3 copies the formula down the column, it automatically adjusts the row numbers in the formula. So @SUM(B7..G7) in H7 becomes @SUM(B8..G8) in cell H8, and so on, for each of the formulas that are copied into the cells.

USING THE COPY COMMAND

To make a copy of a cell, put the cursor on the cell and type /C . The computer first asks for the address of the original cell that you want copied, as in Figure 4-8. This sometimes is called the **FROM range** or the **source range**. Lotus 1-2-3 guesses that you want to copy the cell where the cursor currently is located. If this is the case, simply press the Enter key. If you wish to make a copy of some other cell, you can type the address of the other cell. (Note that Lotus 1-2-3 does allow you to enter a range here. This enables you to copy an entire row down the screen. For now, we will describe how to copy a single cell.)

After you have entered the address of the source for the copy, Lotus 1-2-3 asks for the destination, for the range of addresses where you wish the copies to be placed. Here you either can type the range or you can point to the range. In this example, the formulas are to be placed in cells H8..H12, as indicated in Figure 4-9. This sometimes is called the **TO range** or the **target range**. After the TO range has been entered, Lotus 1-2-3 makes the copies as requested. The result is shown in Figure 4-10.

The next step in the example would be to enter the formula @SUM(B7..B12) into B14. Then you would copy from B14 to C14..H14.

To review the steps in the Copy command:

1. Enter the original formula into a cell.
2. Copy the formula down the column or across the row, as follows
   a) Type /C.
   b) Enter the address of the cell that contains the original formula.
   c) Enter the *range* of addresses for the copies.

```
H7: @SUM(B7..G7)                                                    POINT
Enter range to copy FROM: H7..H7
          A         B       C       D       E       F       G       H
 1
 2
 3                        SALES SUMMARY BY REGION
 4
 5                  JAN     FEB     MAR     APR     MAY     JUN    TOTAL
 6
 7   AFRICA         4.6     3.4     4.2     5.4     3.9     4.9    26.4
 8   ANTARCTICA     1.1     0.8     0.7     1.3     0.9     1.3
 9   ASIA          43.2    46.4    45.4    47.8    47.1    46.3
10   EUROPE        32.5    33.7    34.1    33.8    33.5    35.2
11   LATIN AMERICA 14.7    13.8    13.4    17.5    15.2    18.9
12   NORTH AMERICA 39.5    41.3    40.8    42.4    38.7    43.5
13
14   TOTAL
15
16
17
18
19
20
```

FIGURE 4-8 After we issue the command / C, Lotus 1-2-3 asks for the address or addresses of the source of the copies, the "range to copy FROM". 1-2-3 guesses that we want H7, the current location of the cursor.

```
H12:                                                                POINT
Enter range to copy TO: H8..H12
          A         B       C       D       E       F       G       H
 1
 2
 3                        SALES SUMMARY BY REGION
 4
 5                  JAN     FEB     MAR     APR     MAY     JUN    TOTAL
 6
 7   AFRICA         4.6     3.4     4.2     5.4     3.9     4.9    26.4
 8   ANTARCTICA     1.1     0.8     0.7     1.3     0.9     1.3
 9   ASIA          43.2    46.4    45.4    47.8    47.1    46.3
10   EUROPE        32.5    33.7    34.1    33.8    33.5    35.2
11   LATIN AMERICA 14.7    13.8    13.4    17.5    15.2    18.9
12   NORTH AMERICA 39.5    41.3    40.8    42.4    38.7    43.5
13
14   TOTAL
15
16
17
18
19
20
```

FIGURE 4-9 Lotus 1-2-3 requests the range of addresses where the copies are to be placed. Be sure to enter a *range* rather than a single cell.

```
H7: @SUM(B7..G7)                                                      READY

        A          B        C        D        E        F        G        H
 1
 2
 3                         SALES SUMMARY BY REGION
 4
 5                 JAN      FEB      MAR      APR      MAY      JUN    TOTAL
 6
 7  AFRICA         4.6      3.4      4.2      5.4      3.9      4.9     26.4
 8  ANTARCTICA     1.1      0.8      0.7      1.3      0.9      1.3      6.1
 9  ASIA          43.2     46.4     45.4     47.8     47.1     46.3    276.2
10  EUROPE        32.5     33.7     34.1     33.8     33.5     35.2    202.8
11  LATIN AMERICA 14.7     13.8     13.4     17.5     15.2     18.9     93.5
12  NORTH AMERICA 39.5     41.3     40.8     42.4     38.7     43.5    246.2
13
14  TOTAL
15
16
17
18
19
20
                              UNDO
```

FIGURE 4-10 The formula in H7 has been copied to H8..H12. Lotus 1-2-3 automatically adjusted the row addresses in the formula as it was copied down the column.

The most common mistake that people make with the Copy command is to enter only the address of the final cell of the range for the copies rather than the entire range. That is, in the example in Figure 4-9, people mistakenly enter only H12 rather than H8..H12. Entering H12 for the TO range rather than H8..H12 results in a copy of the formula being placed only in H12 rather than in H8 through H12. If the Copy command does not seem to be working for you, try it again and be sure to enter the entire destination range.

It is possible to copy labels as well as formulas. An example is given in Exercise 4-2.

PAPER AND PENCIL EXERCISE

4-1 Consider the following spreadsheet.

```
          A          B         C         D
1
2
3          86        -4        -8       fun
4         -47         5        26        37
5         2.3         7      Lotus      198
6    computer        18       4.6         3
7          56       102                 -19
8
```

What would be the result of evaluating each of the following formulas? Write out your answers on paper. Do not use the computer. The point of this exercise is to ensure that *you* understand what the functions do.

(a) @SUM(A4..D4)

(b) @COUNT(A4..D4)

(c) @AVG(A4..D4)

(d) @MAX(A4..D4)

(e) @MIN(A4..D4)

(f) @AVG(B6..D7)

(g) @COUNT(A6..D6)

(h) @SUM(@AVG(B3..B6),@MAX(B3..B6),@MIN(B3..B7))

(i) @SUM(3*B3,B3..C6,@MAX(A4..C6),2*@MIN(A3..B5))

COMPUTER EXERCISES

4-2 This exercise helps you become familiar with the Copy command and with pointing.

(a) Enter the word HELLO in cell B2.
Type /C.
Lotus 1-2-3 now asks for the location of the cell to be copied. Type B2 Enter.
Lotus 1-2-3 now asks for the range of addresses for the copies. Type F1..F20 Enter.

The word HELLO now should appear 20 times, as you have copied it to F1..F20.

(b) Enter the word GOODBYE in cell C3.

Type /C.

For the FOR range type C3 Enter.

For the TO range type A15..J15 Enter.

The word GOODBYE should be repeated across row 15 on the screen.

(c) Enter the word LOTUS in cell D1.

Be sure the cursor is on D1.

Type /C.

When Lotus 1-2-3 requests the FOR range, it should guess D1..D1 so you simply can press the Enter key.

When Lotus 1-2-3 requests the TO range point to the range, as follows:

- Use the right arrow key to move the cursor to G1
- Type the period key (This "anchors" the range.)
- Use the down arrow key to move the cursor to G20. (The range should be highlighted as you move the cursor down.)
- Press the Enter key. The word LOTUS should appear in each cell from G1 through G20.

(d) Copy the word LOTUS from D1 to A17..J17. Point to the TO range.

4-3 Enter the following spreadsheet, adding the appropriate formulas. Use the built-in functions and the Copy command. Test the spreadsheet by changing some of the numbers and checking the bottom two rows and the right two columns. Save and print the spreadsheet.

SALES ANALYSIS

PRODUCT	WINTER	SPRING	SUMMER	FALL	TOTAL MAX
GOLF	32000	62000	57000	39000	
TENNIS	47000	52000	71000	29000	
SKIING	37000	21000	11000	52000	
SURFING	12000	21000	29000	13000	
TOTAL					
AVERAGE					

4-4 Set up a spreadsheet to help you track the amount of time you spend on the computer this semester. Use the built-in functions and the Copy command.

```
                    HOURS SPENT ON PC'S

WEEK     MON    TUES   WED    THUR   FRI    SAT    SUN    TOTAL
  1
  2
  3
 ...
 14
 15


TOTAL:

AVERAGE:

MAX:

MAXIMUM NO. HOURS SPENT IN ANY ONE DAY DURING THE SEMESTER:
```

4-5 The following spreadsheet shows the U.S. government receipts and outlays for 1980, 1985, and 1990. Enter the spreadsheet into the computer. (A long label entered into a single cell will show if the cell(s) to its right are blank.) Add formulas for the TOTAL RECEIPTS, TOTAL OUTLAYS, and SURPLUS. Use the @SUM function and the Copy command.

U.S. GOVERNMENT RECEIPTS AND OUTLAYS IN BILLIONS OF DOLLARS

	1980	1985	1990
RECEIPTS			
INDIVIDUAL INCOME TAXES	244	335	467
CORPORATE INCOME TAXES	65	61	94
SOCIAL INSURANCE TAXES	158	265	380
EXCISE TAXES	24	36	35
OTHER	26	37	56
TOTAL RECEIPTS			
OUTLAYS			
NATIONAL DEFENSE	134	253	299
SOCIAL SECURITY	119	189	249
INCOME SECURITY	87	128	147
MEDICARE	32	66	98
ALL OTHER GOVERNMENT	166	181	275
INTEREST	53	129	184
TOTAL OUTLAYS			
SURPLUS (DEFICIT)			

4-6 Create a spreadsheet to calculate the wages for hourly employees.

(a) Start off with a heading, the names of the employees, and the hours worked each day. Fill in the numbers. Use different numbers for each employee.

```
PAYROLL

WEEK OF

LAST      FIRST    MON   TUES   WED   THUR   FRI    SAT    SUN

ABEL      ANN
JONES     JOHN
SMITH     SAM
WALL      JOAN
```

(b) Add a column at the end to calculate total hours worked for each employee. Use the @SUM function.

(c) Add a column with the hourly wage for each employee. Use a different wage for each employee. Be generous.

(d) Add a column to calculate automatically the gross wages earned for the week.

(e) Add a column for tax withholdings of 20%.

(f) Add a column for take-home pay (gross wages minus tax withholding).

(g) Add rows at the bottom for the total and the average of each of the columns. Use the @SUM and @AVG functions and the Copy command.

5

COMMON
COMMANDS

Some of the commands in Lotus 1-2-3 are rarely used; some are used all the time. In this chapter we will discuss some of the more commonly used commands and operations in Lotus 1-2-3.

COLUMN WIDTHS

Initially all columns in the Lotus 1-2-3 worksheet are set to a width of 9 characters. If you type a label that is longer than 9 characters into a cell, Lotus 1-2-3 will display the entire label if the cells to the right are blank. This is illustrated in Figure 5-1. The label in cell C3 is 23 characters long. The cells to the right are blank, so the entire label shows. Similarly, the label

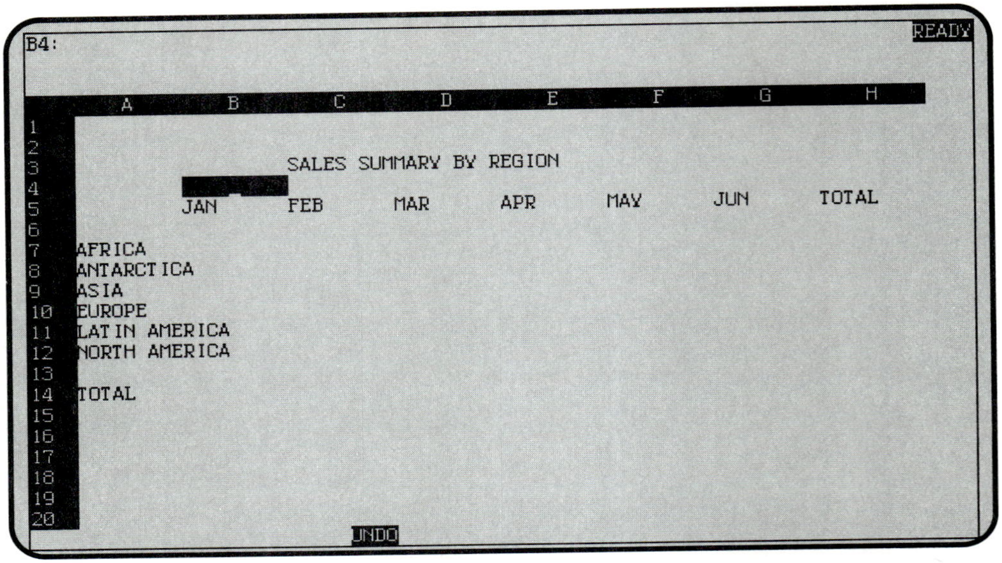

FIGURE 5-1 Labels longer than the cell width show in their entirety if the cells to the right are blank.

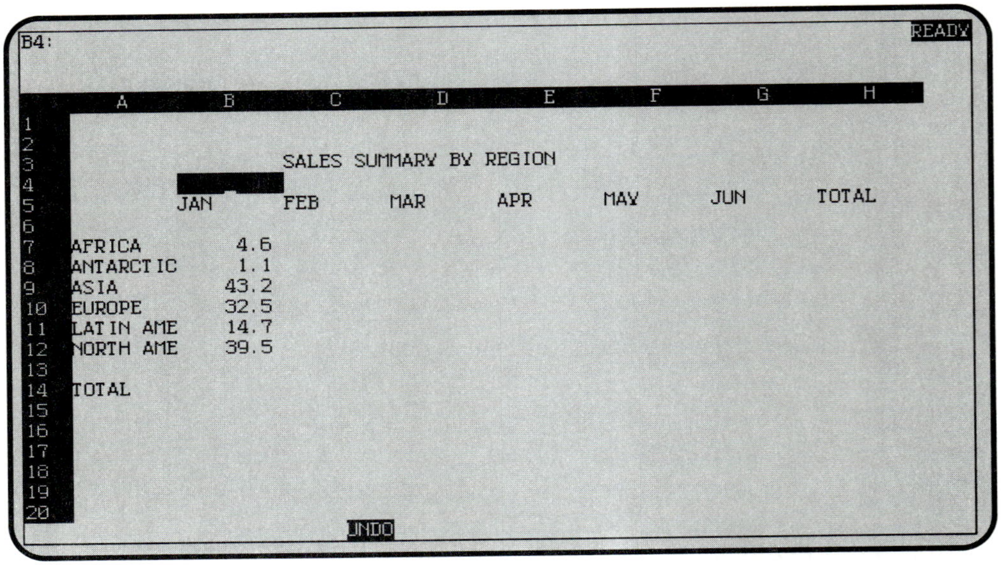

FIGURE 5-2 When the numbers in column B are entered, the labels in column A are cut off at nine characters, the width of the cell.

LATIN AMERICA in cell A11 is 13 characters long. As cell B11 is blank, the entire label shows. However, if we fill numbers into column B, then the labels in column A will be cut off at 9 characters, as in Figure 5-2. To remedy this, we can widen column A.

There are two commands for changing the width of columns.

To change the width of a single column, first move the cursor to any cell in the column. Then select / Worksheet Column Set-Width. Lotus 1-2-3 asks you to enter the column width. You either can type a number from 1 to 240, or you can use the right and left arrow keys to widen and shrink the column one character at a time. In the spreadsheet in Figure 5-3, the width of column A has been changed to 15 characters so that the all of the labels in column A show. The arrow keys are convenient to use if you are not sure how wide to make the column but would like everything to show. Just keep pressing the arrow keys until the screen looks best.

The price that is paid for wider columns is that fewer columns fit on the screen. The computer screen is 80 characters wide. Lotus 1-2-3 leaves a boundary of 4 characters to the left for the row number and 4 more characters to the right. There are up to 72 characters on the screen for the spreadsheet itself. Initially the columns are all 9 characters wide so eight columns (A through H) fit on the screen. If column A is widened to 15 characters, then column H no longer fits on the screen at the same time. If the columns are narrowed, then more columns can fit on the screen.

To determine whether the width of a column has been set using / Worksheet Column Set-Width, place the cursor in a cell in the column. On the top line of the screen, between the address of the cell and the contents of the cell, Lotus 1-2-3 will indicate [W15] if the column width has been set to 15, as in Figure 5-3.

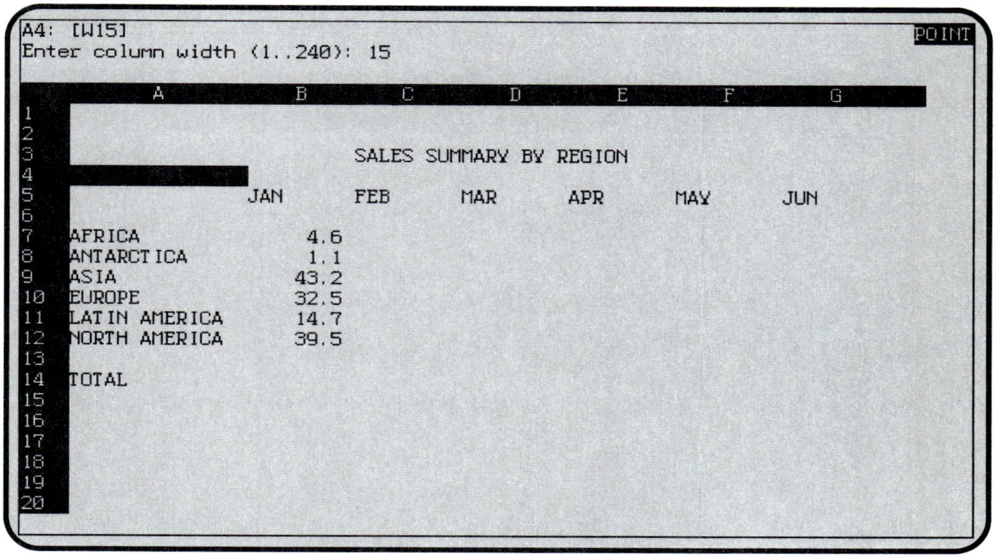

```
A4: [W15]                                                         POINT
Enter column width (1..240): 15

                A          B       C       D       E       F       G
 1
 2
 3                              SALES SUMMARY BY REGION
 4
 5                      JAN     FEB     MAR     APR     MAY     JUN
 6
 7    AFRICA            4.6
 8    ANTARCTICA        1.1
 9    ASIA             43.2
10    EUROPE           32.5
11    LATIN AMERICA    14.7
12    NORTH AMERICA    39.5
13
14    TOTAL
15
16
17
18
19
20
```

FIGURE 5-3 The width of column A is changed to 15. Now the full labels show, but column H no longer fits on the screen.

The second command for changing column widths is / Worksheet Global Column-Width, which changes the default column-width for all of the columns in the worksheet. That is, this command changes the width of all columns that have not been explicitly set with /WCS .

Note that /WCS overrides /WGC . If the width of column C has been set to 12 using /WCS but the global column-width is set to 7, then the width of column C will be 12. To reset the width of column C to the global column-width, place the cursor in a cell in column C and select / Worksheet Column-Width Reset. Now the width of the cells in column C will change with the global column-width.

In the spreadsheet in Figure 5-3, we can select / Worksheet Global Column-Width 8. This reduces the global column width from 9 to 8. Now the totals in column H fit on the screen.

LABEL ALIGNMENT

In Lotus 1-2-3, labels are aligned on the left side of a cell. Numbers are aligned on the right side of a cell. This often makes it difficult to read a spreadsheet. For example, in the spreadsheet in Figure 5-4, it is difficult to determine at a glance whether the 5.4 in cell E7 is the figure for Africa for April or for May. The 5.4 is on the right side of cell E7. The label APR is on the left side of cell E5. We would like each column heading to be directly above the numbers in the column so we can read the spreadsheet easily.

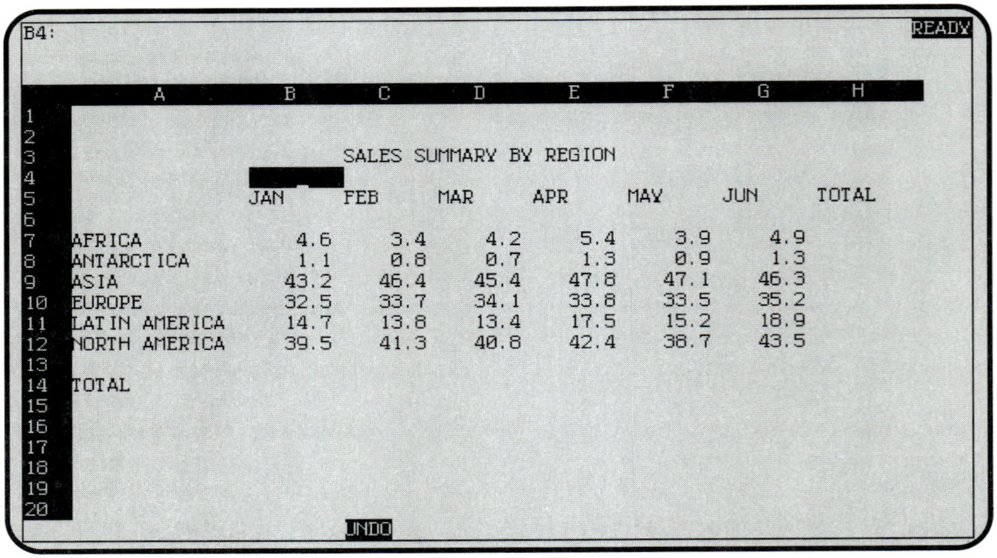

FIGURE 5-4 Labels are placed on the left side of the cell, numbers on the right. This can make the spreadsheet difficult to read.

In Lotus 1-2-3, numbers always remain on the right side of the cells. If you try to force a number to be aligned toward the left of the cell by beginning it with a space, then the "number" actually will be a label and will be treated as a label in any calculations.

The solution is to align the month name labels on the right of the cells so that they line up with the numbers in the cells beneath them.

To align existing labels on the right of their cells, use the command / Range Label Right and then enter the range of the cells that you wish to adjust. In this case we would select / Range Label Right B5..G5 and press the Enter key. This would result in a spreadsheet with the month names on the right side of the columns, directly above the corresponding numbers, as in Figure 4-1. Other possibilities in the / Range Label command are to Center the labels and Left align the labels in the cells.

When typing an individual label it is possible to specify that the label is to be aligned on the right side of the cell by preceding the label with a quote mark ("). To indicate to Lotus 1-2-3 that the label about to be typed is to be centered, begin it with a caret (^) (Shift-6). Similarly, you can force a label to be left aligned by beginning the label with an apostrophe (').

Some people force the placement of a label in a cell by beginning the label with a certain number of spaces. This seems to work, but if the width of the cell is changed, the label might no longer line up with the numbers beneath.

There is another command that affects the placement of labels within a cell. The command / Worksheet Global Label-Prefix allows you to specify the alignment of all future labels. This command does not change the placement of any current labels. If you enter the command / Worksheet Global Label-Prefix Right, then all future labels automatically will be aligned on the right of the cells.

Lotus 1-2-3 is a very well-designed, well thought out program that has gone through several revisions. Millions of dollars have been spent on its design and implementation. Why implement the program so that column headings do not align with the numbers in the columns? Why force people to issue a command to realign the column headings? Like all design decisions, this one involves a trade-off.

The advantage of placing labels on the left of the cell and numbers on the right of the cell is that it allows the user to see at a glance which cells are labels and which cells are numbers. In particular, many people who learned typing on typewriters are used to pressing a lowercase el (l) for a one (1). On most typewriters and on most computer screens, the two are almost indistinguishable. Yet they can have dramatically different results in Lotus 1-2-3. If you want to enter the number 10 into a cell and you type el zero, Lotus 1-2-3 regards this as a label because it begins with a letter! If this "number" is in the range of an @SUM function, it will be regarded as a label and, hence, as a zero. This is illustrated in Figure 5-5. The "number" in cell C11 is really a label, the "one" is really an "el." The same is true in E11. The decision by Lotus to have the program automatically left-align labels and right-align numbers makes it easy to scan a column of numbers to find the entries that really are labels.

INSERT AND DELETE

The command / Worksheet Insert Row enter will insert a blank row at the cursor. The row that includes the cursor and every row below is moved down. The command / Worksheet Insert

```
E14: @SUM(E9..E12)                                                    READY

        A         B         C         D         E         F         G
 1
 2              ALIGNING LABELS ON THE LEFT AND VALUES ON THE RIGHT
 3                   ALLOWS YOU TO DETERMINE AT A GLANCE
 4              WHICH ENTRIES ARE LABELS AND WHICH ENTRIES ARE VALUES
 5
 6
 7
 8                      Labels Left         Labels Right
 9                           22                  22
10                           33                  33
11  Contains el 3 ->         13                  13      <- Contains el 3
12                           20                  20
13                       ----------          ----------
14                           75                  75
15
16
17
18
19
20
                              UNDO
```

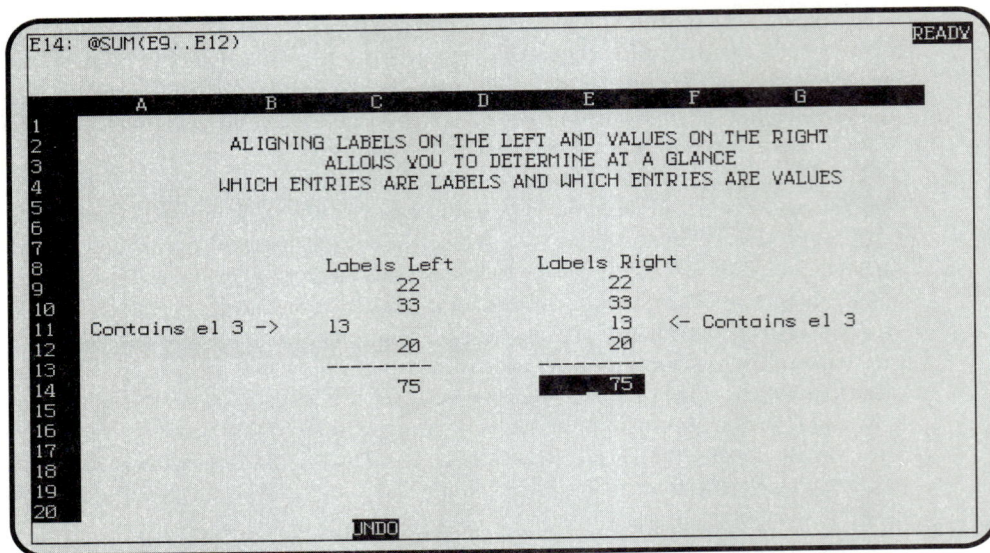

FIGURE 5-5 C11 and E11 really are labels because they begin with an el. Each of the cells acts as a zero in the evaluation of the @SUM functions.

Column enter inserts a blank column at the cursor. The column that includes the cursor and every column to the right is moved right. These commands are more sophisticated than they may appear. When you insert a row or column, Lotus 1-2-3 must go through all the formulas and adjust references to cells that have been moved.

The command / Worksheet Delete Row enter deletes the row containing the cursor. The command / Worksheet Delete Column enter deletes the column containing the cursor. Again, Lotus 1-2-3 moves the appropriate cells and adjusts the formulas.

However, if there is a formula that explicitly references a cell that has been deleted, then Lotus 1-2-3 replaces the reference with ERR. For example, in the simple spreadsheet in Figure 5-6, cell B5 contains the formula +B2+B3. After row 3 is deleted, cell B5 is moved up to B4. Lotus 1-2-3 goes through the formulas to make adjustments. Cell B3 has been deleted, so Lotus 1-2-3 changes the formula in B5 from +B2+B3 to +B2+ERR. Evaluating this formula causes ERR to appear in the cell, as in Figure 5-7.

To insert or delete more than one row or column at a time, simply press the arrow keys to move the cursor over the number of rows or columns desired before pressing the final Enter key.

FORMATTING NUMBERS

The commands for formatting numbers allow you to change how numbers are displayed in the spreadsheet. For example, you can specify that numbers be displayed as dollars and cents or with one place after the decimal point or as a percentage.

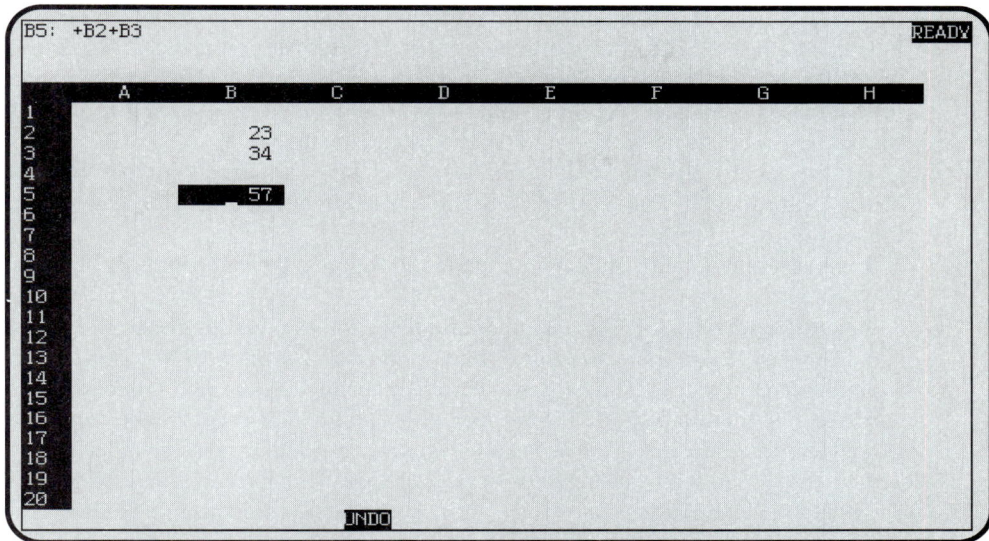

FIGURE 5-6 A formula that refers to a cell in a row that is about to be deleted.

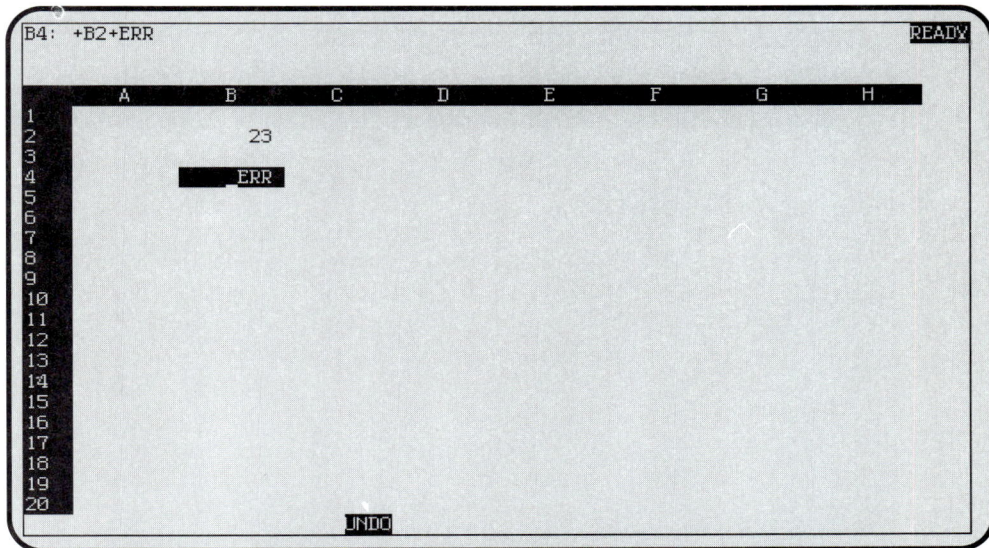

FIGURE 5-7 After row 3 is deleted, cell B5 becomes B4. The formula +B2+B3 becomes +B2+ERR because B3 has been deleted.

There are two commands for formatting numbers. The command / Worksheet Global Format sets the default format for the entire spreadsheet. The command / Range Format allows you to specify the format for some range or rectangular portion of the spreadsheet. A Range format takes precedence over the Global format. A cell is formatted according to the Global format only if it has not been included in a Range format.

After selecting / Worksheet Global Format or / Range Format you are presented with a choice of formats, as indicated in Figure 5-8. The effect of various formats is illustrated in Figure 5-9.

Fixed format displays the number in the cell rounded off to the number of decimal places you select.

Scientific format displays a number as a power of 10. The number in cell C9 1.235E+03 should be read "1.235 times 10 to the third power" or "1.235 times 1000". This format provides a compact method of displaying very large numbers and very small numbers.

Currency format displays the number with a dollar sign in front, with commas, and with a fixed number of decimal points. Negative numbers are displayed surrounded by parentheses. The currency sign can be changed from a dollar sign using the command / Worksheet Global Default Other International Currency (surely one of the best hidden commands in Lotus 1-2-3).

A number that is too large to fit in the cell in a specified format is displayed as a cell full of asterisks. This occurred in cell G10 in Figure 5-9. The inclusion of the dollar sign and commas caused the number to exceed the width of the cell. The number 21987654.321 is still in the cell and can be used in arithmetic. The number just is too large to be displayed in currency format with two decimal places in a cell of width 14.

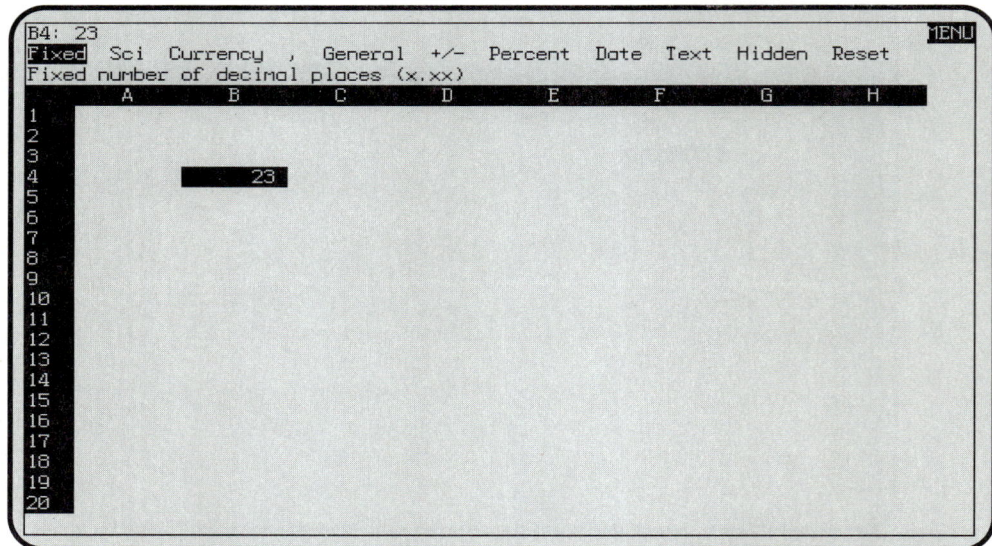

FIGURE 5-8 The choice of formats in the / Range Format command.

```
C10: (C2) [W14] 1234.567                                              READY

            A           B        C         D         E       F       G
 1
 2                            NUMERIC FORMATS
 3
 4
 5                                 1234.567          -1234.567       21987654.321
 6
 7   FIXED 2 PLACES                1234.57            -1234.57       21987654.32
 8   FIXED 0 PLACES                   1235               -1235       21987654
 9   SCIENTIFIC 3 PLACES         1.235E+03          -1.235E+03       2.199E+07
10   CURRENCY 2 PLACES           $1,234.57         ($1,234.57)      **************
11   , (COMMA) 2 PLACES          1,234.57          (1,234.57)       21,987,654.32
12   GENERAL                     1234.567           -1234.567       21987654.321
13   HIDDEN
14
15
16
17
18
19
20
                          UNDO
```

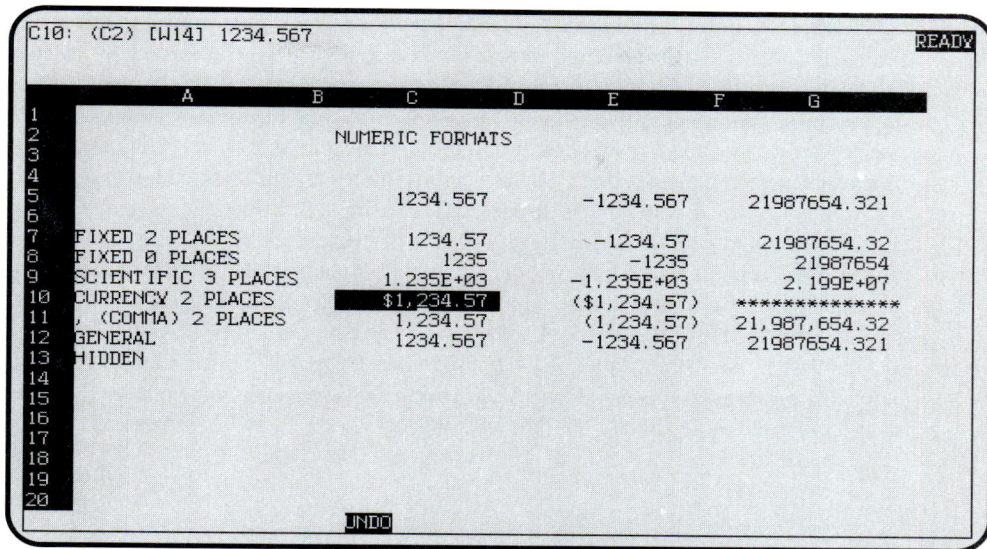

FIGURE 5-9 Numeric formats illustrated for three different numbers in columns of width 14.

Comma format is the same as Currency format except numbers are displayed without the dollar sign.

General format is the format assumed when you start up Lotus 1-2-3 or start with a new worksheet. In General format the number is displayed with no commas and with as many decimal places as entered or calculated that fit in the cell.

The +/- **format** can be used to create a simple bar chart. The number 4 would be displayed as four plus signs. The number -3 would be displayed as three minus signs. The number 3.6 would be displayed as three plus signs.

A number displayed in the **Percent format** is multiplied by 100 in the display and followed by a percentage sign. That is, the number 0.345 in a cell could be displayed as 34.5%.

In **Date format** a number is treated as a date serial number. This is covered in detail in Chapter 12.

Text format is extremely useful. In Text format the formula is displayed in a cell rather than the result of evaluating the formula. Displaying cells in Text format is an excellent tool for finding the errors in a spreadsheet, for documenting a spreadsheet, and for understanding someone else's spreadsheet. A spreadsheet in Text format was shown in Figure 2-3.

In **Hidden format**, cells are hidden, not displayed. The values still are in the cells and can be used in formulas in other cells; they just do not appear on the spreadsheet. The Hidden format is useful for hiding sensitive information. For example you might have a budget spreadsheet that includes specific salaries. You want to use the salaries in the calculations but you do not want them to display. You can format the column of salaries as Hidden so they do not show.

The **Reset** option appears only in the / Range Format command. Reset undoes any previous Range format in the cells specified and causes them to be displayed according to the Global format.

To determine whether the format of a cell has been set using / Range Format , place the cursor on the cell. On the top line of the screen, Lotus 1-2-3 indicates the format, if any, in parentheses after the address of the cell. For example, in Figure 5-9, the cursor is on cell C10. The (C2) on the top line of the screen indicates that C10 has been formatted as Currency with two decimal places.

Remember, the number that is displayed can be slightly different than the number that actually is in a formatted cell. This can seem to cause discrepancies. If you check the arithmetic in a spreadsheet by hand or with a calculator, you might not obtain exactly the same numbers that appear in the spreadsheet. This is illustrated in Figure 5-10. Cell C9 contains the formula +C6+C7. The formula appears to evaluate to 5. Cell C6 appears to contain the number 2. Cell C7 appears to contain the number 2. The sum of 2 plus 2 is 4, not 5. In fact, C6 and C7 both contain 2.4. The spreadsheet has been formatted as Fixed with zero places using / Worksheet Global Format. The numbers in the three cells are 2.4, 2.4, and 4.8 but they are displayed as 2, 2, and 5 because of the format.

THE @ROUND FUNCTION

In some cases, we don't just want the value in a cell to appear to have two places after the decimal point. We want the value actually to be rounded to two places after the decimal point. The @ROUND function will round a value to any desired accuracy.

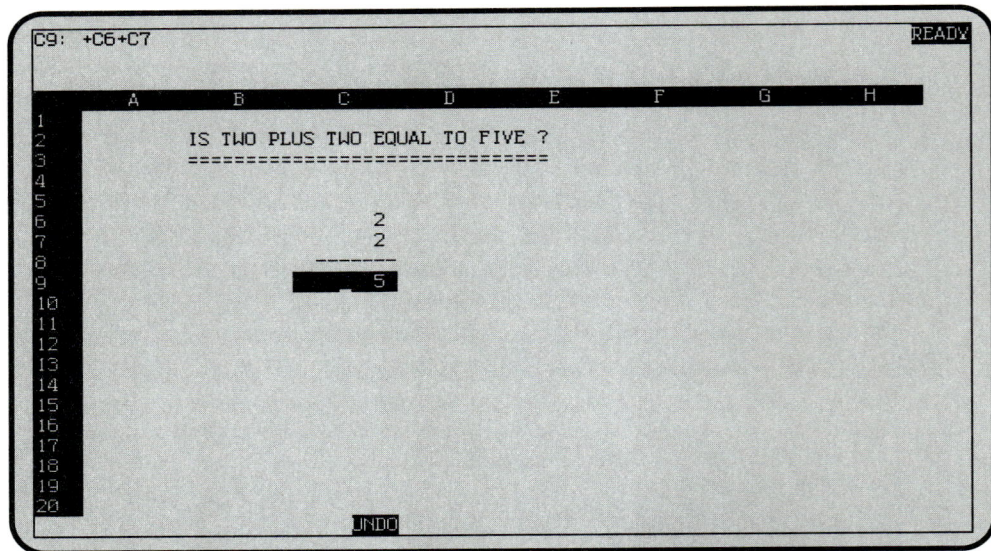

FIGURE 5-10 There appears to be an error. Can you solve the mystery?

The @ROUND function has two arguments:

$$@ROUND(value, places)$$

As illustrated in Figure 5-11, the first argument is the value to be rounded. The second argument is the number of places the value is to be rounded. The difference between using the @ROUND function and formatting a value to some number of decimal places is that using the @ROUND function actually changes the value itself, while formatting the value only changes the appearance of the value.

The @ROUND function can have another function as an argument. For example, suppose we are adding up a column of numbers with the formula @SUM(F6..F23). If we want the result to display to the nearest dollar we could format the cell as Currency with zero places. If, for other calculations, we want the result actually to include no fractions of a dollar, we could change the formula to @ROUND(@SUM(F6..F23),0).

RANGE NAMES

In larger spreadsheets it is easy to forget which cells contain which quantities. When reading the formulas in a larger spreadsheet, it can be cumbersome to determine which quantities are referred to by cell addresses in the formulas. Lotus 1-2-3 provides the capability of giving names

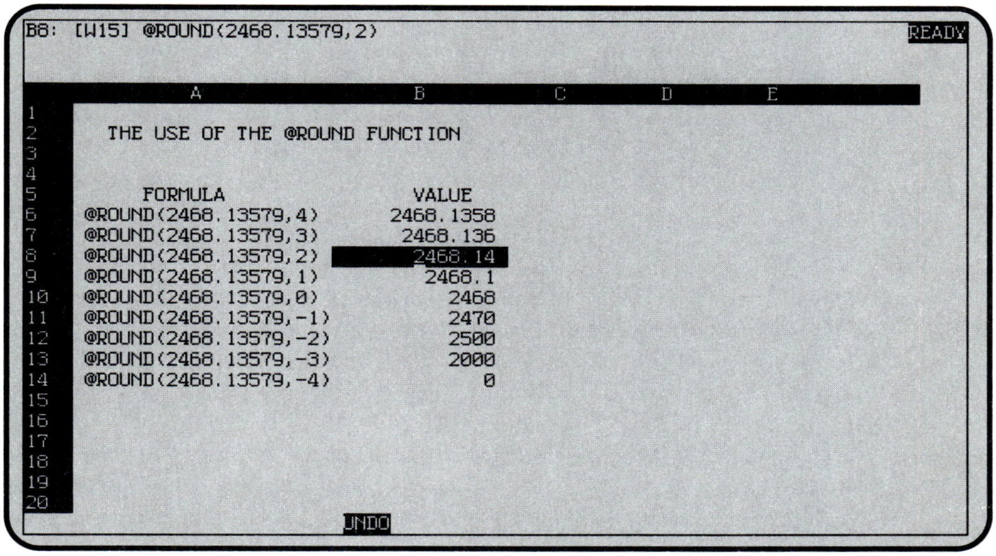

FIGURE 5-11 The use of the @ROUND function.

to cells and ranges of cells and using these names in formulas instead of the cell addresses. It is considered good practice to name key cells in larger spreadsheets.

For example, suppose cell F10 contains the quantity purchased and cell F12 contains the unit price. The formula in cell F14 is

$$+F10*F12$$

We could name cell F10 as QUANTITY and cell F12 as UNITPRICE. Now the formula in F14 could be

$$+QUANTITY*UNITPRICE$$

Similarly, in the monthly sales by region spreadsheet in Figures 4-1 and 5-4, we could name the range B7..G12 as SALES. Then the formula in H14 could be

$$@SUM(SALES)$$

The command for naming a cell or range is / Range Name Create . After you select / Range Name Create you are asked to enter (1) the name to be used and (2) the address of the cell or range of cells to be named.

Range names must be 15 characters or less. The names can include letters, digits, and underlines (Shift-Hyphen) but not spaces or arithmetic operators or most punctuation characters. Do be careful in naming ranges. Select a name that makes sense, that you will remember. Do not be overly clever and name cell D7 as B5.

It is useful to document the names that are used in a spreadsheet and the addresses to which they refer. This information can be included directly on the spreadsheet using the / Range Name Table command. After issuing the command you specify a currently blank range that is two cells wide and long enough to hold every range name in the spreadsheet. Lotus 1-2-3 then fills in each name and the addresses to which it refers.

MOVE

The Move command allows you to move a cell or range of cells.

For example, even though the Lotus 1-2-3 worksheet is 256 columns by 8192 rows, people often cram their spreadsheet way up in the top left corner of the worksheet. If you notice that you have done this and you wish to move the cells you have entered, you could use the Move command.

After selecting / Move you are first asked to "Enter range to move FROM:". Here you type or point to the cell or range of cells you wish to move. Next you are asked to "Enter range to move TO:". When Lotus 1-2-3 asks you to enter the TO range, you actually can enter just the address of the top left corner of the range.

For example, if you type /M B2..C7 Enter D12 Enter, then Lotus 1-2-3 will move the contents of B2..C7 to D12..E17. Anything that was in D12..E17 before will be wiped out. All formulas and range names will be adjusted. For example, a formula that referred to B5 before now will refer to D15.

F2 EDITING

Function key **F2** is the **Edit** key. If you put the cursor on a cell and press F2, Lotus 1-2-3 displays the word EDIT as the mode indicator in the top right of the screen and enters Edit mode. In Edit mode, the label or formula or number in the current cell becomes available for editing. The entry in the cell can be modified without retyping the entire cell. You also can be deposited in Edit mode involuntarily if you type an illegal formula, for example, by including spaces within the formula, into a cell.

In Edit mode you can edit the current cell just as you would edit a line using a word processor. The left and right arrow keys move the cursor left and right through the characters in the cell. The Backspace key deletes the character to the left of the cursor. The Del key deletes the character on the cursor. Letters that are typed are inserted at the cursor. The Enter key terminates editing and enters the revised contents into the cell.

The following keys have special meaning in Edit mode.

← or →	Moves the cursor left or right one character.
Ctrl-← or Ctrl-→	Moves the cursor left or right five characters.
Home or End	Moves the cursor to the beginning or end of the entry.
Backspace	Erases the character to the left of the cursor.
Del	Erases the character on which the cursor is positioned.
Esc	Erases all the characters in the entry.
Ins	Switches between inserting and overstriking characters.
Alt-F1	Allows you to create characters not available on the keyboard.
F2	Switches back to Value or Label mode.
F9	Converts a formula to its current value.
Enter	Completes the entry.
↑ or ↓	Completes the entry and moves the cell pointer up or down.

F2 editing is very convenient for making minor changes in a long formula or label.

COMPUTER EXERCISES

5-1   Enter the following spreadsheet exactly as shown. Only the first nine characters of the entry in cell A7 will show.

```
              A                       B              C                D

 1
 2                          STOCK PORTFOLIO
 3
 4      STOCK                     SHARES          PRICE            TOTAL
 5
 6      IBM                          500             99
 7      LOTUS DEVELOPMENT           2759           28.5
 8      MICROSOFT                    837         93.625
 9
10      TOTAL
11
```

(a) Widen column A so all of LOTUS DEVELOPMENT shows, as follows. Put the cursor in column A. Enter the command / Worksheet Column Set-Width . Now press the right arrow key until the entire entry shows in A7. Press the Enter key.

(b) Align the column headings on the right sides of the cells, as follows. Put the cursor in cell B4. Enter the command / Range Label Right . Now press the right arrow key two times to point to the range of labels to be aligned. When the range is B4..B6, press the Enter key. The column headings should be aligned to the right of the cells.

(c) Enter the formulas for column D for the TOTAL for D6, D7, D8, and D10. Use the @SUM function with a range in D10.

(d) We have just purchased 1250 shares of Intel at $39.875 per share. (Incidentally, Intel is a major chip company that makes the central processing unit for the IBM PC, PS/2, and most compatibles. Microsoft is a major software company that makes DOS as well as Excel, the major rival to Lotus 1-2-3.) Insert a new row between IBM and LOTUS as follows. Put the cursor at A7. Enter the command / Worksheet Insert Row and press the Enter key. Fill in the new row 7 with appropriate entries, including a formula in cell D7. Inspect the formula in cell D11. Does the formula need to be adjusted? What happened to the formula when you inserted the row?

(e) Format the share prices in column C so they are displayed with dollar signs and three places to the right of the decimal point, as follows. Place the cursor in C6. Enter the command / Range Format Currency 3 and press Enter. Now press the down arrow three times so the range specified is C6..C9 and press the Enter key.

(f) Format the totals in column D so they are displayed with dollar signs and with 2 decimal places to the right of the decimal point. Use the / Range Format Currency command. What happened? The cells in column D should be filled with asterisks. The asterisks indicate that the cells are not wide enough to accommodate the numbers in the format specified. Use the / Worksheet Column Set-Width command to widen column D so that all the numbers show.

(g) Save the spreadsheet on the disk. Print the spreadsheet.

(h) Next day, the stock prices are as follows: IBM 99.25, Intel 39.875, Lotus Development 28.625, Microsoft 93.875. Change the spreadsheet appropriately. Do the numbers in D6..D9 add up to the number in D11? What is going on here?

(i) Print the spreadsheet.

(j) The stocks were purchased for the following amounts: IBM 109.5, Lotus 23.25, Microsoft 98.625. Add a new column that lists the purchase price for each. Add another column that indicates how much each stock has gone up or down from the purchase price. Finally, add another column that indicates the percentage gain or loss from the purchase price. Format the numbers in this column as percentages with two decimal places.

5-2 Create and print the exact spreadsheet in Figure 5-9, which illustrates various numeric formats. To accomplish this, you should enter the numbers in C5, E5, and G5 and then copy them down their respective columns. The rows should be formatted as indicated. Columns will need to be widened appropriately.

THE PRINT COMMAND

CHAPTER 6

There are three basic ways to print a spreadsheet in Lotus 1-2-3. The simplest method is to use the PrintScreen key. Pressing the PrintScreen key instructs the computer to print the screen. While PrintScreen is quick and easy, the printout contains the row numbers and column letters, the mode indicator, the address and contents of the current cell, and any other text that appears on the screen as well as the spreadsheet on the screen. If the spreadsheet is larger than the screen, it must be printed in multiple snapshots. PrintScreen works, but it does not produce a very formal printout of the type that would be included in a report. In this chapter we will look at the Print command. The Print command is the "real" way to print spreadsheets in Lotus 1-2-3. In Chapter 17 we will examine Allways. Allways is an "add-in" program that produces even more professional looking Lotus 1-2-3 printouts than does the Print command.

THE FUNDAMENTALS OF THE PRINT COMMAND

The basic operation of the Print command is quite simple. You simply need to specify the range of the spreadsheet to be printed and then tell Lotus 1-2-3 to go ahead and print it.

The Print command is in the main Lotus 1-2-3 command menu. After selecting / Print, you must choose between Printer or File. Here, Lotus 1-2-3 is asking you whether you would like the output to be printed directly on the printer or saved in a text file. Normally, you would select Printer. We will discuss printing to a file at the end of this chapter.

After selecting / Print Printer, you are shown the current print settings, as in Figure 6-1. Chances are the current print settings are fine. We will be discussing the various options for print settings in this chapter. On the top of the screen is the Print menu. The most important selection to be made now is the Range. When you select Range, Lotus 1-2-3 displays the spreadsheet again and asks you to type or point to the range of the spreadsheet that is to be printed. You must specify a print range or nothing will be printed. If you would like the entire spreadsheet to be printed, just type A1 followed by .. followed by the address of the bottom right corner of the spreadsheet.

Once you have specified the print range, you are returned to the print menu. Now simply select Go to print. Select Quit to leave the print menu and return to Ready mode.

If the range that you specified is too large to fit on a single page, Lotus 1-2-3 automatically prints it out on several pages.

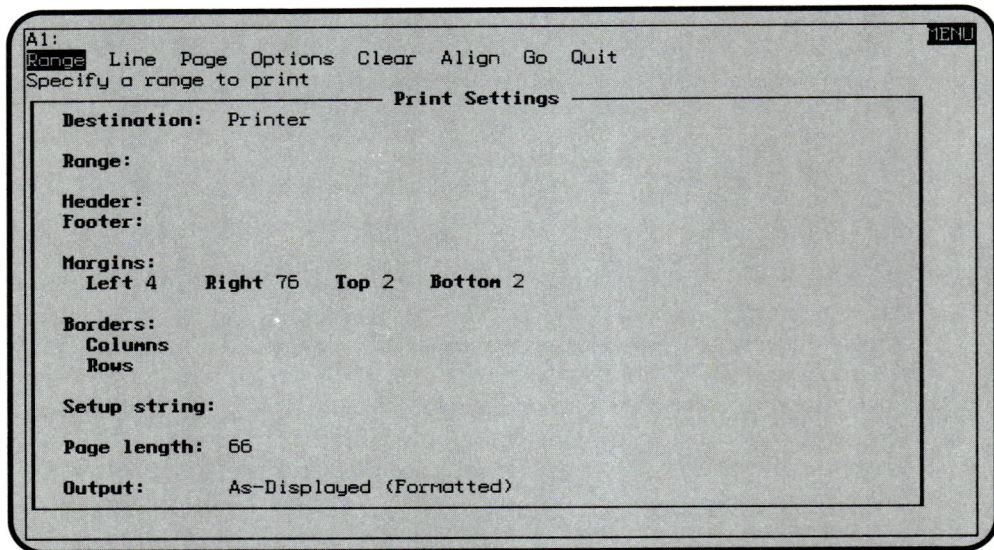

```
A1:                                                             MENU
Range  Line  Page  Options  Clear  Align  Go  Quit
Specify a range to print
                         ──── Print Settings ────
   Destination:  Printer

   Range:

   Header:
   Footer:

   Margins:
     Left 4      Right 76   Top 2    Bottom 2

   Borders:
     Columns
     Rows

   Setup string:

   Page length:  66

   Output:       As-Displayed (Formatted)
```

FIGURE 6-1 The Print Settings sheet is displayed automatically after you select / Print Printer.

At its simplest, the procedure for printing is as follows:

1. Select / Print Printer.
2. Specify the print range by selecting Range and then entering the range to be printed.
3. Select Go to begin the printing.
4. Select Quit to exit from the print menu and return to Ready mode.

For example, we would like to print the monthly sales by region spreadsheet from the previous two chapters. We follow the preceding procedure entering A1..H14 for the print range. The result is the printout in Figure 6-2.

A frequent problem encountered when printing is that the text is not aligned with the paper. For example, the text might run across the perforations at the bottom of the pages. To prevent this problem from occuring we can add some commands for controlling the printer to our procedure for printing.

CONTROLLING THE PRINTER

The most common type of printer used with personal computers is the **dot matrix printer**. Typically, a dot matrix printer is a mechanical impact printer where pins in a print head strike an ink ribbon to form the letters on the page. The print head sweeps across the page and then the paper advances and the print head sweeps across again. Dot matrix printers usually use continuous fanfold paper. You start the printing. The paper advances through the printer. After the printing stops, you tear off the paper at the fold. The print quality of the output is only fair. The printers are noisy. The paper tends to jam in some printers. However, by and large, dot matrix printers are inexpensive and reliable. The Print command in Lotus 1-2-3 is designed for dot matrix printers.

```
                    SALES SUMMARY BY REGION

                JAN     FEB     MAR     APR     MAY     JUN     TOTAL

AFRICA          4.6     3.4     4.2     5.4     3.9     4.9      26.4
ANTARCTICA      1.1     0.8     0.7     1.3     0.9     1.3       6.1
ASIA           43.2    46.4    45.4    47.8    47.1    46.3     276.2
EUROPE         32.5    33.7    34.1    33.8    33.5    35.2     202.8
LATIN AMERICA  14.7    13.8    13.4    17.5    15.2    18.9      93.5
NORTH AMERICA  39.5    41.3    40.8    42.4    38.7    43.5     246.2

TOTAL         135.6   139.4   138.6   148.2   139.3  150.1     851.2
```

FIGURE 6-2 The printout of the monthly sales by region spreadsheet using the Print command.

A basic problem with using dot matrix printers is that the computer cannot sense where the folds (perforations) are in the paper. That is, the computer cannot determine when it begins printing whether the print head is at the top of the page or in the middle of the page. If the print head is not at the top of the page when the computer begins printing, you might find your output printed across the fold. It is up to you to be sure that the print head is located on the top of the page, just below the perforation, and that the computer is so informed. After the print range has been selected, but before actually printing, you should adjust the paper on the printer so the print head is at the top of the page and then so inform Lotus 1-2-3 by selecting the Align command in the Print menu. After the output has been printed, you should advance the paper to the top of the next page using the Page command. You also can advance the paper from the keyboard one line at a time using the Line command.

The second most common type of printer used with personal computers is the **laser printer**. A laser printer basically is a photocopier that receives its input from a computer. Like a photocopier, a laser printer takes a stack of 8.5- by11-inch paper (rather than continuous fanfold paper) and prints out a page at a time. Laser printers are quiet, relatively fast, and produce high-quality output. They also are more expensive than dot matrix printers, though the prices of laser printers keep dropping. The Print command in Lotus 1-2-3 works fine with laser printers but really does not take advantage of many of the features of most laser printers. With laser printers you still should issue the Align command before actually printing. You may need to issue the Page command to finish printing the final page of your output and eject it from the printer.

Printers sometimes fail and the computer can get hung up waiting for the printer. Sometimes the only remedy is to turn off the computer and the printer and start again. Experience teaches that it is good practice to save a spreadsheet on the disk right before trying to print it. If the spreadsheet is saved and you are forced to turn off the computer you can retrieve the spreadsheet from the disk after starting up the computer. If the spreadsheet is not saved you can lose hours worth of work.

PROCEDURE FOR PRINTING

We now can state the normal procedure for printing :

1. Save the spreadsheet on the disk using / File Save.
2. Select / Print Printer.
3. Specify the print range by selecting Range and then entering the range to be printed.
4. Adjust the paper if necessary so that the print head is at the top of the page. Select Align to inform Lotus 1-2-3 that all is ready for a new print job.
5. Select Go to begin the printing.
6. Select Page to advance the paper to the top of the next page.
7. Select Quit to exit from the print menu and return to Ready mode.

HEADERS AND FOOTERS

Suppose you were printing out a large spreadsheet and the printout would take several pages. You would like the date of the printout, a title for the printout, and the page number to appear on each page of the printout. This would help identify the pages in the printout and keep them in the proper order. Lotus 1-2-3 provides the ability to print information automatically on each page of a printout in headers and footers.

A **header** is a line of text that appears at the top of each page of a printout. A **footer** is a line of text that appears at the bottom of each page of a printout. A header or footer might contain the title of the report, the date, the page number, your name, or whatever. This is information that is not necessarily in the spreadsheet but that does appear on the pages of the printout.

Headers and footers can be specified in the Print Options menu. To specify a header select / Print Printer Options Header . Whatever line of text you now enter will appear at the top of each page of your printout.

To be a bit more sophisticated, headers and footers can have three **fields**. The first field appears aligned to the left of the line. The second field is centered on the line. The third field is aligned on the right of the line. The fields are separated by a split vertical bar (Shift-Backslash). Further, an @ in a header or footer signifies the current date. A # signifies the page number.

For example, we might specify the header to be

```
@ | WORLDWIDE INDUSTRIES | PAGE #
```

Here we are instructing Lotus 1-2-3 to print a line of text on the top of each page of the printout. On the left in the header will be today's date. In the center will be the words WORLDWIDE INDUSTRIES. On the right in the header will be the word PAGE followed by the actual page number. Thus, the header will be

```
09-Feb-92            WORLDWIDE INDUSTRIES                 PAGE 1
```

for the first page. Subsequent pages will have identical headers except they will be numbered sequentially.

CHANGING THE SIZE OF THE PRINTOUT ON THE PAGE

Lotus 1-2-3 assumes that you are using 8.5- by 11-inch paper. The initial Print settings are shown in Figure 6-1. The Print settings can be read as follows:

Left margin	4 characters from the left edge of the paper
Right margin	76 characters from the left edge of the paper
Top margin	2 lines from the top of the paper
Bottom margin	2 lines from the bottom of the paper
Page length	66 lines

With a left margin of 4 and a right margin of 76 there are 72 characters per line on the page. This corresponds exactly to the width of the screen in Lotus 1-2-3.

With a page length of 66 lines, a top margin of 2 lines and a bottom margin of 2 lines, there are 62 lines of text on the page. Three lines are reserved on the top for the header, 1 for the header itself and 2 blank lines between the header and the spreadsheet. Three lines are reserved on the bottom for the footer, 2 blank lines between the spreadsheet and the footer and 1 for the footer itself. These lines are reserved whether or not you specify a header or footer. Thus, with the initial settings, there are 56 lines for the spreadsheet itself on each page.

How large of a range in a Lotus 1-2-3 spreadsheet will fit on a single page of paper? With a normal column-width of 9 characters and with the default print settings above, a print range 8 columns wide and 56 rows long will fit on a single printed page.

There are various ways to fit more cells on the page. Clearly, you could change the left, top, and bottom margins to 0 and the right margin to 80 if your printer allows.

Some printers have wide carriages and allow for 14- by 11-inch paper. To instruct Lotus 1-2-3 to print on wide paper you would change the right margin to 128 or to the width suggested in you printer manual.

There are two sets of commands for changing the margins. If you would like to change the margins permanently use the / Worksheet Global Default Printer command, and then issue / Worksheet Global Default Update. If you would like to change the margins just temporarily, use the / Print Printer Options Margins command.

Some printers allow you to print in "compressed" (or "condensed") mode. In compressed mode, characters are narrower on the page. Compressed characters are more difficult to read, but more fit per line. To print in compressed mode you need to perform two actions. First, use the Margins Right command in the / Print Printer Options submenu to change the right margin to 132 or 220 (for 14-inch-wide paper) or whatever is suggested in your printer manual. This changes the number of characters per line that will be printed. Second, you must instruct your printer to switch over to compressed mode. This usually is accomplished by having the computer issue a **setup string** to the printer. A setup string is a magical incantation that is not printed on the printer but rather causes the printer to change the manner in which the characters are printed. The setup string for switching over to compressed printing varies from printer to printer. A common setup string for switching to compressed printing is \015 (backslash zero one five). To issue a setup string to the printer, use the Setup command in the / Print Printer Options submenu and then enter the setup string. A common setup string for switching back to noncompressed mode is \018. If these setup strings do not work, you will need to consult your printer manual or a local computer guru.

Some printers also allow you to print 8 lines per inch vertically, rather than the normal 6 lines per inch. This is "vertically compressed" printing. To print 8 lines per inch you would need to (1) use the Pg-Length command in the / Print Printer Options submenu to change the page length to 88 lines per page and (2) use the Setup command in the / Print Printer Options submenu to issue the appropriate setup string to the printer. Subsequent printouts would be printed 8 lines per inch.

PRINTING FORMULAS

A printout of the formulas in a spreadsheet provides a very useful record of the spreadsheet and a key part of its formal documentation. Auditors often require formula printouts so they can trace through the underlying logic of a spreadsheet. If you are using this book in a course, your instructor might well want a printout of the formulas to determine if you completed an exercise correctly. Just obtaining the right answers for one set of numbers does not guarantee that the formulas in the spreadsheet are correct and will work for any set of numbers. Finally, if you lose your disk copies of the spreadsheet, you always can reenter the spreadsheet from the printed formulas.

There are two methods for obtaining printouts of the formulas in a spreadsheet.

The first approach to printing the formulas is to format all the cells in the spreadsheet in Text format, as discussed in Chapter 5. To accomplish this, first you would save the spreadsheet on the disk. Then you would / Range Format Reset any cells that previously had been formatted using / Range Format. This command undoes the range formats and returns the format of all cells to the global format. Now you would select / Worksheet Global Format Text. All the formulas should show in the cells rather than the values that result from evaluating the formulas. You now may need to widen the columns using / Worksheet Global Column-Width or / Worksheet Column Set-Width . Finally, print out the spreadsheet using / Print Printer, as described earlier. The resulting printout for the monthly sales by region spreadsheet is shown in Figure 6-3. To restore the spreadsheet to its original condition, it is easiest just to read it back from the disk.

For smaller spreadsheets it is often best to print the formulas by formatting the spreadsheet as Text as described in the previous paragraph and then printing the screen using the PrintScreen key rather than the / Print Printer command. The advantage of using the PrintScreen key here is that the row numbers and column letters are printed as well, so it is easier to determine to which cells the formulas refer.

The second method of printing the formulas makes use of a gold nugget of a command that is hidden deep inside the print menu. Issuing the command / Print Printer Options Other Cell-Formulas Quit instructs Lotus 1-2-3 to change the entire format of the printout so that the formulas in the cells are printed out one cell per line. The resulting printout for our monthly sales by region spreadsheet is shown in Figure 6-4. Note that this method also prints the format of each cell and the column width of each cell, if any have been set.

The procedure for printing the formulas one cell per line is as follows.

1. Save the spreadsheet on the disk using / File Save.
2. Select / Print Printer.
3. Specify that the formulas should be printed by selecting Options Other Cell-Formulas Quit (That last Quit gets you out of the Print Options menu).
4. Specify the print range by selecting Range and then entering the range to be printed.
5. Adjust the paper if necessary so that the print head is at the top of the page. Select Align to inform Lotus 1-2-3 that all is ready for a new print job.
6. Select Go to begin the printing.
7. Select Page to advance the paper to the top of the next page.
8. Specify that future printouts should be of the cells as displayed by selecting Options Other As-Displayed Quit (This sequence returns Lotus 1-2-3 to the normal mode of printing).
9. Select Quit to exit from the print menu and return to Ready mode.

```
                    SALES SUMMARY BY REGION

                   JAN           FEB           MAR           APR

AFRICA             4.6           3.4           4.2           5.4
ANTARCTICA         1.1           0.8           0.7           1.3
ASIA               43.2          46.4          45.4          47.8
EUROPE             32.5          33.7          34.1          33.8
LATIN AMERICA      14.7          13.8          13.4          17.5
NORTH AMERICA      39.5          41.3          40.8          42.4

TOTAL        @SUM(B7..B12) @SUM(C7..C12)  @SUM(D7..D12)  @SUM(E7..E12)


        MAY          JUN         TOTAL
        3.9          4.9      @SUM(B7..G7)
        0.9          1.3      @SUM(B8..G8)
        47.1         46.3     @SUM(B9..G9)
        33.5         35.2     @SUM(B10..G10)
        15.2         18.9     @SUM(B11..G11)
        38.7         43.5     @SUM(B12..G12)


   @SUM(F7..F12) @SUM(G7..G12)   @SUM(H7..H12)
```

FIGURE 6-3 The result of printing the spreadsheet formatted as Text.

It seems as if it should be easier to print the formulas than to go through all of these steps. In Chapter 18 we will see how to create a macro that will automate this procedure.

PRINTING TO A FILE VERSUS PRINTING TO THE PRINTER

As soon as you issue /Print, you must select between Printer or File. If you select Printer, Lotus 1-2-3 will print your output directly on the printer. If you select File, you will be asked for a file name. Your output will not be printed, but rather will be saved in a file on the disk under the name that you entered.

Printing to a file is a very convenient way to move information from Lotus 1-2-3 to a word processing program. Suppose you are producing a report that will contain a spreadsheet as an exhibit. You have created the spreadsheet in Lotus 1-2-3. Now you would like to move the relevant portion of your spreadsheet over to the word processing program so that you can incorporate it into the report you are writing. In general, the easiest way to move the spreadsheet from Lotus 1-2-3 into a word processing program is to "print" the spreadsheet the

```
C3: 'SALES SUMMARY BY REGION
B5: "JAN
C5: "FEB
D5: "MAR
E5: "APR
F5: "MAY
G5: "JUN
H5: "TOTAL
A7: [W15] 'AFRICA
B7: 4.6
C7: 3.4
D7: 4.2
E7: 5.4
F7: 3.9
G7: 4.9
H7: @SUM(B7..G7)
A8: [W15] 'ANTARCTICA
B8: 1.1
C8: 0.8
D8: 0.7
E8: 1.3
F8: 0.9
G8: 1.3
H8: @SUM(B8..G8)
A9: [W15] 'ASIA
B9: 43.2
C9: 46.4
D9: 45.4
E9: 47.8
F9: 47.1
G9: 46.3
H9: @SUM(B9..G9)
A10: [W15] 'EUROPE
B10: 32.5
C10: 33.7
D10: 34.1
E10: 33.8
F10: 33.5
G10: 35.2
H10: @SUM(B10..G10)
A11: [W15] 'LATIN AMERICA
B11: 14.7
C11: 13.8
D11: 13.4
E11: 17.5
F11: 15.2
G11: 18.9
H11: @SUM(B11..G11)
A12: [W15] 'NORTH AMERICA
B12: 39.5
C12: 41.3
D12: 40.8
E12: 42.4
F12: 38.7
G12: 43.5
H12: @SUM(B12..G12)
```

FIGURE 6-4 The printout using / Print Printer Options Other Cell-Formulas. In the printout, **[W15]** means the width of the cell has been set to 15 characters.

way you would like it to appear using the Print command, but to print it to a text file instead of to the printer. That is, you would select / Print File, enter the name of the print file, and then go through all the steps you would need to print the desired report. After you select Go, the report would be saved on your disk as a text file under the name you indicated rather than being printed on the printer. Then you can quit out of Lotus 1-2-3, open up your word processing program, and read the text file directly into the word processing program.

Files created using / Print File automatically are given an extension (second name) of .PRN by Lotus 1-2-3. These files are text files that are designed to be read by word processing programs rather than worksheet files that contain formulas and are designed to be read back into Lotus 1-2-3.

▨ COMPUTER EXERCISE

6-1 Retrieve the stock portfolio spreadsheet from Exercise 5-1.

(a) Print the spreadsheet using the PrintScreen key.

(b) Print the spreadsheet using the / Print command, as follows:
> Select   / Print Printer
> Select   Range A1..E15 and press the Enter key.
> If you are using fanfold paper, adjust the printer so the perforation is right above the print head.
> Select   Align
> Select   Go   to print the spreadsheet
> Select   Page   to eject the paper
> Select   Quit   to return to Ready mode

(c) Print the formulas in the spreadsheet, as follows
> Select   / Print Printer
> Select   Options Other Cell-Formulas Quit   to select formulas
> Select   Align Go Page   to print the formulas
> Select   Options Other As-Displayed Quit to not print the cell formulas in future printouts

(d) Print with headers and footers, as follows:
> Select   Options Header
> Type in the following header: Your name | Exercise 6-1 | @ and press the Enter key
> Select   Footer
> Type in the following footer: | Page # | and press the Enter key
> Select   Quit to return to the main print menu
> Select   Align Go Page to print the spreadsheet with a header and footer
> Select   Quit   to return to Ready mode

RELATIVE VERSUS ABSOLUTE ADDRESSING

What makes the Copy command so powerful in copying formulas is that Lotus 1-2-3 adjusts the addresses in the formulas as it makes the copies. For example, if the formula in H7 is @SUM(C7..G7) and we copy the formula down the column, then the formula in H8 will be @SUM(C8..G8), the formula in H9 will be @SUM(C9..G9), and so on. In Chapter 4, we referred to this as an "intelligent" Copy command. The Copy command as described usually works fine. However, there are some cases where we do not want the address in the formula to be adjusted as the formula is copied, where changing the address causes an error in the formula. In this brief but important chapter we will examine how to instruct Lotus 1-2-3 not to change an address in a formula when copying the formula.

AN EXAMPLE WHERE THE COPY COMMAND SEEMS TO FAIL

We would like to know the proportion of the world's population in each continent. Some research in the library yields the population for each continent shown in the spreadsheet in Figure 7-1. To find the total population of the planet, we put the formula

$$@SUM(C8..C13)$$

into cell C15. There are approximately 5234 million people on the planet, of whom 646 million live in Africa. To calculate the proportion of people in Africa, we divide the population of Africa by the total population for the planet. The formula in E8 can be

$$+C8/C15$$

as in Figure 7-2. Thus 0.1234, or approximately one-eighth, of the world's population lives in Africa.

Now we would like to Copy the formula down the column to calculate the proportion of the world's population living in each of the other continents. Here is the key point. Copying the formula in E8 down the column yields the spreadsheet in Figure 7-3. What has happened? The cells into which we copied the formula are full of ERRs. If we look at the formula in E9, we see

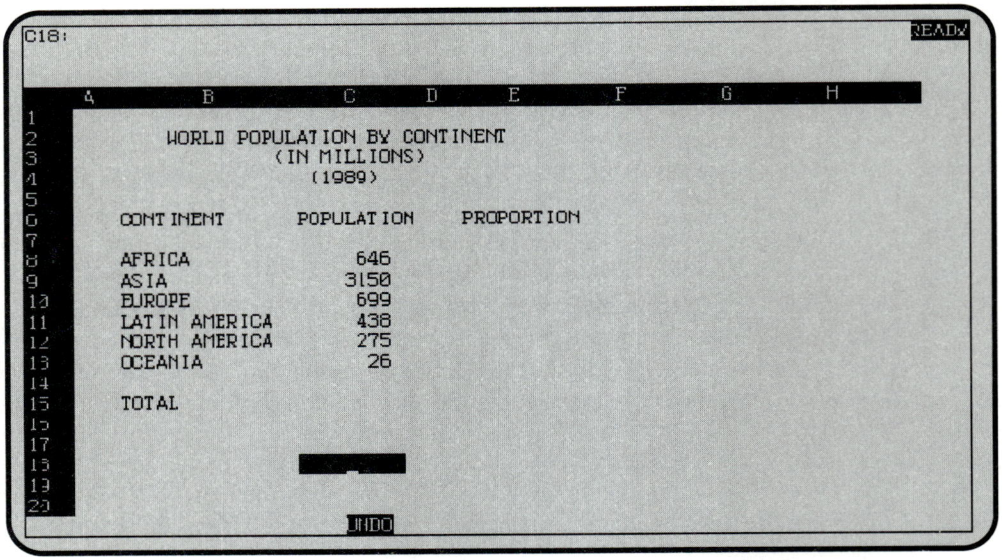

FIGURE 7-1 A spreadsheet for determing the proportion of the world population in each continent. Mexico is included as part of Latin America in these figures.

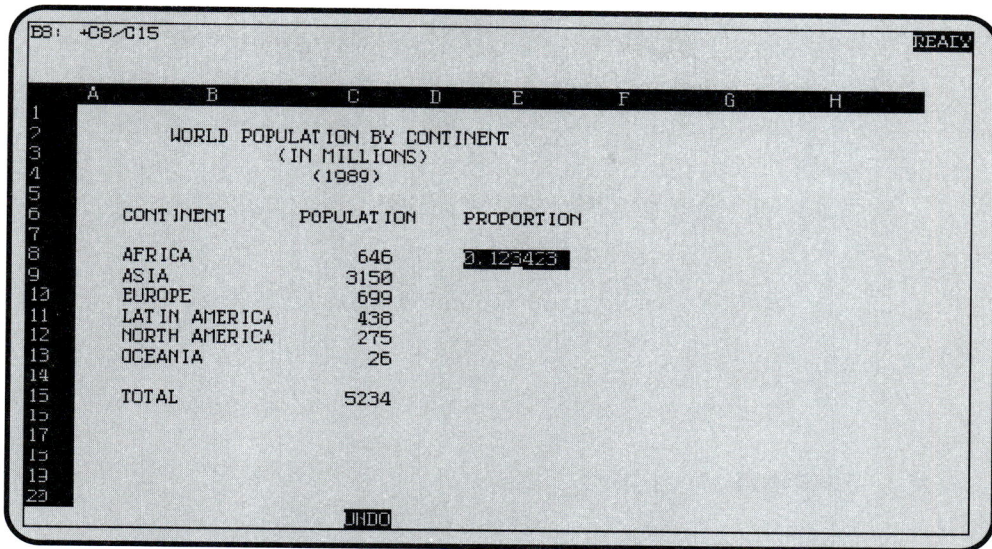

FIGURE 7-2 To find the proportion of the population in Africa divide the Africa Population by the total Population.

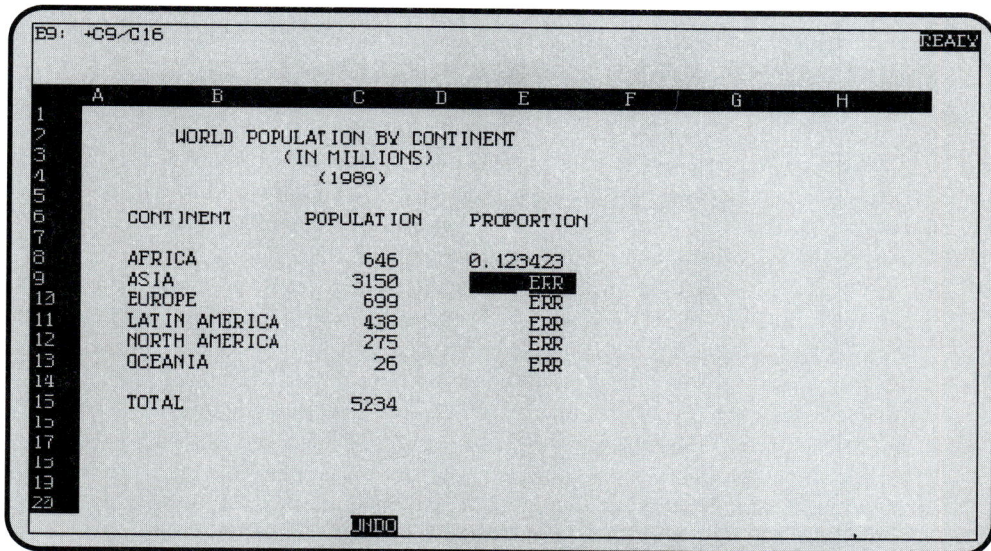

FIGURE 7-3 Copying the formula just entered in E8 produces a very instructive error.

that it is +C9/C16. But C16 is a blank cell. In evaluating the formula +C9/C16, the computer divides 3150, the number in C9, by 0, the "number" in C16. Dividing any number by 0 yields ERR.

What should the formula in E9 be? We would like it to be the population of Asia divided by the total population, +C9/C15 , rather than +C9/C16. What happened in Figure 7-3? When the formula +C8/C15 in cell E8 was copied down the column, both of the addresses were adjusted by the Copy command. So +C8/C15 in E8 became +C9/C16 in E9 became +C10/C17 in E10, and so on. We wanted +C8/C15 in E8 to become +C9/C15 in E9 to become +C10/C15 in E10, and so on. That is, we want the Copy command to adjust the first address C8 in the formula in +C8/C15 but not the second address C15. The cell address for the total population should remain unchanged. Lotus 1-2-3 has an "intelligent" Copy command but not a brilliant Copy command. Lotus 1-2-3 must be told which addresses to adjust and which to keep the same when a formula is copied.

ABSOLUTE ADDRESSING

An address written in the normal way (for example, C15) automatically is adjusted by Lotus 1-2-3 and is called a **relative address** or **relative reference**. To instruct Lotus 1-2-3 that an address in a formula is not to be changed when copied, the address is written with dollar signs before the column name and row name, for example, as $C$15. An address that is not to be adjusted when copied is called an **absolute address** or **absolute reference**. The dollar signs here have nothing to do with money or currency. For reasons not apparent, the dollar signs were selected by the designers of Lotus 1-2-3 to denote an absolute address.

Returning to our example, we now see that the formula in cell E8 should be written

$$+C8/\$C\$15$$

When copied down the column, this formula becomes +C9/$C$15 in E9, which becomes +C10/$C$15 in E10, and so on, as in Figure 7-4. The $C$15 is evaluated in the formula just the same as is C15, as the value in cell C15. The only difference in using an absolute address rather than a relative address occurs when the formula is copied.

Why are the terms "relative address" and "absolute address" used? Consider, again, the original formula in cell E8 in Figure 7-2. The formula +C8/C15 in E8 can be interpreted as "Take the number two columns to the left and divide it by the number in the cell two columns to the left and seven rows down" because the addresses are adjusted when the formula is copied. Hence the addresses C8 and C15 are "relative addresses." In contrast, the formula +C8/$C$15 in E8 can be interpreted "Take the number two columns to the left and divide it by the number in cell C15" because the address C8 is adjusted as the formula is copied but the address $C$15 remains the same. Hence, the address C8 is relative, but the address $C$15 is absolute.

To complete the example, we can format the cells in column E as Percent with one decimal place and add up the percentages in E15. The final spreadsheet is shown in Figure 7-5.

```
E10:  +C10/$C$15                                                    READY

        A         B          C        D       E       F       G       H
 1
 2            WORLD POPULATION BY CONTINENT
 3                  (IN MILLIONS)
 4                     (1989)
 5
 6        CONTINENT      POPULATION      PROPORTION
 7
 8        AFRICA              646        0.123423
 9        ASIA               3150        0.601834
10        EUROPE              699        0.133549
11        LATIN AMERICA       438        0.083683
12        NORTH AMERICA       275        0.052541
13        OCEANIA              26        0.004967
14
15        TOTAL              5234
16
17
18
19
20
                            UNDO
```

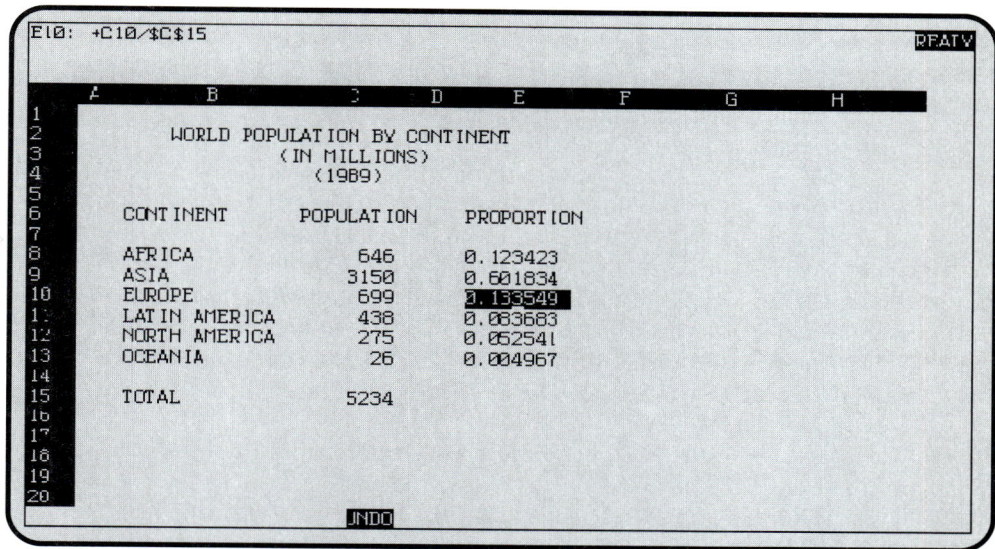

FIGURE 7-4 We do not want the reference to cell C15 to be adjusted when the formula in E8 is copied so we use absolute addressing.

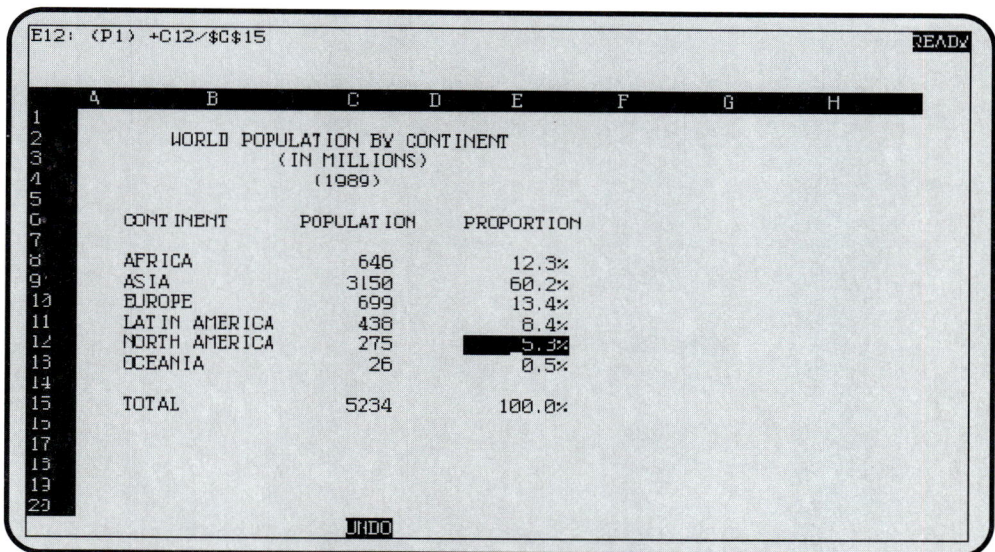

```
E12:  (P1) +C12/$C$15                                               READY

        A         B          C        D       E       F       G       H
 1
 2            WORLD POPULATION BY CONTINENT
 3                  (IN MILLIONS)
 4                     (1989)
 5
 6        CONTINENT      POPULATION      PROPORTION
 7
 8        AFRICA              646          12.3%
 9        ASIA               3150          60.2%
10        EUROPE              699          13.4%
11        LATIN AMERICA       438           8.4%
12        NORTH AMERICA       275           5.3%
13        OCEANIA              26           0.5%
14
15        TOTAL              5234         100.0%
16
17
18
19
20
                            UNDO
```

FIGURE 7-5 The completed spreadsheet for calculating the percentage of the population on each continent.

PETER MINUIT

Absolute addressing is especially important in spreadsheets where key numbers are put into separate cells. To illustrate this, let's do another example.

Peter Minuit was the director-general of the Dutch West Indies Company's settlements in North America. In 1626 he negotiated a deal with the local Indian chiefs and purchased the island of Manhattan from them for pieces of bright cloth, beads, and other trinkets valued at 60 guilders, or about $24. Today the island of Manhattan forms the core of New York City and is worth a fortune. But did Peter make such a great deal? Suppose Peter had taken the money and put it into a money market account at the Dutch National Bank. How much would it be worth today? What would be the value of the investment each year from 1626 to 2000?

We need one more piece of information. What interest rate would Peter have received on his money over 365 years? For now, let us assume a constant 3% per year. We will change this assumption later.

Figure 7-6 is a start toward a spreadsheet that calculates what Peter's investment would be worth. The years from 1626 through 2000 will be in column B. The corresponding value of the investment each year will be in column D. First, how can we obtain the years in column B ? We could type each one of them, but who wants to type 375 numbers ? A good solution is to put a formula into B10 and then copy the formula down the column. Each number in column B is to be one greater than the number in the cell above. So in cell B10 we will put the formula +B9+1. When we copy the formula down the column from B10 to B11..B383, the formula in B11 will

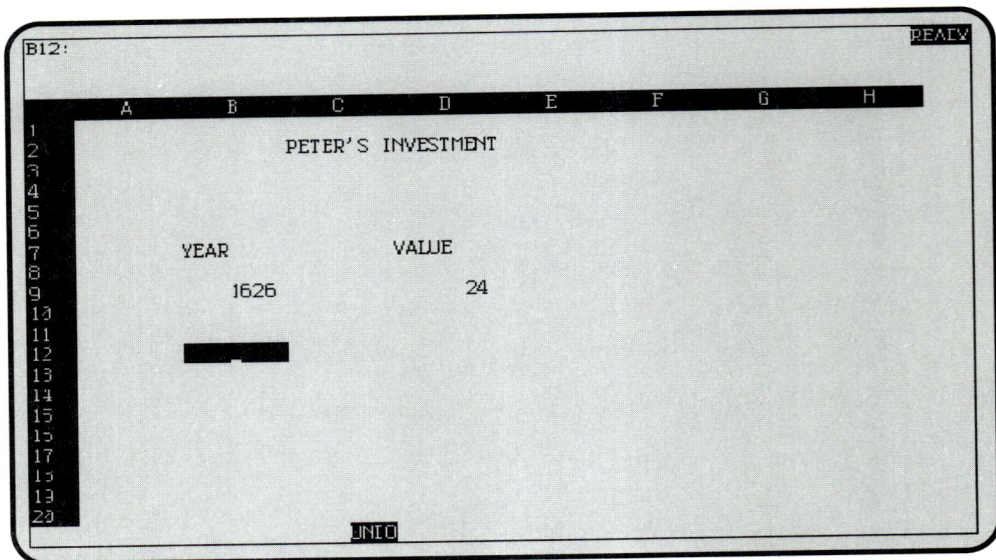

FIGURE 7-6 Beginning the spreadsheet to calculate what the value of the $24 would be if Peter Minuit had deposited it in a bank instead of purchasing Manhattan island.

be +B10+1, the formula in B12 will be +B11+1, and so on. There will be a chain of formulas down the column, each adding one to the value of the cell above. The years from 1626 through 2000 should appear in column B.

How can we obtain the value of the investment each year in column D? We will follow the same idea of entering a formula for the cell in row 10 and then copying the formula down the column. How much money would Peter have in 1627? Peter would have the amount from the previous year plus the interest the money earned during the year. At 3% interest the formula for D10 would be

$$+D9+0.03*D9.$$

We copy the formula from D10 to D11..D383. We format the values in column D (/ Range Format Currency 0 enter D9..D383 enter), widen the cells in column D (place the cursor in column D and then / Worksheet Column Set-Width 20 enter), and align the column headings to the right of the cells (/ Range Label Right B7..D7 enter). The resulting spreadsheet is shown in Figure 7-7. Using the GoTo key to move the cursor to A370 (F5 A370 enter), we can see the bottom of the spreadsheet in Figure 7-8. What would Peter's investment of $24 in 1626 be worth today if he received 3% interest per year? A little over $1 million. What does a little over $1 million buy in Manhattan today? A condo, an apartment in a nice building. It looks like Peter was wise in purchasing Manhattan. (Of course, the British took over the city from the Dutch in 1664 and changed the name from New Amsterdam to New York. If the 60 guilders had been invested in the bank, at least the Dutch still would have had their money.)

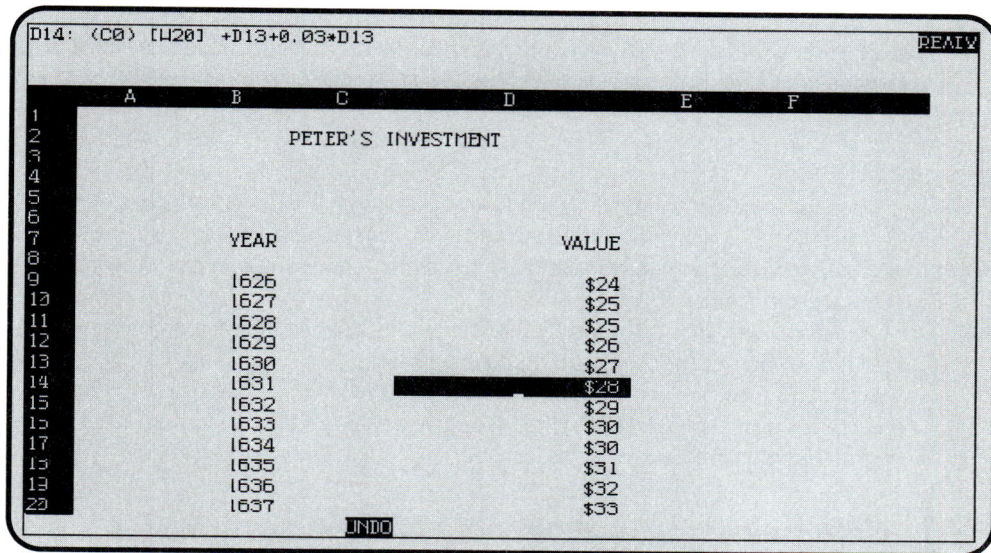

FIGURE 7-7 Calculating the value of the investment assuming a 3% interest rate.

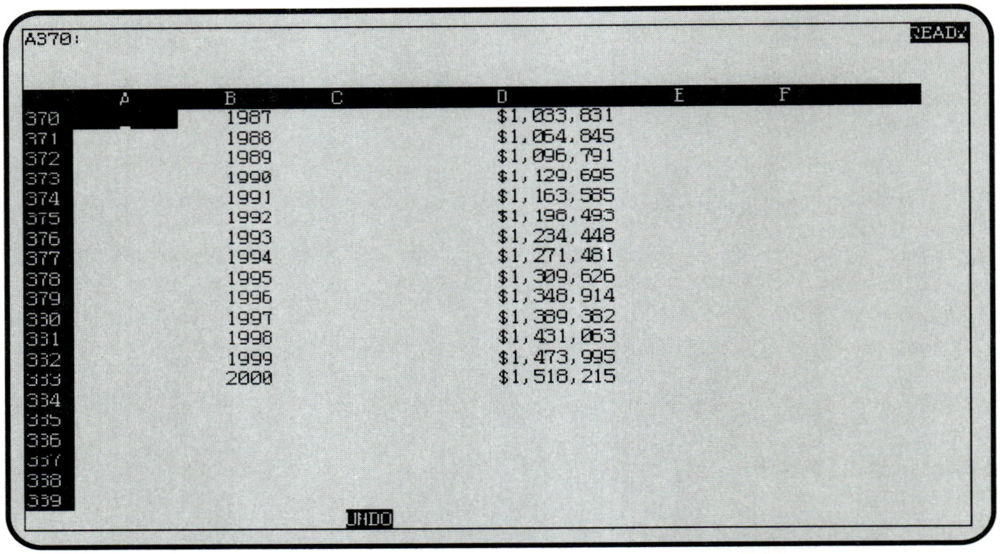

A370: READY

	A	B	C	D	E	F
370		1987		$1,033,831		
371		1988		$1,064,845		
372		1989		$1,096,791		
373		1990		$1,129,695		
374		1991		$1,163,585		
375		1992		$1,198,493		
376		1993		$1,234,448		
377		1994		$1,271,481		
378		1995		$1,309,626		
379		1996		$1,348,914		
380		1997		$1,389,382		
381		1998		$1,431,063		
382		1999		$1,473,995		
383		2000		$1,518,215		
384						
385						
386						
387						
388						
389						

UNDO

FIGURE 7-8 Peter's investment would be worth a little over $1,000,000 today at 3% interest.

But what if Peter had received 5% annual interest rate instead of 3%? What would Peter's account be worth now? To answer this question, we must change the spreadsheet. In particular, we need to change the formulas in column D. The formula in D10 could be changed to

+D9+0.05*D9

Then the formula would be copied from D10 to D11..D383. But suppose we then wanted to see what the value of the investment would be if the annual interest rate were 7% or 9% or 11%. To change the interest rate we would have to change the formula in D10 and then copy the new formula down the column each time.

An easier approach is to put the interest rate in a separate cell and refer to that cell in the formulas in column D. Now if we want to see what would happen with a different interest rate we would just need to change the number in the cell rather than changing all 375 of the formulas. This approach is shown in Figure 7-9. The Annual Interest Rate is in cell D5, which has been formatted to percentage with two decimal places. The formula in D10 is

+D9+$D$5*D9

This formula has been copied from D10 to D11..D383. We refer to the interest rate as an absolute address ($D$5) so that the address is not adjusted as the formula is copied down the

```
D12: (C0) [W20] +D11+$D$5*D11                                    READY

        A        B        C           D            E       F
1
2                      PETER'S INVESTMENT
3
4
5       ANNUAL INTEREST RATE:              5.00%
6
7              YEAR                       VALUE
8
9              1626                        $24
10             1627                        $25
11             1628                        $26
12             1629                        $28
13             1630                        $29
14             1631                        $31
15             1632                        $32
16             1633                        $34
17             1634                        $35
18             1635                        $37
19             1636                        $39
20             1637                        $41
                           UNDO
```

FIGURE 7-9 A better approach is to place the annual interest rate in a separate cell and refer to the cell in the formulas using absolute addressing.

column. In Figure 7-9 the cursor is on D12 and indeed we can see that the formula in D12 is

$$+D11+\$D\$5*D11.$$

THE / WORKSHEET WINDOW COMMAND

Wouldn't it be nice to be able to change the interest rate and see immediately the resulting value of the investment today? In Lotus 1-2-3 the Worksheet Window command allows the screen to be divided into two windows on the spreadsheet. From the spreadsheet in Figure 7-9, we select / Worksheet Window Horizontal. The screen is divided into two portions, called **windows**, at the location of the cursor. The two windows can be vertically scrolled independently. To move the cursor from one window to the other use function key F6, the Window key. By moving the cursor to the bottom window using function key F6 and then using the GoTo key F5 to move the cursor to A373, we can see the two portions of the screen shown in Figure 7-10. At 5% interest, Peter's investment of $24 in 1626 would be worth a little over $1 billion today. With a little over $1 billion you could buy a large office building or two in Manhattan.

In Chapter 1 we discussed how electronic spreadsheets were developed to facilitate "What if" analysis. Here is an example. We can easily determine "What if" Peter received some annual interest rate on his investment. To see "What if" we change the number in D5 to the annual

```
D375: (C0) [W20] +D374+$D$5*D374                              READY

        A       B       C          D            E       F
1
2                    PETER'S INVESTMENT
3
4
5      ANNUAL INTEREST RATE:              5.00%
6
7             YEAR                        VALUE
8
9             1626                         $24
10            1627                         $25
11            1628                         $26
        A       B       C          D            E       F
373           1990              $1,239,127,807
374           1991              $1,301,084,198
375           1992              $1,366,138,408
376           1993              $1,434,445,328
377           1994              $1,506,167,595
378           1995              $1,581,475,974
379           1996              $1,660,549,773
380           1997              $1,743,577,262
                            UNDO
```

FIGURE 7-10 The / Worksheet Window command allows you to display two parts of the spreadsheet at once.

interest rate we wish to try. As soon as we enter the new rate, the new values for the investment go rippling down the screen. With the spreadsheet designed so that the annual interest rate is in a separate cell and with the screen divided into two windows, we can change the interest rate to 7% and see almost instantaneously that Peter's investment of $24 in 1626 now would be worth over $1 trillion (Figure 7-11). Now we're talking about some money!

In the / Worksheet Window command you can set up Vertical windows or Horizontal windows, but not both at the same time. In Lotus 1-2-3 Release 2.2 you can have no more than two windows at a time. In either case, the screen will divide at the cursor, so usually you would place the cursor toward the middle of the screen before selecting / Worksheet Window.

To clear the windows and return to the usual screen, issue / Worksheet Window Clear .

ABSOLUTE ADDRESSING WITH A NAMED RANGE

In Chapter 5 we discussed the benefits of naming cells or ranges of cells. In the spreadsheet in Figure 7-9, we could use the command / Range Name Create to give cell D5 the name INTEREST_RATE . Now the formula in cell D10 would be

$$+D9+\$INTEREST\_RATE*D9$$

To specify an absolute reference to a named cell or range of cells, a dollar sign is placed before the name in a formula.

```
D5: (P2) [W20] 0.07                                                   READY

         A         B       C          D            E          F
 1
 2                     PETER'S INVESTMENT
 3
 4
 5   ANNUAL INTEREST RATE:                      7.00%
 6
 7              YEAR                         VALUE
 8
 9              1626                          $24
10              1627                          $26
11              1628                          $27
         A         B       C          D            E          F
373            1990        $1,190,985,075,095
374            1991        $1,274,354,030,351
375            1992        $1,363,558,812,476
376            1993        $1,459,007,929,349
377            1994        $1,561,138,484,404
378            1995        $1,670,418,178,312
379            1996        $1,787,347,450,794
380            1997        $1,912,461,772,349
                         UNDO
```

FIGURE 7-11 At 7% interest you might prefer the bank account over Manhattan island. What would 9% produce? 11%?

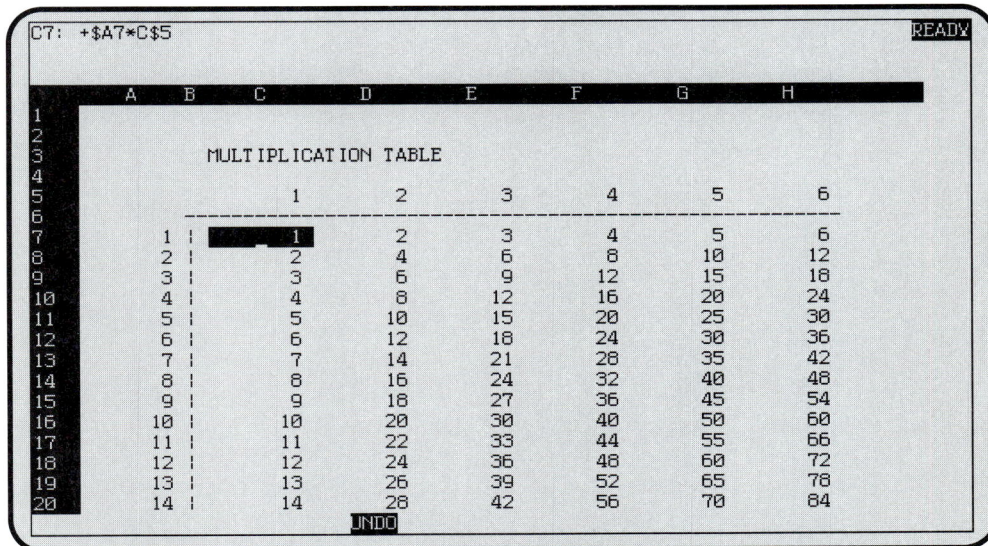

```
C7: +$A7*C$5                                                          READY

       A    B    C      D      E      F      G        H
 1
 2
 3             MULTIPLICATION TABLE
 4
 5                 1      2      3      4      5        6
 6             ------------------------------------------
 7        1  |      1      2      3      4      5        6
 8        2  |      2      4      6      8     10       12
 9        3  |      3      6      9     12     15       18
10        4  |      4      8     12     16     20       24
11        5  |      5     10     15     20     25       30
12        6  |      6     12     18     24     30       36
13        7  |      7     14     21     28     35       42
14        8  |      8     16     24     32     40       48
15        9  |      9     18     27     36     45       54
16       10  |     10     20     30     40     50       60
17       11  |     11     22     33     44     55       66
18       12  |     12     24     36     48     60       72
19       13  |     13     26     39     52     65       78
20       14  |     14     28     42     56     70       84
                         UNDO
```

FIGURE 7-12 A simple spreadsheet that uses mixed addressing.

MIXED ADDRESSING

On rare occasions we might want the column part of the address of a cell in a formula to remain absolute and the row part of the address to be relative. Or we might want the column part of the address of a cell in a formula to be relative and the row part of the address to be absolute. An address in a formula that is to be absolute in one dimension and relative in the other dimension is called a **mixed address** or **mixed reference**.

The spreadsheet in Figure 7-12 illustrates a double use of mixed addressing. Each cell in the range C7..H20 is the product of the number in column A for the row and the number in row 5 for the column. Thus the formula in C7 is

+$A7*C$5

The body of the table is produced by then copying from C7 to C7..H20. As a check on your understanding, what would be the resulting formula in, say, cell G18? In the first address in the formula column A is absolute while the row is relative. In the second address in the formula the column is relative while row 5 is absolute. So the formula copied into cell G18 would be

+$A18*G$5

PENCIL AND PAPER EXERCISE

7-1   The widget industry is dominated by two companies. United Widget (UW) had total sales of $87.2 million in 1990. However, their sales are *decreasing* by 0.8% per year. Widgets International (WI) had sales of $53.4 million in 1990. Their sales are *increasing* by 3.2% each year. We have developed a spreadsheet (using the Copy command) that shows their future performance if this trend continues. The growth rates are in separate cells. Changing one of the growth rates causes the numbers below to change appropriately.

```
A1:                                                              READY

        A        B        C        D        E      F      G      H
1
2                       WIDGET  INDUSTRY  FORECAST
3
4    GROWTH RATE:      -0.8%       3.2%
5
6                 YEAR      UW       WI      TOTAL
7                 1990     87.2     53.4     140.6
8                 1991     86.5     55.1     141.6
9                 1992     85.8     56.9     142.7
10                1993     85.1     58.7     143.8
11                1994     84.4     60.6     145.0
12                1995     83.8     62.5     146.3
13                1996     83.1     64.5     147.6
14                1997     82.4     66.6     149.0
15                1998     81.8     68.7     150.5
16                1999     81.1     70.9     152.0
17                2000     80.5     73.2     153.6
18
19               TOTAL    921.7    691.0    1612.7
20
                                UNDO
```

What is the *formula* in each of the following cells: B12, C12, D12, E12, C19, E19?

COMPUTER EXERCISES

7-2   There are eight students in your math class. They all took a quiz. Enter the eight names in one column and eight (different) scores in an adjoining column. At the bottom of the column calculate the class average. Now add a new column that calculates the points above or below the class average for each student. Use the Copy command. Change one of the scores. Do the class average and all of the points above or below change accordingly?

7-3   In the example in the text on the value of Peter Minuit's investment if he placed the money in a bank account, we assumed that there would be one interest rate for all 375 years. Set up a spreadsheet that is similar to the one in the chapter except that it has an extra column for the interest rate. For each year the corresponding cell in the column would give the interest rate for the year. What would be the value of Peter's investment if from 1626 through 1970 he received 3% and from 1971 through now he received 7%?

7-4   The top 10 vehicle manufacturers in the world are shown below.

Producer	Millions of Vehicles Sold in 1989	Millions of Vehicles Sold in 1988
General Motors	7.95	8.11
Ford	6.41	6.52
Toyota	4.45	3.85
Nissan	3.01	2.71
Volkswagen	2.93	2.85
Fiat	2.44	2.14
Chrysler	2.38	2.57
Peugeot-Citroen	2.22	2.08
Renault	2.05	1.94
Honda	1.86	1.78
Total for all producers (not just top 10)	49.52	47.67

(a) Enter this data into a spreadsheet.

(b) Add a column that shows the change in the number of vehicles sold from 1988 to 1989 for each producer. Use the Copy command.

(c) Add a column that shows the percentage change from 1988 to 1989 for each producer. Use the Copy command.

(d) Add a column that shows the percentage of the total market for 1989 sold by each producer. Use the Copy command.

(e) Add a column that shows the number of vehicles sold in 1989 by each producer as a percentage of the number of vehicles sold by General Motors in 1989. Use the Copy command.

7-5   You are planning to deposit a fixed amount at the beginning of each year in a bank account for 20 years. Assume that you will earn a constant interest rate on your money. Design and implement a spreadsheet that will show you how much you will have accumulated at the end of each of the 20 years. You should have separate, well-labeled cells for the amount of your annual deposit and for the interest rate. If you change either of these cells, all the accumulations should change automatically.

Try your spreadsheet on

(a) a deposit of $5000 per year and an interest rate of 5% per year

(b) a deposit of $5000 per year and an interest rate of 10% per year

(c) a deposit of $10,000 per year and an interest rate of 5% per year

(d) a deposit of $10,000 per year and an interest rate of 10% per year

(e) How much do you need to deposit each year to have exactly $1,000,000 in 20 years assuming that you earn 8% interest per year?

(f) What annual interest rate would you need to obtain in order to accumulate $1,000,000 at the end of 20 years if you deposit $10,000 per year?

7-6 The cost of a college education has been rising rapidly, as I am sure you are aware. You would like to estimate what it will cost to put your children through college. First, we will need to gather some data and make some assumptions. Find out the current cost of attending your favorite college or university in terms of (1) tuition and (2) all other expenses. If you have no children now, assume that your first child will be born five years from now and your second child will be born three years later. Assume that your children will enter college at age 18 and that they will attend for four years each and then graduate with high honors. (Of course they will be model students.) Further, we will assume that there will be a single annual rate of increase over the years for tuition and other expenses.

Your spreadsheet will have a separate section at the top for parameters and data that might be changed. In particular, there should be well-labeled cells for current tuition, current other expenses, and rate of increase. The body of the spreadsheet should have four columns: year, tuition, other expenses, total expenses. The values that appear in these columns of course will depend in part on the values in the input section of the spreadsheet. At the bottom (or top) of the spreadsheet there should be a well-labeled output cell that gives the total projected cost of sending your two children to college.

Try your spreadsheet with an annual rate of increase of 6%. Now change the annual rate of increase to 9%. Do all of the appropriate numbers change? Don't worry. You will have a terrific job. The money you spend on college expenses for your children will be small change.

7-7 Compsys is a start-up computer company. This quarter management expects Sales of $550,000. They expect Sales to grow at a rate of 9% per quarter. Cost of Goods Sold is running at 34% of Sales and is expected to stay at that rate. Selling Costs are 12% of Sales and are expected to stay at that rate. General and Administrative Costs (including Research and Development) are $420,000 this quarter and are scheduled to rise at 2% per quarter.

(a) Design and implement a spreadsheet to make a 20-quarter income statement projection for Compsys. You should have a separate input area with well-labeled separate cells for each of the numbers above. You should have a separate row for each item in the income statement and a separate column for each quarter. The final row should be for Earnings Before Taxes. Use the Copy command wherever possible.

In the initial quarters, Compsys should show operating losses (negative Earnings Before Taxes). Under the assumptions given, what is the first quarter in which Compsys shows an operating profit (positive Earnings Before Taxes)?

(b) Suppose Sales grow at 12% per quarter. Now in what quarter would Compsys first show an operating profit ?

(c) Suppose Sales grow at 9% per quarter and General and Administrative Costs grow at 6% per quarter and Selling Costs are 15% of sales. Now in what quarter will Compsys first show an operating profit ?

7-8 The Fibonacci series is named after Leonardo Fibonacci, an Italian mathematician of the thirteenth century. The Fibonacci series is an infinite series of numbers 0, 1, 1, 2, 3, 5, 8, 13, ... The first two numbers in the series are 0 and 1. Subsequent numbers are formed by adding the two previous numbers in the series. The Fibonacci series appears in many unexpected places. Indeed, there is a regularly published journal that is devoted to applications of the Fibonacci series.

What proportioned rectangle is the most aesthetically pleasing? What is the ratio of height to width that people most prefer in a rectangle? Since the Renaissance it has been claimed that The Golden Ratio is the most aesthetically pleasing ratio for a rectangle. The Golden Ratio has been shown to appear often in Western art. The Golden Ratio usually is defined as the proportion that results from dividing a line in two sections such that the ratio of the length of the smaller section to the larger section is the same as the ratio of the length of the larger section to the length of the line as a whole. Another way of computing the Golden Ratio is to take the ratio of successive terms of the Fibonacci series. Thus 0/1, 1/1, 1/2, 2/3, 3/5, 5/8, ... form closer and closer approximations of the Golden Ratio. (So, a 3 x 5 card or a 5 x 8 piece of paper should seem aesthetically pleasing rectangles.)

Create a spreadsheet with three well-labeled columns. In the first column should be the numbers 0, 1, 2, 3, 4, through 20. In the second column should be the successive terms of the Fibonacci series. In the third column should be the successive approximations to the Golden Ratio, printed as a decimal between 0 and 1. Use the Copy command for all three columns.

7-9 Averosas are a new breed of small furry animal that resemble guinea pigs. They are becoming all the rage as pets. You have decided to make some extra money by raising averosas in your room. For Christmas you ask Santa Claus to help you out. You must have been good this year because, sure enough, on Christmas morning under the tree you find a one-month old male and a one-month old female averosa in a cage.

Averosas are quite prolific, and predictably so. They have their first litter at six months of age. Every three months from then on, each female has a litter of on average four baby averosas (assume two males and two females). Of course these babies will go through the same breeding cycle.

At the end of each quarter (three months) you plan to sell all the averosas that have reached two years of age to the local pet stores. This is how you will make your fortune. You won't have any expenses, as your roommate works in a restaurant, and you figure your roommate can bring home the leftovers from the salad bar to feed the animals.

This sounds like a great scheme, but your roommate would like to know (1) how many averosas will be born in your room each quarter and, more important, (2) how many averosas will be living in the room each quarter! You would like to know (3) how many averosas you'll be able to sell at the end of each quarter so you can plan what to do with all the money you'll earn. Incidentally, your roommate will be (somewhat) relieved to learn that averosas don't smell too bad if their cages are cleaned often.

Set up a Lotus 1-2-3 spreadsheet to answer these three questions. Assume you will have the averosa colony for the next five years. Of course you will use the Copy command wherever possible. Use several columns. Label all columns well. Assume the quarter ends at January 1, April 1, July 1, and October 1.

Assuming everything goes as planned, what is the total number of averosas you will have owned during the five years? What is the maximum number of averosas that will be in your room at any one time? How long will it be before your roommate leaves?

7-10 The accompanying spreadsheet gives the interest for different principal amounts and interest rates. The amounts of the interest rates at the tops of the columns in row 9 are determined by the entries in D5 and E5. For example, if the number in E5 is changed to 0.015 (which would display as 1.5%), then the values in row 9 would change to 8.0%, 9.5%, 11.0%, 12.5%, 14.0%, 15.5%, and the values in B11..G20 would change accordingly. Similarly, the values in A11..A20 are determined by the entries in D6 and E6. Thus B9..G9 and A11..A20 contain formulas as do B11..G20. The formulas in B11..G20 were created using a single Copy command and contain formulas with mixed addressing. Your task is to reconstruct the spreadsheet accordingly. Use the Copy command.

INTEREST TABLE

		START	INCREMENT
INTEREST RATE		8.0%	1.0%
PRINCIPAL		$5,000	$1,000

INTEREST RATE

PRINCIPAL	8.0%	9.0%	10.0%	11.0%	12.0%	13.0%
$5,000	400	450	500	550	600	650
$6,000	480	540	600	660	720	780
$7,000	560	630	700	770	840	910
$8,000	640	720	800	880	960	1040
$9,000	720	810	900	990	1080	1170
$10,000	800	900	1000	1100	1200	1300
$11,000	880	990	1100	1210	1320	1430
$12,000	960	1080	1200	1320	1440	1560
$13,000	1040	1170	1300	1430	1560	1690
$14,000	1120	1260	1400	1540	1680	1820

Change the PRINCIPAL START to 900 and the PRINCIPAL INCREMENT to 150.
Do all the numbers in the table change appropriately?

8

Commands
for Larger
Spreadsheets

In this chapter we discuss some of the commands of Lotus 1-2-3 that are helpful for constructing and working with larger spreadsheets.

REPEATING LABELS

It often is convenient to separate different parts of a spreadsheet with rows or boxes of asterisks, dashes, equal signs, or some other character. To enter a cell of asterisks, you could type `**********`. But what would happen if you later widen the column? The asterisks would no longer fill the cell.

In Lotus 1-2-3 if you type * (backslash asterisk) into a cell, the cell always will be filled with asterisks, whatever the width of the cell. Beginning a cell entry with a backslash specifies a **repeating label**. Whatever characters are typed after the backslash will be used to fill the cell. If the cell width subsequently is changed, the cell still will be filled with the characters. For example, the spreadsheet in Figure 8-1 contains three repeating labels. Cell B2 contains *. Cell B4 contains \ABC. Cell B6 contains \-+ .

To create a line of repeating labels, the cell can be copied across the screen.

FREEZING TITLES

When moving through a large spreadsheet, it is not unusual to be confronted with a screen full of numbers that are difficult to identify. For example, the spreadsheet in Figure 8-2 shows monthly sales figures by country, but it is almost impossible to determine which numbers are associated with which countries for which months.

Lotus 1-2-3 provides us with the capability of freezing the titles on the screen so that they stay in place on the screen wherever the cursor moves. To lock in the titles, we move the cursor back to the top left part of the worksheet so that the row titles are in the left part of the screen and the column titles are in the top of the screen. In Figure 8-3, row 5 is at the top of the screen. Column A is in the left of the screen. The cursor is in B10. We select /Worksheet Titles and are confronted with the menu in Figure 8-3. We select Both, and the rows above the cursor are locked on the screen and the columns to the left of the cursor are locked on the screen. Wherever we move the cursor, rows 5, 6, 7, 8, 9 and column A remain on the screen. When we move the cursor back

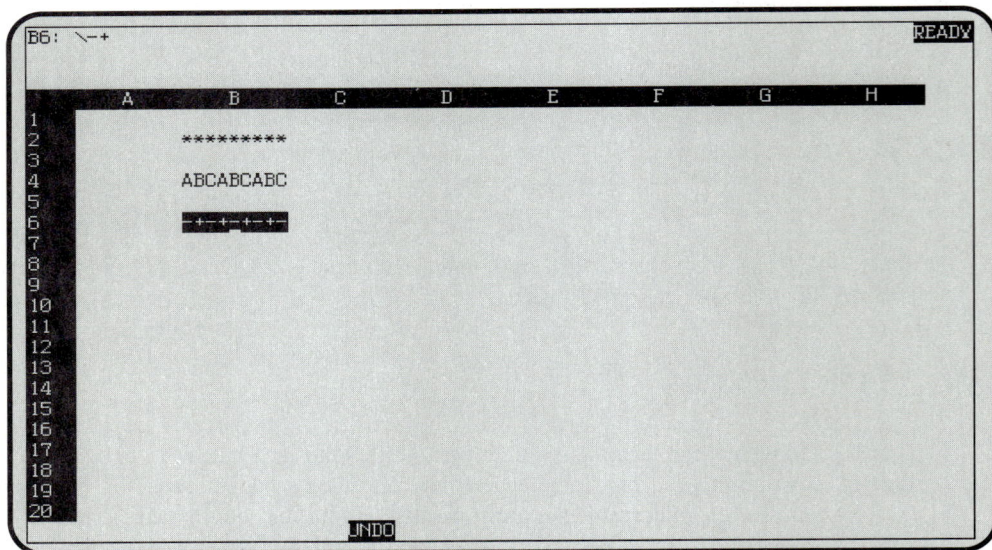

FIGURE 8-1 Three repeating labels.

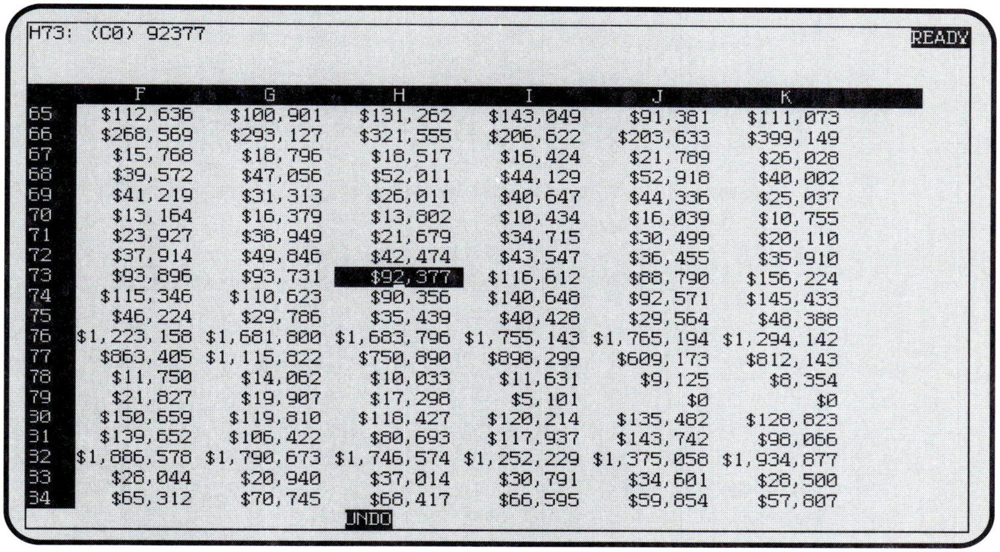

H73: (C0) 92377 READY

	F	G	H	I	J	K
65	$112,636	$100,901	$131,262	$143,049	$91,381	$111,073
66	$268,569	$293,127	$321,555	$206,622	$203,633	$399,149
67	$15,768	$18,796	$18,517	$16,424	$21,789	$26,028
68	$39,572	$47,056	$52,011	$44,129	$52,918	$40,002
69	$41,219	$31,313	$26,011	$40,647	$44,336	$25,037
70	$13,164	$16,379	$13,802	$10,434	$16,039	$10,755
71	$23,927	$38,949	$21,679	$34,715	$30,499	$20,110
72	$37,914	$49,846	$42,474	$43,547	$36,455	$35,910
73	$93,896	$93,731	$92,377	$116,612	$88,790	$156,224
74	$115,346	$110,623	$90,356	$140,648	$92,571	$145,433
75	$46,224	$29,786	$35,439	$40,428	$29,564	$48,388
76	$1,223,158	$1,681,800	$1,683,796	$1,755,143	$1,765,194	$1,294,142
77	$863,405	$1,115,822	$750,890	$898,299	$609,173	$812,143
78	$11,750	$14,062	$10,033	$11,631	$9,125	$8,354
79	$21,827	$19,907	$17,298	$5,101	$0	$0
80	$150,659	$119,810	$118,427	$120,214	$135,482	$128,823
81	$139,652	$106,422	$80,693	$117,937	$143,742	$98,066
82	$1,886,578	$1,790,673	$1,746,574	$1,252,229	$1,375,058	$1,934,877
83	$28,044	$20,940	$37,014	$30,791	$34,601	$28,500
84	$65,312	$70,745	$68,417	$66,595	$59,854	$57,807

UNDO

FIGURE 8-2 Lost in the middle of a large spreadsheet.

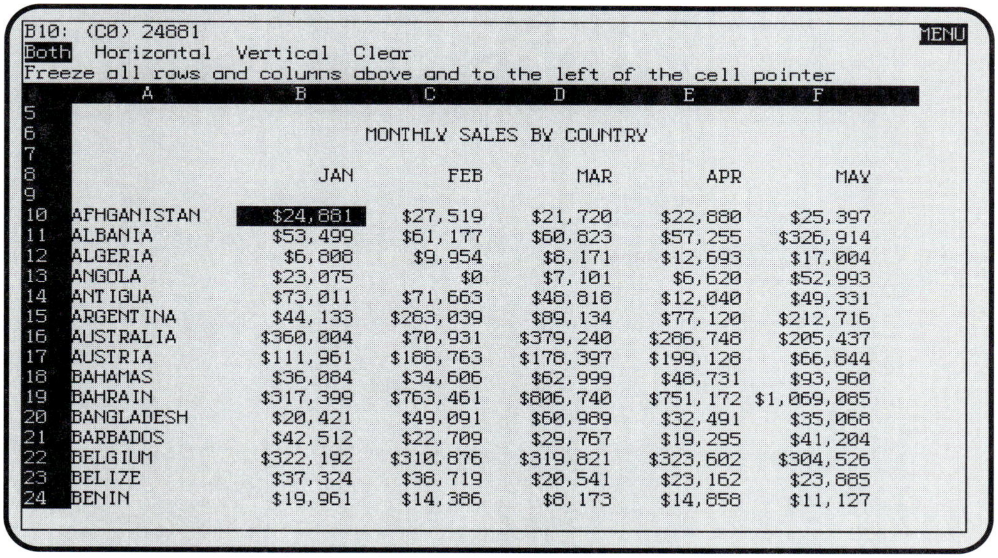

B10: (C0) 24881 MENU
Both Horizontal Vertical Clear
Freeze all rows and columns above and to the left of the cell pointer

	A	B	C	D	E	F
5						
6			MONTHLY SALES BY COUNTRY			
7						
8		JAN	FEB	MAR	APR	MAY
9						
10	AFHGANISTAN	$24,881	$27,519	$21,720	$22,880	$25,397
11	ALBANIA	$53,499	$61,177	$60,823	$57,255	$326,914
12	ALGERIA	$6,808	$9,954	$8,171	$12,693	$17,004
13	ANGOLA	$23,075	$0	$7,101	$6,620	$52,993
14	ANTIGUA	$73,011	$71,663	$48,818	$12,040	$49,331
15	ARGENTINA	$44,133	$283,039	$89,134	$77,120	$212,716
16	AUSTRALIA	$360,004	$70,931	$379,240	$286,748	$205,437
17	AUSTRIA	$111,961	$188,763	$178,397	$199,128	$66,844
18	BAHAMAS	$36,084	$34,606	$62,999	$48,731	$93,960
19	BAHRAIN	$317,399	$763,461	$806,740	$751,172	$1,069,085
20	BANGLADESH	$20,421	$49,091	$60,989	$32,491	$35,068
21	BARBADOS	$42,512	$22,709	$29,767	$19,295	$41,204
22	BELGIUM	$322,192	$310,876	$319,821	$323,602	$304,526
23	BELIZE	$37,324	$38,719	$20,541	$23,162	$23,885
24	BENIN	$19,961	$14,386	$8,173	$14,858	$11,127

FIGURE 8-3 Freezing titles using the / Worksheet Titles command. If we now select Both then column A and rows 5, 6, 7, 8, 9 will be frozen on the screen wherever we move the cursor.

to the original position of Figure 8-2, we now can see the countries and months for the sales figures, as in Figure 8-4.

To unfreeze the titles, select / Worksheet Titles Clear .

The / Worksheet Titles is very useful for making sense of the contents of large spreadsheets. We also could use the / Worksheet Window command discussed in the previous chapter for this purpose.

USE OF THE END KEY

In Chapter 3 we examined several ways of moving the cursor around the worksheet. The arrow keys move the cursor one cell at a time. The PgDn and PgUp keys move the cursor vertically one screen at a time. The Tab and Shift-Tab keys move the cursor horizontally one screen at a time. The Home key moves the cursor back to cell A1. The GoTo key F5 allows you to move the cursor to any cell in the worksheet by typing the cell address.

One cursor movement key we did not discuss in Chapter 3 is the End key. The End key is especially useful for moving around larger spreadsheets.

Assume that Lotus 1-2-3 is in Ready mode. Pressing the End key by itself does not move the cursor anywhere. Rather, when you press the End key, the END indicator lights up in the bottom right corner of the screen and Lotus 1-2-3 awaits the next key press. The End key is followed by a second key press to move the cursor.

```
H73: (C0) 92377                                                      READY

        A           F           G           H           I           J
5
6
7
8                 MAY         JUN         JUL         AUG         SEP
9
65  GHANA        $112,636    $100,901    $131,262    $143,049     $91,381
66  GREECE       $268,569    $293,127    $321,555    $206,622    $203,633
67  GRENADA       $15,768     $18,796     $18,517     $16,424     $21,789
68  GUATEMALA     $39,572     $47,056     $52,011     $44,129     $52,918
69  GUINEA        $41,219     $31,313     $26,011     $40,647     $44,336
70  GUINEA-BISSAU $13,164     $16,379     $13,802     $10,434     $16,039
71  GUYANA        $23,927     $38,949     $21,679     $34,715     $30,499
72  HAITI         $37,914     $49,846     $42,474     $43,547     $36,455
73  HONDURAS      $93,896     $93,731     $92,377    $116,612     $88,790
74  HUNGARY      $115,346    $110,623     $90,356    $140,648     $92,571
75  ICELAND       $46,224     $29,786     $35,439     $40,428     $29,564
76  INDIA     $1,223,158  $1,681,800  $1,683,796  $1,755,143  $1,765,194
77  INDONESIA   $863,405  $1,115,822    $750,890    $898,299    $609,173
78  IRAN          $11,750     $14,062     $10,033     $11,631      $9,125
79  IRAQ          $21,827     $19,907     $17,298      $5,101         $0
                            UNDO
```

FIGURE 8-4 The rows displayed are 5 through 9 and then 65 through 79 and the columns displayed are A, F, G. H, I, J. Can you determine the year of the sales figures?

```
K73: (C0) 156224                                                    READY

          A           K          L          M          N          O
5
6
7
8                   OCT        NOV        DEC                   TOTAL
9
65  GHANA        $111,073   $146,826   $148,542             $1,493,468
66  GREECE       $399,149   $365,641   $224,455             $3,578,635
67  GRENADA       $26,028    $23,293    $27,204               $294,941
68  GUATEMALA     $40,002    $57,326    $33,913               $552,475
69  GUINEA        $25,037    $43,541    $25,813               $416,180
70  GUINEA-BISSAU $10,755    $12,677    $13,157               $157,881
71  GUYANA        $20,110    $21,635    $38,075               $330,955
72  HAITI         $35,910    $46,244    $43,578               $486,561
73  HONDURAS     $156,224   $152,305   $102,744             $1,500,186
74  HUNGARY      $145,433    $89,478   $136,018             $1,390,500
75  ICELAND       $48,388    $34,226    $48,013               $480,571
76  INDIA     $1,294,142 $1,516,360 $1,444,005            $18,059,104
77  INDONESIA   $812,143 $1,058,216   $616,417             $9,287,849
78  IRAN          $8,354    $12,482    $15,203               $135,492
79  IRAQ              $0         $0         $0               $147,521
                         UNDO
```

FIGURE 8-5 Pressing the End key followed by the right arrow key would move the cursor to M73, the first non-blank cell to the right that is followed by a blank cell.

Pressing the End key and then the Home key moves the cursor to the bottom right corner of the active area of the worksheet. The **active area** of the worksheet is the smallest rectangular range from A1 that contains all of the nonblank cells. Pressing End Home moves the cursor to the bottom right corner of that rectangle.

Pressing the End key followed by the right arrow key basically moves the cursor to the right end of the spreadsheet. Specifically, pressing End followed by the right arrow moves the cursor to the first nonblank cell to the right that has a blank cell to its right. For example, in Figure 8-5 the cursor is in K73. If we press the End key followed by the right arrow key, then the cursor will move to the right to M73, the first nonblank cell in row 73 to the right of column K that is followed by a blank cell. Assuming that there are no entries to the right of the TOTAL column, pressing the End key followed by the right arrow key again would move the cursor to the right to O73. Pressing End followed by right arrow again would move the cursor to IV73, the rightmost cell in row 73 in the worksheet. If the cursor already is in the rightmost nonblank cell of the row, then pressing End right arrow moves the cursor out to column IV, the rightmost column of the spreadsheet.

Pressing the End key followed by the left arrow, up arrow, or down arrow acts similarly. For example, if the cursor is in K73 as in Figure 8-5, pressing the End key followed by the up arrow key will move the cursor up to K10 because K9 is blank.

Using the End key is a convenient way to navigate around large spreadsheets, as it takes you directly to the end of a large block of data. For example, the End key can be useful when pointing to a wide row of numbers in the argument in an @SUM function.

MANUAL RECALCULATION

A large spreadsheet can take Lotus 1-2-3 a while to recalculate. Lotus 1-2-3 normally recalculates formulas in a spreadsheet whenever a cell is changed. In a large spreadsheet, this can mean an annoying wait whenever a piece of data is entered.

Suppose the monthly sales by country spreadsheet in Figure 8-3 contains formulas for calculating row and column totals and averages, deviations from goals, and a multitude of other statistics. When we are entering the country by country sales figures for a new month, after each entry Lotus 1-2-3 would go through and recalculate statistics. This means that after each of the 192 entries for the month, there could well be a noticeable delay while the recalculation is performed. What we would prefer is to type in the data as quickly as we can and only then, after all of the sales figures for the month have been entered, have the formulas calculated.

Lotus 1-2-3 allows us to suppress automatic recalculation by selecting / Worksheet Global Recalculation Manual. Under **manual recalculation**, formulas are not automatically recalculated after a cell entry is changed. Rather, formulas are recalculated when F9, the Calc key, is pressed. Under manual recalculation we could enter all of our data for the month without waiting between each entry for formulas to be recalculated. After all of the data has been entered, we press F9 and the statistics are brought up to date. Under manual recalculation, Lotus 1-2-3 places the word CALC at the bottom of the screen if there are formulas in the spreadsheet that need to be recalculated.

To return to automatic recalculation, select / Worksheet Global Recalculation Automatic.

CELL PROTECTION

Cell protection is an important capability of Lotus 1-2-3 that should be used with almost all spreadsheets. Cell protection prevents the user from inadvertently changing or erasing cells in the spreadsheet. There are two steps in protecting the cells in a spreadsheet.

The first step in protecting cells is to inform Lotus 1-2-3 which cells you wish to be able to change, which cells should be unprotected. For example, in the spreadsheet that calculates the proportion of the world's population in each continent in Figures 7-1 through 7-5, cells C8..C13 would be unprotected, as those are the only cells that should be changed. Perhaps cell C4, the year, should be unprotected as well. In the spreadsheet for Peter Minuit's investment in Figures 7-9 through 7-11, the interest rate in D5 would be unprotected. The command for informing Lotus 1-2-3 what cell or range of cells should be unprotected is / Range Unprotect. To unprotect two groups of cells, the command would be selected twice. All cells that are unprotected are displayed differently on the screen. Sometimes the text in the unprotected cells is darkened, sometimes it is displayed in green, depending on the type of screen on your computer.

The second step is to enable (turn on) the cell protection. Cell protection is turned on by specifying the command / Worksheet Global Protection Enable. Once this command is issued, cells that were not unprotected cannot be changed. If you try to enter a new value in a cell that is protected, Lotus 1-2-3 will beep and the mode indicator will change to ERROR. To exit from the ERROR mode, press the Escape key.

The conventions for cell protection take a while to get used to. Basically, you first unprotect the cells you want to be able to change. Then you enable the cell protection. You can think of the first step as building an electric fence around the cells that can be changed. The second step is turning on the electric power in the fence. If you simply enable protection without first unprotecting specific cells, then all the cells will be protected. In this case, nothing in the spreadsheet could be changed.

The command / Worksheet Global Protection Disable stops cell protection. After this command has been issued, any cell in the worksheet can be changed.

The cell protection mechanism in Lotus 1-2-3 does not provide high security. Cell protection can be disabled by anyone by selecting the command / Worksheet Global Protection Disable. The cell protection mechanism does prevent beginners (who do not know the / Worksheet Global Protection Disable command) from changing cells they are not supposed to change, and it does prevent experienced users from accidentally changing cells.

PASSWORD PROTECTION

Lotus 1-2-3 allows you to save a worksheet file on the disk under password security so that no one (including yourself) can retrieve the file without knowing the password.

To initiate password security, select / File Retrieve, as normal. However, follow the name of the file with a space and then a p. Lotus 1-2-3 will ask you to type the desired password twice, just to be sure you do not make a typing mistake. Thereafter when you attempt to retrieve the file using / File Retrieve, you will be asked for the password.

Password protection allows you to prevent other people from reading your spreadsheets off the disk. Unfortunately, many people have been prevented from reading their own files because they forgot the passwords.

LINKING FILES

Rather than having one huge spreadsheet for our global sales, we might want to enter the data into different spreadsheets and then link the information in these spreadsheets into a master spreadsheet.

A **linking formula** is a formula that refers to a cell in another file. Lotus 1-2-3 Release 2.2 provides the capability for simple linking. This capability was not provided in Release 2.01 and earlier releases.

As an example of file linking, in a cell in a spreadsheet we could have the formula

+<<ASIAJUN>>D23

The value in the cell would be the value that is in the cell D23 in the spreadsheet called ASIAJUN that is stored in the default directory on the disk. That is, when Lotus 1-2-3 encounters a linking formula in the spreadsheet, it looks in the disk file indicated and returns the value in the indicated cell.

In Release 2.2, a linking formula must be of the following form:

+<<file reference>>cell reference

The formula begins with a plus sign followed by two left angle brackets (less than signs) followed by a file reference followed by two right angle brackets (greater than signs) followed by a cell reference. The file reference can include a path name and a file extension. The cell reference can be either a cell address or the name assigned to a cell. For example, the following are legal linking formulas:

+<<BUDG93.WK1>>K49

+<<\123\DATA\BUDG93.WK1>>K49

+<<C:\123\DATA\BUDGET\BUDG93>>TOTALSALARY

Linking references cannot be used as part of larger formulas. For example, this formula would be *illegal* in Release 2.2:

+P57-<<BUDG93>>K49

(As you may have guessed from the prose, this formula would be legal in some other Lotus 1-2-3 versions, for example in Release 3 and Release 3.1.) To perform this calculation in Release 2.2 would require two cells, one to link to the spreadsheet and the second to subtract the value obtained from P57.

A spreadsheet can contain as many linking formulas to as many different files as you wish. If Lotus 1-2-3 cannot find the file named in a linking formula, the word ERR will appear as the value in the cell. You can obtain a list of all the files linked to in the current worksheet using the / File List Linked command.

File linking is a powerful capability that allows you to create systems of spreadsheets that refer to each other. If you update one of the spreadsheets, each of the other spreadsheets will be updated automatically when it is retrieved from the disk.

THE / FILE COMBINE COMMAND

Another approach to relating the values in two or more different spreadsheets is to use the / File Combine command. The / File Combine command allows you to take a range of values in a spreadsheet on the disk and copy them into the current spreadsheet or add them into the current spreadsheet or subtract them from the current spreadsheet.

For example, consider the spreadsheet in Figure 8-6. This spreadsheet gives monthly sales figures by region for Product Family 1. We have eight Product Families and, hence, eight similar spreadsheets on the disk, one for each Product Family. We would like to combine the eight spreadsheets into a consolidated spreadsheet that has the total sales for all of the products for each month and region.

```
E17: [W7]                                                                READY

         A           B       C       D       E       F       G       H
 1
 2  PRODUCT FAMILY 1
 3                                SALES BY REGION
 4
 5                  JAN     FEB     MAR     APR     MAY     JUN    TOTAL
 6
 7  AFRICA          1.1     0.8     1.2     1.7     0.9     1.4     7.1
 8  ANTARTICA       0.3     0.2     0.1     0.4     0.2     0.4     1.6
 9  ASIA           10.6    11.0    12.4    11.8    11.6    10.9    68.3
10  EUROPE          8.1     8.7     8.5     7.8     8.7     9.6    51.4
11  LATIN AMERICA   2.4     3.7     3.4     4.3     3.8     4.8    22.4
12  NORTH AMERICA  10.7    10.2    10.2    10.5     9.9    10.6    62.1
13
14  TOTAL          33.2    34.6    35.8    36.5    35.1    37.7   212.9
15
16
17
18
19
20
                         UNDO                                    CAPS
```

FIGURE 8-6 We have eight spreadsheets like this on the disk that we would like to add together.

To create this Totals spreadsheet we will start with the spreadsheet for Product Family 1. We then will add in the 36 sales numbers in B7..G12 in the spreadsheet for Product Family 2. To this new combined spreadsheet we will add in the 36 sales numbers in B7..G12 in the spreadsheet for Product Family 3. And so on.

We begin with the spreadsheet for Product Family 1 shown in Figure 8-6. We move the cursor to B7. The cursor must be placed in the top left cell of the target range of data in the current spreadsheet. We select / File Combine Add. Our next menu choice is Entire-File or Named/Specified-Range. We type N for Named/Specified-Range because we want to add in only a portion of the spreadsheet that is on the disk. Lotus 1-2-3 then asks us to "Enter range name or address: ". We type in B7..G12 Enter because that is the range in the worksheet file on the disk that contains the numbers to be added. If the range had been assigned a name using / Range Name Create before the spreadsheet had been saved on the disk then we could have typed that name in here. We next enter in the name of the file that contains the sales data for Product Family 2. When we press the Enter key the 36 numbers are read off the disk and added into the same-sized range in the current spreadsheet beginning at the current location of the cursor.

We repeat this process for each of the other six files. The result will be a spreadsheet that looks like the one in Figure 8-6 but that has total sales figures for all eight Product Families in each of the cells. Cell A2 still will contain the label PRODUCT FAMILY 1. We need to change the cell to TOTALS FOR ALL EIGHT PRODUCT FAMILIES.

Incidentally, this is exactly the type of problem for which Lotus 1-2-3 Release 3 and the more graphical Release 3.1 were developed. The Release 3 family are three-dimensional spreadsheet programs whereas Release 2.2 is a two-dimensional spreadsheet program. The spreadsheet in

Release 3 can be thought of as a book where each page is a two-dimensional spreadsheet. In Release 3 the pages are "numbered" A, B, C, and so on. There can be up to 256 pages of spreadsheets at a time. Ranges can be three-dimensional rectangular solids rather than just two-dimensional rectangles as in Release 2.2. To solve the consolidation problem just discussed, in Release 3 the spreadsheet for Product Family 1 would be on page A; the spreadsheet for Product Family 2 would be on page B, and so on through page H. Page I would contain the the Totals spreadsheet. The formula in cell I:B7 (that is, in cell B7 in page I) would be @SUM(A:B7..H:B7). That is, the formula would add the January Africa sales figures in B7 for each of the eight spreadsheets in the third dimension into the screen. It is much easier to use Release 3 of Lotus 1-2-3 for problems that are inherently three dimensional rather than Release 2.2. Unfortunately, Release 3 requires a much more powerful computer than does Release 2.2 and is slower calculating most strictly two-dimensional spreadsheets.

There are two other variations of the / File Combine command. If you select / File Combine Subtract then the values in the file on the disk will be subtracted from the values in the current spreadsheet. For example, the values in the file on the disk might represent Returns that should be subtracted from Sales. If you select / File Combine Copy, then the values in the file on the disk will replace the values in the current spreadsheet.

COMPUTER EXERCISE

8-1 We Love Plants, Inc., is a small company in the house plant care business. People can arrange for the company to come into their apartment or house to care for their plants when they are traveling or on vacation or full year around. The company has begun offering the same service to businesses and offices.

For 1991 the income statement for the company looks as follows.

WE LOVE PLANTS, INC.
Income Statement
For the Year Ended December 31, 1991

Revenues		
Home plant care revenue	$67,329	
Office plant care revenue	15,544	
Total revenues		$82,873
Expenses		
Salaries expense	32,488	
Payroll tax expense	2,803	
Rent expense for office	4,800	
Utilities expense	2,377	
Advertising expense	2,103	
Automobile expense	5,292	
Supplies expense	4,550	
Insurance expense	3,500	
Total expenses		57,913
Pretax income		24,960
Income tax expense		4,992
Net income		$19,968
Earnings per share		$4.99

The company pays 20% in income taxes. There are 4000 shares of stock.

Create a spreadsheet for the income statement. All the numbers in the right column should be the results of formulas. The numbers should be formatted as they appear. All cells should be protected except for the numbers in the middle column and the year. Do the best you can with the underlines.

9

DEVELOPING SPREADSHEETS

In the first eight chapters, we looked at the basics of creating Lotus 1-2-3 spreadsheets. Now it is time to step back a little and look at the process of developing Lotus 1-2-3 spreadsheets to help solve problems.

THE SPREADSHEET DEVELOPMENT PROCESS

The spreadsheet development process usually involves five phases.

1. PROBLEM DEFINITION
What is the problem to be solved? What are we trying to accomplish? What information would we like to have? It is very important that you understand the problem before trying to solve

it. You do not want to spend hours developing and perfecting a spreadsheet that solves the wrong problem.

2. DESIGN

Is a spreadsheet the right tool to use to solve the problem? Sometimes people become so enamored with Lotus 1-2-3 that they try to use the program to solve problems that would be better solved by other means. There is an old saying, "To a person with a hammer, everything looks like a nail." Lotus 1-2-3 is a powerful and useful tool, but it is not the solution to every problem. If a calculation is to be performed only once, sometimes it is easier just to do the calculation by hand, to use paper and pencil and a calculator. For problems that are better solved using the computer, there are several different types of personal computer software available. Many problems are better solved using, say, a data base program rather than 1-2-3 or by using some specialized software. For example, if you would like the computer to help you keep the books of a small business, you could create custom spreadsheets, but you might save a lot of time and trouble by simply buying one of the several small business accounting programs available. If you are using the computer to perform sophisticated statistical analyses, you might be better off with a statistics program.

Once you decide that Lotus 1-2-3 is the right tool to use, it is best to design the spreadsheet on paper first. What are the inputs to the spreadsheet? What information needs to be provided? What are the outputs of the spreadsheet? What are we trying to learn? What should be the format of the outputs? Are there any special printed reports that need to be produced? What should they look like? How do you get from the inputs to the outputs? Are there any key formulas to be developed? Could you perform the calculations by hand given enough time and a calculator? You want to be sure that there is nothing mystical in your spreadsheet design, no key steps that need to be calculated but that you do not know how to specify.

As we saw in the Peter Minuit example in Chapter 7, an important principle for designing effective spreadsheets is that any number that might be changed should be placed into a separate cell. Do not put numbers that might be changed, like interest rates, directly into formulas. Rather, put them into separate cells and always refer to these cells in the formulas. All the numbers that might be varied should be placed together in a separate well-labeled input area of the spreadsheet.

In designing a spreadsheet you might have four separate areas: introduction, input, calculations, output. The introduction contains a description of the spreadsheet, the name of the developer, the date, instructions to the user, and documentation. The input area contains all of the cells that need to be changed by the user. In a spreadsheet for "What if" analysis, the input area would contain all the assumptions, all the numbers that might be varied. The calculations area contains the formulas. The output area pulls the results of special interest out of the calculations area. The output area might be located next to the input area for easy viewing.

3. IMPLEMENTATION

Normally it is best to have the spreadsheet designed on paper before proceeding to the computer. Implementation should be straightforward. It is useful to name the important cells and ranges and to use these names in the formulas. Names should remind you of the contents of the cell or range. If a formula is going to be copied, be careful about using relative or absolute addressing. Think about whether the address is relative, whether it is to be adjusted as it is copied, or whether the address is absolute, always referring to the same cell or range of cells. Use the cell protection capability of Lotus 1-2-3 to protect all the cells except the input cells from being changed by mistake.

It is customary to store a frequently used spreadsheet as a **template**. A template is a spreadsheet where all the input values are set to zero. The user would retrieve the template spreadsheet from the disk, enter in the input values, and save the filled-in spreadsheet on the disk under a new name. The template would remain on the disk unchanged.

4. TESTING

Beginners often expect their spreadsheets to work correctly the first time. Sometimes the spreadsheets do, but even the best planned and designed spreadsheets may have errors. It is best to assume that a new spreadsheet is full of errors and then test it extensively to make sure it is correct. Testing a spreadsheet involves working the numbers out ahead of time with pencil, paper, and calculator before trying them on the computer. It is important that the spreadsheets be tested on a wide variety of inputs, on typical inputs and on extreme inputs.

There are several types of errors in spreadsheets that can be uncovered. There can be errors in your understanding of the problem. Sometimes you create a spreadsheet and then you realize that you did not understand the problem properly. The spreadsheet might "work", but it does not produce the answers you need. In this case, you would need to go back to step 1 to reanalyze the problem. There can be errors in your design of the spreadsheet. You might have used an erroneous formula. You might have built a number that needs to be changed into a formula in the spreadsheet. You might not have foreseen some condition that might occur in the spreadsheet. In this case, you would need to go back to step 2 to modify your design for the spreadsheet. There can be errors in your implementation of the spreadsheet. You might have a number that is too large for the width of the column. You might forget to use absolute addressing where it is required. You might have made an error in typing a formula or pointing to an address. These errors in step 3 can be corrected right on the computer.

5. DOCUMENTATION

Documentation is the part of the spreadsheet development process that involves making the spreadsheet understandable by people, rather than just by the computer. Documentation includes external paper documentation as well as instructions on the spreadsheet itself. In a sense, documentation includes everything in a spreadsheet except for the numbers and the formulas themselves. Documentation should not be an afterthought but rather an integral part of the entire development process.

The extent of the documentation required depends on the uses to which your spreadsheet will be put.

If you are the only person who ever will use your spreadsheet, then you should provide yourself with sufficient labels and instructions so that the spreadsheet will be understandable to you six months in the future.

If the spreadsheet is being handed in as an assignment, then your instructor will determine the level of documentation required. Certainly you should include your name, the date, and the assignment number at the top of each spreadsheet. You should indicate any extra assumptions you have made and explain any tricky aspects of your spreadsheet. Your instructor might ask you to hand in printed documentation, including printouts of the spreadsheet and its formulas, or you might submit disks, or you might submit the spreadsheets and documentation electronically over a computer network.

A spreadsheet produced for class generally is seen by just two people—yourself and the person who grades the assignment. In industry there often are several people who will use and modify the spreadsheets you create.

In industry, spreadsheets often are used by people other than the creator of the spreadsheet. These people may have only a superficial understanding of Lotus 1-2-3 and its commands. It is important to include explicit instructions with your spreadsheets in these situations. The instructions should include where the data should be entered, how and where to save the spreadsheet, and how to print out reports. Important instructions are best included as text in the spreadsheet itself as well as on a separate piece of paper. Paper instructions can be separated from the spreadsheet or lost altogether. The cell protection capabilities should be used so that only input cells can be modified easily.

In industry, spreadsheets often are improved by people other than the creator of the spreadsheet. You create a spreadsheet as part of your job and then you are rapidly promoted twice. Someone else is hired for your old position. This person inherits your spreadsheets. Can this person make sense of them? Where did this data come from? What is this formula? What are the assumptions underlying the spreadsheet? What happens at the end of the year? Here you would like the spreadsheet to be transparent, self-explanatory. List assumptions for the spreadsheet. List sources for data. Explain unusual formulas. Give explicit instructions. Put yourself in the place of the person who will succeed you. Could you understand this spreadsheet the way it is written if you hadn't developed it yourself?

With important spreadsheets in industry it is customary to create a full documentation booklet for the spreadsheet. The documentation booklet could include

- a description of the problem the spreadsheet is designed to solve
- a general discussion of the spreadsheet, its design and operation
- full, detailed instructions for a novice user of the spreadsheet
- full documentation for someone who will modify the spreadsheet, including any assumptions, a discussion of formulas and macros, any pitfalls or possible errors in the spreadsheet, features that might be added to the spreadsheet
- a full printout of the spreadsheet with values displayed
- a full printout of the spreadsheet with formulas displayed (using either Text format or /PPOOC)
- two semi-sealed, write-protected disks containing the spreadsheet to be used for emergency backup. The disks also should contain files containing the documentation itself.

Many people tend to provide too little documentation for their spreadsheets. The reason is simple. It takes a long time and a lot of effort to produce good documentation for a spreadsheet. It can take as long to document a spreadsheet as it does to identify the problem, design the spreadsheet, implement the spreadsheet, and test the spreadsheet all combined. A little extra effort with documentation can save users of your spreadsheet hours of work.

COMPUTER EXERCISES

9-1 Do you live with other people and share a telephone? If so, create a spreadsheet to determine how much each person owes. Follow the rules you use to divide up the bill. Perhaps you split the cost of the basic service charge and pay for your own long-distance calls. Perhaps unclaimed long distance calls are split evenly. You should have an entry in your spreadsheet for each separate entry that appears on your phone bill. Don't forget the tax. Prepare the spreadsheet as a template that is stored on the disk and can be filled in each month. In the spreadsheet all cells should be protected except for the input cells. Go through the spreadsheet development process of problem definition, design, implementation, testing, and documentation.

9-2 Your courses each have different requirements—different types of assignments, quizzes, exams, and so on. Create a spreadsheet to keep track of all the grades you receive. Every grade should appear in the spreadsheet along with a description of what it is for, and the date received. Your spreadsheet should calculate your average in each class, if possible using the weighting system of the instructor. In the spreadsheet all cells should be protected except for the input cells. Go through the spreadsheet development process of problem definition, design, implementation, testing, and documentation.

9-3 Create a spreadsheet to help keep track of a checking account. There should be separate entries for each check, deposit, and service charge. These entries should include the date, the amount, the check number (if any), the payee (if any), and the purpose. The spreadsheet should keep track of the balance in your account and help you check for errors in the statement you receive from the bank each month. Go through the spreadsheet development process of problem definition, design, implementation, testing, and documentation.

9-4 Create a spreadsheet that helps you budget income and expenses for each month. Include separate entries for income and expense items. Allow for both budgeted and actual. You may use fictional data if you wish. Go through the spreadsheet development process of problem definition, design, implementation, testing, and documentation.

9-5 If you have a car, how much does it cost to operate? Create a spreadsheet that will allow you to track operating expenses for your car for a year. Your spreadsheet should allow you to record money spent for gas, oil, repairs, insurance, registration, and any other expenses. For each expense, you should record the date, the odometer mileage, the payee, a description of the expense, and an amount. The spreadsheet should calculate subtotals for each type of expense, the total amount of money spent, and the cost per mile and the cost per day to drive your car. Go through the spreadsheet development process of problem definition, design, implementation, testing, and documentation.

9-6   Perhaps you belong to a group, for example a campus organization or a church group, that is considering undertaking an activity, say, a picnic, dance, or raffle. Create a spreadsheet that will allow you to model the financial aspects of the activity. You might have cells for the number of tickets sold and the price of the tickets and for any other revenue variables and for each of the different expense variables. The spreadsheet should allow you to try out different scenarios. For example, what would happen if all of the tickets are sold? What would happen if only 20 tickets are sold? What would be the financial consequences if it rains the day of the picnic? In the spreadsheet all cells should be protected except for the input cells. Go through the spreadsheet development process of problem definition, design, implementation, testing, and documentation.

9-7   Read through the first six exercises for this chapter. Create a spreadsheet that would be useful to you in whatever area you would like. Go through the spreadsheet development process of problem definition, design, implementation, testing, and documentation.

P
A
R
T

FEATURES

GRAPHING

Graphs have visual impact. People often respond better to graphs than to tables of numbers. An important part of Lotus 1-2-3 is the ability to turn tables of numbers into bar charts and pie charts and other types of graphs. Graphing in Lotus 1-2-3 is easy, useful, and fun.

FUNDAMENTALS OF GRAPHING

In Lotus 1-2-3 graphs are made from ranges of numbers in the current spreadsheet. Basically one needs to specify (1) the type of graph and (2) the portion of the spreadsheet that contains the values to be graphed.

As an example, consider the simple spreadsheet in Figure 10-1. There are several different graphs that could be drawn from this spreadsheet. Suppose we want to draw a bar graph that has

FIGURE 10-1 A spreadsheet to graph.

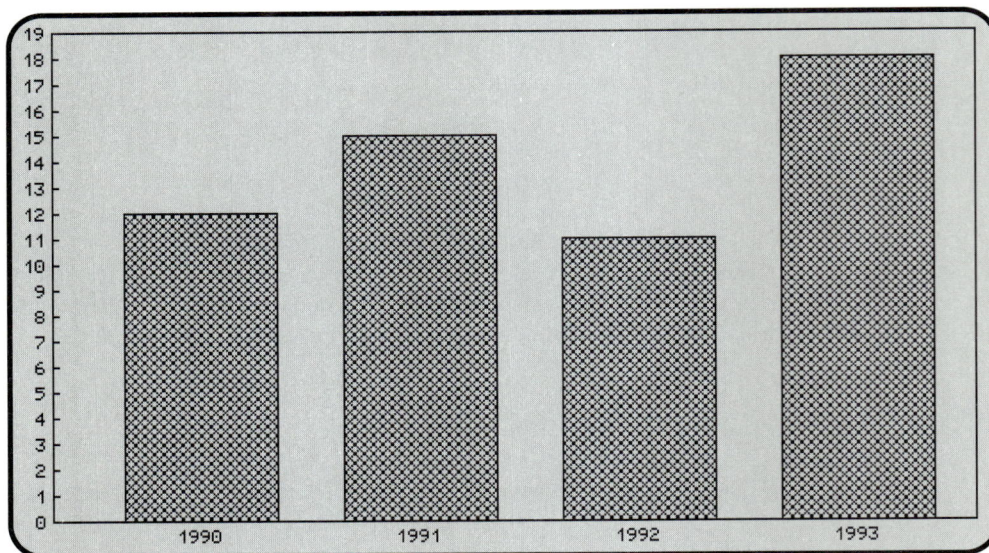

FIGURE 10-2 A simple bar graph.

```
E15:                                                              ГЕНU
Type  X  A  B  C  D  E  F  Reset  View  Save  Options  Name  Group  Quit
Line  Bar  XY  Stack-Bar  Pie
                            ─── Graph Settings ───
    Type: Line                    Titles: First
                                          Second
       X:                                 X axis
       A:                                 Y axis
       B:
       C:                                         Y scale:      X scale:
       D:                                 Scaling Automatic     Automatic
       E:                                 Lower
       F:                                 Upper
                                          Format  (G)           (G)
    Grid: None         Color: No          Indicator Yes         Yes

       Legend:             Format:     Data labels:          Skip: 1
    A                      Both
    B                      Both
    C                      Both
    D                      Both
    E                      Both
    F                      Both
```

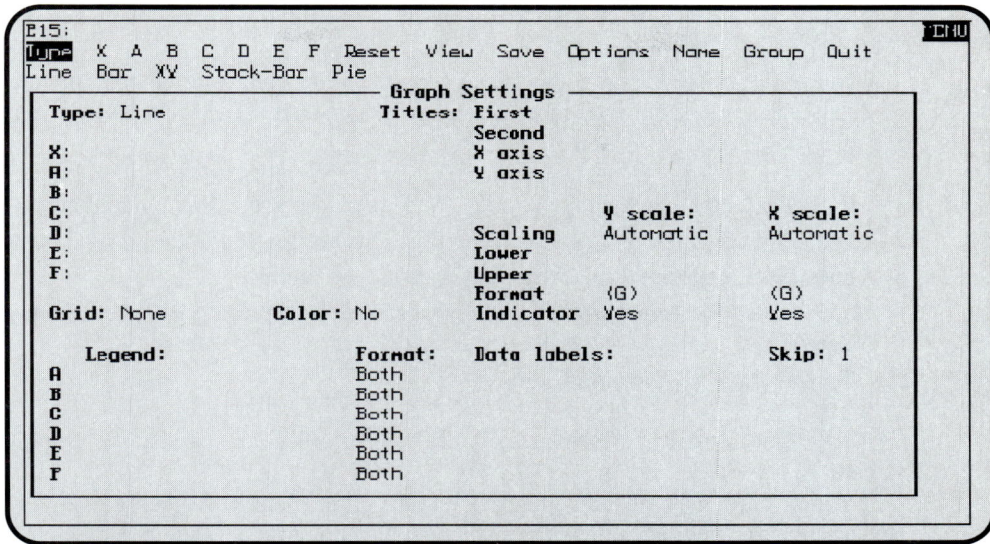

FIGURE 10-3 The default graph settings sheet.

the years along the horizontal axis and the sales of apples as the height of the bars, as in Figure 10-2.

Before beginning with graphing, it is always a good idea to save the spreadsheet using / File Save.

All commands for creating graphs are issued through the / Graph command. After selecting the / Graph command, one is confronted with the / Graph menu on the top of the screen. At the same time, the **graph settings sheet** is displayed in the main part of the screen in place of the current spreadsheet, as in Figure 10-3. The graph settings sheet shows the current settings for specifying the graph to be drawn.

In Lotus 1-2-3 Release 2.2, there are five graph types: line, bar, XY, stack-bar, and pie. To select a graph type, use the Type command in the graph menu. The default type is line. To specify that we want to draw a bar graph as in Figure 10-2, we would select Type Bar from the graph menu.

After selecting the type of graph to be drawn, we inform Lotus 1-2-3 of where the data to be graphed is located in the spreadsheet. The X command in the graph menu is used to specify the **X data range**, the values for the X or horizontal axis of the graph. In the example in Figures 10-1 and 10-2 we would specify B6..E6 as the range for the X axis, as this is the range that contains the years.

In Lotus 1-2-3 up to six sets of data can be graphed at the same time. The first set of data to be graphed is called the **A data range**. The second set of data is called the **B data range**, and so on. In this graph we are interested only in graphing one set of data, the sales data for Apples.

To specify this data range we would issue the A command in the graph menu and then specify B8..E8 for the A data range.

To have the graph drawn on the screen issue the View command in the graph menu.

Thus, to draw the graph in Figure 10-2 given the spreadsheet in Figure 10-1 we went through the following steps:

1. Enter the Graph command by typing /G. This places you in the / Graph menu.
2. Specify a bar graph by selecting Type Bar. This returns you to the / Graph menu.
3. Specify the horizontal axis by typing X B6..E6 Enter.
4. Specify that the Apple sales data is to be graphed by typing A B8..E8 and pressing Enter.
5. See the graph by selecting View.

Notice that Lotus 1-2-3 automatically scales the vertical axis so that the graph fits in the screen.

To return from viewing the graph back into the graph menu press the Enter key, the Escape key, or any other key. Then to exit from the graph menu back to Ready mode, select Quit from the graph menu.

Once a graph has been specified, the values in the spreadsheet can be changed and the graph easily redrawn. Lotus 1-2-3 remembers the most recent graph settings. To redraw the currently specified graph with newly entered or calculated values in the spreadsheet one can select / Graph View or, more easily, just press function key F10, the **Graph key**. Thus one can specify a graph, change a number in the spreadsheet, see the resulting graph by pressing F10, change a number in the spreadsheet, see the new graph by pressing F10, and so on. Graphs can become an integral part of the "What if" analysis process. Again, use the Graph key F10 to draw a graph if you are in Ready mode and all of the Graph settings are fine. If you are in Ready mode and you would like to change some of the Graph settings, select /Graph, change the settings, and then select View in the graph menu to draw the resulting graph.

MORE SOPHISTICATED GRAPHS

A fancier graph for this spreadsheet is shown in Figure 10-4. Here we have specified the Peach sales in B9..E9 as data set B using the B command in the graph menu and the Pear sales in B10..E10 as data set C using the C command in the graph menu. When specifying the X data set and the A to F data sets, be sure that each range contains the same number of cells.

The graph in Figure 10-4 exhibits some of the features that can be specified in the / Graph Options submenu.

The boxes and identifying labels on the bottom of the graph are called **legends**. Legends are specified in the / Graph Options submenu. That is, to specify the legend for the A data set, issue the command / Graph Options Legend A and then enter either the text for the legend (Apples) or a backslash followed by the address of a cell in the spreadsheet that contains the legend (\A8).

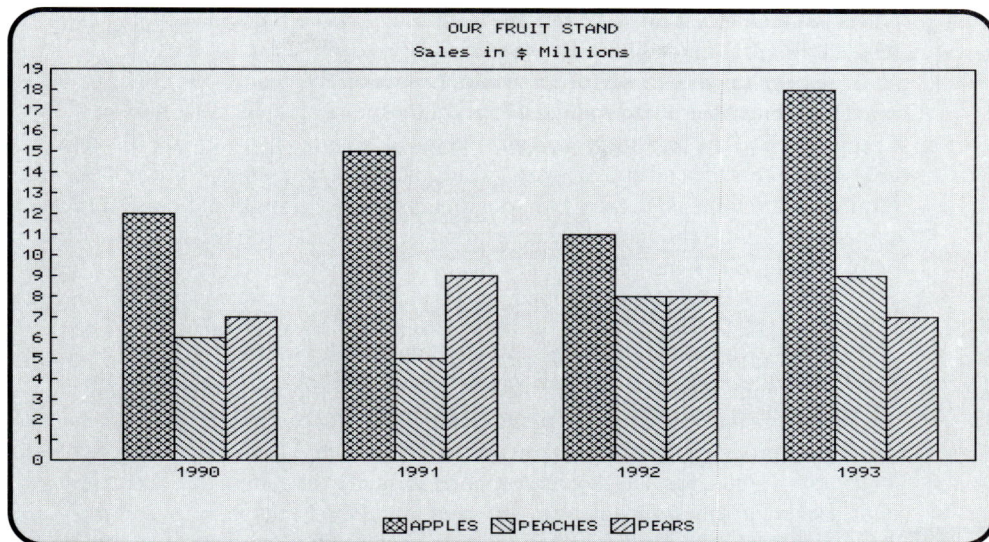

FIGURE 10-4 A fancier bar graph for the spreadsheet in Figure 10-1.

The legends for the B and C data sets can be entered similarly. If the legends that are to appear in the graph all are located in a range in the spreadsheet, you can specify them all at once using the Legend Range command in the / Graph Options submenu. For the graph in Figure 10-4 the legends were specified by Legend Range A8..A10 in the / Graph Options submenu.

The two lines of text on the top of the graph are the **First Title** and the **Second Title**. These are set in the Title First command and the Title Second command in the / Graph Options submenu. The title is specified either by typing a line of text or by typing a backslash followed by the address of a cell that contains the desired title. Titles for the X Axis and for the Y Axis can be specified similarly.

If you have a color screen on your computer, the graph can be viewed in color by issuing the Color command in the / Graph Options submenu. To switch from color to the black-and-white cross-hatchings, issue the B&W command in the / Graph Options submenu.

A COMMON PROBLEM

A common problem when you first try to use a version of Lotus 1-2-3 to display a graph on a computer is for the screen to go blank when you instruct Lotus 1-2-3 to View the graph.

The most likely cause of the problem is simply that you have not properly selected the data to be graphed. Press the Escape key. If you see the graph settings sheet, then check the X data set and the A data set to be certain that the proper ranges have been selected. Make any necessary changes by selecting the X command or the A command in the graph menu and entering the correct ranges. Try again to View the graph. If you see a graph, you can skip the next two paragraphs.

If no graph is drawn even if the settings are correct, then there might be a more serious problem. Sometimes the computer freezes at this point and you must re-boot the system either by pressing Ctrl-Alt-Del (hold your fingers on the keys labeled Ctrl and Alt and while these are held down press the Del key) or even by turning off the computer, waiting 30 seconds, and then turning on the computer again. Either of these actions will result in Lotus 1-2-3 and the current spreadsheet being erased from primary memory. Hence, it is a good idea to save the spreadsheet before trying to draw a graph.

The cause of this problem is either that your computer is not capable of displaying graphs or, more likely, that Lotus 1-2-3 is not set up properly to draw graphs on your computer. Before ou can use Lotus 1-2-3 to draw or print graphs, you must "install" the proper "drivers" for your computer setup. **Drivers** are low-level programs for printing and display that vary from computer type to computer type. **Install** is a program that accompanies 1-2-3 that allows you to specify the proper Lotus 1-2-3 drivers for your computer. If your screen goes blank when you try to draw a graph, first check your computer manual to be certain that your computer is capable of displaying graphics. If it is, you will need to run the Lotus 1-2-3 Install program to specify the screen display (and graphics printer) on your computer. The installation process is described in the Lotus 1-2-3 manual accompanying the software you purchased.

THE STACKED BAR GRAPH

A variation on the bar graph is the stacked bar graph. The stacked bar graph for the fruit stand spreadsheet is shown in Figure 10-5. Here the corresponding bars for the data sets are stacked on top of each other. This graph facilitates a visual comparison of the total sales for each year while still allowing the viewer to see the components of each year's sales. The command Type Stack-Bar in the / Graph menu selects a stacked bar graph.

THE LINE GRAPH

A line graph for the fruit stand example is shown in Figure 10-6. Visually, line graphs emphasize the continuity of data and are useful for plotting data values over time. The graph in Figure 10-6 contains both symbols (the small square, plus, diamond) at the data values plotted and lines between the data values. It is possible to display the graph with just symbols and no connecting lines or with just lines and no symbols by using the Format command in the / Graph Options submenu.

THE XY GRAPH

The XY graph is very similar to the line graph except the X data set must be numeric and is graphed accordingly. The difference between the line graph and the XY graph is subtle. In a line

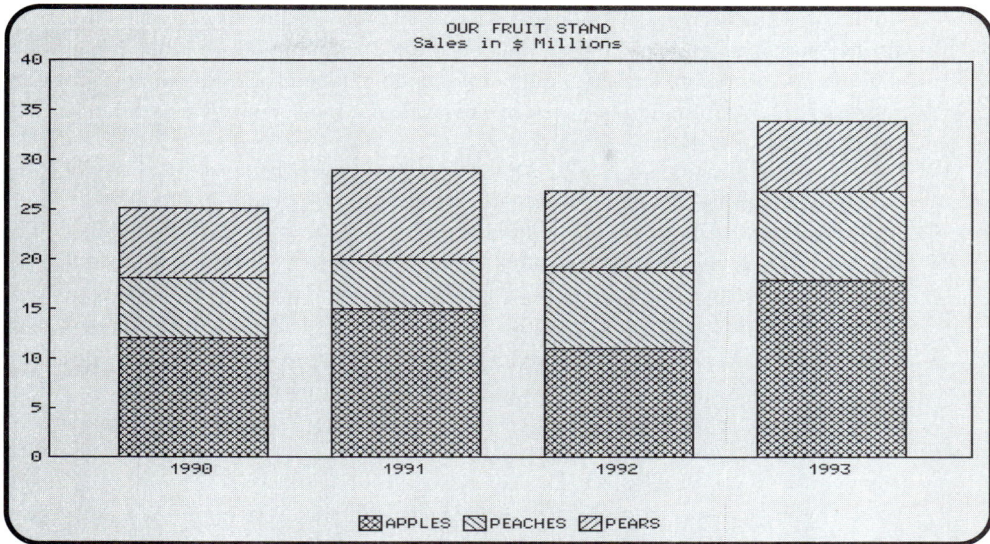

FIGURE 10-5 The same data graphed as a Stacked Bar graph.

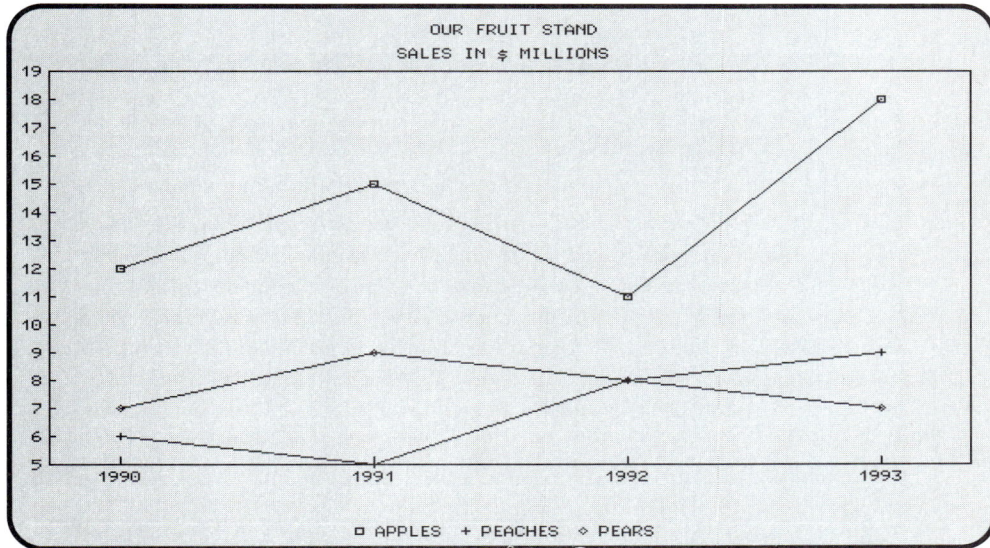

FIGURE 10-6 And as a Line graph.

graph the values in the X data range basically are treated as labels and are spaced equally along the horizontal axis in the order they appear, whatever their values. In the XY graph the values in the X data range are treated as numbers and are graphed accordingly. An XY graph is useful in showing the correlation between two numeric data sets. One of these would be specified as the X data set, the other as the A data set.

For example, suppose we would like to see how Peach sales correlate with Pear sales. That is, we are interested in seeing whether in years when Pear sales are high, Peach sales are high also. We could create an XY graph like the one in Figure 10-7. In this graph, Pear sales are plotted along the X axis. Peach sales are plotted along the Y axis. The data points are labeled with the year. To obtain this graph requires a lot of maneuvering. Let's trace through the process.

To obtain the graph in Figure 10-7, we specify Type XY. We specify the X data range as B10..E10, the Pear sales. We specify the A data range as B9..E9, the Peach sales. Normally, an XY graph will be drawn like a line graph, with straight lines connecting the data points. To draw just symbols at the data points, with no lines connecting them, we next select Options Format Graph Symbols Quit. This returns us to the /Graph Options submenu. We select Titles First and enter PEACH VS. PEAR SALES. We select Titles Second and enter (IN $ MILLIONS). We select Titles X-Axis and enter PEAR SALES. We select Titles Y-Axis and enter PEACH SALES.

If we were to View the graph now, we would see that Lotus 1-2-3 would select 5 through 9.5 for the Y axis scale and would select 7 through 9 for the X axis scale. We would like these scales to appear uniform as 0 through 10. We need to override the automatic selection of scales. In the

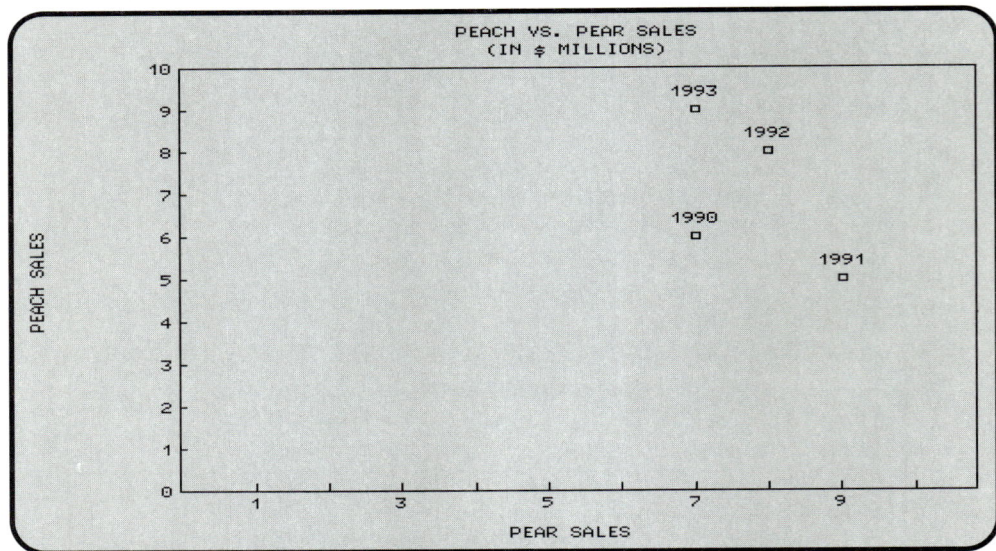

FIGURE 10-7 An XY graph showing annual Peach sales vs. Pear sales.

/ Graph Options menu we select Scale Y-Scale Lower 0 enter Upper 10 enter Manual Quit . This informs Lotus 1-2-3 that we would like the lower value of the Y scale to be 0, the upper value to be 10, and that we wish to override the automatic selection of scales manually. We then repeat the process for the X axis and select Scale X-Scale Lower 1 enter Upper 10 enter Manual Quit. The Manual command is necessary to override the automatic selection. The Scale commands work for bar graphs and line graphs, as well as for XY graphs.

We would like to label the data points with the years. In the / Graph Options menu we select Data-Labels A B6..E6 enter Above Quit Quit . This informs Lotus 1-2-3 that the labels for the data points are in B6..E6 and that we would like these data labels to appear above the actual data points. The Data-Labels command allows us to label the data points on bar charts and line charts, as well as XY charts.

The screen shows the / Graph settings sheet as in Figure 10-8. Now, finally, when we select View we see the graph in Figure 10-7.

OTHER GRAPH OPTIONS

Numbers that mark off the X axis or Y axis can be formatted, for example, as Currency, using the Scale X-Scale Format command or the Scale Y-Scale Format command in the / Graph Options submenu.

Horizontal and vertical grid lines can be placed across the graph using the Grids command in the / Graph Options submenu.

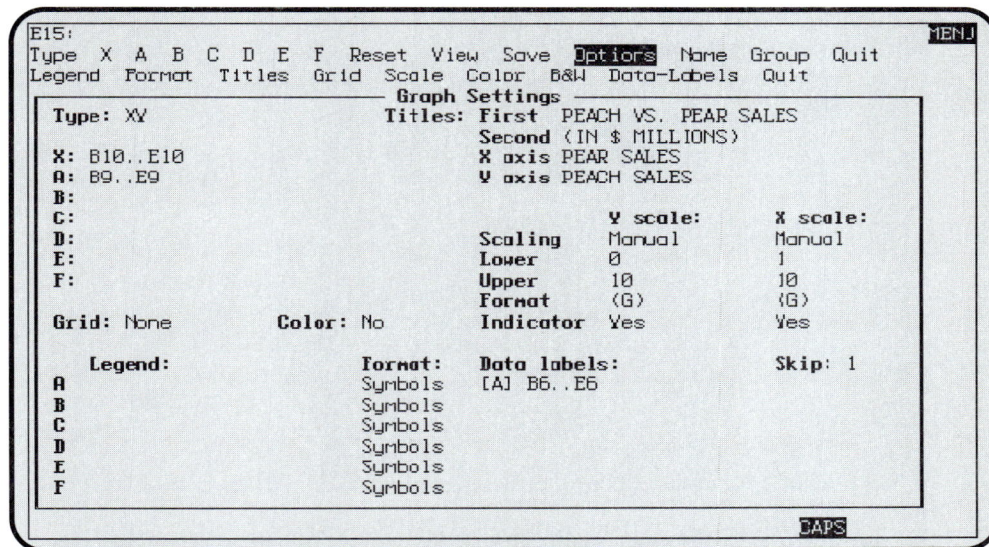

```
E15:                                                                    MENU
Type  X  A  B  C  D  E  F  Reset  View  Save  Options  Name  Group  Quit
Legend  Format  Titles  Grid  Scale  Color  B&W  Data-Labels  Quit
─────────────────────── Graph Settings ───────────────────────
 Type: XY                        Titles: First  PEACH VS. PEAR SALES
                                         Second <IN $ MILLIONS>
 X: B10..E10                             X axis PEAR SALES
 A: B9..E9                               Y axis PEACH SALES
 B:
 C:                                                  Y scale:      X scale:
 D:                                      Scaling     Manual        Manual
 E:                                      Lower       0             1
 F:                                      Upper       10            10
                                         Format      <G>           <G>
 Grid: None         Color: No            Indicator   Yes           Yes

    Legend:              Format:    Data labels:            Skip: 1
 A                       Symbols    [A] B6..E6
 B                       Symbols
 C                       Symbols
 D                       Symbols
 E                       Symbols
 F                       Symbols

                                                                      CAPS
```

FIGURE 10-8 The / Graph settings for the XY graph in Figure 10-7.

THE PIE CHART

A **pie chart** for the fruit stand spreadsheet is shown in Figure 10-9. In a pie chart only one set of numbers, the A data set, is graphed. For the pie chart in Figure 10-9 the A data set was changed to the 1990 sales in B8..B10. The X data set was changed to the fruit names in A8..A10. The values in the X data set are used to label the slices in the pie chart.

For this pie chart, the data in the fruit stand spreadsheet was organized vertically instead of horizontally. If we had kept the A data set as the Apple sales in B8..E8, then the pie chart would have had four slices, one for each year of Apple sales. (It would have been an Apple pie chart?) But graphing time-based data in a pie chart usually does not work well (and the pun would have been too dreadful to bare) so the data sets were changed accordingly.

You can control the hatch patterns of the slices in a black and white pie chart and the colors of the slices in a color pie chart by specifying values for the B data set. To obtain the pie chart in Figure 10-7, put 1 in G8, 2 in G9, and 103 in G10. Then specify the B data set as G8..G10. In the resulting pie chart, the slice for APPLES is cross-hatched in pattern 1, the slice for PEACHES is cross-hatched in pattern 2, and the slice for PEARS is cross-hatched in pattern 3. Furthermore, since the B data set item that corresponds to PEARS is 103 (rather than just 3), the slice is **exploded**, that is, separated from the rest in the pie chart. This is strange and arbitrary, but nonetheless the way that Lotus 1-2-3 was designed.

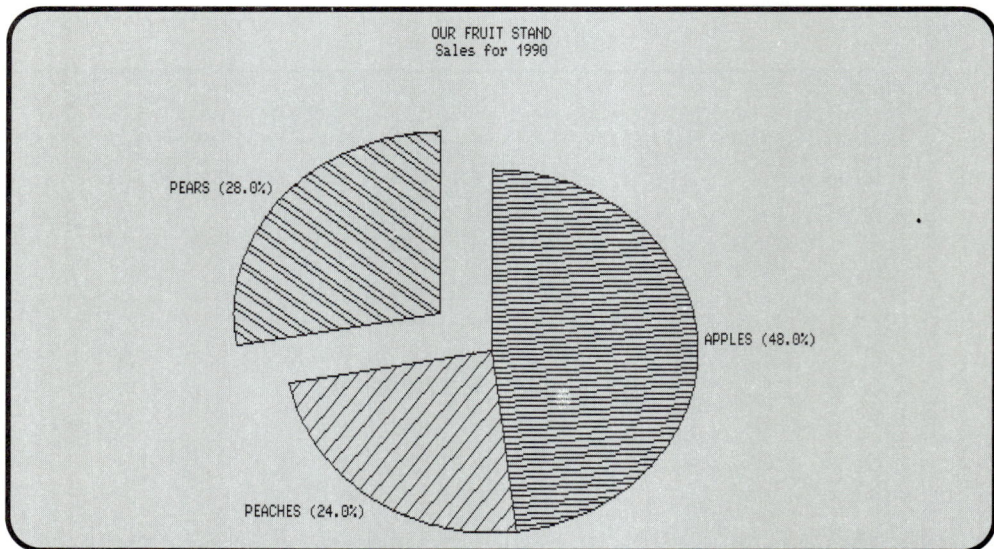

FIGURE 10-9 A pie graph based on the fruit sales spreadsheet. The data sets have been changed for this graph. The X data set is the fruit names in A8..A10. The A data set is the 1990 sales in B8..B10. The B data set is a new column that has been added.

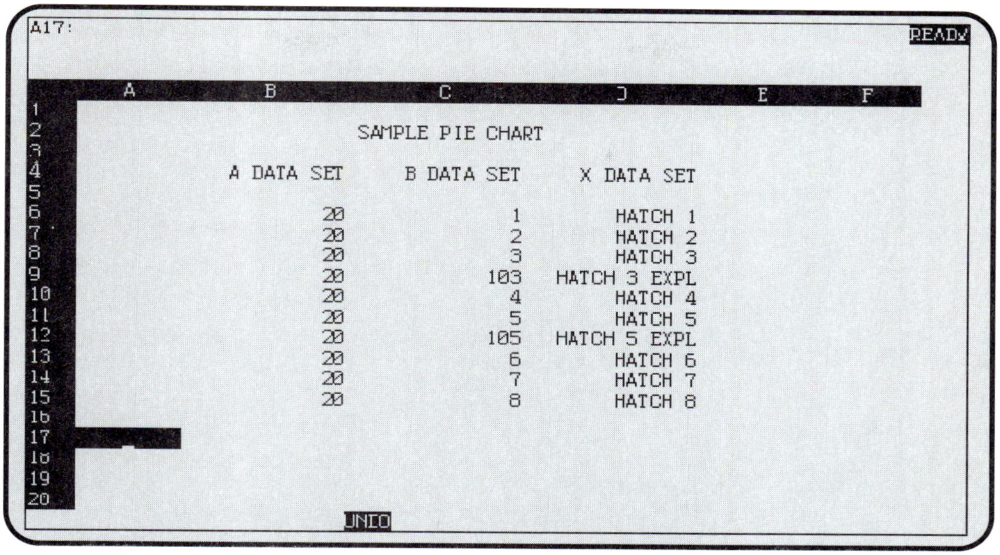

FIGURE 10-10 A spreadsheet to graph.

There are eight different possible hatch patterns and eight corresponding colors. The hatch pattern (or color) for a slice is determined by the number in the corresponding cell in the B data set. If 100 is added to the number, then the slice is "exploded." To change the PEACHES slice to cross-hatch pattern 4, change the number in G9 to 4. If no B data set is specified, then all the slices will be drawn with hatch pattern 8, which is blank. Specifying hatch pattern 0 is the same as specifying hatch pattern 8.

The use of the values in the B data set to control the appearance of the slices in a pie chart is illustrated in Figures 10-10 and 10-11. To draw the pie chart in Figure 10-11 using the spreadsheet in Figure 10-10 the A data set is specified as B6..B15. The B data set is specified as C6..C15. The X data set is specified as D6..D15.

The A data set in a pie chart determines the relative sizes of the slices. The B data set determines the hatching of the slices and whether the slices are "exploded." The X data set determines the explanatory text written besides the slices.

PRINTING GRAPHS

Naturally you will want to print the graphs you create. There are three possible approaches to printing graphs: (1) the PrintScreen key, (2) the PrintGraph program in 1-2-3, and (3) the Allways add-in program.

The PrintScreen key normally allows you to print only text screens and not graphics screens, not screens containing pictures. On some computer systems you can enable the PrintScreen key

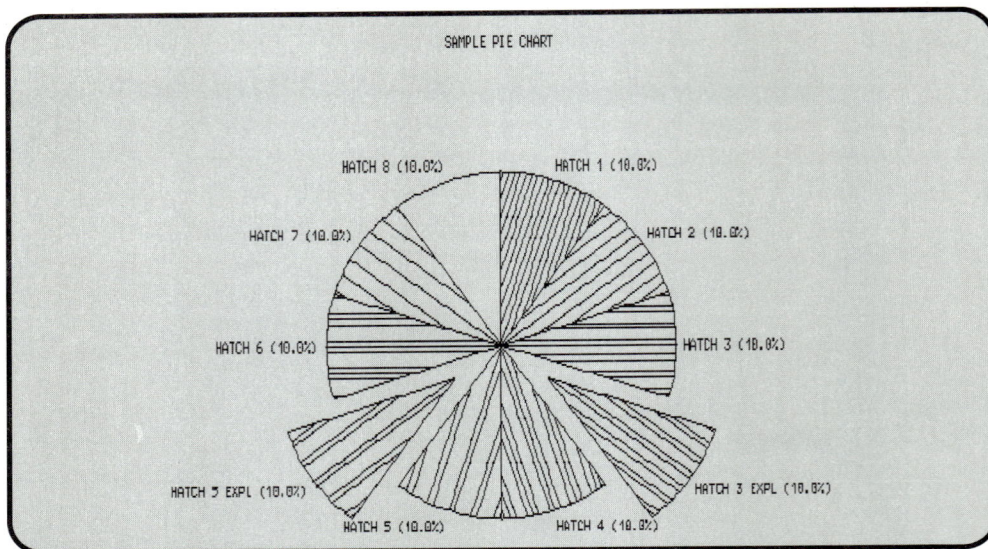

FIGURE 10-11 The pie chart that results from the spreadsheet in Figure 10-10.

to print graphs by issuing the Disk Operating System command GRAPHICS. You would type GRAPHICS Enter in DOS before starting up Lotus 1-2-3. Whether this would enable the PrintScreen key to print graphs depends on the type of printer and the version of DOS you are using.

In Lotus 1-2-3 Release 2.2 the / Print command does not work for graphs. The official way of printing graphs is to use the PrintGraph program, which is part of the 1-2-3 system. The procedure for using the PrintGraph program is discussed in the next section.

The third approach to printing graphs is to use the Allways add-in program. Allways provides the most flexibility, allowing you to print a graph as an integral part of a spreadsheet. Allways is discussed in Chapter 17.

PRINTGRAPH

PrintGraph is a separate program that comes as part of the 1-2-3 package. The sole purpose of the PrintGraph program is to print out graphs that were created in Lotus 1-2-3. PrintGraph can be entered through the Lotus 1-2-3 Access System. The procedure for using PrintGraph to print a graph is somewhat involved. Basically, to print a graph using PrintGraph you must first save your graph on the disk and then exit from 1-2-3 and then run PrintGraph. Let's go through the process step by step.

Assume that we just have specified a graph in Lotus 1-2-3 and that we currently are viewing the graph on the screen. First, press a key to return to the / Graph menu. Now we need to save the graph on the disk. Saving the graph is different from saving the spreadsheet. Here we are not interested in saving the formulas; rather we are just interested in saving the picture of the graph itself. We select the Save command in the / Graph menu to save the picture of the current graph on the disk. Later when we enter the PrintGraph program,we will have the computer retrieve this picture file from the disk. In the / Graph Save command, Lotus 1-2-3 asks us for the name of the picture to be saved. Again, the name we give a file must be eight characters or less and may consist of letters, digits, and possibly underscores (Shift-Hyphens) but may not include spaces or most punctuation marks. Lotus 1-2-3 automatically assigns an extension (second name) to the file of **.PIC** as this is a picture file.

After saving the graph on the disk, we Quit from the / Graph menu, which returns us back to Ready mode. Now we save the spreadsheet itself using / File Save . Lotus 1-2-3 saves the current graph settings in the file as well, so later when we retrieve the spreadsheet file we will not need to respecify the current graph. With the graph saved using / G S and the spreadsheet saved using / F S, we quit out of 1-2-3 by selecting / Quit Yes and enter into the Lotus 1-2-3 Access System. (If quitting out of 1-2-3 deposits you back into DOS, then you can enter the Lotus 1-2-3 Access System by typing LOTUS and pressing Enter.)

The screen for the Lotus 1-2-3 Access System was shown in Figure 2-5. You may not have realized it, but the Lotus 1-2-3 Access System uses a menu system just like the rest of 1-2-3. To run the PrintGraph program, select PrintGraph in the Lotus 1-2-3 Access System.

After selecting PrintGraph the PrintGraph copyright screen is displayed briefly and then the main PrintGraph menu screen shown in Figure 10-12 is displayed. The specific settings shown

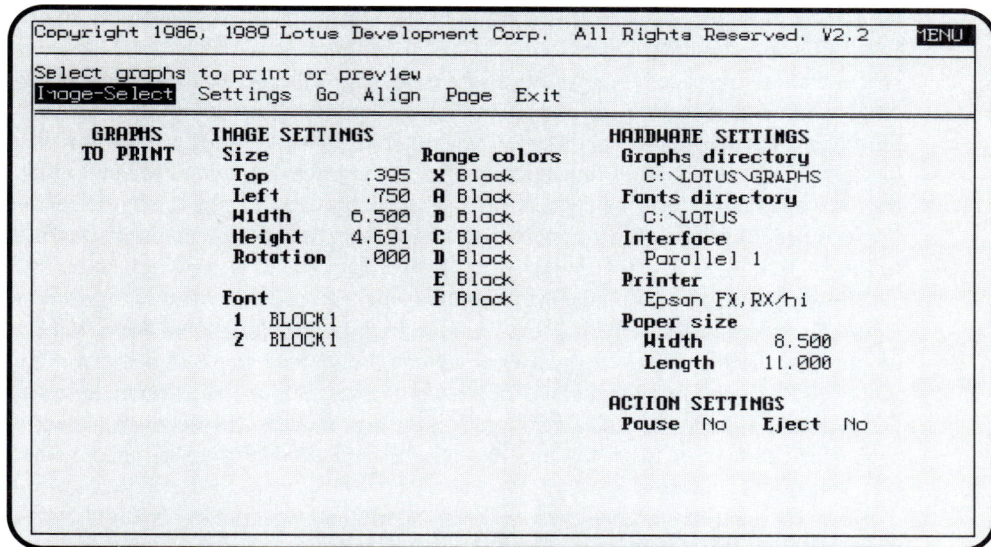

FIGURE 10-12 The PrintGraph Main Menu. Your settings may differ.

OUR FRUIT STAND

Sales in $ Millions

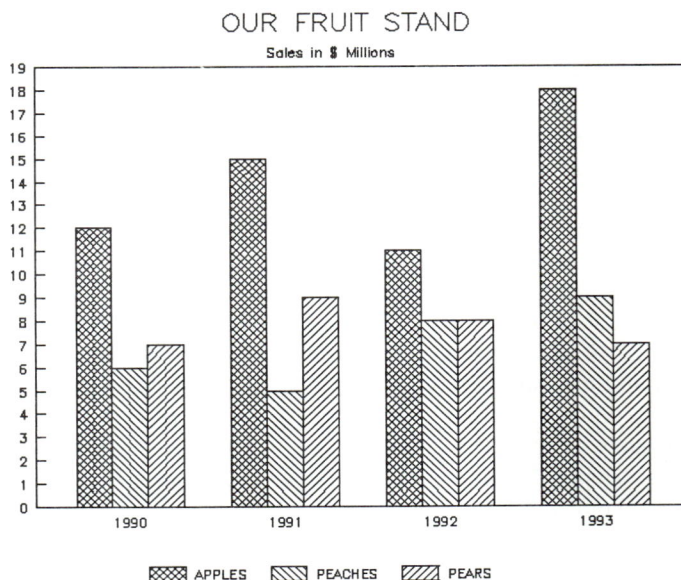

FIGURE 10-13 The result of printing the spreadsheet in Figure 10-4 using the Lotus PrintGraph program.

on your screen, for example the printer type or the Graphs Directory, may be different. Most of these settings were established when the system was installed using the Install program.

The basic procedure within the PrintGraph program is to select the graph file to be printed, align the paper, and then go ahead and print the graph. We issue the Image-Select command in the PrintGraph menu and then select the .PIC file in the current Graphs Directory that we wish to print. Now we adjust the paper in the printer so the print head is just below the perforation and issue the Align command. At last, we issue the Go command to instruct the computer to go ahead and print the graph. Depending on your computer and printer it may take a while for the computer to process the graph picture and for the printer to actually print the graph. Be patient. After the graph is printed, the Page command ejects the page and advances the print head to the top of the next page.

The result of printing the graph in Figure 10-4 using the Lotus PrintGraph program is shown in Figure 10-13.

The Settings command in the PrintGraph menu allows you to customize the way your graph is printed. For example, selecting Settings Hardware Graph-Directory allows you to change the directory on the disk where the graph files are to be found. Selecting Settings Image Font 1 allows you to change the font, the typeface, of the top line of the Title in the graph. Selecting Settings Image Font 2 allows you to change the font of the rest of the text in the graph. Selecting Settings Image Size allows you to specify the size of the printed graph on the page and whether the graph is to be printed sideways.

If when you print the graph you discover some small flaw in the graph that was saved, you must exit from PrintGraph to the Lotus Access System, reenter 1-2-3, retrieve the spreadsheet from the disk, specify the correct graph, save the new graph on the disk, exit from 1-2-3, reenter PrintGraph, select the graph file on the disk, and print the new version of the graph. Whew.

COMPUTER EXERCISES

10-1 Enter the fruit stand spreadsheet in Figure 10-1. Duplicate the graphs that appear in Figures 10-2, 10-4, 10-5, 10-6, and 10-7, and 10-9.

10-2 The following spreadsheet was used in Exercise 4-3. Either enter the spreadsheet with formulas or retrieve the spreadsheet from your disk.

```
                      SALES ANALYSIS

PRODUCT    WINTER    SPRING    SUMMER    FALL    TOTAL    MAX

GOLF       32000     62000     57000     39000
TENNIS     47000     52000     71000     29000
SKIING     37000     21000     11000     52000
SURFING    12000     21000     29000     13000

TOTAL

AVERAGE
```

All the following graphs should be as understandable as possible and should be well identified with titles, legends, and so on.

(a) Create a bar graph of total sales by season. Here, the total sales row would be the A data set and the season names would be the X data set. There should be four bars in the graph (and, hence, four cells in the A data set range and four cells in the X data set range).

(b) Create a bar graph of sales for each of the different products by season. The four golf sales figures should form the A data set, the four tennis sales the B data set, and so on. The season names should be the X data set. There should be 16 bars in the final graph.

(c) Display the graph in (b) as a stacked bar chart.

(d) Display the graph in (b) as a line chart.

(e) Which of the three graphs is most effective? Why?

(f) Display the sales for summer as a pie chart.

(g) Control the hatch patterns in the pie chart by establishing a new column of numbers with different values between 1 and 8 and specifying this column as the B data range. "Explode" the slice for skiing by adding 100 to the corresponding value in the B data set column.

(h) Is there any relationship between sales for tennis and sales for golf? Display an XY chart with tennis sales as the A data set and golf sales as the X data set. Do not use any legends in this chart but do label the X and Y axes appropriately. Label the data points with the season of the data point.

10-3 Produce a graph that illustrates how the square of numbers increases compared to the cube of the numbers, that is, graph x^2 versus x^3.

Create a spreadsheet that has three columns. In the first column type in the numbers from 1 to 12. (For reasons that will become clear below, type in the numbers explicitly rather than using a formula.) In the second column calculate the squares of the corresponding numbers in the first column. In the third column, calculate the cubes of the corresponding numbers in the first column.

Each of the following graphs should be well labeled and self-explanatory.

(a) Produce a line graph of the data where the numbers from 1 to 12 are the X range, the squares of the numbers are the A range, and the cubes of the numbers are the B range.

(b) Produce an XY graph of the same data. In the XY graph, lines should connect the two sets of data points.

(c) Produce a bar graph of the same data.

(d) Try a pie chart of the data. (Remember that a pie chart only graphs the A data set.)

Now change the number 4 in the first column to a 10. The corresponding square and cube should change as well. The first column now should contain 1 2 3 10 5 6 7 8 9 10 11 12.

(e) Produce the line graph of the data.

(f) Produce the XY graph of the data.

(g) Describe the difference between a line graph and an XY graph.

10-4 Produce a well-labeled graph that shows the Sine curve versus the Cosine curve.

10-5 Produce a well-labeled graph that illustrates the difference in obtaining fixed annual interest rates of 5%, 10%, and 15% on an investment of $100,000 over the course of 10 years. Your graph should show three curves: the value of the investment growing at 5% per year, the value of the investment growing at 10% per year, and the value of the investment growing at 15% per year.

10-6 Create a spreadsheet that keeps track of your major living expenses over the past five months. Include at least four different categories of expenses (for example, room and board, school, transportation, clothing, miscellaneous). Fill in numbers. You may use fictional numbers if you wish. Calculate row and column totals. Print the spreadsheet. Create and print five well-labeled graphs, as follows:

(a) A pie chart of your expenses for the most recent month.

(b) A line chart of your total expenses over the past five months.

(c) A stacked bar chart showing all the categories of expenses over the past five months.

(d) An XY chart comparing two of the categories of expenses over the past five months. One of the expense categories should form the X data set. The other category should form the A data set. No lines should connect the points. The data points should be labeled with the months.

(e) A bar chart of your choice.

10-7 You have been asked to make a presentation to the U.S. Congress about the U.S. budget and its trends over the past 10 years. The relevant data is included in the spreadsheet in Exercise 4-5.

(a) Use the spreadsheet to prepare four graphs that best capture the most important points to be made about the U.S. budget. Your graphs should be well thought out, well labeled, and self-explanatory.

(b) Prepare the text of your testimony. State in English the important points that your graphs illustrate.

10-8 Obtain a recent financial statement or annual report for your college or university or for a company or organization with which you are familiar. Use the financial data to prepare four graphs that best capture the most important points to be made about the financial situation of the organization. Your graphs should be well thought out, well labeled, and self-explanatory.

11

SELECTION FUNCTIONS: @IF, LOOKUP

Sometimes we would like a cell to display one of two or more alternative values. If you sell over $2 million, you receive a bonus of $1,000; otherwise, you receive no bonus. People caught driving at a speed over 80 miles per hour (mph) on the Interstate owe a fine of $100; people caught driving between 66 mph and 80 mph owe $40; otherwise, no fine. In this chapter we will look at three functions—@IF, @VLOOKUP, and @HLOOKUP—that are designed to solve the problem of selecting among alternatives.

THE @IF FUNCTION

For orders under $100 there is a $5 Shipping and Handling charge. For orders of $100 or more there is no charge for Shipping and Handling. Consider the spreadsheet in Figure 11-1. What formula should be entered into cell D37 so that the appropriate number is calculated from the total in cell D35? This simple problem cannot be solved with what we have covered so far.

The solution is to use the @IF function, as follows:

@IF(D35<100,5,0)

The @IF function always has three arguments:

@IF(condition, result-if-true, result-if-false)

The first argument is a **condition.** A condition is an expression that evaluates to ***True*** or ***False***. In this case the condition is D35<100. If D35 is less than 100, then the condition is *True;* otherwise, the condition is *False*.

Conditions usually contain one or more of the following **comparison operators**:

Operator	Meaning
<	less than
<=	less than or equal to
=	equal to
>=	greater than or equal to
>	greater than
<>	not equal to

```
D42:                                                              READY

              A          B          C          D      E      F      G
     34
     35             Total                     $28.95
     36
     37             Shipping and Handling     $5.00
     38
     39             Grand Total               $33.95
     40
     41
     42
     43
     44
     45
     46
     47
     48
     49
     50
     51
     52
     53
                                    UNDO
```

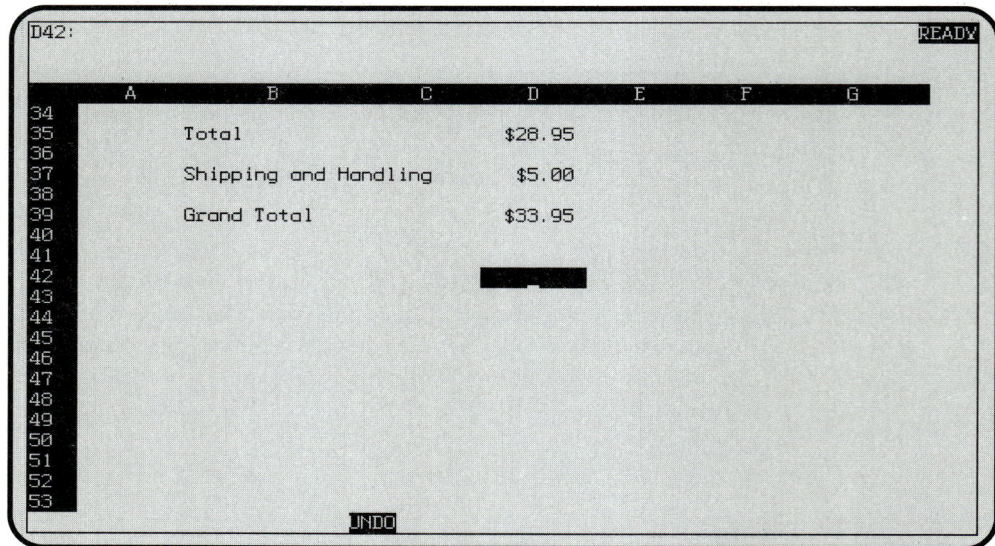

FIGURE 11-1 If the Total is under $100 then Shipping and Handling is $5.00. Otherwise there is no charge for Shipping and Handling. What is the formula for Shipping and Handling in D37?

Note that the operators <= >= <> are formed by two consecutive keystrokes.

The second argument in an @IF function is the result if the condition is *True*. The third argument is the result if the condition is *False*. That is, the result of evaluating an @IF function is always either the second argument or the third argument. If the first argument is *True*, then the @IF function evaluates to the second argument. If the first argument is *False*, then the @IF function evaluates to the third argument.

In the example, if the value in cell D35 becomes 200, then the condition becomes False and the value displayed in cell D37 changes to 0, as in Figure 11-2.

The second and third arguments in the @IF function can be any formula. For example, suppose orders under $100 are charged 5% for shipping. Then the formula in cell D37 would be @IF(D35<100,0.05*D35,0).

ANOTHER EXAMPLE

Suppose that salespeople who sell at least $2,000,000 are entitled to a free trip to Hawaii. The names of the salespeople and their sales figures are listed in the spreadsheet in Figure 11-3. What formula should be entered into cell E15 (and copied down) so that the cell contains FREE TRIP TO HAWAII if the person is eligible and appears blank otherwise? The answer is

@IF(C15>=$F$9,"FREE TRIP TO HAWAII"," ")

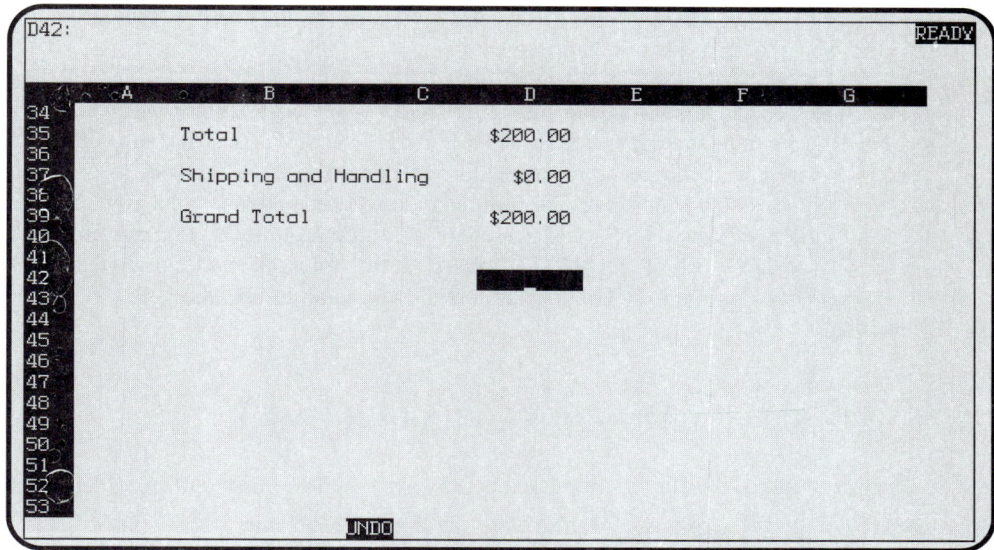

FIGURE 11-2 When the value in D35 is changed to 200, the value in D37 becomes 0.

```
E20: [W20] @IF(C20>=$F$9,"FREE TRIP TO HAWAII"," ")          READY

            A         B          C          D          E          F
5
6                         Salesperson Summary
7
8
9              Minimum sales required for free trip to Hawaii: $2,000,000
10
11
12                        Annual
13            Name        Sales                 Result
14
15            Aaron        $552,030
16            Baker         $23,400
17            Brown      $7,358,800          FREE TRIP TO HAWAII
18            Carey      $1,488,900
19            Chu        $3,500,400          FREE TRIP TO HAWAII
20            Church       $995,000          ████████████████  █
21            Dark       $1,557,100
22            Davis          $7,560
23            Delaney    $5,922,000          FREE TRIP TO HAWAII
24            Denning      $481,120
                          UNDO
```

FIGURE 11-3 Salespeople whose sales are at least $2,000,000 are entitled to a free trip to Hawaii.

The second and third arguments are character strings that are enclosed in quotation marks. Thus if the condition C15>=2000000 is *True*, then the result of evaluating the function is the label FREE TRIP TO HAWAII. If the condition is *False*, the result of evaluating the function is the label that consists of a single space.

Text must be enclosed in quotation marks. The formula @IF(C15>=$F$9,FREE TRIP TO HAWAII," ") will not work. If the quotation marks were absent from the second argument, then Lotus 1-2-3 would attempt to interpret FREE TRIP TO HAWAII as the name of a cell. Since no cell has that name (and, indeed, since the phrase contains a space it would be an illegal name anyway) if you try to leave the quotes off, the computer would beep at you and put you into Edit mode.

An @IF function always must have exactly three arguments. For example, the formula @IF(C15>=$F$9,"FREE TRIP TO HAWAII",) will not work. If you try to leave out the third argument, the computer would beep at you and put you into Edit mode so you can correct the mistake.

USING @IF FUNCTIONS IN EXTRA COLUMNS

@IF functions are useful in some unexpected ways. Suppose you would now like to find out how many salespeople sold $2,000,000 or more, that is, how many qualify for the free trip to Hawaii.

A good solution is to add an extra column to the spreadsheet. The column will contain a 1 for each salespeople with sales of at least $2,000,000 and a 0 for each salesperson who sold under $2,000,000, as in Figure 11-4. The formula in F15 will be

```
F18: [W12] @IF(C18>=$F$9,1,0)                                    READY

      A       B           C          D          E              F
 6                     Salesperson Summary
 7
 8
 9          Minimum sales required for free trip to Hawaii: $2,000,000
10
11
12                   Annual                                 Tally the
13          Name     Sales            Result               Hawaii-bound
14
15          Aaron    $552,030                                    0
16          Baker    $23,400                                     0
17          Brown    $7,358,800    FREE TRIP TO HAWAII           1
18          Carey    $1,488,900                                  0
19          Chu      $3,500,400    FREE TRIP TO HAWAII           1
      A       B           C          D          E              F
88          Young    $79,500                                    0
89          Zak      $3,668,300                                  1
90
91          Total who qualify for trip to Hawaii:              21
92
                              UNDO
```

FIGURE 11-4 Finding the number of salespeople who qualify for the trip to Hawaii using an extra column.

$$@IF(C15>=\$F\$9,1,0)$$

which will be copied down. In cell E82 we will put the formula

$$@SUM(F15..F89)$$

and that will tell us the answer.

If you do not want the 1's and 0's to show, you could place the formulas in them way off to the right, say, in column X, or you could hide the contents of the column using / Worksheet Column Hide.

An alternative formula for F15 would be

$$@IF(E15=``FREE\ TRIP\ TO\ HAWAII",1,0)$$

A CELL CAN CONTAIN JUST A CONDITION

A cell can contain just a condition by itself; that is, a cell could contain the formula (D23<>4), or a cell could contain (X17>(0.05*Q55)). Lotus 1-2-3 represents *True* as a 1 and *False* as a 0. If a cell contains just a condition by itself, the value in the cell will be a 1 if the condition is *True* and a 0 if the condition is *False*.

This leads to an even shorter, though not as intuitive, solution to the problem of counting up how many salespeople sold at least $2,000,000. Thus, F15 alternatively could contain the formula

(C15>=$F$9)

This also could be written

+C15>=$F$9

(Incidentally, the @DCOUNT function also could be used to solve this problem. The @DCOUNT function is covered in Chapter 16.)

NESTED @IF FUNCTIONS

Suppose that salespeople who sell under $100,000 are to be fired. Now there are three choices for the cells in column E. Cell E15 should contain FREE TRIP TO HAWAII if cell C15 contains a value of at least $2,000,000. Cell E15 should appear blank if cell C15 contains a value between $100,000 and $2,000,000. Cell E15 should contain FIRED if cell C15 is under $100,000. This is illustrated in Figure 11-5.

```
E20: [W20] @IF(C20>=$F$9,"FREE TRIP TO HAWAII",@IF(C20<$F$8,"FIRED"," "))   READY

        A        B         C          D           E              F
5
6                     Salesperson Summary
7
8               People who sell under this amount are fired:    $100,000
9               Minimum sales required for free trip to Hawaii: $2,000,000
10
11
12                       Annual
13              Name     Sales         Result
14
15              Aaron    $552,030
16              Baker     $23,400      FIRED
17              Brown  $7,358,800      FREE TRIP TO HAWAII
18              Corey  $1,488,900
19              Chu    $3,500,400      FREE TRIP TO HAWAII
20              Church   $995,000      ███████████████
21              Dark   $1,557,100
22              Davis      $7,560      FIRED
23              Delaney $5,922,000      FREE TRIP TO HAWAII
24              Denning  $481,120
                              UNDO
```

FIGURE 11-5 People with sales under $100,000 are fired. Now there are three alternatives.

So far, @IF functions have allowed us to create formulas that select between two possibilities depending on a condition. In this example, we need a formula that allows us to select among three possibilities. The following formula will correctly select among these three possibilities:

@IF(C15>=$F$9,"FREE TRIP TO HAWAII",@IF(C15<$F$8,"FIRED"," "))

This formula contains **nested** @IF functions. This means that one @IF function contains another @IF function. The key to working with nested @IF functions is to remember that @IF functions always must have exactly three arguments.

The formula just given can be read as follows: "If C15 is greater than or equal to F9, then this cell should show FREE TRIP TO HAWAII. Otherwise, if C15 is less than F8, then this cell should show FIRED otherwise this cell should appear blank."

What are the arguments here? The outer @IF function has three arguments:

1. The condition: C15>$F$9
2. The result if the condition is *True*:   "FREE TRIP TO HAWAII"
3. The result if the condition is *False*:   @IF(C15<$F$8,"FIRED"," ")

The inner @IF function is the third argument. It, too, clearly has three arguments:

1. The condition: C15<$F$8
2. The result if the condition is *True*:   "FIRED"
3. The result if the condition is *False*:   " "

YOU TRY

A spreadsheet for tabulating the results of the Tiger football season is given in Figure 11-6. We would like the cells in column G to say WIN if the Tigers won, TIE if the number of points each scored was equal, and LOSE if the Tigers lost the game. What should be the formula in G7?

There are several possible correct answers. A good solution would be

@IF(D7>E7,"WIN",@IF(D7=E7,"TIE","LOSE"))

Here the computer first checks to see if D7 is greater than E7. If that is *True*, then the answer is WIN and the evaluation is over. If D7 is not greater than E7, then the computer evaluates the third argument, the inner @IF function. Now the computer checks the first argument of the inner @IF function. The computer checks to see if D7 equals E7. If D7 does equal E7, then the answer is TIE. If the first condition is *False* and then the second condition is *False*, then the answer is LOSE. With nested @IF functions, the computer always makes its way from the outside in.

You could rearrange the order, for example, by checking for a tie first:

@IF(D7=E7,"TIE",@IF(D7>E7,"WIN","LOSE"))

There are four other similar rearrangements that would work.

```
G19:                                                                    READY

          A         B          C          D          E       F        G
1
2                              Tiger Football Season
3
4                                         Tiger    Opponent
5        Game      Date       Opponent    Score     Score           Result
6
7          1      Sep  5      Eagles        27        31            LOSE
8          2      Sep 12      Scorpions     17        17            TIE
9          3      Sep 19      Wimps         10        35            LOSE
10         4      Sep 26      Panthers      33        21            WIN
11         5      Oct  3      Hawks         14         7            WIN
12         6      Oct 10      Madmen        21         3            WIN
13         7      Oct 17      Bears         17        10            WIN
14         8      Oct 24      Gators         9         6            WIN
15         9      Oct 31      Warlocks      20        21            LOSE
16        10      Nov  6      Daisies        3        34            LOSE
17        11      Nov 13      Braves        21        17            WIN
18
19
20
                              UNDO
```

FIGURE 11-6 What formula has been placed into G7 and copied down?

Suppose we want the cells in column G to contain the name of the team that won (or the word "Tie") as in Figure 11-7. What formula would you put in cell G7?

Here what we would need to do is to change two of the arguments, as follows:

$$@IF(D7>E7,\text{"Tigers"},@IF(D7=E7,\text{"Tie"},C7))$$

The cell C7 contains the name of the opponent. Of course, when this formula is copied down, the row numbers of C7, D7, and E7 will be adjusted accordingly.

If you wanted to choose among four alternatives, then you would need three nested @IF functions. There can be as many nested @IF functions as you would like. The only limit is that a formula cannot exceed 240 characters in length. Of course, all @IF functions must have three arguments. Any of these arguments can be other @IF functions.

LOGICAL OPERATORS

At the Tropical Resort there are 600 guest rooms. The guest rooms are classified as suites, doubles, or singles. Some face the beach; some face the pool; some face inland (the parking lot). The resort manager has decided to charge $159 per night for suites facing the beach. All other rooms will be $139 per night. The spreadsheet in Figure 11-8 shows a list of the guest rooms. Each cell in column F should contain the price of the room. What formula should appear in cell F8?

```
G19:                                                                    READY

         A           B            C          D          E         F        G

1
2                              Tiger Football Season
3
4                                           Tiger     Opponent
5        Game       Date       Opponent     Score      Score             Result
6
7          1        Sep  5     Eagles        27         31               Eagles
8          2        Sep 12     Scorpions     17         17               Tie
9          3        Sep 19     Wimps         10         35               Wimps
10         4        Sep 26     Panthers      33         21               Tigers
11         5        Oct  3     Hawks         14          7               Tigers
12         6        Oct 10     Madmen        21          3               Tigers
13         7        Oct 17     Bears         17         10               Tigers
14         8        Oct 24     Gators         9          6               Tigers
15         9        Oct 31     Warlocks      20         21               Warlocks
16        10        Nov  6     Daisies        3         34               Daisies
17        11        Nov 13     Braves        21         17               Tigers
18
19
20
                                     UNDO
```

FIGURE 11-7 We would like the name of the winner to appear in column G or the word "Tie" if there is a tie. What is the formula in cell G7?

```
A1:                                                                         READY

         A         B          C          D          E            F        G         H

1
2
3                          Tropical Resort Room Charges
4
5
6                   Room       Type       View                 Rate
7
8                   101       Double     Inland                139
9                   102       Suite      Beach                 159
10                  103       Single     Inland                139
11                  104       Single     Beach                 139
12                  105       Suite      Inland                139
13                  106       Single     Beach                 139
14                  107       Suite      Pool                  139
15                  108       Double     Beach                 139
16                  109       Single     Pool                  139
17                  110       Single     Beach                 139
18                  111       Double     Pool                  139
19                  112       Suite      Beach                 159
20                  114       Double     Beach                 139
                                    UNDO
```

FIGURE 11-8 Suites that face the beach are $159 per night. All other rooms are $139 per night. What formula has been placed in F8 and copied down?

Clearly, we want to use an @IF function here as there are two alternatives. The @IF function would have the basic form

@IF(condition,159,139)

Now we need to fill in the condition. There are two parts to the condition, both of which must be *True* for the condition as a whole to be *True*. That is, for the room to cost $159, the room both must be a suite and must face the beach.

First, we can check whether a cell contains a specific label with a condition like (D8="Suite"). This condition will be *True* if D8 contains the word "Suite" and *False* otherwise.

Lotus provides the operator **#AND#** for the purpose of combining two parts of a condition. The completed formula would be

@IF((D8="Suite")#AND#(E8="Beach"),159,139)

The condition is (D8="Suite")#AND#(E8="Beach"). This condition will be *True* only if both D8 contains the word "Suite" *and* E8 contains the word "Beach".

The operator #AND# is called a **logical operator** or **Boolean operator**. (George Boole was an English mathematician who developed key ideas of symbolic logic. His best known book is *The Laws of Thought*, which was published in 1854.) Logical operators work on operands that are *True* or *False* just the way that arithmetic operators like addition or multiplication work on numbers.

The #AND# operator corresponds closely to the meaning of the word "and" in English. The result of the #AND# operator is *True* only if both of its operands are *True* as follows:

Expression	Value
True#AND#*True*	*True*
True#AND#*False*	*False*
False#AND#*True*	*False*
False#AND#*False*	*False*

There are two other logical operators: **#OR#** and **#NOT#**.

If we wrote the formula @IF((D8="Suite")#OR#(E8="Beach"),159,139) then a room would cost $159 if it is a suite *or* if it faces the beach or both.

The #OR# operator also corresponds closely to the meaning of the word "or" in English. The result of the #OR# operator is *True* if either or both of its operands is *True* as follows:

Expression	Value
True#OR#*True*	*True*
True#OR#*False*	*True*
False#OR#*True*	*True*
False#OR#*False*	*False*

The #NOT# operator transforms *True* into *False* and *False* into *True*.

Expression	Value
#NOT#*True*	*False*
#NOT#*False*	*True*

The #NOT# operator has only a single operand that follows it. The #AND# and #OR# operators must have two operands that appear on either side of it.

ANOTHER EXAMPLE

Suppose the manager decides that suites facing the beach will be $159. All other suites will be $139. Doubles not facing inland will be $139. All other rooms will be $119. (See Figure 11-9.) Now we have three possibilities. The formula for cell D6 could have the form

$$@IF(Condition1,159,@IF(Condition2,139,119))$$

Now we need to fill in the conditions. *Condition1* is the same as before, namely (D8="Suite")#AND#(E8="Beach").

```
F8: @IF((D8="Suite")#AND#(E8="Beach"),159,@IF((D8="Suite")#OR#((D8="Double"READY

          A       B       C         D        E        F        G         H
1
2
3                      Tropical Resort Room Charges
4
5
6                Room    Type      View            Rate
7
8                101     Double    Inland           139
9                102     Suite     Beach            159
10               103     Single    Inland           119
11               104     Single    Beach            119
12               105     Suite     Inland           139
13               106     Single    Beach            119
14               107     Suite     Pool             139
15               108     Double    Beach            139
16               109     Single    Pool             119
17               110     Single    Beach            119
18               111     Double    Pool             139
19               112     Suite     Beach            159
20               114     Double    Beach            139
                         UNDO
```

FIGURE 11-9 Suites that face the beach are $159 per night. All other suites are $139 per night as are doubles that do not face inland. All other rooms are $119. What formula has been placed into F8?

The tough one is *Condition2*. *Condition2* consists of two parts joined by an #OR#. The first part of *Condition2* is (D8="Suite"). The second part of *Condition2* is (D8="Double")#AND#(#NOT#(E8="Inland")). So the entire formula would be

@IF((D8="Suite")#AND#(E8="Beach"),159,@IF((D8="Suite")#OR#
((D8="Double")#AND#(#NOT#(E8="Inland"))),139,119))

All the parentheses are included so there is no doubt as to the order in which operations are to be performed. This practice is strongly recommended in complicated conditions. Alternatively, the formula could be written

@IF((D8="Suite")#AND#(E8="Beach"),159,@IF((D8="Suite"),139,
@IF((D8="Double")#AND#(#NOT#(E8="Inland")),139,119)))

Here we have treated the two parts of *Condition2* separately. Another nested @IF has been added to accommodate this extra condition. This formula resembles the original statement of the problem on the previous page. Do you see how these two formulas are equivalent? If not, you might take a few minutes to work through the two formulas by writing out the arguments for each of the @IF functions and applying the formulas to the examples in Figure 11-9.

Formulas can be continued beyond 80 characters, as long as they do not extend beyond 240 characters. You just keep typing and Lotus takes care of it. Note that Lotus 1-2-3 does not allow any spaces to be included in a formula, even though spaces might make complicated formulas easier to read.

LOOKUP FUNCTIONS

It often is convenient to express a multiway selection in a table. For example, we might have a tax rate table that indicates that if you earned so much money then your tax rate is such and such. Or we might give volume discounts, where the more you purchase, the lower the price. This could be expressed in a volume discount table that indicates how much you must purchase to qualify for the different discounts. Lotus provides the special functions @VLOOKUP and @HLOOKUP especially for making selections by looking up values in a table.

The @VLOOKUP function has three arguments. The first argument is the number you want to look up. The second argument is the location of the **vertical lookup table**. The third argument indicates which column in the table contains the answer, the value to be returned by the function.

Suppose that the photocopy center charges are based on the number of photocopies ordered, as follows:

Photocopy Prices

Number of Copies	Price per Page
1 to 19	0.06
20 to 99	0.05
100 to 499	0.04
500 to 999	0.035
1000 or more	0.03

In cell D15 we have the number of copies. We would like the price per page to appear in cell D17. What formula should go into cell D17?

We could solve this problem using a nested @IF function. The cell would contain the formula

@IF(D15<20,0.06,@IF(D15<100,0.05,@IF(D15<500,0.04,@IF(D15<1000,0.035,0.03))))

This formula works, but it is cumbersome and does not indicate the price table explicitly in the spreadsheet. If the price changes, we would need to find and change the formula. An alternative approach to solving this problem uses a vertical lookup table and the @VLOOKUP function, as in Figure 11-10. The formula in cell D17 is

@VLOOKUP(D15,F20..G24,1)

This formula instructs the computer to look up the number in cell D15 in the vertical lookup table located in cells F20 through G24.

A vertical lookup table has a definite organization. The values in the first column must be in *ascending* order. The computer takes the number in D15 and compares it to the top left cell in the lookup table. If the number in the cell is less than or equal to D15, then the computer proceeds to the next cell down. The computer keeps chugging down the left column until it finds a number that is greater than the value in D15. At that point it goes up one cell and over to the right the number of cells indicated by the third argument in the @VLOOKUP function call. The third argument is called the **column-offset**. This may sound confusing at first, but it works well.

In the example in Figure 11-10, the number to be looked up in the table is 325. The computer compares 1 against 325. The number 1 is less than 325 so the computer moves down a cell. The number 20 is less than 325 so the computer moves down another cell. The number 100 is less than 325 so the computer moves down a cell. At last, 500 is greater than 325. The computer moves up one cell. This is the row with the answer. Then it moves over one cell to the right (as the third argument is 1). Finally the computer returns the number 0.04. The number 0.04 is the result of evaluating the @VLOOKUP function in cell D17.

Suppose the number in cell D15 were 700. The result of evaluating the @VLOOKUP function in D17 would be 0.035.

Suppose the number in cell D15 were 5000. The result of evaluating the @VLOOKUP function in D17 would be 0.03. If the number to be looked up is larger than any number in the first column of the table, then the computer stops at the last row in the table.

```
D17: @VLOOKUP(D15,F20..G24,1)                                    READY

            A        B         C         D       E       F        G        H
     14
     15              Number of copies        325
     16
     17              Price per page        0.04                Price Table
     18
     19                                                     #Copies    $/Page
     20                                                           1     0.06
     21                                                          20     0.05
     22                                                         100     0.04
     23                                                         500     0.035
     24                                                        1000     0.03
     25
     26
     27
     28
     29
     30
     31
     32
     33
                                   UNDO
```

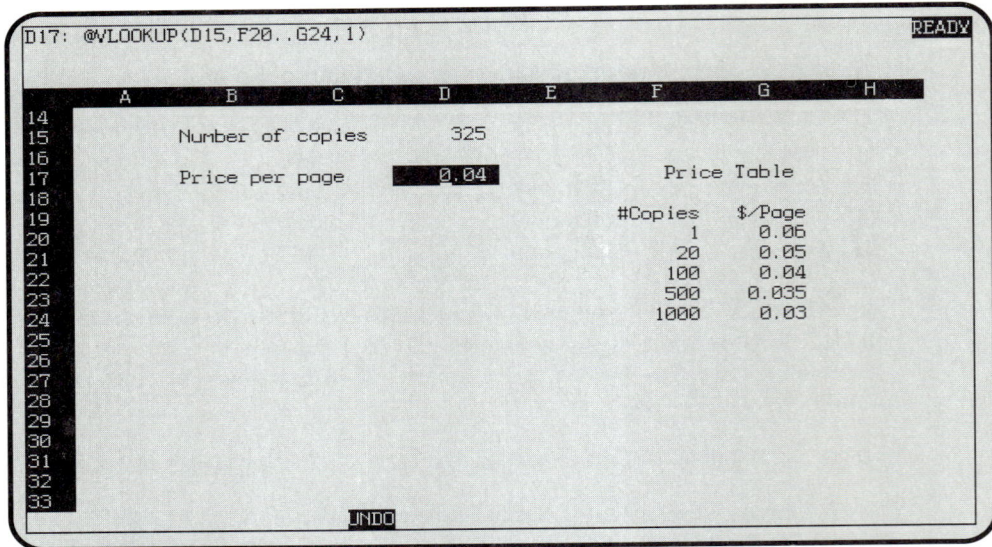

FIGURE 11-10 The computer uses the vertical lookup table in F20..G24 to find the price per page for the number of copies in D15.

Suppose the number in cell D15 were -25. The result of evaluating the @VLOOKUP function in D17 would be ERR. If the number to be looked up is less than the first value in the table, then the computer would indicate an error.

Suppose the number in cell D15 were 100. The result of evaluating the @VLOOKUP function in D17 would be 0.04. In this case the first number in the column that would be larger than the number we are looking up would be 500. The computer would then go up one cell and over one cell.

A major advantage of using a lookup table is that the numbers in the table become an apparent part of the spreadsheet. The person using the spreadsheet can see the table rather than having the values hidden inside a nested @IF formula. If the pricing policy changes, you can change the numbers in the table rather than trying to edit a complicated formula. For example, if the price per page for 100 to 499 copies is raised to $0.045, the number in cell G22 can be changed to 0.045. In the spreadsheet in Figure 11-10 the result of evaluating the formula in D17 would become 0.045.

What is the purpose of the third argument, the column-offset? Suppose we had two classes of customers, regular and preferred, and two sets of rates. We could assign regular customers a code of 1 and preferred customers a code of 2. Now we could determine the rate by making the code be the column offset, as in Figure 11-11. Here our formula would be

@VLOOKUP(D15,F20..H24,D12)

Note that we extended the lookup table over to column H in the formula.

```
D17: @VLOOKUP(D15,F20..H24,D12)                                    READY
```

```
          A        B          C         D        E        F        G         H
11
12                 Class code                 2
13                 (1=regular, 2=preferred)
14
15                 Number of copies          325
16
17                 Price per page        0.035              Price Table
18                                                          Regular  Preferred
19                                             #Copies      $/Page    $/Page
20                                                   1       0.06      0.05
21                                                  20       0.05      0.05
22                                                 100       0.04      0.035
23                                                 500       0.035     0.03
24                                                1000       0.03      0.025
25
26
27
28
29
30
                              UNDO
```

FIGURE 11-11 The lookup table with two classes of customers.

This same technique would work for income tax tables where there are different rates for single taxpayers, married taxpayers filing jointly, and so on.

It often is useful to name a lookup table (using / Range Name Create) as well as the other key cells. The formula in D17 could be

$$@VLOOKUP(COPIES,PRICE\_TABLE,CLASS\_CODE)$$

Warning! If a @VLOOKUP function is to be copied down a column, do be sure that the table location is expressed as an absolute address. Otherwise, the address of the table will change as the formula is copied ! This is a common but subtle error when using lookup functions.

The @HLOOKUP function is the same as the @VLOOKUP function except that it works horizontally, scanning across the top row of the table. The equivalent spreadsheet using an @HLOOKUP function is shown in Figure 11-12.

LOOKING UP LABELS

It is possible to search for labels in a lookup table as well as values. An example is shown in the phone directory spreadsheet in Figure 11-13. Enter a name in D8. The computer then looks up the name in the table and responds with the telephone number. The formula in D10 is

$$@VLOOKUP(D8,C14..D87,1)$$

```
D17:  @HLOOKUP(D15,C22..G24,D12)                                    READY

        A          B          C        D        E        F        G
11
12              Class code                 2
13              (1=regular, 2=preferred)
14
15              Number of copies          325
16
17              Price per page        [ 0.035 ]
18
19
20  Price Table
21
22              #Copies        1       20      100      500     1000
23  Regular     $/Page       0.06     0.05    0.04     0.035    0.03
24  Preferred   $/Page       0.05     0.04    0.035    0.03     0.025
25
26
27
28
29
30                        [ UNDO ]
```

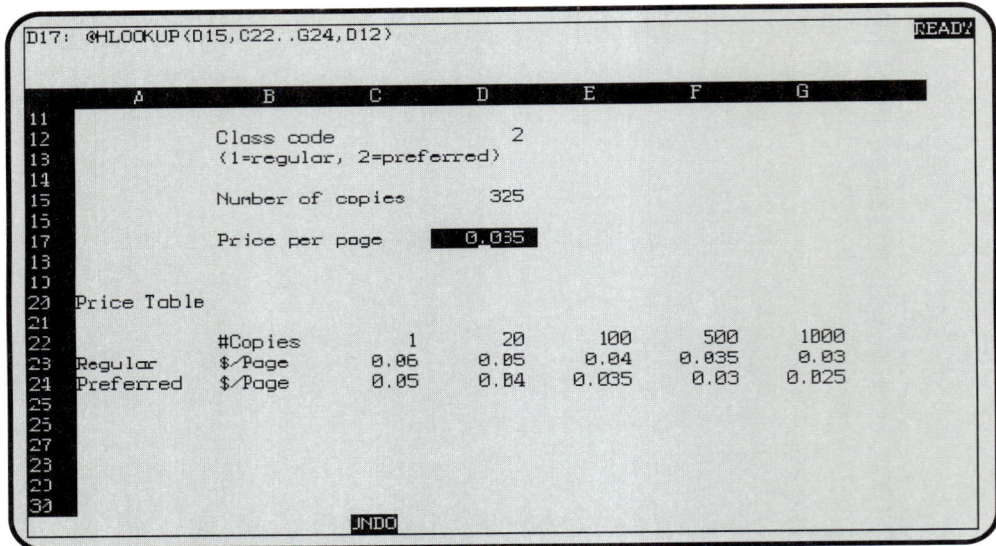

FIGURE 11-12 Solving the problem using a horizontal lookup table.

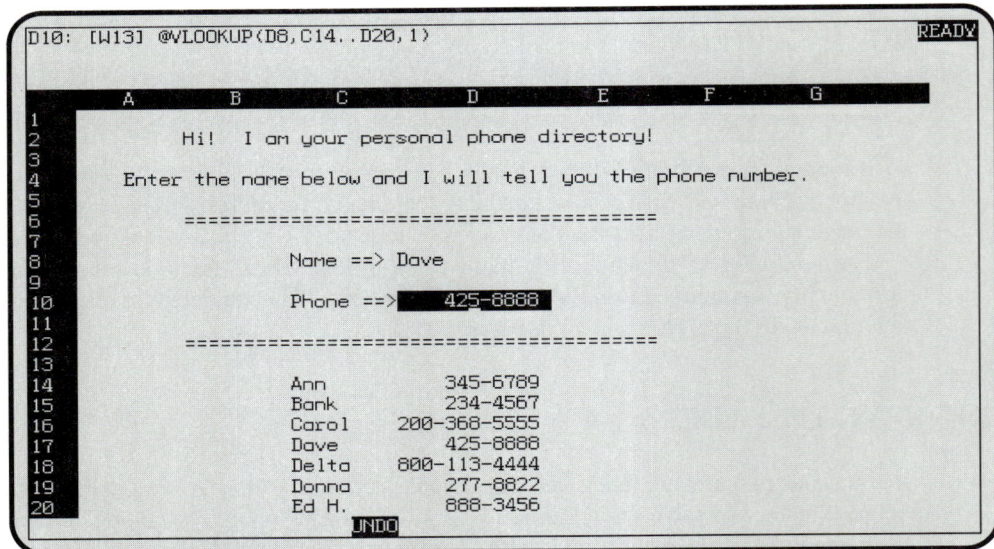

```
D10:  [W13] @VLOOKUP(D8,C14..D20,1)                                 READY

        A          B          C        D        E        F        G
1
2             Hi!  I am your personal phone directory!
3
4       Enter the name below and I will tell you the phone number.
5
6            ========================================
7
8                 Name ==> Dave
9
10                Phone ==> [ 425-8888 ]
11
12           ========================================
13
14                Ann         345-6789
15                Bank        234-4567
16                Carol     200-368-5555
17                Dave        425-8888
18                Delta     800-113-4444
19                Donna       277-8822
20                Ed H.       888-3456      [ UNDO ]
```

FIGURE 11-13 Looking up labels in a personal phone directory.

Lotus 1-2-3 treats a lookup table with labels in the left column somewhat differently than it treats lookup tables with numbers. When Lotus 1-2-3 is looking up a label, it must find an *exact* match. If we typed "Bob" in D8, the computer would respond with ERR in D10. In contrast, remember that when looking up numbers Lotus 1-2-3 stops when it reaches a number that is greater than the number being looked up.

TESTING SELECTION FUNCTIONS

Testing spreadsheets that contain selection functions presents a challenge.

Consider the spreadsheet for salespeople in Figure 11-5. The spreadsheet basically contains one nested @IF function that has been copied down column E. To test this spreadsheet you should try Annual Sales values of (1) a number more than $2,000,000 (for example $5,000,000), (2) the number $2,000,000 exactly, (3) a number between $2,000,000 and $100,000 (for example $995,000), (4) the number $100,000 exactly, and (5) a number below $100,000 (for example $23,400). You also should try varying the value in C15 (the top cell in the column) and the value in C89 (the bottom cell in the column) and the value in a cell between just to be sure that the formula was copied correctly. You also should try changing the threshold values in F8 and F9.

@IF functions with complicated conditions require careful testing. Spreadsheets with many independent @IF functions require very extensive testing to make sure that they are correct.

Similarly, with spreadsheets that contain lookup functions, it is important to test the spreadsheet with a wide variety of values, with a value below the lowest value to be looked up, with a value above the highest value to be looked up, and with a number of values in between. If a formula containing a lookup function has been copied, it is important to check that absolute addressing was used in referring to the lookup table.

It is quite possible and common for a spreadsheet with selection functions to work correctly most of the time but to fail when certain relatively unlikely conditions are true.

PENCIL AND PAPER EXERCISES

11-1 Consider the following spreadsheet:

	A	B	C	D
1				
2				
3	86	-4	-8	fun
4	-47	5	26	37
5	2.3	7	Lotus	198
6	computer	18	4.6	3
7	56	102		-19
8				

What would be the result of evaluating each of the following formulas? Write out your answers on paper. Do not use the computer.

(a) @IF(B5>6,"YES","NO")

(b) @IF(B4<D6,C5,A6)

(c) @IF(@SUM(B4..D4)>=D5,A4,"NOPE")

(d) (B5<A3)

(e) (2*B6)>(C4+10)

(f) @IF(B3=12,47,@IF(C4<D5,59,B7))

(g) @IF(C4=26,@IF(B5=19,2,4),@IF(A7=56,6,8))

(h) ((A7>A5)#AND#(D6<B6))

(i) @IF((B4=7)#OR#((C5="Lotus")#AND#(#NOT#(B6>20))),44,33)

(j) @VLOOKUP(12,B3..C7,1)

(k) @HLOOKUP(A4+A7,A4..D7,C3/B3)

11-2 We are writing a spreadsheet to select stocks for our clients. We have gathered some of the relevant data in the following spreadsheet. (The P/E Ratio is the closing price divided by this year's earnings.)

	A	B	C	D	E	F	G
1							
2			Our Stock Recommendations				
3							
4							
5	Stock	Earnings	Earnings	Earnings	Closing	P/E	We
6		2 yrs ago	Last yr	This yr	Price	Ratio	Recommend
7							
8	AA Electronic	$3.47	$3.59	$3.83	$48.50	12.7	
9	Aarvark Intl	$0.69	$1.24	$0.53	$15.75	29.7	
10	Abaco	$4.23	$5.89	$5.92	$33.25	5.6	
11	Abandon Mines	$0.12	$0.15	$0.23	$2.25	9.8	
12	Abernathy	$1.27	$1.31	$0.98	$21.00	21.4	

What formula would go into cell G8 and be copied down for each of the following recommendations? Each of the cells in column G should contain BUY, HOLD, SELL, or appear blank. When no recommendation is made, the cell should appear blank. I have answered part (a) just to give you the basic idea. Each part is independent of the others.

(a) BUY if the P/E Ratio is below 10.   *answer: @IF(F8<10,"BUY"," ")*

(b) BUY if the earnings have increased this year.
SELL if the earnings have decreased this year.

(c) BUY if the earnings have increased for each of the two years and the P/E Ratio is below 10.
SELL if the earnings have decreased for each of the two years.

(d) BUY if this year's earnings are up over 20% from last year and this year's earnings are up over 30% from two years ago or if the P/E ratio is below 8.
SELL if this year's earnings are down over 20% from last year or if the P/E ratio is above 20.
HOLD otherwise.

COMPUTER EXERCISES

11-3 At Hill University, students who register for at least 12 credits are considered Full Time students and pay a flat $4320 tuition. Students who register for under 12 credits are considered Part Time students and pay $360 per credit.

Create a spreadsheet that allows you to enter a student's name and the number of credits for which the student is registering. The spreadsheet should then display (1) the status of the student (Full Time or Part Time) and (2) the amount of tuition owed.

11-4 At the county courthouse speeders pay a fine of $30 plus $2 for every mile per hour above the speed limit. Anyone caught driving 90 mph or over pays an extra $100.

Create a spreadsheet that will allow you to enter a driver's name, the speed limit on the road where the driver was caught, and the driver's speed. If the driver's speed did not exceed the speed limit, then the spreadsheet should display SORRY! NO FINE. Otherwise, the spreadsheet should display the fine owed.

11-5 An employee is eligible for retirement if he or she satisfies at least one of the following criteria:

1. The employee has worked here at least 40 years.
2. The employee is 65 or over.
3. The employee has worked here at least 30 years and is 60 or over.

(a) Create a spreadsheet that allows one person to enter in his or her age and the number of years worked here. A cell in the spreadsheet should respond either CONGRATULATIONS! YOU ARE ELIGIBLE FOR RETIREMENT or BACK TO WORK.

(b) Add a cell that will indicate how many years it will be until the employee is eligible for retirement if he or she is not now eligible.

You may use extra cells in your spreadsheet.

11-6 Salespeople receive $10,000 base salary plus a commission of 1.5% of sales. Anyone who sells over $3 million receives a free vacation in Tahiti for two people. Anyone who sells over $5 million receives an additional $4,000 bonus. At the end of the year salespeople are rated as follows: under $2 million DUD, $2 million through $5 million STAR, over $5 million SUPERSTAR. Create a spreadsheet that allows you to enter a salesperson's name and annual sales amount and then calculates the following:

```
SALESPERSON SUMMARY

NAME:                          (input)
ANNUAL SALES:                  (input)

BASE SALARY:                   $10,000
COMMISSION:                    (formula)
BONUS:                         (formula)
TOTAL PAY:                     (formula)

FREE VACATION?                 (formula)

STATUS:                        (formula)
```

11-7 The Weather Bureau would like a spreadsheet to help it keep track of some simple statistics. In column B from B8 through B38, put the numbers from 1 through 31. In column C from C8 through C38, put the highest temperature recorded for your town for each day during the last month. (You can make up these temperatures, if you like.) In the top lines of the spreadsheet put appropriate titles and column headings.

Beginning in cell B40 and continuing down put the following labels:

```
AVERAGE TEMPERATURE FOR MONTH:
HIGHEST TEMPERATURE:
DAY OF HIGHEST TEMPERATURE:
SECOND HIGHEST TEMPERATURE:
DAY OF SECOND HIGHEST TEMPERATURE:
```

Widen column B appropriately (using / Worksheet Column Set). Your task is to enter formulas so that the appropriate statistics are calculated automatically in C40 through

C44. The DAY OF THE HIGHEST TEMPERATURE would be 23 if the highest temperature occurred on the 23rd of the month. In case of tie, select the latest day. Do not use the Sort command. You may use extra columns. Of course, your spreadsheet should work for any sequence of temperatures.

11-8 Create a spreadsheet that gives a price quote. You will enter (1) an item name and (2) the quantity of that item purchased. Your spreadsheet should look up the item name in the Price Table to find the unit price. Then it should calculate the total amount. Then look up this amount in the Discount Table to find the quantity discount percent. Then it should calculate the discount amount, the total, add in 6% sales tax, and give the final amount due for the order.

```
PRICE QUOTES                        _____

                                         PRICE TABLE
ITEM:            (input)                        UNIT
QUANTITY:        (input)             ITEM        PRICE $
                                     CONNECTORS    3.98
UNIT PRICE:                          GROMMITS     15.99
TOTAL BEFORE DISCOUNT:               HAPSES        0.35
DISCOUNT %:                          WIDGETS       8.79
DISCOUNT AMOUNT:                     _____


TOTAL AFTER DISCOUNT:                    DISCOUNT TABLE
SALES TAX:
                                     AMOUNT$     DISCOUNT
TOTAL:                                    0          0%
                                        100          5%
                                        500         10%
                                       1000         15%

                                     _____
```

11-9 In your history course there are three different hour exams, a paper, and a final exam. Each of these is graded between 0 and 100. In determining the final grade, the professor has decided to drop each student's lowest hour exam grade. The two highest hour exam grades will count one-sixth each, the paper will count one third, and the final exam will count one third in determining the overall average for the course. The final letter grade for the course will be based on the overall average, as follows: below 60 is an F, 60 to 65 is a D, 65 to 75 is a C, 75 to 80 is a B-, 80 to 90 is a B, 90 to 95 is an A-, 95 and above is an A.

(a) There are 10 students in the course. Create a spreadsheet that automatically calculates and displays the overall average and final letter grade for each student. Enter 10 names and sets of grades that fully test the formulas in the spreadsheet. You should enter a name, three hour exam grades, a paper grade, and a final exam grade for each student. Everything else should be calculated automatically.

(b) In deciding the Grade Point Average, an A is worth 4 points, a B is worth 3 points, a C is worth 2 points, a D is worth 1 point, and an F is worth 0 points. An A- is worth 3.666 points and a B- is worth 2.666 points. Add formulas to your spreadsheet so that the course Grade Point Average is calculated and displayed. For example, the average grade of the 10 students in the course might be 2.8.

(c) To further encourage students to work hard on their papers, the professor has decided that whoever receives the highest grade on the paper will receive at least an A- in the course whatever the student's grades on the exams. Modify your spreadsheet so that the student who receives the highest grade on the paper automatically receives at least an A-.

11-10 Form 1040EZ is the simplest Internal Revenue Service form for filing your income taxes. The form is intended for people who are single with no dependents and who had taxable income of less than $50,000 including taxable interest income of $400 or less. Obtain a copy of the form from your bank, post office, or library.

For this exercise you are to replicate this form as a spreadsheet in Lotus 1-2-3. In calculating the tax owed use the equivalent Schedule X (rather than the tax tables they give):

Taxable Income	Tax Owed
$0–$19,450	15%
$19,450–$47,050	$2,917.50 + 28% of the amount over $19,450
$47,050– $97,620	$10,645.50 + 33% of the amount over $47,050

11-11 The administration and faculty at New Ivy University have thought long and hard about their admission criteria. They have decided to forget about activities, athletics, parents who graduated from NIU, interviews, recommendations, and so on in deciding which high school students should be admitted. NIU is going to decide admission strictly on academics. Only standardized test scores and grades will count.

Applicants will not have to write essays. All they will have to submit are five numbers: three test scores (Math SAT score, Verbal SAT score, and an Achievement test score), rank in graduating class, and number of students in graduating class. SAT and Achievement test scores always range from 200 to 800.

The following criteria are used in deciding admissions:

1. If an impossible number is submitted, the applicant is refused admission.
2. If any test score is 800, the applicant is accepted.
3. If any of the test scores is below 300, the applicant is refused admission.
4. If the two SAT scores average above 600 and the applicant is in the top quarter of the graduating class, the applicant is accepted.
5. If any two of the test scores are below 400 or the applicant is in the bottom quarter of the graduating class, the applicant is refused admission.
6. Otherwise, the applicant is put on the waiting list.

These criteria are applied in order. Thus, any impossible number disqualifies an applicant. If the five numbers are valid, then any test score of 800 means acceptance, regardless of the other numbers. If the first two criteria do not hold, then check the third criterion. And so on.

For this exercise you are to create a spreadsheet to decide whether an applicant is admitted. Your spreadsheet should be designed to accept the information for a single applicant. Thus a visiting high school senior could enter the information into your spreadsheet and find out the admission decision. In your spreadsheet you should have a different cell for each criterion. Then you should combine all six criteria into a final decision.

Try your spreadsheet on each of the following 11 applicants:

Student	Math SAT	Verbal SAT	Achievement	Rank	Class Size
A	520	480	450	103	298
B	643	121	800	3	137
C	256	302	800	492	506
D	593	602	720	352	440
E	598	800	740	193	160
F	650	680	240	53	800
G	598	702	550	120	410
H	310	520	390	42	77
I	430	290	453	10	240
J	470	510	423	- 15	137
K	602	723	934	210	982

DATES AND TIMES

The calendar we use was developed 2000 years ago by Julius Caesar and improved slightly by Pope Gregory XIII in 1582. We are so used to the system of 12 months per year and 28, 29, 30, or 31 days per month and leap days almost every fourth year that we don't think twice about it. Still, it is difficult to perform calculations in the calendar system. How many days is it until Christmas? A payment was due on November 27. When will the payment be 60 days overdue? How many days have you been alive? (Not surprisingly, the calculations are difficult in the same way that doing arithmetic with Roman numerals is difficult.)

Similarly, we are used to the division of the day into 24 hours (usually expressed as 12 hours AM and 12 hours PM), the hour into 60 minutes, and the minute into 60 seconds. But calculations using this time notation system are awkward too. How many minutes are there between 9:38 AM and 3:32 PM? A movie that is 2 hours and 27 minutes long begins at 8:46 PM. When will the movie end? How many seconds are there in a day?

The capabilities provided in Lotus 1-2-3 greatly simplify date and time calculations. The secret lies in the use of serial numbers to represent dates and times.

SERIAL NUMBERS

In Lotus 1-2-3 each day between January 1, 1900 and December 31, 2099 is assigned a sequential serial number. January 1, 1900 is serial number 1. January 2, 1900 is serial number 2. February 1, 1900 is serial number 32. January 1, 1901 is serial number 367. June 19, 1992 is serial number 33774. December 31, 2099 is serial number 73050. And so on.

Time of day is represented by a fraction of a serial number. The serial number 33774.5 is noon on June 19, 1992. The serial number 33774.75 is 6:00 PM on June 19, 1992. The serial number 33774.6650694444 is 3:57:42 PM on June 19, 1992. Strictly speaking, the serial number 33774 is actually 12:00 AM (midnight) at the beginning of June 19, 1992.

Can you see how serial numbers make date and time calculations easier? To determine the number of days between two dates, just subtract one serial number from the other.

AN ERROR IN LOTUS 1-2-3

As you may have noticed, the developers of Lotus 1-2-3 made a minor error in assigning serial numbers. The serial number 60 is assigned to February 29, 1900. But that day never existed! There was no leap day in 1900, as 1900 was not a leap year. Years ending in 00 are not leap years unless they are divisible by 400. Thus, all dates after February 29, 1900 are assigned serial numbers one greater than they should be. If you think about it, this error is only rarely consequential. Calculations of the length of time between a date in January or February 1900 and a date in March 1900 or later are off by a day. All other calculations are unaffected. Still, in such a well-designed program, any known error is worth noting, if only for some future trivia question.

DATE FUNCTIONS FOR CONVERTING TO SERIAL NUMBERS

How can we calculate how many days there are between September 23, 1992 and January 14, 1993? The short answer is to subtract their serial numbers. But how can we determine the serial numbers for those dates? Two built-in functions are provided for converting from dates to serial numbers.

The **@DATE** function has three arguments: a year, a month number, and a day of the month. The result of evaluating the date function is the corresponding serial number. Thus the formula @DATE(93,1,14) calculates the serial number for January 14, 1993, which is 33983. The year 1993 must be written as 93. The year 2054 would be written as 154. Thus the following formula calculates the number of days between September 23, 1992 and January 14, 1993

$$@DATE(93,1,14)-@DATE(92,9,23)$$

Entering this formula into a cell in Lotus 1-2-3 yields an answer of 113.

The **@DATEVALUE** function converts a date written as a character string or label to its corresponding serial number. For example, the formula @DATEVALUE("14-Jan-93") evaluates to 33983, the serial number for January 14, 1993. Another formula for calculating the number of days between September 23, 1992 and January 14, 1993 would be

$$@DATEVALUE(``14\text{-}Jan\text{-}93")-@DATEVALUE(``23\text{-}Sep\text{-}92")$$

The argument for the @DATEVALUE function must be a character string and so the date must be enclosed in quotation marks. The date can be written in any of the five date formats discussed below: "14-Jan-93" or "01/14/93" or "14-Jan" or "Jan-93" or "01/14". If the date in the argument of a @DATEVALUE function is written in some other manner the function will evaluate to ERR. In the formats where the year is left out, the current year is assumed. In the format where the day of the month is left out, the first day of the month is assumed. Either the date can be written explicitly as the argument in the @DATEVALUE function call or the date can be written as a label in a cell and the address of the cell can appear as the argument to the @DATEVALUE function call. That is, if C7 contains the label '14-Jan-93, then D11 could contain the formula @DATEVALUE(C7).

THE @NOW FUNCTION AND THE SYSTEM CLOCK

The **@NOW** built-in function evaluates to the serial number for the date and time right now according to the system clock. Every computer has a system clock that keeps track of the current date and time. Some computers have system clocks with batteries that keep track of the date and time even when the computer is shut off. On computers without battery-powered system clocks, you are asked to enter the date and time each time you start up the computer. The @NOW function reads the current date and time from the system clock and converts it into a serial number.

Warning! If you are asked for the date and time when you start up the computer, be sure to enter the date and time correctly. If you skip over the questions or answer incorrectly, @NOW will give the wrong serial number.

The @NOW function yields a new value every time the formulas in the spreadsheet are recalculated. The @NOW function has no arguments and is written without the parentheses.

How many days have you been alive? Suppose your birthdate is July 4, 1971. The following formula will calculate your age in days

$$@NOW-@DATEVALUE(``4\text{-}Jul\text{-}71")$$

Furthermore, the computer will keep updating the answer whenever any cell in the spreadsheet is changed and formulas are recalculated.

THE @INT FUNCTION

The @NOW function gives the serial number for right now. Unless it is exactly midnight, there will be a fractional part to the serial number that corresponds to the fraction of the day that has passed. Thus the formula given will evaluate to 7211.4423, or whatever. Suppose we would like the answer to be a whole number. We would like the answer to be 7211 rather than 7211.4423. The @INT function in Lotus 1-2-3 calculates the integer portion of a number. Thus, @INT(32.4) is 32. The @INT function truncates rather than rounds, so @INT(32.87) also is 32. The result of @INT(@NOW) is today's serial number without the fractional part. So to calculate the number of whole days that someone born on July 4, 1971 has lived we could use the formula

$$@INT(@NOW)-@DATEVALUE(\text{``4-Jul-71''})$$

The @INT function is not a date function but a general numerical function that often is used with date functions.

USING / SYSTEM TO RESET THE SYSTEM CLOCK

The @NOW function obtains the current date and time from the system clock of the computer. What if the system clock is not set to the proper date and time? It is possible to reset the system clock by temporarily entering the Disk Operating System (DOS), resetting the date and time, and then returning to Lotus 1-2-3. Let's go through the process step by step. First, save your spreadsheet, just to be safe. Next, select / System. The / System command instructs the computer to place you temporarily in DOS while Lotus 1-2-3 and your spreadsheet are preserved. In DOS you will receive the current DOS prompt of C> or A> or whatever. To change the date, type DATE Enter and then the new date in the form 11/26/93 Enter . To change the time, type TIME Enter and then the new time in the form 15:43 Enter. While in DOS through the / System command you can issue most other DOS commands, too, if you wish. For example, you could create a new directory or format a new disk. To return back to Lotus 1-2-3 and your current spreadsheet type EXIT Enter.

DATE FORMATS

Suppose we would like to date stamp our spreadsheet so that the current date always occurs in, say, cell B3 in the spreadsheet. That way, all our printouts of the spreadsheet would be date stamped, too. We could put @NOW in B3. So far, so good, but what is displayed in cell B3 is a number like 33071.59, the serial number for the current date and time. Serial numbers are fine for the computer, but they are difficult for people to translate. We would like the computer to display a serial number in a cell as a date that we can understand.

Lotus 1-2-3 provides the capability of formatting numbers as dates. One of the options in the / Range Format menu (and / Worksheet Global Format menu) is Date. Selecting / Range

Format Date yields the submenu in Figure 12-1. There are five different date formats, known as D1, D2, D3, D4, and D5. Two of these date formats, D1 and D4, are **long date formats**. A long date format displays the month, day, and year. The other three formats are **short date formats**, which display either the day and month or the month and year. The five formats are illustrated in the spreadsheet in Figure 12-2. To display a long date format the cell must be widened to at least 10 characters.

The important point to remember about a cell formatted as a date is that the cell contains a number. Cell D7 in Figure 12-2 appears as 17-Jul-90, but it really contains the number 33071.59 displayed in format D1. You can use the cell D7 directly in arithmetic in a formula because the cell contains the number 33071.59. This is where it can get confusing. Another cell could contain the label "17-Jul-90. The two cells would appear the same in the spreadsheet. Cell D7 contains a number and can be used directly in a calculation. The other cell contains a label and would have to be transformed into a serial number by the @DATEVALUE function before it could be used in a calculation.

The date formats only work for numbers between 1 and 73050. These numbers correspond to the dates January 1, 1900 and December 31, 2099. If you try to format a number that is less than 0 or greater than or equal to 73051 in a date format the cell will display as all asterisks, whatever its width. Date formats ignore the fractional part of a number in a cell. The date format for 33576.847 is the same as the date format for 33576.

Different countries and different cultures use different formats for writing dates. It is possible to change D4 (the "Long International Date Format") and D5 (the "Short International Date Format") using the / Worksheet Global Default Other International Date command.

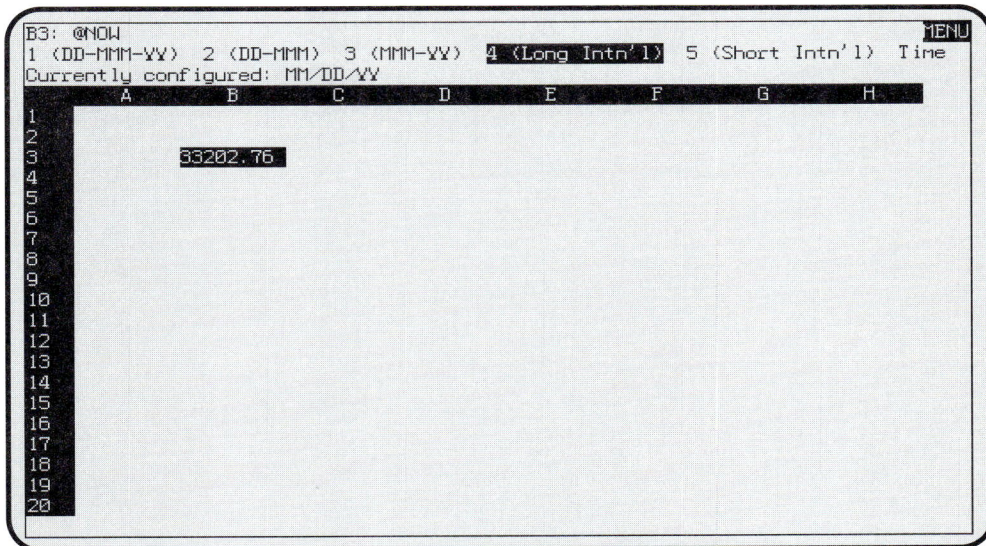

FIGURE 12-1 The / Range Format Date menu shows the five date formats.

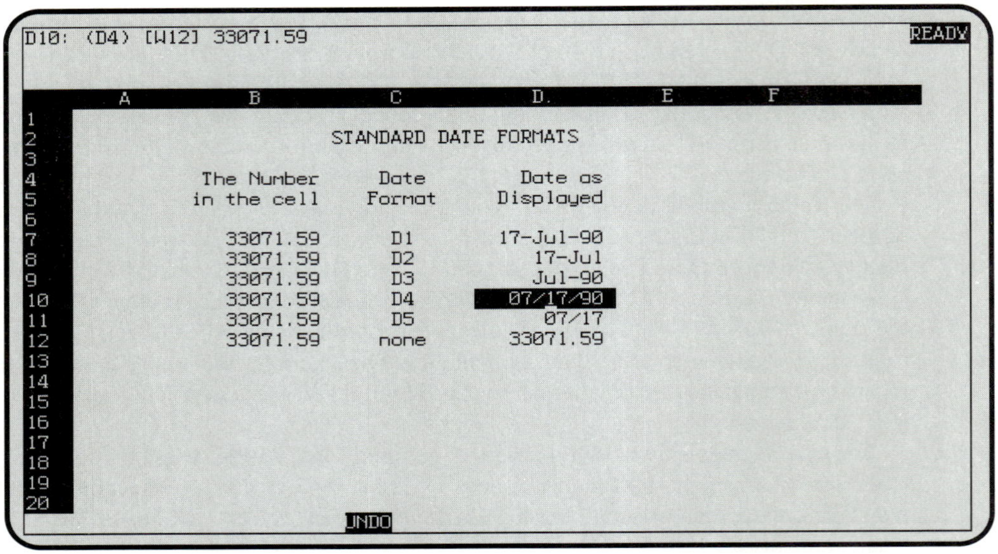

```
D10:  (D4) [W12] 33071.59                                    READY

        A         B          C            D.        E      F
1
2                      STANDARD DATE FORMATS
3
4                  The Number    Date      Date as
5                  in the cell   Format    Displayed
6
7                     33071.59    D1      17-Jul-90
8                     33071.59    D2         17-Jul
9                     33071.59    D3         Jul-90
10                    33071.59    D4       07/17/90
11                    33071.59    D5         07/17
12                    33071.59    none     33071.59
13
14
15
16
17
18
19
20
                            UNDO
```

FIGURE 12-2 The five standard date formats illustrated in a spreadsheet.

DATE FUNCTIONS FOR CONVERTING FROM SERIAL NUMBERS

There are three date functions that convert a serial number into the corresponding year, month, and day of the month.

The **@YEAR** function converts a serial number into the corresponding year. For example, @YEAR(33996.847) is 93 because the serial number falls in 1993.

The **@MONTH** function converts a serial number into the corresponding month of the year. For example, @MONTH(33996.847) is 1 because the serial number falls in January.

The **@DAY** function converts a serial number into the corresponding day of month. For example, @DAY(33996.847) is 27 because the serial number falls in January 27, 1993.

If the argument to any of these three functions is not a valid serial number, that is, if the argument is less than 0 or greater than or equal to 73051, then the function will evaluate to ERR.

EXAMPLE: HOW MANY DAYS UNTIL JULY 1?

Our organization uses a July 1 budget year. Budgets begin and end at midnight (at the beginning) of July 1. We would like to be able to calculate how many days are left before our current budget expires. If the current budget year ends on July 1, 1992, we could write the formula

@DATE(92,7,1)-@NOW

The only problem is that each year we would have to adjust the first argument in the @DATE function. How could we write the formula so it always automatically works whatever the current year? As a first try, we could substitute the current calendar year for the 92 in the formula given, as follows.

$$@DATE(@YEAR(@NOW),7,1)-@NOW$$

(@YEAR(@NOW) evaluates to the current calendar year, to 93 if this is 1993. The formula works if the current month is January through June, if we are in the same calendar year as the budget end. However, if this were October then the formula would be incorrect. If the month were July through December the formula would evaluate to a negative number because @DATE(@YEAR(@NOW),7,1) would yield the serial number of July 1 in the current calendar year, of the previous July 1 rather than the next July 1. To solve this problem, we could use an @IF function where the condition is *True* if today's month is before July and *False* if today's month is July or after.

$$@IF(@MONTH(@NOW)<7,(@DATE(@YEAR(@NOW),7,1)-@NOW),$$
$$(@DATE(@YEAR(@NOW)+1,7,1)-@NOW))$$

If the month is before July the computer calculates the serial number of July 1 of this year minus today's serial number. Otherwise, if the month is July or after, the computer calculates the serial number of July 1 of next year minus today's serial number.

HOURS, MINUTES, AND SECONDS

Serial numbers represent days. The fractions of a serial number represent fractions of a day. For example, 0.5 represents 12 hours. An hour is 0.0416666667, which is 1/24. A minute is 0.0006944444, which is 1/(24*60). A second is 0.0000115741, which is 1/(24*60*60) of a day.

The same types of built-in functions and display formats are provided for times as are provided for dates.

TIME FORMATS

There are four formats for displaying times in Lotus 1-2-3. The time formats are reached through the /Range Format Date menu (or, much more rarely, the /Worksheet Global Format Date menu). The time format menu that results from specifying /Range Format Date Time is shown in Figure 12-3. There are four time formats, known as T1, T2, T3, and T4, as shown in Figure 12-4. The first two time formats use AM and PM. The latter two time formats are known as "International" time formats and use 24-hour clocks. Formats T1 and T3 are "long" formats that display hour, minutes, and seconds. Formats T2 and T4 are "short" formats that display only hours and minutes. To display format T1, the cell must be widened to at least 12 characters.

```
B3: @NOW                                                                 MENU
1 (HH:MM:SS AM/PM)  2 (HH:MM AM/PM)  3 (Long Intn'l)  4 (Short Intn'l)
Currently configured: HH:MM:SS (24 hour)
          A        B        C        D        E        F        G        H
 1
 2
 3              33202.76
 4
 5
 6
 7
 8
 9
10
11
12
13
14
15
16
17
18
19
20
```

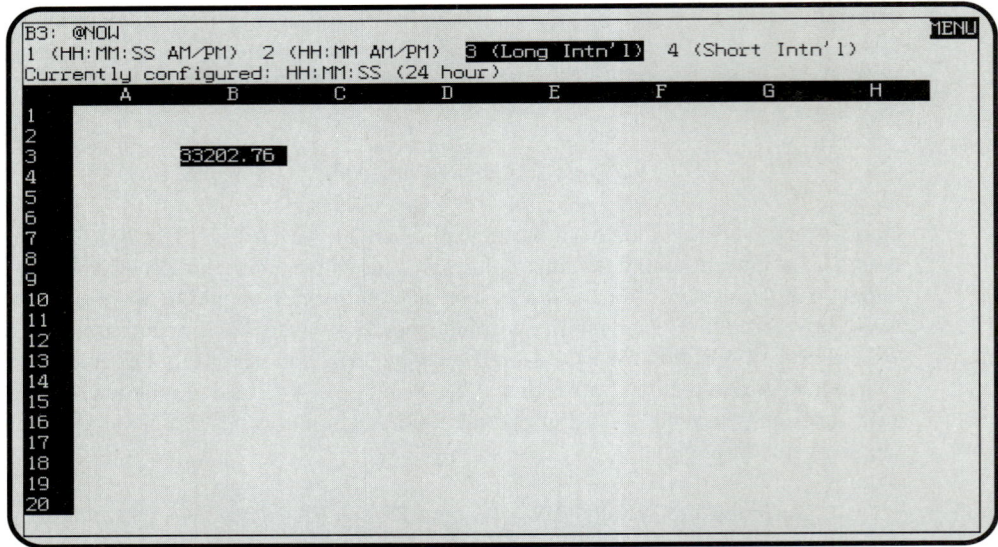

FIGURE 12-3 The / Range Format Date Time menu shows the four time formats.

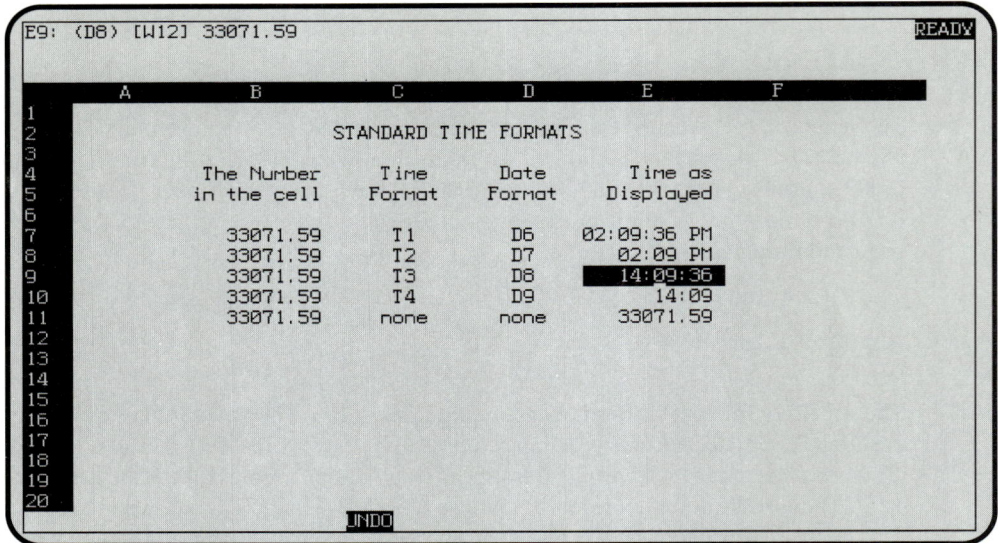

```
E9: (D8) [W12] 33071.59                                                  READY

          A        B        C        D        E        F
 1
 2                     STANDARD TIME FORMATS
 3
 4               The Number    Time     Date      Time as
 5               in the cell   Format   Format    Displayed
 6
 7                33071.59      T1       D6      02:09:36 PM
 8                33071.59      T2       D7         02:09 PM
 9                33071.59      T3       D8         14:09:36
10                33071.59      T4       D9            14:09
11                33071.59     none     none       33071.59
12
13
14
15
16
17
18
19
20                          UNDO
```

FIGURE 12-4 The four standard time formats illustrated in a spreadsheet. These are also known as formats D6, D7, D8, and D9.

When a cell is displayed in a time format, the digits to the left of the decimal point in the number in the cell are ignored. Only the fractional part of the number is used to determine what is displayed. Thus a cell with the number 65.59 would appear the same as a cell with the number 42051.59 if the cells have the same time format.

We would like to both time stamp and date stamp our spreadsheet. We would like the current time to appear in B2 and the current date to appear in B3. We put @NOW in both B2 and B3. The column is widened to 10 characters by putting the cursor in column B and selecting / Worksheet Column Set-Width 10 enter. We format cell B2 to show the hour and minute and AM or PM by selecting / Range Format Date Time 2 B2 enter. We format cell B3 to show the current day, month name, and year by selecting / Range Format Date 1 B3 enter. Now the current time and date will appear in B2 and B3. These cells will be updated every time the formulas in the spreadsheet are recalculated.

The "International" formats T3 and T4 normally have colons separating the hours, minutes, and seconds. It is possible to command Lotus 1-2-3 to use periods or commas as separators in formats T3 and T4 through the / Worksheet Global Default Other International Time command. This command also allows you to establish the interesting format of using the letters "h," "m," and "s" as separators, as in 14h09m36s for T3 and 14h09m for T4.

TIME FUNCTIONS FOR CONVERTING TO SERIAL NUMBERS

There are two functions for converting times to their equivalent serial numbers.

The **@TIME** function has three arguments—the hour based on a 24 hour clock, the minute, and the second. The result of evaluating the @TIME function is the equivalent serial number. For example, @TIME(19,12,0) evaluates to 0.8.

The movie began at 8:46 PM. The movie is 2 hours and 27 minutes long. When will the movie be over? The formula for determining the answer is

$$@TIME(20,46,0)+@TIME(2,27,0)$$

The answer that appears in the cell is 0.9673611111. Formatting the cell as T1 we find out that the movie is over at 11:13:00 PM.

The **@TIMEVALUE** function converts a time written as a character string or label to its corresponding serial number. For example, we also could have found out when the movie ended with the formula

$$@TIMEVALUE("08:46 PM")+@TIMEVALUE("02:27")$$

The time in the argument of the @TIMEVALUE function must be written in the exact style of one of the four current Time formats or the function will evaluate to ERR. In the formula given, the argument "08:46 PM" in the first function call is in format T2. The argument "02:27" for the second function call is in format T4.

EXAMPLE: RIDING THE ROLLER COASTER

John loves riding on roller coasters. His lifetime dream is to set the world endurance record for riding a roller coaster and have his achievement be recorded in the *Guinness Book of World Records*. Now John has his chance. The local amusement park is excited about supporting John for the publicity his great accomplishment will bring. According to the book, the current record is 503 hours set in Montreal, Canada, in 1983. John would like to ride for 510 straight hours, just to be safe. If he begins on June 15 at 10:30 AM when would he be finished?

To determine the date and time when John would finish, we set up the spreadsheet in Figure 12-5. In cell D5 we put the label '15-Jun. In cell D6 we put the label '10:30 AM. In cell D8 we put the number 510.

In cells D11 and D12 we want to put the formulas for calculating the serial number of the time and date when John will be finished riding the roller coaster. Serial numbers represent days. This serial number can be calculated by adding the starting serial number to the number of days he will be riding. The serial number for the moment John will start riding can be calculated by

$$@DATEVALUE(D5)+@TIMEVALUE(D6)$$

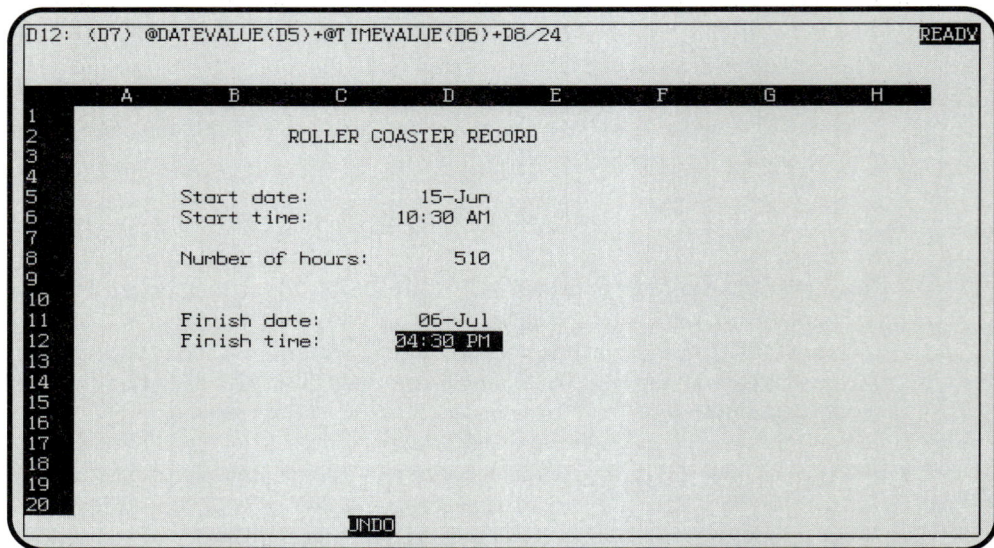

```
D12: (D7) @DATEVALUE(D5)+@TIMEVALUE(D6)+D8/24                        READY

         A       B         C         D         E        F        G        H
  1
  2                        ROLLER COASTER RECORD
  3
  4
  5              Start date:            15-Jun
  6              Start time:            10:30 AM
  7
  8              Number of hours:         510
  9
 10
 11              Finish date:           06-Jul
 12              Finish time:           04:30 PM
 13
 14
 15
 16
 17
 18
 19
 20
                               UNDO
```

FIGURE 12-5 John is going for the World's Record for longest consecutive roller coaster ride. If he begins at 10:30 AM on June 15 and rides for 510 hours, when will John be finished?

Since we have left off the year in D5, Lotus 1-2-3 will assume the current year. The number of days John will be riding the roller coaster can be calculated by

$$+D8/24$$

Hence the serial number for the moment when he will complete his ride can be calculated by

$$@DATEVALUE(D5)+@TIMEVALUE(D6)+D8/24$$

This formula is placed in both D11 and D12, but the cells are formatted in different ways. We format cell D11 as date type D2. We format cell D12 as time type T2 (which is the same as date type D7). The first cell tells us that the date when John will be finished is 06-Jul. The second cell tells us that he will be finished at 04:30 PM. Bon voyage.

TIME FUNCTIONS FOR CONVERTING FROM SERIAL NUMBERS

There are three time functions that convert a serial number into the corresponding hour, minutes, and seconds.

The **@HOUR** function converts a serial number into the corresponding hour of the day. For example, @HOUR(33996.847) is 20 because the serial number falls between 8 PM and 9 PM.

The **@MINUTE** function converts a serial number into the corresponding minute of the hour. For example, @MINUTE(33996.847) is 19 because the serial number falls between 8:19 PM and 8:20 PM.

The **@SECOND** function converts a serial number into the corresponding second of the minute. For example, @SECOND(33576.847) is 41 because the serial number corresponds to 8:19:41 PM on January, 27, 1993.

DISPLAY OF THE TIME AND DATE BELOW THE SPREADSHEET ON THE SCREEN

In Lotus 1-2-3 Release 2.2 the current date and time normally are displayed on the bottom left of the screen, below the spreadsheet. These readings are taken from the system clock and are the same as those used for @NOW. The format of this display can be changed to the current "International" date and time format through the / Worksheet Global Default Other Clock command. The same command can be used to eliminate the clock display altogether, as has been done in the screens displayed in this book, or, more interestingly, to display the name of the current file. That is, you can display the name of the most recently retrieved or saved file in the bottom left of the screen instead of the current date or time.

PENCIL AND PAPER EXERCISE

12-1 Write down the formula that calculates each of the following quantities. Then identify the format in which the cell is to be displayed. You may use the computer to check the formulas. (You do not need to write down the result of evaluating each formula. You just need to write down the formula itself and the format in which the answer will be displayed.) I have answered part (a) just to give you the general idea.

(a) The date which is 90 days after December 23, 1991.
Answer: The formula is @DATEVALUE("23-Dec-91")+90
The format is Date 1

(b) The number of days Franklin D. Roosevelt was president. FDR was inaugurated as president on March 4, 1933. He died in office on April 12, 1945.

(c) The date that is 1000 days from now.

(d) The date that was 1000 hours ago.

(e) The number of days until the year 2000.

(f) The date of serial number 10000.

(g) The serial number for April 3, 2046.

(h) The year for serial number 50000.

(i) The date of the 200th day of 1992.

(j) The number of days you have been alive.

(k) The number of hours between 11:52 AM on 05-Nov-92 and 8:07 AM on 25-Dec-92.

(l) The time 1000 hours from now.

(m) The hours:minutes:seconds between 6:46:32 AM and 10:23:15 PM.

(n) The number of minutes in the 1990s.

(o) The exact time 60% through the day.

(p) The time and date 100,000 minutes after 4:12 PM on November 12, 1992.

COMPUTER EXERCISES

12-2 Use the @NOW function to create the following spreadsheet. Your spreadsheet should work automatically whatever the day.

```
   A        B           C           D        E
1
2
3
4  Today is     21-Feb-93
   This is day          52  of the year    1993
   There are          313  days remaining in the year
```

12-3 NASA has commissioned you to create a spreadsheet for Mission Control. The design is given here. The time and date of launch should be entered as labels in D6 and E6. (Type the time and date of launch in the format shown, but begin each entry with a quote or apostrophe.) The spreadsheet should display the current time and date using @NOW. The elapsed length of the mission so far should be calculated and displayed in two ways: (1) in terms of days in E12 and then hours, minutes, and seconds in G12 and (2) in terms of hours and fractions of hours in E14. To update the display, you will press F9, the Recalculation key.

```
     A        B        C        D        E        F        G
1
2                OFFICIAL MISSION CLOCK
3
4  =================================================================
5
6      Mission Launch:     19:34:10   04-Jul-92
7
8      Current Time:       16:12:36   21-Feb-93
9
10 =================================================================
11
12 Current Mission Length:                    232 days 20:38:26
13
14 Current Mission Length in Hours:     5,564.64
15
16 =================================================================
17
```

12-4 The local department store has hired you to create a well-labeled spreadsheet that displays in four cells the number of days, hours, minutes, and seconds from now until Christmas.

12-5 Create a spreadsheet that allows you to enter in any date as a label and then in separate cells gives the date 30, 60, 90, and 120 days from the entered date.

12-6 At the local medical center patients can schedule appointments at 10 minute intervals from 8:30 AM to 4:50 PM. Create a blank daily appointment book. Put a heading at the top. Cell A6 should contain a formula and be formatted so the cell shows 08:30 AM. Put a formula in cell A7 based on A6 so cell A7 shows 08:40 AM. The last entry in column A should show 04:50 PM. Use the copy command. Widen column B for the patient names.

12-7 You have taken a part-time job as manager of the Happy Hamburger Stand. The stand is open from 6 AM to 11 PM. Employees work all different odd schedules. Employees are paid at the rate of $6.00 per hour from the moment they check in to the moment they check out. So, for example, an employee who checked in at 6:00 PM and checked out at 9:15 PM would make $19.50 for the day.

(a) Create a well-labeled spreadsheet that accepts two labels, the check-in time and the check-out time, as inputs. The output should be the amount of money the employee is to be paid for the day. No other inputs are allowed.

(b) The stand is so popular under your management that you decide to stay open until 3 AM. Modify the spreadsheet so that it accepts check-in and check-out times between 6 AM and 3 AM. Still, the only two cells used for input should be the labels for the check-in time and the check-out time.

(c) The stand is doing a booming business at dinner time, but you are having a hard time hiring employees to work then. You decide to pay $8.00 per hour for any time worked between the hours of 5 PM and 8 PM. For example, an employee who checked in at 6:00 PM and checked out at 9:15 PM now would make $23.50 for the day. Modify your spreadsheet accordingly. Your spreadsheet should work for any check-in time and check-out time. You may use extra cells to hold partial results, but clearly label the final answer. Still, the only two inputs should be the labels for the check-in time and the check-out time.

12-8 You have been hired by Club 2000 to design and implement a spreadsheet for the "greeter" at the door to use to determine whether people are old enough to enter. Create a well-labeled spreadsheet that allows the greeter to enter into three cells the numbers of the month, day, and year of the person's birthdate as listed on the person's driver's license. In a separate cell should appear either WELCOME if the person is at least 21 years old or SORRY, YOU ARE UNDERAGE otherwise. Use @NOW and @IF.

12-9 Create a spreadsheet that has as input any date between 1901 and 2099 and as output the day of the week (MONDAY, TUESDAY, etc.) of the date. The date should be entered as a label in the form 04-Jul-76. No other inputs are allowed. Hint: Use the @MOD function described in Appendix E. You may use extra cells as you wish.

FINANCIAL FUNCTIONS

Lotus 1-2-3 is often used to help analyze financial problems.

A basic concept in finance is the **time value of money**. The value of money changes over time because of the potential of earning interest on the money. Which is more valuable, $1000 today or $1001 two years from now? The $1000 today is more valuable because with almost no risk you could put the $1000 in the bank, earn interest, and have over $1100 two years from now.

Furthermore, if you leave the money in the bank, then the interest compounds. During the second year you earn interest not just on the amount you deposited in the bank but also on the interest that you earned the first year. Suppose you decide to start saving for a down payment for a house. You open a bank account that pays 8% per year. Every year you put $2500 into the account. How much money will you have in four years? How long will it be before you have $20,000?

Suppose you have $10,000 that you would like to invest for four years. The bank will guarantee you 8% interest per year. Your cousin has this great idea for starting a business. If you invest the $10,000 with her, she promises to pay you $2000 after one year, $3000 after two years, $4000 after three years, and $5000 at the end of four years. Which investment would pay the higher rate of interest? In making the decision of what to do with your money you may decide to invest in the bank because it is much less risky or you may decide to invest with your cousin because she is family, but at least you ought to be able to figure out how the options compare in terms of the rate of return on your money.

The calculations in financial analyses can be quite complex. A lot of money can be riding on making the correct calculations. To help in this important application area, eight financial functions are provided in Lotus 1-2-3. These functions facilitate many calculations involving the time value of money.

CALCULATING LOAN PAYMENTS USING @PMT

Wouldn't it be nice to drive around town in a bright red Ferrari Testarossa? Here is one advertised in the paper for only $199,000. Not bad. I can scrape up $3000. My buddy just got an auto loan at 12% annual interest. Maybe I could take out a loan and then pay it back over 5 years. I wonder what the monthly payment would be on a $196,000 loan.

When borrowing money for an automobile loan or for the mortgage for a house or condo, the money usually is paid back in equal monthly payments. Part of these payments covers the interest that is owed. Part of the payments goes to pay off the principal. The principal of a loan is the amount of money that was borrowed. After each payment, the amount owed on the principal is decreased, until after the final payment, the loan is paid off. The formula for calculating the fixed monthly payment is built into the @PMT function.

The @PMT function has three arguments: the principal, the periodic interest rate, and the number of periodic payments:

@PMT(principal, interest rate, number of payments)

When using the @PMT function, or any financial function for that matter, the first step is to decide on the period. All figures must be expressed in terms of a common period of time. If the payments are to be made each month, then the period would be a month. This means that the second argument to the @PMT function, the interest rate to be paid, must be stated as the monthly interest rate. The third argument, the term of the loan, would be the number of monthly payments to be made.

How much would the monthly payment be for the Ferrari? The principal, the amount borrowed, would be 196000. As usual in Lotus 1-2-3, the number must be entered without dollar sign and without commas. The interest rate is 12% per year. The monthly interest rate would be 12%/12 or 1%. This could be written in the formula either as 1% or as 0.01. We would make monthly payments for five years, for a total of 60 payments. So the formula for calculating the monthly payment for the Ferrari would be

@PMT(196000, 0.01, 60)

Entering this formula into a cell and formatting the cell as currency with two places yields a monthly loan payment of $4359.11. Taxes, insurance, gas, and tune-ups are extra. You know, I've always wanted an eight-year-old Chevy.

Rather than entering the numbers for the loan directly into the formula, we could put them into separate cells and refer to the cells in the formula, as in the spreadsheet in Figure 13-1. The advantage of this approach, of course, is that to change the specifics for the loan, we would just need to change the numbers in the cells rather than going in and editing the formula. Also, these numbers show on the spreadsheet and in a printout of the spreadsheet. Most lending institutions state the interest rate and the length of the loan in years so the spreadsheet in Figure 13-1 was designed accordingly. The interest rate and length of the loan are converted to monthly figures in the formula. The actual data in the spreadsheet in Figure 13-1 shows the figures for a $200,000 mortgage at 9% per year over 30 years.

The formula in the @PMT function assumes that payments are made at the end of the period, as is usual, rather than at the beginning.

SOLVING COMPOUND INTEREST PROBLEMS WITH @CTERM AND @RATE

Suppose you place $2000 in the bank and receive 8% interest per year. How long will it take until you have $5000? This is the type of problem that @CTERM was designed to solve. The $2000

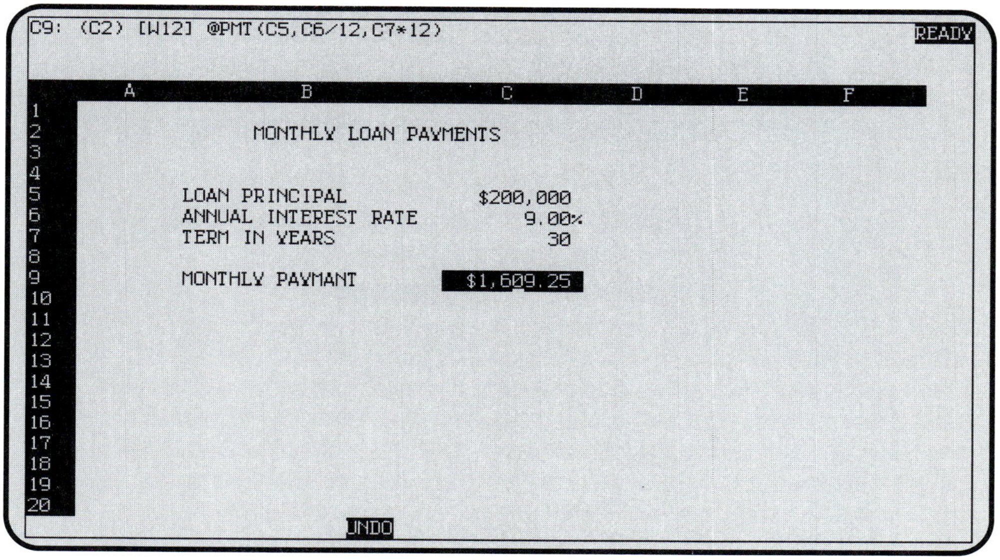

```
C9: (C2) [W12] @PMT(C5,C6/12,C7*12)                              READY

        A            B              C         D      E      F
1
2                  MONTHLY LOAN PAYMENTS
3
4
5            LOAN PRINCIPAL        $200,000
6            ANNUAL INTEREST RATE     9.00%
7            TERM IN YEARS              30
8
9            MONTHLY PAYMANT       $1,609.25
10
11
12
13
14
15
16
17
18
19
20
                           UNDO
```

FIGURE 13-1 A spreadsheet for calculating the monthly payment for a loan. In this case the loan is for $200,000 for 30 years.

initial investment is called the present value. The 8% is the interest rate. The $5000 is the future value of the investment. The @CTERM function calculates the term, the number of periods, required for the initial investment earning the specified interest rate to grow to the future value. The @CTERM function has three arguments,

@CTERM(interest rate, future value, present value)

The arguments must be typed in that order. The spreadsheet in Figure 13-2 shows that to grow a $2000 investment into $5000 at 8% interest per year requires 11.91 years.

The **@RATE** function is used to solve a related type of problem. Suppose we have $2000 and we would like to grow it into $5000 in five years. What interest rate would we need to receive? The @RATE function calculates the interest rate required for an initial investment to grow into a future value in some fixed period of time. The @RATE function has three arguments

@RATE(future value, present value, number of periods)

The spreadsheet in Figure 13-3 shows that to grow a $2000 investment to into $5000 in 5 years we need to earn 20.11% per year.

Both of these functions are designed for isolated investments where the present value will be left for the full number of periods and the interest rate will remain constant. There will be no further payments or withdrawals. The formulas built into the functions are based on the general

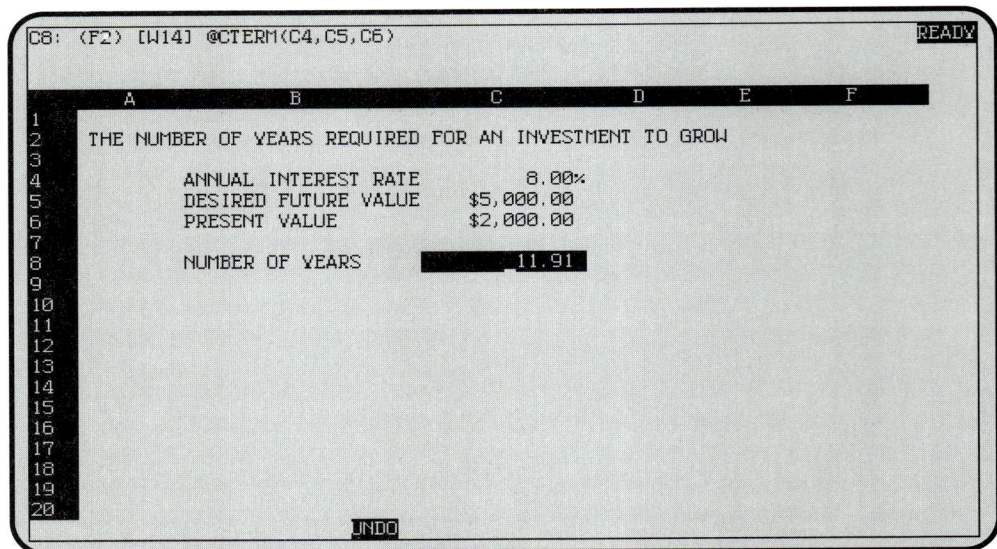

```
C8: (F2) [W14] @CTERM(C4,C5,C6)                                    READY

       A              B              C            D        E        F
1
2     THE NUMBER OF YEARS REQUIRED FOR AN INVESTMENT TO GROW
3
4           ANNUAL INTEREST RATE            8.00%
5           DESIRED FUTURE VALUE      $5,000.00
6           PRESENT VALUE             $2,000.00
7
8           NUMBER OF YEARS                  11.91
9
10
11
12
13
14
15
16
17
18
19
20
                              UNDO
```

FIGURE 13-2 How many years will it take $2000 to grow into $5000 at 8% interest?

compound interest formula for determining the future value (FV) of an investment given the present value (PV), the periodic interest rate (INTEREST), and the term or number of periods (N):

$$FV = PV * (1 + INTEREST) \wedge N$$

In Chapter 7 we calculated what the value of Peter Minuit's investment of $24 would be if he had put the money into a bank account rather than using it to purchase Manhattan island. In these spreadsheets we calculated year by year the growing value of the investment. We could calculate directly the value in 1996 of $24 invested in 1626 at 5% interest using the formula

$$+24*(1+0.05)\wedge370$$

This formula yields the same answer for 1996 as appears in Figure 7-10, namely, $1,660,549,773. Note that there is no built-in function in Lotus 1-2-3 for calculating the future value of an isolated investment. Rather, you must use the formula just given.

We could calculate the annual interest rate needed to grow $24 into 1 trillion in 370 years using the formula

$$@RATE(1000000000000,24,370)$$

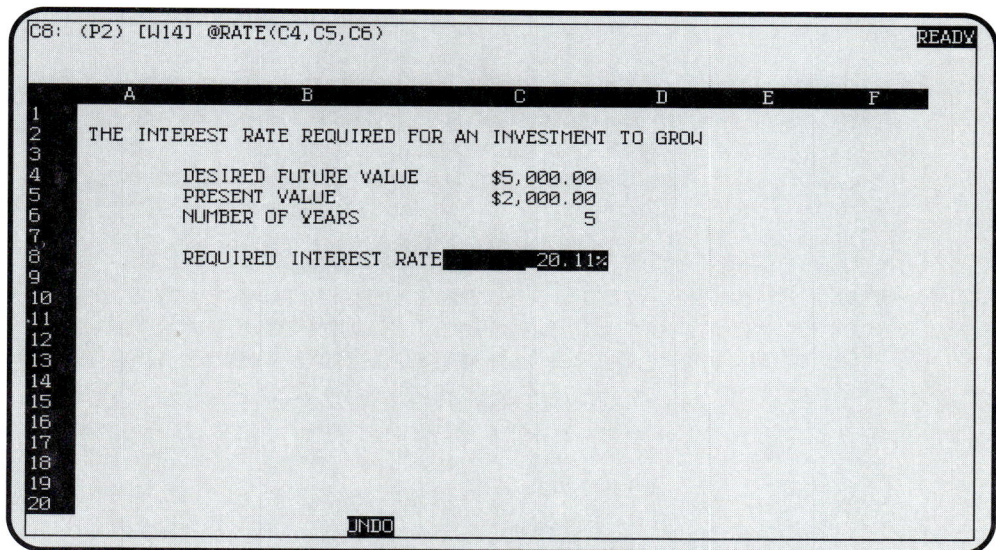

```
C8: (P2) [W14] @RATE(C4,C5,C6)                                    READY

         A              B                C          D      E      F
 1
 2      THE INTEREST RATE REQUIRED FOR AN INVESTMENT TO GROW
 3
 4              DESIRED FUTURE VALUE       $5,000.00
 5              PRESENT VALUE              $2,000.00
 6              NUMBER OF YEARS                    5
 7
 8              REQUIRED INTEREST RATE        20.11%
 9
10
11
12
13
14
15
16
17
18
19
20
                            UNDO
```

FIGURE 13-3 What annual interest rate is requied to grow $2000 into $5000 in 5 years?

Entering this formula into a cell yields the answer of 6.83%, which is in accord with the spreadsheet in Figure 7-11. Alternatively, we could have changed the values in cells C4, C5, and C6 in Figure 13-3.

SOLVING ANNUITY PROBLEMS WITH @FV, @PV, AND @TERM

Every year Mary deposits $2000 into a bank account earning 9% per year. How much will her investment be worth in 20 years? This problem is different than those discussed in the previous section. Here Mary is making a deposit each year. In the previous section the investment was isolated: no deposits or withdrawals were made after the initial investment. An investment where there are fixed periodic payments is called an annuity. In Lotus 1-2-3 there are three built-in functions for solving problems involving annuities.

To solve the problem stated, the future value of depositing $2000 each year for 20 years into an account earning 9% per year, we could use the @FV function. The @FV function calculates the future value of an investment with fixed periodic payments earning a certain interest rate. The @FV function has three arguments:

$$@FV(payment, interest\ rate, number\ of\ periods)$$

Each of the three arguments must be based on the same time period. If Mary is making a deposit every month, then the interest rate must be monthly and the third argument must give

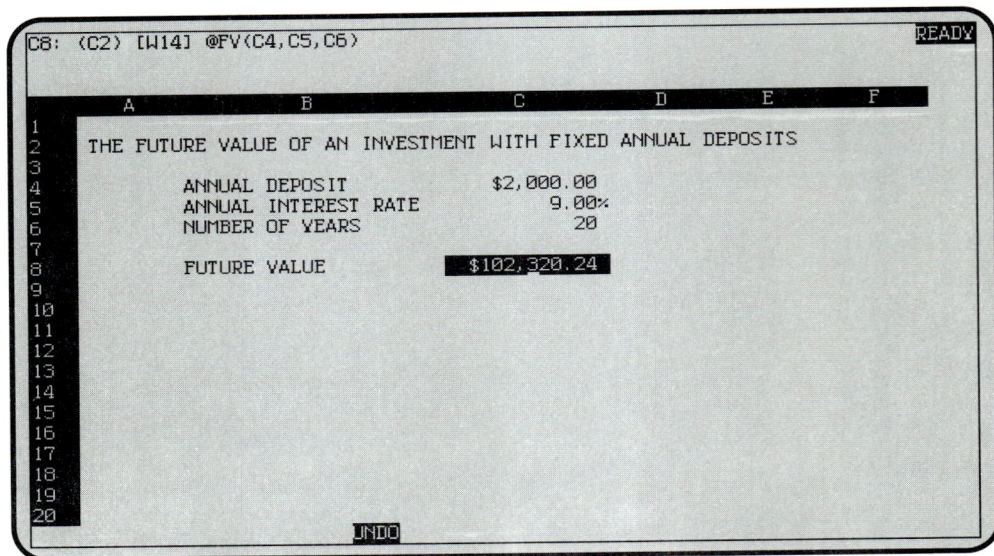

```
C8: (C2) [W14] @FV(C4,C5,C6)                                    READY
          A            B              C          D      E      F
 1
 2   THE FUTURE VALUE OF AN INVESTMENT WITH FIXED ANNUAL DEPOSITS
 3
 4        ANNUAL DEPOSIT              $2,000.00
 5        ANNUAL INTEREST RATE            9.00%
 6        NUMBER OF YEARS                    20
 7
 8        FUTURE VALUE             $102,320.24
 9
10
...
                          UNDO
```

FIGURE 13-4 The future value of depositing $2000 per year for 20 at 9% annual interest.

the number of months for the investment. In the stated problem, the period is a year. A spreadsheet for solving the problem is shown in Figure 13-4. Mary would have a little over $100,000 after 20 years of depositing $2000 per year in an account earning 9%.

Note that in the design of the @FV function and the other two functions in this section, it is assumed that the payments are made at the end of the period rather than at the beginning of the period. Thus in the spreadsheet in Figure 13-4 it is assumed that the deposits are made at the end of each year, in December if the years are calendar years.

Mike is hoping to spend 18 months on a Greek island writing the Great American Novel (and tasting a little ouzo). Mike figures he will need $1000 per month to live. How much money would Mike need to deposit initially in an account paying 9% interest per year to be able to withdraw $1000 per month for 18 months? Intuitively Mike would need slightly less than $18,000 because the funds will earn some interest while they are in the account. The **@PV** function would be used to calculate the exact amount.

The @PV function calculates the "present value" required to be able to fund fixed period payments if the money earns a certain interest rate. The @PV function has three arguments:

@PV(payment, interest rate, number of periods)

The spreadsheet in Figure 13-5 shows how to calculate the initial amount of money Mike would need to fund his writing. Note that the withdrawals will be made every month, so the period for the calculation is a month. The annual interest rate is given so it must be converted

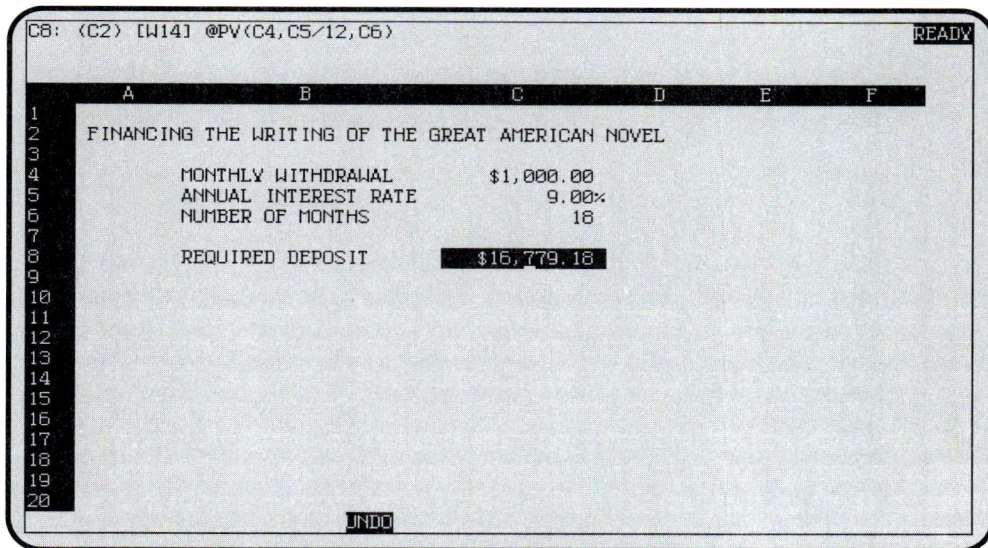

FIGURE 13-5 Mike must start with $16,779.18 to be able to withdraw $1000 per month for 18 months if the money earns interest of 9% per year.

to a monthly interest rate. Mike would need $16,779.18 in the bank to be able to withdraw $1,000 at the end of the month for each of 18 months if the money earns 9% per year.

Suppose Karen would like to save $50,000 to start her own business. If Karen saves $1000 per month and the money earns 10% interest, how long would it be before she has the $50,000? The **@TERM** function calculates the number of periods required to accumulate some future value if one makes fixed payments and the funds earn a certain interest rate each period. The @TERM function has three arguments

@TERM(payment, interest rate, future value)

The spreadsheet in Figure 13-6 shows that 42 months would be required for Karen to accumulate the $50,000 by depositing $1000 per month into an account earning 10% per year. Clearly, of the $50,000 there would be $42,000 from the deposits and $8000 from the accumulated interest.

How does the @TERM function differ from the @CTERM function discussed in the previous section? Use the @TERM function when you are making periodic payments into an account, for an annuity. Use the @CTERM function when you deposit a certain amount of money into an account and just leave it.

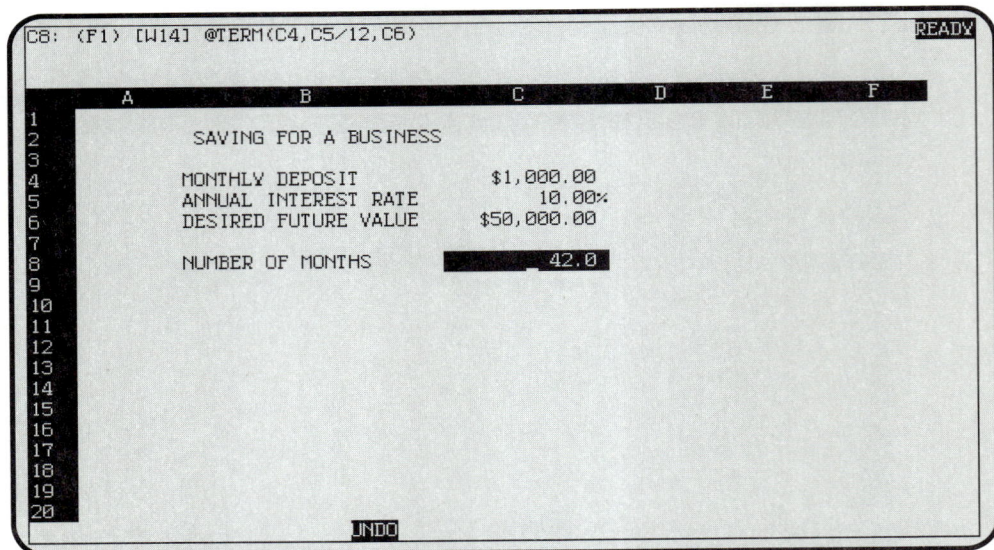

```
C8:  <F1> [W14] @TERM(C4,C5/12,C6)                                    READY

       A          B              C          D       E       F
 1
 2           SAVING FOR A BUSINESS
 3
 4          MONTHLY DEPOSIT         $1,000.00
 5          ANNUAL INTEREST RATE        10.00%
 6          DESIRED FUTURE VALUE   $50,000.00
 7
 8          NUMBER OF MONTHS             42.0
 9
10
11
12
13
14
15
16
17
18
19
20
                            UNDO
```

FIGURE 13-6 How many months does it take to accumulate $50,000 by depositing $1000 each month into an account earning 10% interest per year?

MAKING INVESTMENT DECISIONS USING @IRR AND @NPV

Let's return to the investment decision we posed in the beginning of the chapter. The bank will pay you 8% interest per year if you deposit your $10,000 there for four years. Your cousin says that if you invest the $10,000 in her new business, she promises to pay you $2000 after one year, $3000 after two years, $4000 after three years, and $5000 at the end of four years. Which investment would pay the higher rate of interest? Here we have periodic (annual) payments being made, but the payments are not equal. This is frequently the case in proposed investments in business. Two functions in Lotus 1-2-3 are designed to help analyze situations where there is an arbitrary stream of periodic cash flows.

The **@IRR** function is used to calculate the interest rate returned on an investment involving various positive and negative payments that are made on a regular basis. The @IRR function calculates "internal rate of return."

The use of the @IRR function to calculate the internal rate of return for the investment in your cousin's business is shown in the spreadsheet in Figure 13-7. The cash flows are listed explicitly in column D. Any investments you make, money you pay out, are entered as negative numbers. Any returns on your investment, money you receive, are entered as positive numbers. Using the @IRR function in the spreadsheet we can see that investing in your cousin's business under the terms proposed would result in a rate of return of 12.83%. The bank is paying only 8% so you would receive a higher rate of return from your cousin.

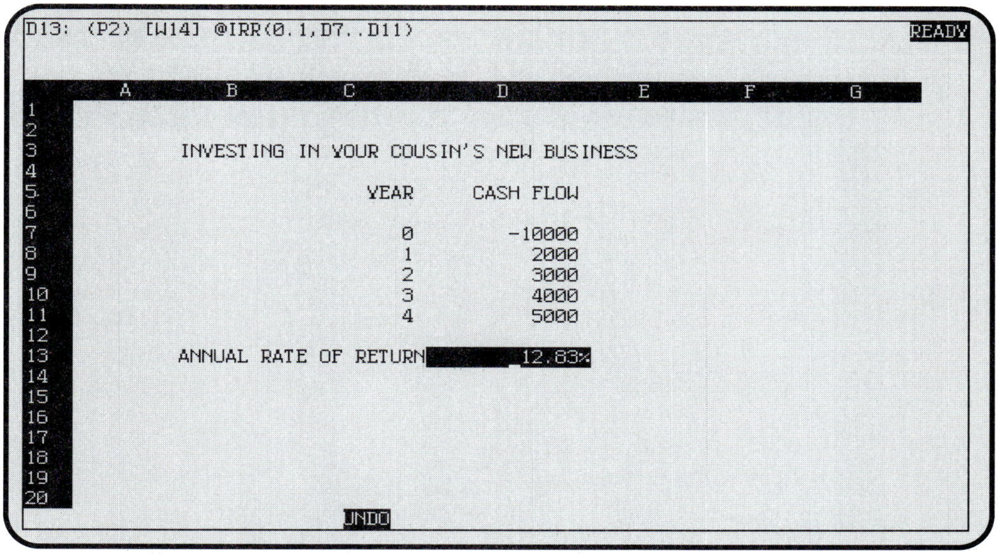

FIGURE 13-7 If you invest $10,000 in your cousin's business now and receive $2000 at the end of the first year, $3000 at the end of the second year, $4000 at the end of the third year, and $5000 at the end of the fourth year then you will be making a 12.83% return on your money.

The @IRR function has two arguments

$$@IRR(guess, cash\ flows)$$

The first argument, the "guess," takes some explaining. The first argument for the @IRR function is a guess as to the correct answer for the rate of return. There is no direct formula for calculating the internal rate of return function. Instead, the rate of return must be calculated iteratively by Lotus 1-2-3, by trial and error. To start the process off, you must supply an initial guess.

In the formula in the spreadsheet the first argument, the initial guess, is 10%. Where did the 10% come from? An initial guess of a return of 10% is a good guess for many real life projects. A guess of 10% also is reasonable given the numbers in the situation. You would be investing $10,000. You would receive $2000 + $3000 + $4000 + $5000, which equals $14,000. For your $10,000 you would receive a profit of $4000 over 4 years. The $4000 represents a total 40% return on your money spread over 4 years, which "averages" out to 10% per year. This 10% is just an approximation as it ignores the fact that you are receiving different amounts each year and that the money received early is more valuable as it can be invested further. At any rate, when you use the @IRR function you must provide an initial guess.

Does the initial guess to the @IRR function matter? Yes. Lotus 1-2-3 can arrive at the wrong rate of return if the initial guess you supply is way off target. This is illustrated in the spreadsheet in Figure 13-8. An initial guess of -50% or -500% results in an erroneous rate of return being calculated for the investment. Lotus 1-2-3 has made a mistake! You need to be careful when using the @IRR function to check the answer given to make sure that it is reasonable.

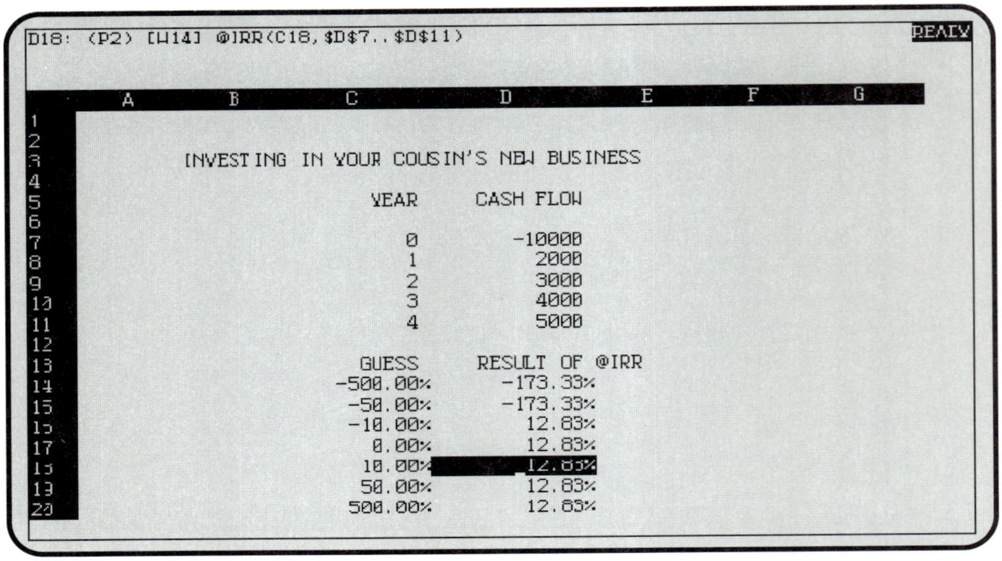

FIGURE 13-8 An inital guess of -50% or -500% yields the wrong answer for the internal rate of return of the investment!

The second argument to the @IRR function is the range of addresses where the series of cash flows is located on the spreadsheet. The cash flows must be in sequential cells, either down a column or across a row. Don't skip any cells between cash flows. Blank cells or cells with labels will count as $0. The period of time from one cash flow to the next must be the same. The resulting rate of return is for that period. That is, if the time between each payment in the cash flows is one year, then the result of evaluating @IRR will be an annual rate of return. If the time between each payment in the cash flows is one month then the result of evaluating @IRR will be a monthly rate of return. Note that in the spreadsheets in Figure 13-7 and Figure 13-8, the year numbers in column C are there just to help make the spreadsheets understandable by people. The numbers in column C are not used by the computer in the @IRR calculations.

The @IRR function assumes that the initial cash flow in the range occurs right now and not at the end of the first period. The initial cash flow usually is negative and represents an initial investment.

Suppose your cousin is so successful in her business and so grateful for your investment that she decides to give you $10,000 back at the end of year 4 instead of $5000. Now what would be the annual rate of return on your investment? To find out we can just change the number in D11 to 10000, as in Figure 13-9. The internal rate of return of the series of cash flows -10000, 2000, 3000, 4000, 10000 is 23.54%. If at the end of the second year you would need to invest another $2000 rather than receiving $3000 then you would change the number in D9 to -2000.

An alternative approach to analyzing an investment in terms of its internal rate of return is to calculate its **net present value**. In a present value calculation you state future cash flows in

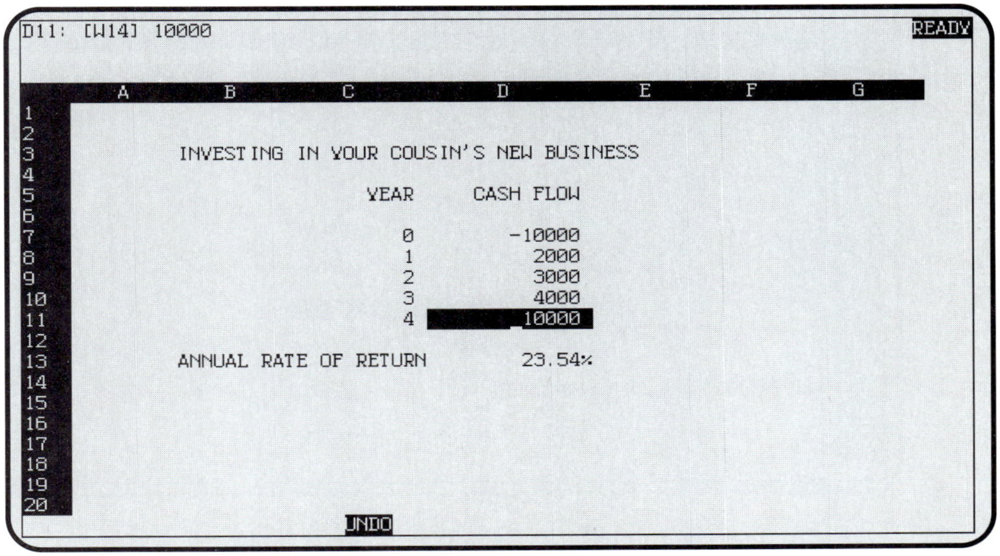

FIGURE 13-9 If your cousin pays you $10,000, then the annual rate of return would be 23.54%

terms of their value in today's dollar. If money earns 10% per year, then $500 today would be worth the same as $550 a year from now. So the present value of $550 a year from now using a discount rate of 10% would be $500. Similarly, the present value of $605 two years from now using a discount rate of 10% would be $500. (1.10 * 500 is 550. 1.10 * 550 is 605.) The net present value of an investment is the total value of each of the cash flows for the investment stated in terms of today's dollars.

When making a present value calculation, you must use a **discount rate**. The discount rate is the rate at which money changes in value each year. Roughly speaking, the discount rate is the interest rate the bank will pay or it is the inflation rate in the economy.

If the net present value of an investment is greater than zero, then it is a good investment relative to the discount rate. If the net present value is less than zero then it is a poor investment relative to the discount rate. Or, alternatively, if you are comparing the merits of two potential investments, you would select the investment with the higher net present value.

A net present value analysis of the investment in your cousin's business is shown in the spreadsheet in Figure 13-10. The net present value of the investment is calculated by finding the present value of the future cash flows and subtracting the $10,000 initial investment.

The **@NPV** function is used to calculate the present value of future cash flows. The @NPV function has two arguments:

$$@NPV(\text{discount rate, cash flows})$$

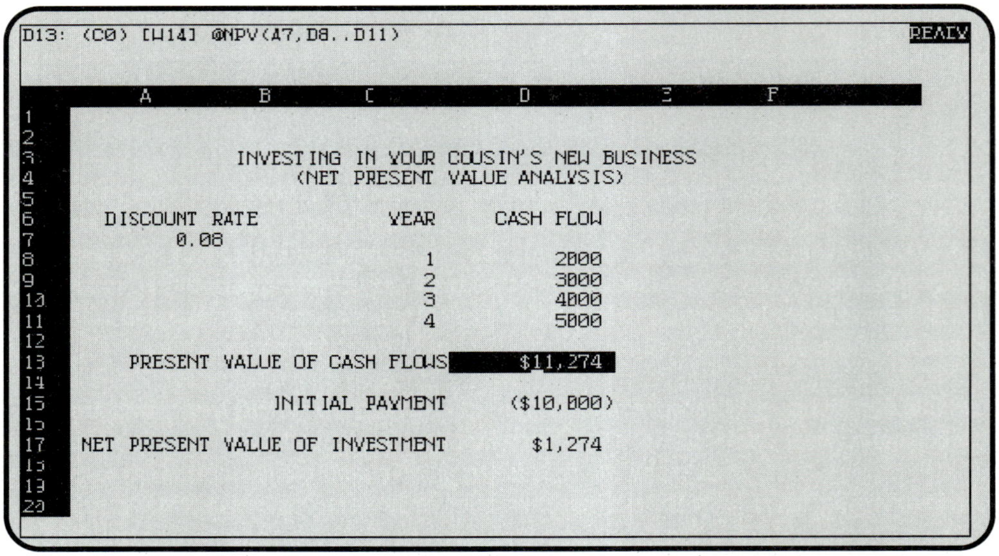

FIGURE 13-10 A net present value analysis of the investment in your cousin's new business shows a positive net present value of $1274 using an 8% discount rate. The investment would make you $1274 in today's dollars.

The first argument is the discount rate, the rate at which money changes value each period. The second argument is the range in the spreadsheet in which the future cash flows are listed. As with the @IRR function, the cash flows must be entered in sequential cells either across a row or down a column.

The @NPV function is similar to the @PV function discussed earlier. However, where the @PV function assumes that the cash flow each period is a constant, the @NPV function allows for different cash flows each period. If each year you would receive $4,000 then you could use the @PV function. If, as is the case in the current example, the cash flows are not the same from year to year, then you must use @NPV to calculate the present value.

In the spreadsheet in Figure 13-10 we used a discount rate of 8% as that is the rate the bank would pay. The net present value for the investment is calculated by taking the present value of the future cash flows and subtracting the initial investment required. In cell D17 we see that the net present value of the investment is $1274. Investing in your cousin's business would be worth $1274 more in today's money than investing the money in the bank at 8% interest.

Unlike the @IRR function the @NPV function assumes that the first of the cash flows occurs at the end of the first period rather than right away. Note that the @NPV function is somewhat misnamed. The @NPV function does *not* calculate the net present value of an investment. Rather the @NPV function calculates the present value of a series of possibly different future cash flows that occur at fixed intervals. The net present value is then calculated by subtracting any initial investment that might be made right now.

The @IRR function and the @NPV function are closely related. The @NPV function is used in the series of calculations made for the @IRR function. Indeed, if we use the internal rate of return of the investment as the discount rate, then the net present value of the investment will be 0.

WINNING THE LOTTERY

We now have covered the eight financial functions available in Lotus 1-2-3. All the functions are designed to facilitate analyses involving the time value of money. These calculations take practice, so let's do one more example.

Many states have initiated state lotteries. Typically you pay $1 to select the numbers you think will be drawn at the end of the week. If you select all the numbers correctly, you win a fortune! But do you? Suppose you have selected your numbers, and the day after the drawing you learn that they have drawn your numbers and you have won $1,000,000! You are the big winner! You head down to the state lottery office to collect your million dollars. But at the office you learn that the lottery commission does not give you the million dollars all at once. Rather, they pay the money to you in 20 equal annual payments. You receive $50,000 now and $50,000 per year at the end of each of the next 19 years.

How much have you really won? Clearly that last $50,000 payment 19 years from now is not going to be worth very much if inflation picks up. Suppose someone offered you $100,000 right now for your ticket (and all the winnings). Would you take it? No, your winnings are worth more than $100,000 even though they are spread out over 20 years. Suppose the person offered you $900,000 right now for your ticket. Yes, $900,000 today is worth more than $1,000,000 paid out in 20 equal annual payments.

```
C12: (C2) [W15] @PV(C10,C7,C6)                                    READY


      A              B                    C           D        E
 1
 2                        WINNING THE LOTTERY
 3
 4             TOTAL AMOUNT YOU WON    $1,000,000.00
 5             IMMEDIATE PAYMENT          $50,000.00
 6       NUMBER OF FUTURE PAYMENTS               19
 7              DISCOUNT RATE                  0.08
 8
 9
10      AMOUNT OF EACH FUTURE PAYMENT     $50,000.00
11
12   PRESENT VALUE OF FUTURE PAYMENTS    $480,179.96
13
14   *****************************************************
15
16      NET PRESENT VALUE OF WINNINGS    $530,179.96
17
18   *****************************************************
19
20
                         UNDO
```

FIGURE 13-11 The net present value of winning $1,000,000 in the lottery paid out in 20 annual payments. The formula in C10 is (C4-C5)/C6. The formula in C16 is +C5+C12.

How can we figure out how much your lottery winnings would be worth in terms of today's money? What we are asking for is the net present value of the winnings. There are two functions that calculate present value—@NPV and @PV. The @NPV function calculates the present value of a series of possibly unequal future cash flows. The @PV function calculates the present value of a series of equal future cash flows. The lottery winnings are paid in equal amounts so @PV is the function to use.

The @PV function calculates the present value of future cash flows. We separate out the payment to be received now and the 19 payments to be received in the future. A spreadsheet for calculating the net present value of winning the lottery is shown in Figure 13-11. The present value of the $50,000 you are receiving now is $50,000. The present value of the 19 future payments of $50,000 each is $480,179.96, assuming an 8% discount rate. So the net present value of winning the lottery is $530,179.96. Another way of looking at the problem is that you would have to deposit $530,179.96 in an account earning 8% per year to be able to withdraw $50,000 today and $50,000 at the end of each of the next 19 years. So if you believe the discount rate to be 8% for the next 19 years, you might want to accept an offer of $550,000 for your winnings and decline an offer of $500,000. Of course, our analysis has not taken into account the income taxes you would have to pay on your winnings.

Look at the situation from the state's point of view. The state can take a million dollars and put it in the bank. If they earn 5% per year, they would make $50,000 per year in interest, which they pay you. At the end of the 20 years the state would still have its $1,000,000 intact.

Understanding the time value of money is critical to being able to analyze many financial situations. The financial functions of Lotus 1-2-3 provide important tools.

PENCIL AND PAPER EXERCISE

13-1 Write down the formula that calculates each of the following quantities. You may use the computer to try your answers. You need only write down the formula. You do not need to calculate the result of evaluating the formula.

(a) the monthly payment on a 30-year mortgage for $4,500,000 at 11% per year

(b) the value of your Rickey Henderson baseball card in 30 years if it is worth $6.50 today and appreciates at 9% per year

(c) the annual rate of increase in the value of Manhattan island, which was purchased for $24 in 1626 and had a total assessed value of $38,928,369,373 in 1989

(d) the value of your retirement account in 50 years if you deposit $2400 each year and receive 9% interest on your money

(e) the value of your retirement account in 50 years if you deposit $200 per month for 50 years and receive 9% interest on your money

(f) the number of years it would take to become a millionaire if you set aside $10,000 each year and accumulated it in investments yielding 15%

(g) The amount of money you would need to accumulate to be able to retire for the rest of your life on $100,000 per year if your money earns 10% per year

COMPUTER EXERCISES

13-2 The Friendly Mortgage Company offers your choice of 10-year, 20-year, and 30-year home mortgages all at the same interest rate. Create a spreadsheet that will allow you to enter the amount of the mortgage and the annual interest rate. For each type of loan the spreadsheet should calculate (a) the monthly payment, (b) the total amount paid back to the mortgage company, and (c) the total amount of interest paid. That is, your spreadsheet should have two cells of input and nine cells of output. Of course, you would expect to pay more interest for the longer-term mortgage as you would have the use of their money longer and the money paid back 30 years from now will be worth much less than the same amount today.

13-3 Your broker suggests that you buy a zero coupon bond ("zero") with a face value of $20,000 maturing in 10 years that sells today for $6237. That is, you pay $6237 today and receive $20,000 10 years from now. You would like to find out the yield—the effective annual interest rate you would receive—on the zero.

(a) Create a spreadsheet for analyzing zeros that allows you to enter the face value, the time to maturity, and the current price. The output should be the yield.

(b) Create a similar spreadsheet that allows you to enter the face value, the actual maturity date, and the current price. The output should be the yield. Use @NOW.

Of course, your spreadsheet should work for any inputs.

13-4 You are presented with a proposal for a project. The bottom line is that it is claimed that if you invest 20 million in a project this year, you will receive 5 million, 18 million, and 12 million over the following three years.

(a) Set up a spreadsheet that will tell you both the net present value of this project assuming a 12% discount rate and the internal rate of return for this project.

(b) You decide that most likely the project will cost 24 million this year and return 4 million, 14 million, and 10 million. Now what would be the net present value and internal rate of return?

13-5 The "Rule of 72" is a very convenient rule of thumb for performing mental calculations on the effect of compound interest. The rule indicates the approximate doubling time for money at a given interest rate or the approximate interest rate required to double your money in a certain period of time.

The Rule of 72 states that to find the time required to double an investment at a given interest rate, divide the interest rate into 72. Equivalently, the Rule of 72 states that to find the interest rate required to double your money in a certain number of years, divide the number of years into 72. For example, the rule states that investments at 6% double in 12 years. Investments at 9% double in 8 years. Investments at 18% double in 4 years.

How is this helpful? What will a $20,000 investment at 14% be worth in 10 years? At 14% the doubling time is approximately 5 years. So in 5 years the investment will double in value to $40,000. In five more years the investment will double again to $80,000. So $80,000 is the approximate answer.

For this exercise you are to check the validity of the Rule of 72. Create a spreadsheet with 3 columns and 72 rows plus column headings and titles. In the first column should be interest rates from 1% through 72%. In the next column should be the actual time for money to double at this interest rate as calculated using the @CTERM function. In the third column should be the amount of time for money to double at this interest rate predicted using the Rule of 72. Is the Rule of 72 reasonably accurate?

13-6 You are considering purchasing a new car. The price would be $14,239. You would pay $2000 now and the rest monthly in a four-year loan. The automobile dealership is offering a sales promotion where either (a) you will receive a $1000 rebate check right now and the annual interest rate on the loan will be 11.9% or (b) the annual interest rate on the loan will be 2.9% but there is no rebate. Create a spreadsheet to compare the two options by calculating the present value of each of the options, assuming an 8% discount rate. Which is the better deal? Write a paragraph to justify your answer.

13-7 You have been asked to analyze the proposed Skopi Project. Initial investment in the project would be $10M ($10,000,000), which would be spent on planning, design, and construction. This phase would take three years. It is proposed that in year 0, $1M be spent; in year 1, $3M be spent; in year 2, $6M be spent.

Revenues would be generated beginning in year 3, as follows:

Year	Revenues
3	$1M
4	$3M
5–13	$6M
14	$3M

At year 14, the project would be scrapped. In year 15, the project would return $2M in the scrap value of the equipment.

Expenses would be as follows. Annual operating expenses for years 3 through 14 are figured at $1.25M for raw materials, $1M for maintenance and repairs, $0.5M for labor, and $0.25M for other expenses.

(a) Develop a spreadsheet that figures out the internal rate of return of this project. You should have a separate input area with separate cells for each of the assumptions. You should have columns for *each* of the years from 0 through 15. You should have separate rows for each of the revenue and expense items and for the total revenues and total expenses. The bottom row should be annual cash flow. You should have a separate well-labeled cell for the rate of return. Sketch the spreadsheet on paper before entering it into the computer. Have your spreadsheet figure the internal rate of return using the assumptions given.

(b) Draw a graph in Lotus 1-2-3 that shows the projected revenues, expenses, and cash flow over the life of the project. Print the graph.

(c) Next try some sensitivity analysis. Print each of the results. Suppose revenues for years 5 through 13 are only $4M. What would be the internal rate of return? Suppose construction costs are $10M in year 2? Suppose labor costs are double those expected?

(d) Put together a professional report on your analysis of the project. The company expects at least a 14% rate of return on its money. What is your recommendation on this project? Include appropriate printouts from the spreadsheet and appropriate graphs. To what parameters is the rate of return most susceptible?

13-8 You have been assigned the task of comparing two sources of energy for a proposed manufacturing plant.

(a) Build a spreadsheet that determines the more economical of the two choices by comparing the present value of the expenses associated with each choice. A basic design for the spreadsheet and some projected data are given below. You may fill in whatever intermediate calculations you wish, but be sure to label these cells clearly. The bottom row of the spreadsheet should use an @IF function to indicate whether Electricity or Fuel Oil is a more economical choice.

```
          COMPARISON OF ENERGY SOURCES

                      Electricity        Fuel Oil

Unit Cost           $0.160 per kwh    $1.45 per gallon
Setup Cost            $15,000           $25,000
Annual Consumption   700,000 kwh       75,000 gallons
Annual Maintenance    $3,000            $2,000
Number of Years          8                 8
Discount Rate          0.12              0.12


(Intermediate Calculations)...          ...


Present Value


More Economical Energy Source:
```

(b) There is some uncertainty in the prices that can be negotiated in a long-term supply contract for the energy sources. Listed below are three possible scenarios. For each scenario, have your spreadsheet determine which choice would be more economical. To do this, you should be able to just change the values in the appropriate cells at the top of your spreadsheet. All other calculations should then be done automatically by the computer.

THREE UNIT COST SCENARIOS

Scenario	Electricity	Fuel Oil
1 (original)	$0.160 per kwh	$1.45 per gallon
2	$0.195 per kwh	$1.75 per gallon
3	$0.125 per kwh	$1.15 per gallon

(c) Write a brief but professional report giving your recommendation on the energy source to select. Include appropriate printouts from your spreadsheet.

13-9 A loan amortization table shows the effect of each payment on the amount of principal still owed. A spreadsheet for constructing loan amortization tables for 48 month loans is shown below. The spreadsheet has two input cells: (1) the principal of the loan (the original amount borrowed) and (2) the annual interest rate. All other numbers in the spreadsheet are calculated. Changing either or both of these input numbers will create a new amortization table.

Note that in the table, the amount of interest owed each month is the monthly interest rate times the amount of the principal still owed at the beginning of the month. The amount of the payment that goes to reducing the principal is the amount of the payment that is left over. If all of the calculations are correct then the principal owed at the end of the 48th month should be 0.

(a) Duplicate the accompanying spreadsheet. Try it on the loan indicated and then on a $53,000 loan at 12% and on a $4,000 loan at 2.9%.

```
A1: [W6]                                                            READY

         A          B           C          D          E          F
1
2          LOAN AMORTIZATION TABLE FOR 48 MONTH LOANS
3
4                        PRINCIPAL:              $16,353.00
5                        ANNUAL INTEREST RATE:        9.90%
6
7          RESULTING MONTHLY INTEREST RATE:           0.825%
8          RESULTING MONTHLY PAYMENT:             $413.97
9
10         PRINCIPAL                                        PRINCIPAL
11            AT         MONTHLY    INTEREST   PRINCIPAL       AT
12 MONTH    BEGINNING    PAYMENT    PAYMENT    PAYMENT    END OF PERIOD
13   1     $16,353.00    $413.97    $134.91    $279.06    $16,073.94
14   2     $16,073.94    $413.97    $132.61    $281.36    $15,792.58
15   3     $15,792.58    $413.97    $130.29    $283.68    $15,508.90
16   4     $15,508.90    $413.97    $127.95    $286.02    $15,222.88
         A          B           C          D          E          F
58   46     $1,221.70    $413.97     $10.08    $403.89     $817.80
59   47       $817.80    $413.97      $6.75    $407.22     $410.58
60   48       $410.58    $413.97      $3.39    $410.58     ($0.00)
```

(b) Construct a similar spreadsheet for 36 month loans. Try the spreadsheet on the same three sets of data.

(c) Construct a spreadsheet that produces an amortization table for any term loan of from 1 to 5 years (60 monthly payments). The spreadsheet should have three input cells: the principal of the loan, the annual interest rate, and the number of years for the loan. This is a bit tricky. While you might have 60 rows of formulas, the table should only appear to have one row for each month of payment. All rows below the final payment should appear blank.

13-10 Mary and John have been married for three years. They both work and their salaries total $65,000 per year. They are currently paying $1200 per month rent plus utilities. Between savings and wedding gifts they have managed to accumulate $36,000, which they have in a money market account.

Mary and John are thinking about buying a house. They have done some looking and after much dispute have settled on a suburban house that costs about $150,000. Annual real estate taxes would be about $2,300. They are asking the age-old questions: Can we afford it? Will we be better off financially 10 years from now if we buy the house instead of continuing to rent?

Your task is to design and implement a spreadsheet that will analyze the financial implication over the next 10 years of buying versus renting.

The issue of home ownership is a complicated one in this society. You can make some assumptions:

1. Assume a fixed rate mortgage of 80% with 20% down. Find out the prevailing mortgage rate by checking in the local newspaper or by calling a bank. John and Mary would use the $36,000 for the down payment, closing costs, and moving expenses.

2. Assume that everything (house values, rents, real estate taxes) goes up with inflation. Have a separate cell for the inflation rate.

Of course, if they buy, Mary and John would no longer receive the interest they receive now from the $36,000 in the money market account.

A very important aspect of home ownership in the United States is the income tax advantage. If Mary and John own their own home, then real estate taxes and the interest (but not the principal) they pay on their mortgage are deductible for income tax purposes. You will need to find out what income tax bracket Mary and John are in, assuming no other dependents, and so on.

From a financial point of view would Mary and John be better off buying a house or continuing to rent? Write a brief report justifying your answer. Include appropriate printouts of the spreadsheet.

CHAPTER 14

@Rand and Simulation

One way of dealing with the complexities of the world is to build a model to simulate a situation or environment. The model then can be tested and manipulated, and these results can be used to predict what will happen in the world. An airplane company wants to know how a proposed new plane will fly, so it builds a model and places the model in a wind tunnel and runs tests. Or it creates a computer program that allows engineers to specify the plane on the screen and then mathematically simulate the plane flying under different conditions.

Of course, the effectiveness of using a model to predict what really will happen depends on how well the relevant aspects of the situation are captured in the model. One certainly can imagine an airplane whose design worked great on the computer but that crashes when it is first flown. There is a saying in the computer field, "Garbage In, Garbage Out," or "GIGO." If you put nonsense into the computer, you will get nonsense out. Don't believe everything that comes out of the computer. Just because "the computer says" something doesn't mean it is right.

People have attempted to create computer models for all kinds of situations. There are computer models of the weather. Enter in the temperature, wind velocity, and so on at many different locations on the earth. The computer predicts what the weather will be like tomorrow or next week. There are computer models of the economy. Suppose we raise the income tax rate. What will be the effect on the economy a year from now or five years from now?

We have seen how Lotus 1-2-3 can be used as a tool for simulation. "What if" analysis is computer simulation. To predict the profitability of a new enterprise, create a Lotus 1-2-3 spreadsheet to model the projected finances and try it out under different scenarios.

Some situations are best modeled probabilistically. One third of the time this will happen; two thirds of the time something else will happen. These situations can be modeled on the computer with the use of "random numbers." Simulations that make use of random numbers often are called **Monte Carlo simulations**. Monte Carlo is a city on the Mediterranean Sea that is the site of a well-known gambling casino.

In this chapter we will discuss random numbers in Lotus 1-2-3 and their use in simulations.

THE @RAND FUNCTION

Random numbers are generated in Lotus 1-2-3 using the @RAND function. The @RAND function has no arguments. The value of the @RAND function is a number between 0 and 1

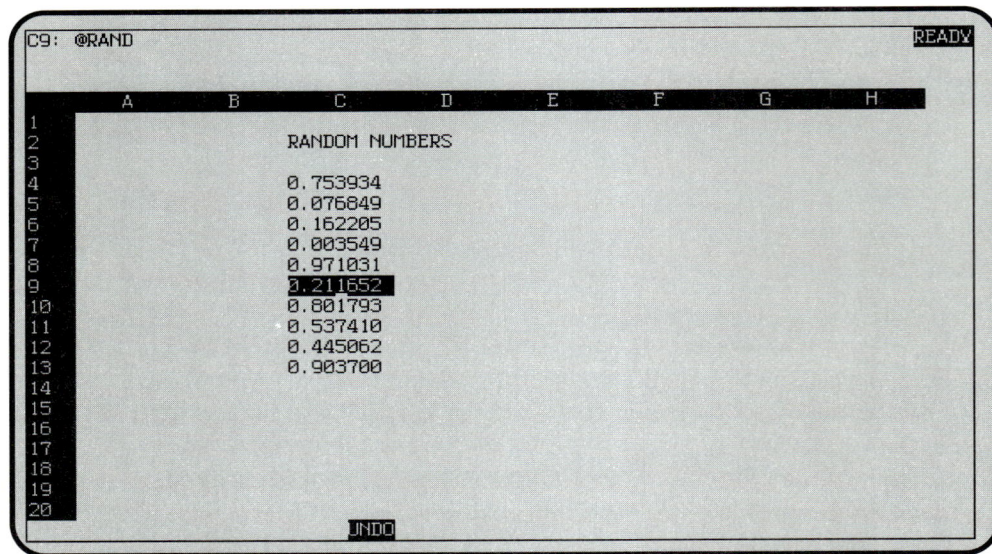

FIGURE 14-1 Ten random numbers. Each time the spreadsheet is recalculated the numbers change.

(but not including 1). The user cannot predict what this number will be. An example of a spreadsheet with ten random numbers is shown in Figure 14-1.

The value of each call to the @RAND function is calculated out to 15 digits to the right of the decimal point. Only six decimal places of each number are displayed in each random number in Figure 14-1 because of the column width. To see the full numbers, we would widen the column to 18 characters and display the number in Fixed format with 15 decimal places.

The @RAND function is a strange beast. Each time the spreadsheet is recalculated, the value of each @RAND changes! Hence, when using the @RAND function, it usually is a good idea to switch over to manual recalculation (/ Worksheet Global Recalculation Manual) as described in Chapter 8. That way the value of each @RAND function will stay until you order the spreadsheet recalculated by pressing the Calc key, F9.

FLIPPING COINS

Suppose we want to simulate flipping a coin in Lotus 1-2-3. Each time we recalculate the spreadsheet (by pressing F9), the computer flips the coin again. The computer will say HEADS or TAILS, but we won't know ahead of time which it will be. We would like HEADS and TAILS each to occur 50% of the time.

To accomplish this, we will use random numbers generated by the @RAND function. We would like half the possible numbers produced by @RAND to be HEADS and the other half of the numbers to be TAILS. Thus, we check the random number against 0.5. If the random number is less than 0.5, we call the result HEADS. Otherwise, we call the result TAILS. The formula is

@IF(@RAND<0.5,"HEADS","TAILS")

The spreadsheet is shown in Figure 14-2. Each time we press F9 a new random number between 0 and 1 is produced by @RAND, and hence a new coin is flipped with equal likelihood of a HEADS or a TAILS. We have no way of knowing ahead of time whether the computer will say HEADS or TAILS.

Suppose that we would like to rig the spreadsheet so that 70% of the time the flip comes out HEADS and only 30% of the time the flip comes out TAILS. We could change the formula, as follows:

@IF(@RAND<0.7,"HEADS","TAILS")

Now 70% of the random numbers (all the numbers between 0 and 0.7) will result in HEADS and only 30% of the random numbers (all the numbers from 0.7 to 1) will result in TAILS.

Suppose we would like three possible outcomes. We would like HEADS 49% of the time, TAILS 48% of the time, and 3% of the time we would like the outcome to be COIN ROLLS AWAY.

The first step is to divide up the numbers between 0 to 1 into three segments that correspond to the desired outcomes. We assign the numbers from 0 to 0.49 to correspond to HEADS. (This

```
C6:  @IF(@RAND<0.5,"HEADS","TAILS")                              READY
        A       B       C       D       E       F       G       H
1
2
3
4              The coin is in the air and it's ...
5
6                      TAILS
7
8
9
10
11
12
13
14
15
16
17
18
19
20
                              UNDO
```

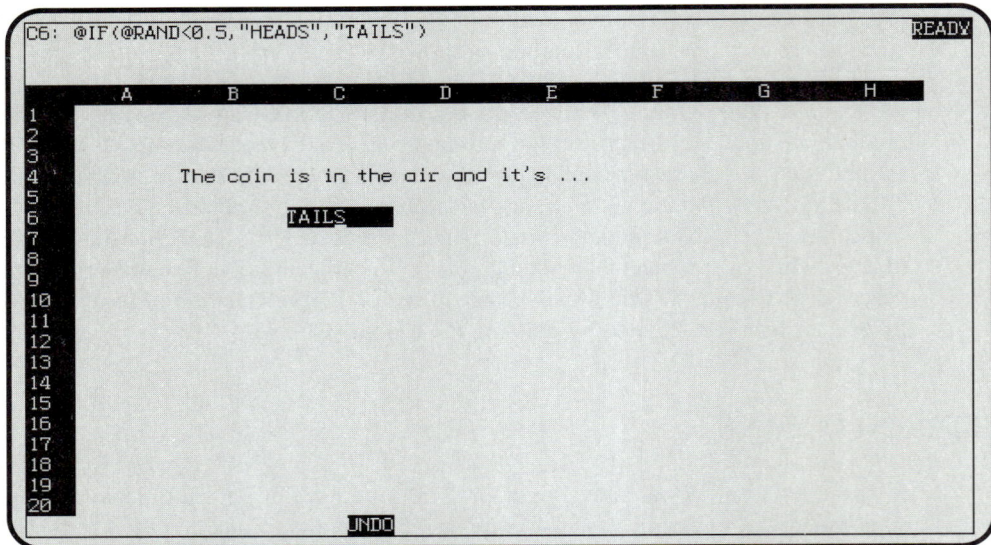

FIGURE 14-2 Flipping a coin.

is 49% of the numbers.) The numbers from 0.49 through 0.97 will correspond to TAILS. (This is 48% of the numbers.) The numbers between 0.97 and 1 correspond to COIN ROLLS AWAY. (This is 3% of the numbers.) This is illustrated in Figure 14-3.

To implement this in the spreadsheet we might first think of writing a formula like @IF(@RAND<0.49,"HEADS",@IF(@RAND<0.97,"TAILS","COIN ROLLS AWAY")). This formula is the right idea, but it has a subtle error. The problem is that each time the @RAND function is called, it returns a different value. Thus the two calls to @RAND in the above formula will return different random numbers and the desired probabilities will not be obeyed.

The remedy is to place the call to @RAND in a different cell, for example, B14, and then refer to that cell in the formula, as in

@IF(B14<0.49,"HEADS",@IF(B14<0.97,"TAILS","COIN ROLLS AWAY"))

This solution is shown in Figure 14-4. Now the same random number is used in both places in the formula. To flip another coin, press F9 to recalculate the spreadsheet. This generates another random number in B14 and another result in C6. If you would like, the actual random number can be placed in a cell off the screen or can be formatted as Hidden so it does not show.

An alternative to using the nested @IF function is to use a lookup table. Lookup tables have the advantage of showing the cutoff points for the random numbers explicitly in the spreadsheet. An equivalent spreadsheet for flipping coins that uses a lookup table is shown in Figure 14-5. To determine the outcome of the coin flip in B6, the random number in B14 is looked up in the table in F13..G15.

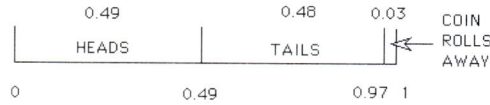

FIGURE 14-3 Dividing up the number line from 0 to 1 so that 49% of the numbers correspond to HEADS, 48% of the numbers correspond to TAILS, and 3% of the numbers correspond to COIN ROLLS AWAY.

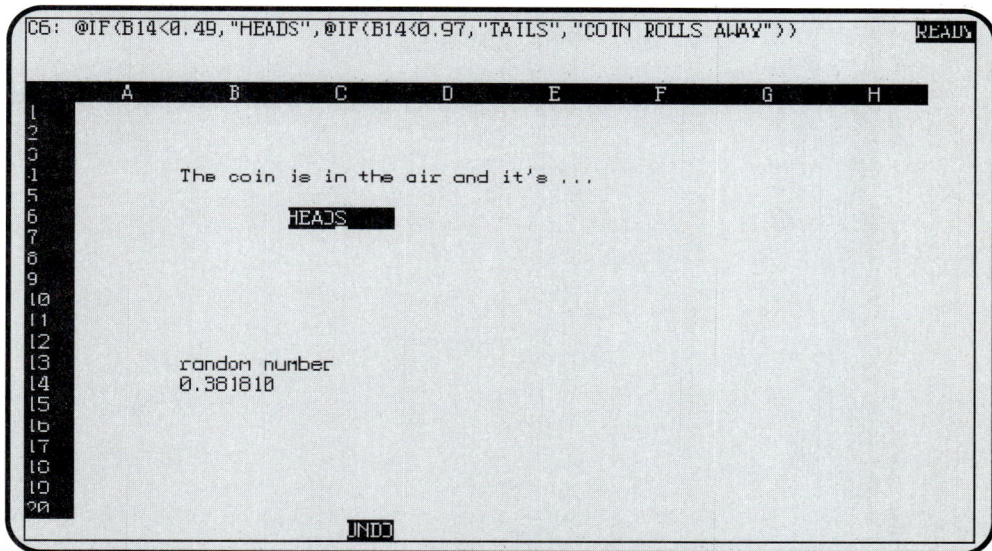

FIGURE 14-4 Flipping a coin with three possible outcomes.

```
C6:  @VLOOKUP(B14,F13..G15,1)                                    READY

           A       B       C       D       E       F       G       H
  1
  2
  3
  4              The coin is in the air and it's ...
  5
  6                    TAILS
  7
  8
  9
 10
 11                                                    lookup table
 12
 13              random number                         0.00 HEADS
 14              0.715027                               0.49 TAILS
 15                                                     0.97 COIN ROLLS AWAY
 16
 17
 18
 19
 20
                              UNDO
```

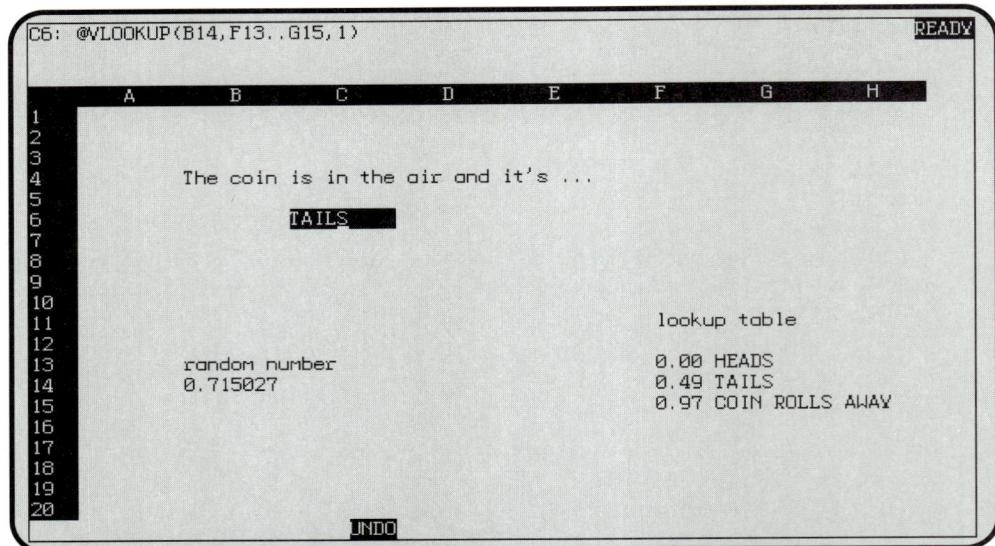

FIGURE 14-5 Flipping a coin with three possible outcomes using a lookup table rather than a nested @IF function.

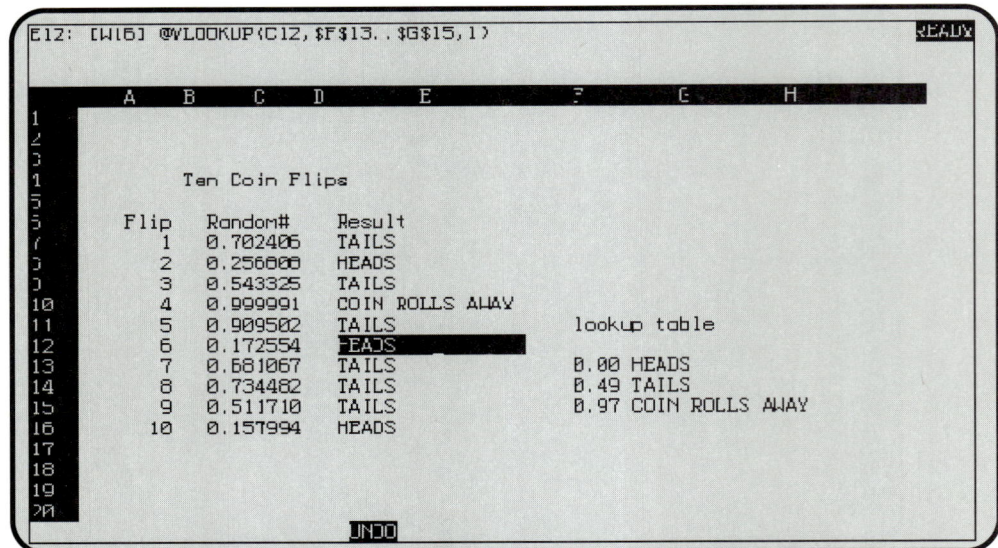

```
E12:  [W16] @VLOOKUP(C12,$F$13..$G$15,1)                         READY

           A    B    C    D       E            F       G       H
  1
  2
  3
  4         Ten Coin Flips
  5
  6     Flip    Random#    Result
  7       1    0.702406    TAILS
  8       2    0.256800    HEADS
  9       3    0.543325    TAILS
 10       4    0.999991    COIN ROLLS AWAY
 11       5    0.909502    TAILS                 lookup table
 12       6    0.172554    HEADS
 13       7    0.681067    TAILS               0.00 HEADS
 14       8    0.734482    TAILS               0.49 TAILS
 15       9    0.511710    TAILS               0.97 COIN ROLLS AWAY
 16      10    0.157994    HEADS
 17
 18
 19
 20
                              UNDO
```

FIGURE 14-6 Ten coin flips.

Now we would like 10 coin flips to appear in one spreadsheet. The spreadsheet in Figure 14-6 simulates 10 coin flips. Here we create a new random number for each coin flip. Each cell in column C contains the formula @RAND. The formulas in the cells in column E look up the corresponding random number in the lookup table. Absolute addressing is used when referring to the lookup table so that the addresses do not change when the formula is copied down column E. Each time we press the recalculation key F9, 10 more coin flips are simulated.

QUEUING PROBLEMS

A common application for Monte Carlo simulation is in queuing problems. A **queue** is a waiting line. People form a queue waiting for a bus, waiting to cash a check in a bank, or waiting to pay for their groceries in a supermarket. In particular, a queue is a line where the first people to arrive in the line are the first to be served. That is, a queue is what people think of as a "fair" waiting line. (A **stack** is a line where the first to arrive are the last to be served. This occurs, for example, if people are lined up for the bus and the bus stops so that the door opens at the end of the line. The last on line would be the first on the bus.) In some situations there is one large master queue (for example, in most banks). In some situations there are multiple queues (for example, in most supermarkets).

People have studied queuing problems for years. How many tollbooths should be built at the entrance to the bridge? If too few are built, the traffic will back up too far. Widening the highway for tollbooths is expensive. If too many tollbooths are built, money will be spent unnecessarily. How many checkout registers should be built in the supermarket? At a busy intersection, for how long should the green light be on in each direction during each cycle? How should tasks be divided up on an assembly line? All these are problems involving queues.

One approach to solving queuing problems is to model the process on the computer. Once the basic model is set up, we can change some of the assumptions and see what the results would be in the model. We can do "What if" analysis with queuing models just as we can with financial models. Of course, the usefulness of the results depends on the fidelity with which the relevant portions of the world have been captured in the model.

SANTA CLAUS'S AFTERNOON

It is late November and you are working as an intern in a local department store. The rival department store across town has set up Santa Claus in a big chair in their store and has invited parents to bring their children in to meet him. Their promotion seems to be working well. Your store manager has asked you to do the same in your store. To make the idea even more attractive to parents, you plan to hire a photographer to take instant photographs of the children sitting on Santa's lap.

You have limited space in the store. The department next to the area where Santa will sit is Fine Jewelry, and the manager of the department does not want a long line of screaming kids winding through the department. You decide to try a quick computer simulation to see how long the line is likely to become.

Santa Claus will be in the store from 2 PM to 5 PM each afternoon. You figure that with each kid sitting down, pulling Santa's beard, saying he or she has been good, telling Santa what he or she wants for Christmas, and having the photographer take a picture, Santa can serve a child in 30 seconds, or two per minute. How many children will arrive each minute? You decide to visit the rival department store with your watch and a pad and to use their arrivals as an estimate for your store. After observing for a while, you decide that in 10% of the minutes no children arrive, in 20% of the minutes 1 child arrives, in 30% of the minutes 2 children arrive, in 30% of the minutes 3 children arrive, and in 10% of the minutes 4 children arrive.

Now we need to translate this into a spreadsheet model. Each row in the model will correspond to a different minute with Santa. We will draw a new random number each minute and use the random number to determine the number of children who arrive using the above distribution. For simplicity, we will assume that all children arrive right at the beginning of each minute. The number of children who see Santa each minute will depend on the number of people still waiting from the previous minute and the number of arrivals. If no children are there, then Santa has the minute off. If there is only one child there then Santa will see the one child. If there are two or more children, then Santa will see two children that minute and any remaining children will wait on line.

The spreadsheet for the simulation is shown in Figure 14-7 and Figure 14-8.

In column A the times are listed from 2:00 PM through 4:59 PM using serial numbers for the times. The formula in A8 is

$$@TIMEVALUE(\text{``2:00 PM''})$$

This formula calculates the serial number for 2:00 PM. The formula in cell A9 adds a minute to the preceding cell, as follows:

$$+A8+1/(24*60)$$

Remember that serial numbers correspond to days and that a minute is 1/(24*60) of a day. This formula is then copied down from A9 to A10..A187 so that the formula in each cell calculates the serial number for the next minute. The cells in A8..A187 are formatted in Time format 2 (HH:MM AM/PM).

Column B is blank and the width is set to three characters. Column C contains the random numbers for calculating the number of arrivals. Each cell in C8..C187 contains the formula

$$@RAND$$

The number of children who arrive at the beginning of each minute is calculated in column D using the lookup table in H9..I13. The lookup table is set up so that there is a 10% chance that no children arrive, a 30% chance that 1 child arrives, a 30% chance that 2 children arrive, a 20% chance that 3 children arrive, and a 10% chance that 4 children arrive. This is illustrated in Figure 14-9. The formula in D8 is

$$@VLOOKUP(C8,\$H\$9..\$I\$13,1)$$

I15: READY

```
            A      B         C         D        E        F      G      H       I
1
2
3               SANTA CLAUS' AFTERNOON
4
5      TIME       RANDOM#   ARRIVALS   SERVED   QUEUE
6                                                                    NUMBER OF
7   start                                         0                  ARRIVALS
8   02:00 PM   0.179098      1          1        0                   PER MINUTE
9   02:01 PM   0.948214      4          2        2      0.00      0
10  02:02 PM   0.454014      2          2        2      0.10      1
11  02:03 PM   0.264295      1          2        1      0.40      2
12  02:04 PM   0.781264      3          2        2      0.70      3
13  02:05 PM   0.073536      0          2        0      0.90      4
14  02:06 PM   0.660229      2          2        0
15  02:07 PM   0.239501      1          1        0
16  02:08 PM   0.604205      2          2        0
17  02:09 PM   0.785791      3          2        1
18  02:10 PM   0.103763      1          2        0
19  02:11 PM   0.624251      2          2        0
20  02:12 PM   0.393336      1          1        0
```

FIGURE 14-7 The beginning of an afternoon for Santa Claus.

I191: READY

```
            A      B         C         D        E        F      G      H      I
179  04:51 PM   0.378866     1          2       12
180  04:52 PM   0.815644     3          2       13
181  04:53 PM   0.785222     3          2       14
182  04:54 PM   0.873956     3          2       15
183  04:55 PM   0.560516     2          2       15
184  04:56 PM   0.967958     4          2       17
185  04:57 PM   0.012967     0          2       15
186  04:58 PM   0.299738     1          2       14
187  04:59 PM   0.457441     2          2       14
188
189  TOTAL CHILDREN:        345
190
191  LONGEST LENGTH OF LINE:                    17
```

FIGURE 14-8 The afternoon does not end so peacefully. There are 14 children in line at the end of the day.

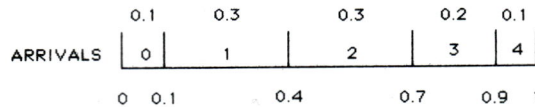

FIGURE 14-9 Dividing up the numbers between 0 and 1 so that 10% correspond to 0 arrivals, 30% correspond to 1 arrival, 30% correspond to 2 arrivals, 20% correspond to 3 arrivals, and 10% correspond to 4 arrivals.

The formula has been copied from D8 to D9..D187. This generates the number of children who arrive each minute.

Remember that we are estimating that Santa Claus will need 30 seconds with each child. If there are no children on line and no children arrive, then Santa sees no children that minute. If there is one child there (number on line plus number who just arrive), then Santa will see the one child. Otherwise Santa will see two children. So the formula in E8 for the number of children served at 2:00 is

$$@IF(F7+D8=0,0,@IF(F7+D8=1,1,2))$$

The cell F7 contains the number of children who are already waiting in line. The cell D8 contains the number of children who just arrive. Thus the formula can be read as "If the number of children waiting in line plus the number of children who arrive that minute equals zero, then Santa Claus will see no children that minute. Otherwise, if the number of children waiting in line plus the number of children who arrive that minute equals one then Santa Claus will see that child during the minute. Otherwise, Santa Claus will see two children during the minute." This formula is copied down column E.

Finally, column F contains the queue, the length of the line each minute. Here we set F7 to 0, assuming that the line would be 0 when Santa begins, though it certainly is possible that people might show up at 1:55 PM to see Santa at 2:00 PM. The length of the line each minute will be the length of the line the previous minute plus the number of arrivals minus the number of children who see Santa. So the formula in F8 is

$$+F7+D8-E8$$

This formula is copied down column F.

At the end of the day in Figure 14-8 we see that there are 14 children waiting in line and that the longest the line has been is 17 children. A total of 345 children have arrived to see Santa during the three hours.

To simulate another day we would press F9 again. A new set of random numbers would appear. For each minute a new set of arrivals would be generated, Santa would see children, the line would grow or shrink.

What can we conclude? Under these assumptions the system is fairly saturated. Santa would be worked close to capacity and there is a danger of quite long lines. The manager of the Fine Jewelry Department has reason to be concerned. You ought to think about ways to improve the situation. Perhaps the visits with Santa could be speeded up a bit, or Santa could be hired for more hours to dissipate the demand, or a second Santa could be hired, or you could go to a reservation system. Forewarned is forearmed.

This exercise was somewhat fanciful and simple-minded, but Monte Carlo simulation has proved useful in understanding a wide variety of queuing problems. In more sophisticated simulations we might model a probabilistic distribution for serving people as well as for arrivals. For example, some children might come with long lists of toys they want and take longer with Santa. Some of those who arrive might leave if the line is too long. The probability distribution for arrivals might change as the day progresses. For example, more people might tend to arrive right after school lets out. We might have multiple lines and multiple servers. All these situations and more could be modeled by expanding the spreadsheet.

GENERATING RANDOM INTEGERS

The @RAND function generates random numbers between 0 and 0.99999... (to 15 decimal places). In some situations it is useful to be able to generate a random set of integers instead. For example, we might want to simulate the rolling of a die by generating the integers 1, 2, 3, 4, 5, 6, with equal probability. We could set up a nested @IF function or a lookup table to accomplish this, but there is a more direct method.

First, we can expand the range of the random numbers by multiplying the @RAND function by a number. For example, the formula +6*@RAND would produce random numbers between 0 and 5.9999.... Since the @RAND function generates numbers from 0 to 0.99999..., the lowest number generated by 6*@RAND would be 0 and the highest would be 5.9999.... This is demonstrated in column C of Figure 14-10. Similarly, the formula 100*@RAND would generate random numbers from 0 to 99.999....

Now we can convert these numbers to integers using the @INT function. The formula @INT(6*@RAND) will generate the integers 0, 1, 2, 3, 4, 5 randomly with equal likelihood. Recall that the @INT function converts the value of its argument into an integer by chopping off the number at its decimal point. Any number between 0 and 0.99999... is converted to 0. Any number between 1 and 1.99999... is converted to 1, and so on. This is illustrated in column D of Figure 14-10. The random numbers in B10..B19 are multiplied by 6 in C10..C19. These numbers are then transformed into integers in D10..D19 using the @INT function.

We have the random integers 0, 1, 2, 3, 4, 5. By adding 1 to the previous formula we can generate the random integers 1, 2, 3, 4, 5, 6. Hence, to simulate a die by generating the random integers 1, 2, 3, 4, 5, 6 we can use the formula

$$@INT(6*@RAND)+1$$

This is illustrated in column E of Figure 14-10.

```
E13:  [W18] @INT(6*B13)+1                                          READY

              A              B           C           D              E
1
2                    TRANSFORMING RANDOM NUMBERS
3
4    FORMULA:              @RAND       6*@RAND   @INT(6*@RAND)   @INT(6*@RAND)+1
5
6    LOWEST VALUE      0.000000    0.000000        0              1
7
8    HIGHEST VALUE     0.999999    5.999999        5              6
9
10   TEN EXAMPLES      0.106944    0.641666        0              1
11                     0.226149    1.356897        1              2
12                     0.823592    4.941550        4              5
13                     0.066432    0.398591        0              1
14                     0.833651    5.001908        5              6
15                     0.544458    3.266748        3              4
16                     0.373392    2.240350        2              3
17                     0.824080    4.944483        4              5
18                     0.298499    1.790991        1              2
19                     0.279146    1.674876        1              2
20
```

FIGURE 14-10 Transforming random numbers. Multiplying a number times @RAND expands the range. Taking the @INT transforms the numbers to integers. Adding a number shifts the range.

```
D8:  @INT(6*@RAND)+1                                               READY

      A       B       C       D       E       F       G       H
1
2
3                      ROLLING THE DICE
4
5              ROLL   DIE #1  DIE #2  TOTAL
6               1       5       1       6
7               2       3       2       5
8               3       6       5      11
9               4       4       3       7
10              5       2       1       3
11              6       4       6      10
12              7       2       4       6
13              8       6       6      12
14              9       3       3       6
15             10       3       1       4
16
17
18
19
20
                          UNDO
```

FIGURE 14-11 Simulating the rolling of a pair of dice ten times.

If we want to simulate the rolling of a pair of dice we can simulate each die separately and then add the two numbers together. The rolling of a pair of dice ten times is shown in the spreadsheet in Figure 14-11.

The general formula for generating a random integer from some sequence of integers is given by

$$@INT(N*@RAND)+L$$

where N is the number of integers in the sequence and L is the value of the lowest integer in the sequence.

For example, if we would like to generate random integers from the sequence 40, 41, 42, ..., 59 we could use the formula

$$@INT(20*@RAND)+40$$

because there are 20 integers in the sequence and the lowest integer is 40.

This method works for generating integers from a sequence where we want each integer to be equally likely to occur. If we do not want the outcomes to occur with equal probabilities then we would need to use nested @IF functions or lookup tables as discussed earlier in the chapter.

PENCIL AND PAPER EXERCISES

14-1 Write out on paper how to use @RAND to generate each of the following distributions. Show all formulas and tables.

(a) 50%   I WIN
    50%   YOU WIN

(b) 80%   I WIN
    20%   YOU WIN

(c) 55%   I WIN
    30%   YOU WIN
    15%   TIE

(d) 35%   I WIN
    25%   YOU WIN
    30%   TIE
    10%   RAINED OUT

(e) 32%   I WIN
    22%   YOU WIN
    25%   WE BOTH WIN
    15%   WE BOTH LOSE
    6%   RAINED OUT

(f) 50%   1
    50%   2

(g) 25%   7
    25%   8
    25%   9
    25%   10

(h) the years (integers) from 1900 through 1999 with equal likelihood

(i) the (integer) temperatures from -37 degrees through 120 degrees with equal likelihood.

(j) the integers 2, 4, 6, 8 with equal likelihood

(k) the numbers 3.0, 3.1, 3.2, ..., 4.9 with equal likelihood

COMPUTER EXERCISES

14-2 Create an Executive Decision Maker. The user will type in a decision that needs to be made. For example, SHOULD WE LAUNCH A TAKEOVER BID OF IBM? Or

SHOULD I ASK PAT OUT FOR A DATE? Your spreadsheet should respond with one of the following answers with the frequencies indicated.

60%	GO FOR IT!
30%	NO. THE TIME IS NOT RIGHT.
10%	PLEASE GATHER MORE INFORMATION.

14-3 For each day in the month of January, the probabilities are

0.19	that it will snow
0.36	that it will be cloudy
0.30	that it will be sunny
0.15	that it will rain

Create a spreadsheet that uses @RAND to "predict" the weather for the month of January. Each time F9 is pressed, the spreadsheet should show a different prediction. The spreadsheet should look like:

```
I PREDICT
JANUARY      1      CLOUDY
JANUARY      2      RAIN
JANUARY      3      CLOUDY
   . . .
JANUARY      31     SUNNY
```

14-4 Your stockbroker suggests you buy 1000 shares of International Electronics. The stock currently is selling at $38.75 per share. From research in the library you discover that the stock is quite volatile and that, based on recent past data, in:

21% of the weeks it goes up $1.00

17% of the weeks it goes up $0.50

10% of the weeks it remains unchanged

35% of the weeks it goes down $0.50

17% of the weeks it goes down $1.00

(a) Create a spreadsheet to simulate the price of the stock and the value of your portfolio for 100 weeks assuming the distribution just given. You should have 100 rows in the main part of your spreadsheet, one for each week. You should have separate columns for the week number, a random number, the price change that week, the closing price of the stock that week, the value of your portfolio. List separately at the top of the spreadsheet the resulting High, Low, and Close for the stock price over the 100 weeks, that is, the highest price the stock reaches, the lowest price the stock reaches, and the closing price after 100 weeks. Run your simulation several times. Based on the past history data and your simulations, is this a good investment?

(b) On telling your broker your findings she suggests that you employ the following strategy: Buy the 1000 shares of stock now. Put in a Sell order for the stock at $43.75 or at 100 weeks, whichever comes first. That way if the stock reaches $43.75 you will sell out and achieve a profit of $5 per share. Otherwise you will sell out at the end of 100 weeks and take whatever profit or loss results. On inquiry your broker tells you that there will be a commission cost to you of $149 for purchasing the stock and another $149 for selling the stock.

Add appropriate formulas to your spreadsheet so that the net profit or loss you would gain by this strategy appears in a separate well-labeled cell.

Run the simulation 10 times and record by hand the consequences of using this investment strategy.

(c) Write a brief report on this investment strategy. Include appropriate printouts and graphs. Would you make money or lose money on average using this strategy? How much on average? Should you invest?

14-5 The game of Rock-Paper-Scissors is played by two people. At the count of three each person puts out a closed fist (Rock), a flat hand (Paper), or two fingers (Scissors). The winner is decided as follows: Rock breaks Scissors. Paper covers Rock. Scissors cuts Paper. If both players make the same selection, it is a tie.

(a) Create a spreadsheet so you can play Rock-Paper-Scissors against the computer. There will be a cell for you to enter in your choice (ROCK, PAPER, or SCIS-SORS). There will be another cell where the computer makes its choice. The computer should choose among the three alternatives randomly using @RAND. Each choice should be equally likely. No fair peeking at the person's choice in this formula! A third cell should indicate the outcome: YOU WIN, I WIN, or TIE. Test your spreadsheet until all nine possible combinations are tried.

(b) What happens in your spreadsheet if the person misspells the entry? Modify your spreadsheet so it says ILLEGAL ENTRY in this case rather than YOU WIN, I WIN, or TIE.

(c) Add cells to your spreadsheet to keep cumulative track of the number of times you win, it wins, and there is a tie. This is a bit tricky as it will involve circular references where the cells refer to themselves in their formulas. Be sure to set your spreadsheet to Manual Recalculation beforehand and save the spreadsheet before trying it.

14-6 Each day during the summer you plan to go downtown, set up a table, and sell pet tarantulas in cages. Your supplier has agreed to make weekly shipments of the tarantulas in their cages. For you to get the best rate, your supplier insists that you contract ahead of time for a fixed number of tarantulas to be shipped at the beginning of each week. You would like to know how many tarantulas to agree to purchase each week.

(a) You plan to work downtown everyday for 10 weeks. You figure that each day you are equally likely to sell 0, 1, 2, ..., or 12 tarantulas.

One of your selling points will be that you offer a money-back guarantee. If the customer (or his or her family) wishes, he or she can bring back the tarantula and cage, and you will refund the money with no questions asked. You figure that each day you work there will be 0, 1, 2, or 3 returns with equally likely probability. These tarantulas can then be resold.

Create a spreadsheet to simulate the summer on a day-by-day basis. At the top of the spreadsheet have a cell for entering the number of tarantulas and cages to be shipped each week. When this number is changed, the rest of the spreadsheet should change accordingly. You should have 70 rows in the main part of your spreadsheet, one for each day. You should have columns at least for the day number, the number of tarantulas received that day (every 7 days you will receive a shipment), the number of tarantulas sold that day, the number of returns that day, the number of tarantulas in inventory at the end of the day. Assume that the shipment arrives early in the morning before you leave for the day. You should use different random numbers for determining the amount sold and the amount returned. As you can see, many inventory problems can be modeled as queuing problems.

At the bottom of the spreadsheet put cells to calculate the maximum and minimum size of the inventory during the summer and the net number of tarantulas sold (sales minus returns).

You would like never to have fewer than 10 tarantulas and never to have more than 100 or so tarantulas on hand in inventory. Certainly, you would like never to run out of tarantulas during the summer. Try different numbers for the shipment size. By pressing F9, simulate several summers. How many tarantulas should you agree to purchase each week assuming the accuracy of the assumptions?

(b) In trying the simulations in part (a) you probably were more likely to run short in the beginning of the summer and to be overstocked toward the end of the summer. One solution is to double the standing order of tarantulas for just the first shipment to use as a base inventory. Change the formula in that cell accordingly. Now how many tarantulas should you agree to purchase each week, assuming the accuracy of the assumptions?

14-7 So that people feel they are getting more value for all the taxes they pay, the U.S. government has decided to hold a giant national lottery. Everyone in the country is entered automatically. Once a month a Social Security number will be selected at random. Whoever has that Social Security number will be given $10,000,000 tax free.

You have been hired to create the spreadsheet that will generate the random Social Security number. Social Security numbers have the form 012-34-5678. Each of the billion possible Social Security numbers should be equally likely to be selected in your spreadsheet.

For you to receive full payment for your work, the government contract officer insists that all 0's in the Social Security number selected appear in your spreadsheet and that the dashes appear in their usual places in the number.

14-8   The game of Chuck-a-Luck is popular at carnivals and fairs and also is played in casinos at Las Vegas and Atlantic City. Chuck-a-Luck is played with three large dice tumbling over in a cage. You can bet on various outcomes. We will assume here that each bet is for $1. Different bets pay different odds if you win. Here are some of the bets available:

1. Single Value. You bet on a number from 1 through 6. If the number appears on one die you win $1. If the number appears on two dice you win $2. If the number appears on all three dice you win $3.
2. Triple. If any number comes up on all three dice you win $30.
3. High-Low. You bet on either High (total of 11 through 17) or Low (total of 4 through 10). You always lose on a triple. Otherwise, you win $1 if you choose correctly.

In this spreadsheet you will play Chuck-a-Luck on the computer. First pick a number from 1 through 6 to bet for Single Value. Next pick HIGH or LOW. We will assume that you will play for 10 rolls with the same bets. On each roll you will bet $1 on Single Value, $1 on Triple, and $1 on High or Low. The spreadsheet will roll the three dice and tally how well you do.

A picture of columns A through H of the spreadsheet follows. Cell F4 contains the number you selected for Single Value. Cell H4 contains HIGH or LOW. Each time you press F9 the three dice are rolled 10 times. The results of your 10 sets of bets are tabulated. Try the spreadsheet several times. Be sure to check your spreadsheet carefully as the @IF functions required are tricky. The spreadsheet below is not typical. As you'll see, it's cheaper to play on the computer than it is at the carnival!

```
D20: (C0) +F19+G19+H19                                              READY

        A        B         C        D     E     F        G        H
 1
 2          CHUCK-A-LUCK                                  BETS
 3                                              ============================
 4      STEP RIGHT UP AND PLACE YOUR BET:            4 =========    HIGH
 5                                              ============================
 6                                              SINGLE            HIGH/
 7      ROLL    DIE #1    DIE #2   DIE #3       VALUE   TRIPLE     LOW
 8       1        1         6        3         ($1)     ($1)      ($1)
 9       2        2         2        2         ($1)     $30       ($1)
10       3        1         2        2         ($1)     ($1)      ($1)
11       4        2         6        2         ($1)     ($1)      ($1)
12       5        2         4        4          $2      ($1)      ($1)
13       6        3         5        2         ($1)     ($1)      ($1)
14       7        2         4        5          $1      ($1)       $1
15       8        5         4        6          $1      ($1)       $1
16       9        5         2        4          $1      ($1)       $1
17      10        6         3        4          $1      ($1)       $1
18                                             -----    -----     -----
19     TOTAL FOR 10 BETS                        $1      $21       ($2)
20     GRAND TOTAL        >>>>>>>>>      $20   <<<<<<<<
```

DATA MANAGEMENT: SORTING AND QUERYING

15

A major use of computers is keeping track of large amounts of data. Airline reservations, personnel, accounts payable and receivable, inventory, and payroll all can involve large amounts of data and all have been profitably automated. Indeed, the major use of mainframe computers is for data management. (**Mainframe** is simply the name given to large computers.)

A special type of software, called **database management systems,** has been developed for data management. There are database management systems for mainframe computers, personal computers, and all types of computers in between. Whereas a word processor can be considered a computerized typewriter and an electronic spreadsheet can be considered a computerized calculator and ledger paper, a database management system can be considered a computerized filing cabinet. Some of the more popular database management systems for the personal computer include dBASE III Plus®, Q&A®, and Paradox®.

Lotus 1-2-3 has some powerful and useful data management features. We are going to explore these capabilities in this chapter and in the next. But before we begin, it is important to point out that Lotus 1-2-3 is not considered a database management system. One major difference is that in a database management system most of the data is kept on the disk, thus allowing the computer to deal with tens of megabytes, or even gigabytes, of data. In Lotus 1-2-3, all the data is in the spreadsheet and must therefore fit in the primary memory of the computer. Thus, database management systems can deal with much larger sets of data than can Lotus 1-2-3. Still, the data management features of Lotus 1-2-3 have proved useful in many different applications.

To use the data management commands in Lotus 1-2-3, the data always must be arranged so that all the information about a single person, object, or transaction occupies a single row and so that each column contains information of the same type. This is illustrated by the real estate spreadsheet in Figure 15-1. Here, each row corresponds to the information about a different house for sale. Column A contains the addresses of the houses. Column B contains the number of bedrooms in the houses, and so on. In database terminology, in Lotus 1-2-3, a row corresponds to a **record** and a column corresponds to a **field**.

Lotus 1-2-3 provides the capability to sort, query, and perform basic statistics on data in spreadsheets. **Sorting** means arranging the rows of the spreadsheet so they are in a certain order. For example, we might rearrange the rows of the real estate spreadsheet so that the properties are in order by cost. **Querying** means that we can find rows in the spreadsheet that satisfy certain criteria. For example, we might want to find all of the houses with four bedrooms or more that sell for under $100,000. The **database functions** allow us to calculate certain statistics on rows that satisfy some stated criteria. For example, we might want to find the average cost of houses

```
H7:                                                                    READY

            A            B     C       D      E      F       G          H
 1                      CURRENT  LISTINGS
 2  ADDRESS            BDRMS BATHS    LOT    HEAT    AGE     COST
 3  12 Bartholomew Sq    5     4     0.25   Gas     48    $290,000
 4  46 Prospect Pl       5     2     0.40   Oil     22     $90,000
 5  690 Rice Ave         3     2     0.60   Oil     25     $92,000
 6  903 Ray Rd           2     1     0.30   Oil     45     $42,000
 7  455 Daniels Rd       2     1     0.25   Elec    16     $47,500
 8  12 Garden St         2     1     0.20   Elec    34     $87,500
 9  203 Somerset Ave     4     2     0.60   Gas     12     $95,000
10  34 Harley Pl         7     5     1.33   Oil     40    $180,000
11  45 Lynwood Dr        3     2     0.30   Gas     45     $55,000
12  11 Pomona Rd         3     1     0.40   Oil     30     $80,000
13  315 Fremont Ave      5     2     0.60   Elec    20    $160,000
14  19 Auburn St         4     2     0.35   Elec    22    $112,500
15  122 Stuyvesant Rd    3     2     1.25   Elec    14    $180,000
16  87 Newbury St        6     2     0.60   Gas     17    $120,000
17  1122 Bellevue        6     3     1.00   Gas      9    $140,000
18  19 Hill Rd           4     2     0.30   Oil     26    $110,000
19  1 Pond Rd            8     5     2.00   Gas     60    $245,000
20
                              UNDO
```

FIGURE 15-1 A spreadsheet showing real estate listings.

with four bedrooms. We will examine sorting and querying in this chapter. We will look at the database functions and some other data management capabilities in Chapter 16.

SORTING

When we sort objects, we alphabetize them or put them in numerical order. For example, when you get your checks back from the bank at the end of the month, you might sort the checks to put them in numerical order or you might sort the playing cards in your hand when you are playing gin or Go Fish. In Lotus 1-2-3 we can instruct the computer to rearrange the rows in a spreadsheet so that the cells in one of the columns are in order. Basically we need to tell the computer (1) the range of the spreadsheet that contains the rows to be rearranged and (2) the column of the spreadsheet that is to be used as the basis for the sort.

Before sorting a spreadsheet, always save the spreadsheet on the disk. It is quite possible to make hash out of a spreadsheet when trying to sort it. It is a comfort always to be able to restore the original version.

Suppose we would like to sort the spreadsheet in Figure 15-1 so that the houses are listed in order by cost. All data management commands in Lotus 1-2-3 are accessed through the / Data command. Selecting / Data Sort yields the / **Data Sort settings sheet** shown in Figure 15-2. The **data range** is the portion of the spreadsheet that is to be sorted. The **primary key** is the column that is to be used as the basis for the sort. These entries in the settings sheet are blank at the start and need to be completed before the spreadsheet can be sorted.

```
H7:                                                                    MENU
Data-Range   Primary-Key  Secondary-Key   Reset   Go   Quit
Select records to be sorted
                            ─── Sort Settings ───
    Data range:

    Primary key:
      Field (column)
      Sort order

    Secondary key:
      Field (column)
      Sort order

11  45 Lynwood Dr        3    2    0.30   Gas    45    $55,000
12  11 Pomona Rd         3    1    0.40   Oil    30    $80,000
13  315 Fremont Ave      5    2    0.60   Elec   20   $160,000
14  19 Auburn St         4    2    0.35   Elec   22   $112,500
15  122 Stuyvesant Rd    3    2    1.25   Elec   14   $180,000
16  87 Newbury St        6    2    0.60   Gas    17   $120,000
17  1122 Bellevue        6    3    1.00   Gas     9   $140,000
18  19 Hill Rd           4    2    0.30   Oil    26   $110,000
19  1 Pond Rd            8    5    2.00   Gas    60   $245,000
20
```

FIGURE 15-2 The / Data Sort settings sheet.

To specify the data range we select Data-Range in the / Data Sort menu and then enter A3..G19 either by typing or pointing. This tells the computer the portion of the spreadsheet that is to be rearranged. A common mistake that people make is to include the column headings in the data range, in this case by entering A2..G19. We do not want the labels in row 2 to be mixed in with the data when it is sorted.

To specify the primary key we select Primary-Key in the Sort menu and then move the cursor to any cell in the column we want to use as the basis for the sort. In this case, we would move the cursor to cell G7 or any other cell in column G, the column with the costs. Then press the Enter key. Next the computer asks us for "Sort order (A or D):". Here the computer is asking whether we want the rows sorted in Ascending order by Cost or in Descending order by Cost. That is, do we want the lowest cost house to appear first and the highest house last (Ascending order), or do we want the houses sorted highest cost to lowest cost (Descending order). Ascending is the default sort order, the order that Lotus 1-2-3 guesses we want. We type D for Descending and press the Enter key.

Now we have specified both the data range and the primary key. To tell the computer to perform the sort we select Go from the Sort menu. The result is the spreadsheet in Figure 15-3.

To sort the spreadsheet by type of heat, we now would select / Data Sort Primary-Key E7 enter Ascending enter Go. The result would be the spreadsheet in Figure 15-4. The program has remembered the data range from the previous sort. Since the primary key column contains labels rather than numbers, the computer automatically sorts on the basis of alphabetical order rather than numerical order. The houses with Electric heat are grouped together and then the houses with Gas heat and then the houses with Oil heat.

```
H7:                                                                    READY

            A              B      C      D      E      F        G          H
 1                       CURRENT LISTINGS
 2    ADDRESS           BDRMS BATHS  LOT   HEAT   AGE    COST
 3    12 Bartholomew Sq   5     4   0.25  Gas    48    $290,000
 4    1 Pond Rd           8     5   2.00  Gas    60    $245,000
 5    34 Harley Pl        7     5   1.33  Oil    40    $180,000
 6    122 Stuyvesant Rd   3     2   1.25  Elec   14    $180,000
 7    315 Fremont Ave     5     2   0.60  Elec   20    $160,000  ███████
 8    1122 Bellevue       6     3   1.00  Gas     9    $140,000
 9    87 Newbury St       6     2   0.60  Gas    17    $120,000
10    19 Auburn St        4     2   0.35  Elec   22    $112,500
11    19 Hill Rd          4     2   0.30  Oil    26    $110,000
12    203 Somerset Ave    4     2   0.60  Gas    12     $95,000
13    690 Rice Ave        3     2   0.60  Oil    25     $92,000
14    46 Prospect Pl      5     2   0.40  Oil    22     $90,000
15    12 Garden St        2     1   0.20  Elec   34     $87,500
16    11 Pomona Rd        3     1   0.40  Oil    30     $80,000
17    45 Lynwood Dr       3     2   0.30  Gas    45     $55,000
18    455 Daniels Rd      2     1   0.25  Elec   16     $47,500
19    903 Ray Rd          2     1   0.30  Oil    45     $42,000
20
                          UNDO
```

FIGURE 15-3 The real estate spreadsheet with the rows sorted in descending order by Cost.

Notice that within each group of houses in Figure 15-4 the order of the houses is arbitrary. The **secondary key** serves as the "tie-breaker," the criteria for sorting the rows if the cells in the primary key column are identical. In the example in Figure 15-4, there was no secondary key specified so there is no order to the rows within each type of heat. Suppose we are interested in a house that is heated by Electricity and that has as much land as possible. We could specify the primary key to be column E, the heat type, and the secondary key to be column D, the lot size. From the spreadsheet in Figure 15-4 we select / Data Sort Secondary-Key D7 enter Descending enter Go. The result is the spreadsheet in Figure 15-5. Within each heat type, properties are sorted in descending order by lot size.

Notice that properties that have the same heat type and lot size, for example, the two properties in the middle of the spreadsheet that are heated by Gas and have 0.60 acres of land, are in arbitrary order. To break this tie would require a "tertiary key," a feature which Lotus 1-2-3 does not now have.

Another word of warning about sorting. A common error that people make is not to specify the full data range. This can be disastrous. Suppose we had specified the data range as A3..E19 rather than A3..G19 and then specified the primary key as column E (heat) and the secondary key as column D (lot size). The computer would sort the rows as before, but only in columns A through E. Columns F and G would remain unchanged. The new address in A3 would be in the same row as the old cost in G3. We would have the houses with the right bedrooms, baths, lot size, and heat type but with the wrong ages and costs. A realtor's nightmare! Before you sort, look twice to be sure that all of the relevant data is included in the data range. Save the spreadsheet right before beginning the sorting process so you can recover if you make a mistake.

```
H7:                                                              READY

            A          B      C      D      E      F       G        H
 1                        CURRENT LISTINGS
 2  ADDRESS         BDRMS BATHS   LOT    HEAT    AGE     COST
 3  315 Fremont Ave     5     2    0.60   Elec    20   $160,000
 4  12 Garden St        2     1    0.20   Elec    34    $87,500
 5  19 Auburn St        4     2    0.35   Elec    22   $112,500
 6  122 Stuyvesant Rd   3     2    1.25   Elec    14   $180,000
 7  455 Daniels Rd      2     1    0.25   Elec    16    $47,500  ████████
 8  45 Lynwood Dr       3     2    0.30   Gas     45    $55,000
 9  1122 Bellevue       6     3    1.00   Gas      9   $140,000
10  203 Somerset Ave    4     2    0.60   Gas     12    $95,000
11  12 Bartholomew Sq   5     4    0.25   Gas     48   $290,000
12  1 Pond Rd           8     5    2.00   Gas     60   $245,000
13  87 Newbury St       6     2    0.60   Gas     17   $120,000
14  690 Rice Ave        3     2    0.60   Oil     25    $92,000
15  11 Pomona Rd        3     1    0.40   Oil     30    $80,000
16  903 Ray Rd          2     1    0.30   Oil     45    $42,000
17  46 Prospect Pl      5     2    0.40   Oil     22    $90,000
18  19 Hill Rd          4     2    0.30   Oil     26   $110,000
19  34 Harley Pl        7     5    1.33   Oil     40   $180,000
20
                        UNDO
```

FIGURE 15-4 The real estate spreadsheet sorted in ascending order by Heat.

```
H7:                                                                    READY

            A          B     C       D      E      F        G        H
1                    CURRENT LISTINGS
2   ADDRESS          BDRMS BATHS    LOT    HEAT   AGE      COST
3   122 Stuyvesant Rd  3     2     1.25   Elec   14     $180,000
4   315 Fremont Ave    5     2     0.60   Elec   20     $160,000
5   19 Auburn St       4     2     0.35   Elec   22     $112,500
6   455 Daniels Rd     2     1     0.25   Elec   16      $47,500
7   12 Garden St       2     1     0.20   Elec   34      $87,500  ████████
8   1 Pond Rd          8     5     2.00   Gas    60     $245,000
9   1122 Bellevue      6     3     1.00   Gas     9     $140,000
10  87 Newbury St      6     2     0.60   Gas    17     $120,000
11  203 Somerset Ave   4     2     0.60   Gas    12      $95,000
12  45 Lynwood Dr      3     2     0.30   Gas    45      $55,000
13  12 Bartholomew Sq  5     4     0.25   Gas    48     $290,000
14  34 Harley Pl       7     5     1.33   Oil    40     $180,000
15  690 Rice Ave       3     2     0.60   Oil    25      $92,000
16  46 Prospect Pl     5     2     0.40   Oil    22      $90,000
17  11 Pomona Rd       3     1     0.40   Oil    30      $80,000
18  903 Ray Rd         2     1     0.30   Oil    45      $42,000
19  19 Hill Rd         4     2     0.30   Oil    26     $110,000
20
                            UNDO
```

FIGURE 15-5 The real estate spreadsheet sorted in ascending order by Heat and within each Heat type in descending order by Lot size.

QUERYING

With sorting we rearranged the rows in a certain order. It also is possible to have the computer look through the data range to find the rows that fulfill some criteria. Suppose we are looking for a house with four bedrooms or more that sells for under $100,000. One approach is to sort the rows, say, with cost as the primary key and bedrooms as the secondary key. A better approach is to use the data querying commands of Lotus 1-2-3 to find or extract the houses that fulfill our criteria. The data query commands are quite involved, perhaps the most complicated commands in Lotus 1-2-3, but they are very powerful.

For our example of finding the houses with four bedrooms that sell for under $100,000, we return to the original real estate spreadsheet in Figure 15-1. We first select / Data Query and are then shown the current / **Data Query settings sheet**, as in Figure 15-6.

The query settings sheet shows the three ranges that can be used in the / Data Query command. We will discuss each of these ranges in detail in the paragraphs that follow, but first a quick overview. The **Input Range** is the location of the data to be searched. The **Criteria Range** gives the location of the criteria to be used in searching through the rows in the Input Range. The **Output Range** gives the location where copies of the rows that are found will be put. The Output Range is used with the / Data Query Extract command, which is discussed shortly.

```
H7:                                                                    MENU
Input  Criteria  Output  Find  Extract  Unique  Delete  Reset  Quit
Specify range that contains records to search
                              ── Query Settings ──
      Input range:

      Criteria range:

      Output range:

7   455 Daniels Rd       2      1    0.25  Elec    16   $47,500  ████████
8   12 Garden St         2      1    0.20  Elec    34   $87,500
9   203 Somerset Ave     4      2    0.60  Gas     12   $95,000
10  34 Harley Pl         7      5    1.33  Oil     40   $180,000
11  45 Lynwood Dr        3      2    0.30  Gas     45   $55,000
12  11 Pomona Rd         3      1    0.40  Oil     30   $80,000
13  315 Fremont Ave      5      2    0.60  Elec    20   $160,000
14  19 Auburn St         4      2    0.35  Elec    22   $112,500
15  122 Stuyvesant Rd    3      2    1.25  Elec    14   $180,000
16  87 Newbury St        6      2    0.60  Gas     17   $120,000
17  1122 Bellevue        6      3    1.00  Gas      9   $140,000
18  19 Hill Rd           4      2    0.30  Oil     26   $110,000
19  1 Pond Rd            8      5    2.00  Gas     60   $245,000
20
```

FIGURE 15-6 The / Data Query settings sheet.

THE INPUT RANGE

From the / Data Query menu in Figure 15-6, we first select Input and specify the Input Range as A2..G19. The Input Range is the section of the spreadsheet through which Lotus 1-2-3 will look for the rows we want. The Input Range is similar to the Data Range in the / Data Sort command but with one important difference: *The Input Range must include the headings of the columns as the top row.* That is, we must be sure to include row 2 as the top row in the Input Range. Further, the column headings must occupy only *one* row and each heading must be unique. That is, each cell in the headings row must be different from all the other cells in the row.

CRITERIA AND THE CRITERIA RANGE

After specifying the Input Range, we need to set up the Criteria Range. We Quit out of the / Data Query menu and return to Ready mode. Now we stake out a portion of the spreadsheet, usually below the Input Range, for the Criteria Range. Rows 23 and 24 will do fine. The first step here is to copy the headings into row 23. The best way to copy the headings is with the / Copy command with the From range set to A2..G2 and the To range set to A23..G23, or even to just A23. This is a variation on the / Copy command that allows us to copy an entire row at once.

It is very important that the headings that appear in the Criteria Range are *identical* to the headings that appear in the Input Range. If a heading is capitalized in the Criteria Range, it must be identically capitalized in the Input Range. The spellings must be identical. Using the Copy command to copy the headings from the Input Range to the Criteria Range is much safer than retyping the headings. Note, also, that only one row of headings is allowed.

In row 24, the row below the headings in the new Criteria Range, we put the criteria we wish to be satisfied in our query. In cell B24 we put the formula

$$(B3>=4)$$

In cell G24 we put the formula

$$(G3<100000)$$

as in Figure 15-7. The criteria we have specified are that we wish the number of bedrooms to be >= 4 and the cost to be <100000. The criteria are logical expressions that evaluate to *True* or *False*. The criteria are placed in the row directly below the headings in the Criteria Range. In the logical expressions we refer to the address of the cell in the top data row in the Input Range, in this case row 3. That is, we use B3 to stand for each of the number of bedrooms for the different properties and G3 to stand for the Cost of each of the different properties. If there are multiple criteria in the same row, it is assumed that we want all of the criteria to be true. That is, in this case, the computer takes the criteria to be bedrooms greater than or equal to 4 *and* cost less than 100000. Once we have entered these formulas into B24 and G24 Lotus 1-2-3 will display 1 or 0 in each of the cells, depending on whether or not those particular

```
G24: [W11] (G3<100000)                                              READY

           A            B     C      D     E      F        G        H
 7   455 Daniels Rd     2     1    0.25   Elec    16    $47,500
 8   12 Garden St       2     1    0.20   Elec    34    $87,500
 9   203 Somerset Ave   4     2    0.60   Gas     12    $95,000
10   34 Harley Pl       7     5    1.33   Oil     40    $180,000
11   45 Lynwood Dr      3     2    0.30   Gas     45    $55,000
12   11 Pomona Rd       3     1    0.40   Oil     30    $80,000
13   315 Fremont Ave    5     2    0.60   Elec    20    $160,000
14   19 Auburn St       4     2    0.35   Elec    22    $112,500
15   122 Stuyvesant Rd  3     2    1.25   Elec    14    $180,000
16   87 Newbury St      6     2    0.60   Gas     17    $120,000
17   1122 Bellevue      6     3    1.00   Gas     9     $140,000
18   19 Hill Rd         4     2    0.30   Oil     26    $110,000
19   1 Pond Rd          8     5    2.00   Gas     60    $245,000
20
21
22
23   ADDRESS          BDRMS BATHS   LOT   HEAT    AGE      COST
24                      1                                         0
25
26
                         UNDO
```

FIGURE 15-7 Setting up the criteria for the query.

expressions are *True* or *False*. The values of 1 or 0 here can be ignored. In a minute Lotus 1-2-3 will be told to apply the criteria to check each of the rows in the Input Range.

The next step is to inform Lotus 1-2-3 of the location of the Criteria Range. To do this, we select / Data Query Criteria and then specify A23..G24.

FINDING

We now have (1) informed Lotus 1-2-3 of the location of the Input Range, (2) set up the criteria in a section of the spreadsheet, and (3) informed Lotus 1-2-3 of the location of this Criteria Range. We are ready to instruct Lotus 1-2-3 to find the rows in the Input Range that satisfy the criteria in the Criteria Range.

In the / Data Query menu we select Find. Lotus 1-2-3 now goes through each of the rows in the Input Range and determines which rows fulfill the conditions in the Criteria Range. The initial result is shown in Figure 15-8. The mode indicator at the top right of the screen says FIND; Lotus 1-2-3 is in Find mode. The computer has highlighted the first row in the Input Range that fulfills the conditions in the Criteria Range. The house at 46 Prospect Place does indeed have at least four bedrooms and costs under $100,000. When we press the down arrow, the computer highlights the next property down that fulfills the criteria. The cells for the property at 203 Somerset Avenue in row 9 are highlighted. Pressing the down arrow again brings a beep as there are no rows lower in the Input Range that fulfill the criteria. We can move back up to the previous

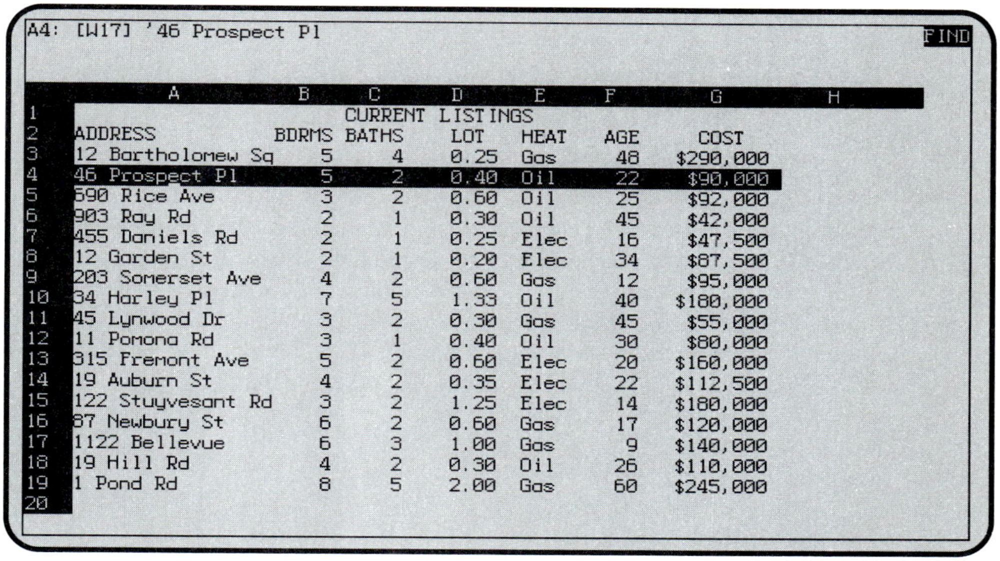

FIGURE 15-8 The initial result of a / Data Query Find when the criteria are a house with at least 4 bedrooms that costs under $100,000.

row that met the criteria by using the up arrow. Thus, in Find mode we use the down arrow and the up arrow to highlight the properties that meet the criteria. We can use the Enter key or the Esc key to exit from Find mode and return to the / Data Query menu.

ALTERNATIVE CRITERIA

Suppose we would now like to find a big old house on a good-sized lot. We Quit out of the / Data Query menu and return to Ready mode. We erase the current criteria using / Range Erase A24..G24. Be sure not to "erase" the cells in the Criteria Range by putting spaces in them. The spaces would tell the computer that you are looking to find a row where the cell in that column contains just a space! Now we enter the new criteria.

We would like at least six bedrooms in the house, so in cell B24 we put the formula

$$(B3>=6)$$

We would like the lot to be at least an acre so in cell D24 we put the formula

$$(D3>=1.0)$$

We would like the house to be at least 40 years old so in F24 we put

$$(F3>=40)$$

Thus our criteria look like

```
        A          B        C       D        E        F        G          H

23 ADDRESS    BDRMS    BATHS    LOT     HEAT     AGE      COST
24            (B3>=6)          (D3>=1.0)        (F3>=40)
```

Now to find the houses that have at least six bedrooms, a lot of at least an acre, and are at least 40 years old, we can select / Data Query Find, or alternatively we can press function key **F7**, which is the **Query key**. Function key F7 instructs Lotus 1-2-3 to issue the most recent Query command. First the cells for 34 Harley Place in row 10 are highlighted. Pressing the down arrow key moves the highlight to 1 Pond Road in row 19.

If we wanted to find the houses with Oil heat we could put the formula

$$(E3="Oil")$$

into the criteria at cell E24. Or, Lotus 1-2-3 lets us abbreviate this formula by just entering

Oil

into cell E24. Whenever you want to match cells in the Input Range against a specific label, you can put just the label itself into the criteria cell.

USING OR IN CONDITIONS

To take the AND of multiple conditions, we put the conditions in cells in the same row. To take the OR of conditions, we put the conditions in separate rows in the Criteria Range. For example, if we wanted a house that either has at least four bedrooms *or* costs under $100,000, we would set up two rows of conditions in the Criteria Range, as follows:

	A	B	C	D	E	F	G	H
23	ADDRESS	BDRMS	BATHS	LOT	HEAT	AGE	COST	
24		(B3>=4)						
25							(G3<100000)	

We now have to instruct Lotus 1-2-3 to expand the Criteria Range by selecting / Data Query Criteria A23..G25 enter. To have Lotus 1-2-3 identify the houses that fulfill the criteria we select Find. Since the conditions are on two rows, the criteria are interpreted as (B3>=4)#OR#(G3<100000), and now every house but one in the Input Range satisfies the criteria since they either have four or more bedrooms or cost under $100,000 (or both).

We could get ever more complicated with the criteria. For example, the Criteria Range

	A	B	C	D	E	F	G	H
23	ADDRESS	BDRMS	BATHS	LOT	HEAT	AGE	COST	
24		(B3>=4)		(D3>1#AND#D3<5)				
25							(G3<100000)	
26			(C3>2)		(E3="Oil")			

would be interpreted as requesting a house that satisfies at least one of the following three criteria:

1. At least 4 bedrooms and on a lot between 1 acre and 5 acres, or
2. Cost of under $100,000, or
3. More than 2 baths and Oil heat

Of course, we would need to expand the Criteria Range again to A23..G26.

Incidentally, if you use a Criteria Range with two or more rows of conditions and then want to use a Criteria Range with only one row of conditions, be sure to use the / Data Query Criteria command to reduce the Criteria Range accordingly.

EXTRACTING

The / Data Query Find operation identifies rows in the Input Range that satisfy the conditions in the Criteria Range. Wouldn't it be nice to be able to put copies of these rows into a separate section of the spreadsheet? That is the purpose of the / Data Query Extract command. The / Data Query Extract command copies each of the rows in the Input Range that meet the conditions in the Criteria Range and puts them into a separate section of the spreadsheet called the Output Range.

Suppose we want to extract the data on each of the houses that have at least four bedrooms and cost under $100,000. We already have identified the Input Range, set up the criteria, and identified the Criteria Range. Now we need to set up the Output Range and identify it as such to the program.

We decide to begin the Output Range in row 29, a few rows below the criteria. We copy the headings from A23..G23 to A29..G29. The Input Range, the Criteria Range, and the Output Range all must have identical headings in their top rows.

To identify the Output Range we select / Data Query Output A29..G49 enter. The copied headings are the top row of the Output Range. We leave 20 rows below, just in case we wish to extract all of the rows from the Input Range.

To perform the actual extraction we select Extract in the / Data Query menu. The result is shown in Figure 15-9. The rows for the two houses in the Input Range that fulfill the conditions in the Criteria Range have been copied into the Output Range. The original data in the Input Range is unchanged. To return to Ready mode we select Quit from the / Data Query menu shown in Figure 15-9.

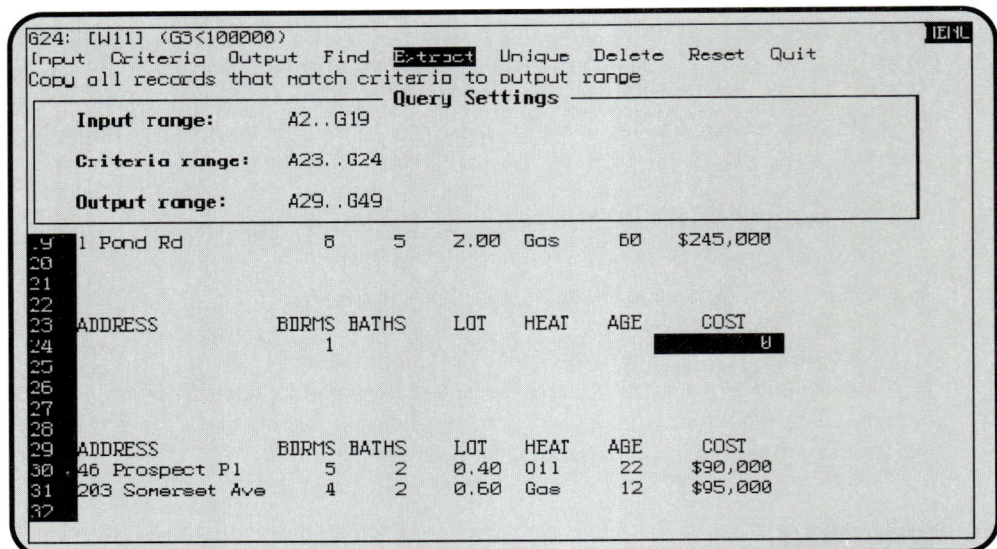

FIGURE 15-9 The result of extracting the rows for the houses with at least four bedrooms that cost under $100,000. To return to Ready mode and erase the Query Settings display, select Quit.

Note that if you leave out one of the column headings in the top row of the Output Range then Lotus 1-2-3 will not copy the data for that column. For example, if we erased the word LOT in D29, then none of the lot sizes would appear in the extracted data below.

To review the process of extracting data:

1. Input Range
   (a) Enter unique column headings in the row above the data.
   (b) Specify the full Input Range to Lotus 1-2-3 using the / Data Query Input command.
2. Criteria Range
   (a) Copy the row of headings to a new portion of the spreadsheet.
   (b) In the row(s) below the headings, state the conditions to be satisfied.
   (c) Specify the full Criteria Range using the / Data Query Criteria command.
3. Output Range
   (a) Copy the row of headings to a new portion of the spreadsheet. Be sure there are sufficient blank rows below the headings.
   (b) Specify the full Output Range using the / Data Query Output command.
4. Initiate the extract operation using the / Data Query Extract command.

DELETING DATA

The Extraction command makes a copy of data that fulfills some criteria. In some applications we might want to delete the data that fulfills the criteria. For example, each row of the data might correspond to a different invoice. We might want to delete each invoice that has been paid. Or we might have a row of data for each current employee in the company. We might want to delete the data for all employees who have quit or retired or been fired.

The / Data Query Delete command deletes each row of data in the Input Range that fulfills the conditions in the Criteria Range. All of the rows of data in the Input Range below the data that are deleted are moved up accordingly. The cells outside of the Input Range are unaffected.

UNIQUE

The / Data Query Unique command is just like the / Data Query Extract command except that it eliminates duplicates in the copies. If there are two or more rows of data in the Input Range that are identical and that meet the criteria in the Criteria Range, then the / Data Query Unique command instructs Lotus 1-2-3 to put just one copy of the row of data in the Output Range.

PENCIL AND PAPER EXERCISE

15-1 Used Car City has created a spreadsheet that contains data on each of the cars on their lot. When a customer comes in, the data on the spreadsheet can be searched for an appropriate car. A portion of the current spreadsheet is shown below. There are 359 cars on the lot now. Assume that the data extends out to column Q.

```
D372:                                                              READY

          A              B             C    D        E         F
 1
 2                            USED CAR CITY
 3
 4                       CURRENT LIST OF CARS ON THE LOT
 5
 6
 7   MAKE           MODEL         YEAR COLOR      MILES   LISTPRICE
 8   ROLLS ROYCE    SILVER SPIRIT 1989 GREEN     10,500    $99,900
 9   TOYOTA         CORONA        1980 BLUE     125,647       $399
10   CHEVROLET      CORVETTE ZR-1 1990 RED        7,468    $55,989
          A              B             C    D        E         F
365  LINCOLN        CONTINENTAL   1988 BLACK     34,255    $16,666
366  DODGE          DYNASTY       1990 BLUE      17,339     $8,499
367
368
369  MAKE           MODEL         YEAR COLOR      MILES   LISTPRICE
370
371
372
373
                            UNDO
```

The Criteria Range begins at A369. Write out exactly (1) the formulas that should appear in the cells and (2) the Criteria Range for each of the following queries. I have answered the first one to give you the general idea.

(a) A 1990 Dodge.
   Answer   A370: DODGE   C370: (C8=1990)
   Criteria Range A369..Q370

(b) A Lincoln.

(b) A 1990 Chevrolet that costs under $8,000.

(c) A 1989 or later car with under 40,000 miles that costs under $3000.

(d) A red or blue car.

(e) A Rolls Royce with under 10,000 miles or any Mercedes-Benz.

(f) A red Ferrari or a white 1976 Cadillac or a brown Yugo.

(g) A red Ford Mustang from the 1960s.

(h) An automobile that is black and has under 40,000 miles. The automobile can be either a 1989 or later Lincoln or a 1989 or later Cadillac or a Rolls Royce of any year.

Now give an English description of the cars found with each of the following criteria:

(i)
```
MAKE      MODEL     YEAR   COLOR      MILES       LISTPRICE
BUICK     REGAL            WHITE  (E8<20000)
```

```
(j)  MAKE        MODEL    YEAR    COLOR         MILES        LISTPRICE
                 (C8>1987)                                   (F8<15000)

(k)  MAKE        MODEL    YEAR    COLOR         MILES        LISTPRICE
     FORD        TAURUS SHO               (E8<30000)
     FORD        MUSTANG GT               (E8<30000)

(l)  MAKE        MODEL    YEAR    COLOR         MILES        LISTPRICE
     LAMBORGHINI                  YELLOW                     (F8<15000)
     FERRARI                      RED                        (F8<15000)
```

COMPUTER EXERCISES

15-2 Each June, *Datamation* magazine publishes a list of the top companies in the computer industry for the year before. Here is the list of the 1989 top 30 companies by Information Systems Revenue ("IS Revenue") published in June 1990.

Rank 1989	Company	Country	IS Revenue	Total Revenue	Rank 1988
1	IBM	United States	60.8	62.7	1
2	Digital	United States	12.9	12.9	2
3	NEC	Japan	11.5	23.4	4
4	Fujitsu	Japan	11.4	18.1	3
5	Unisys	United States	9.4	10.1	5
6	Hitachi	Japan	8.7	49.1	6
7	Hewlett-Packard	United States	7.8	11.9	7
8	Groupe Bull	France	6.5	6.5	11
9	Siemens	Germany	6.0	32.5	8
10	Olivetti	Italy	5.6	6.6	9
11	Apple	United States	5.4	5.4	12
12	NCR	United States	5.3	6.0	10
13	Toshiba	Japan	4.6	28.9	13
14	Canon	Japan	3.8	9.8	15
15	Matsushita	Japan	3.7	40.9	14
16	Compaq	United States	2.9	2.9	24
17	AT&T	United States	2.9	36.1	21
18	NV Philips	The Netherlands	2.8	27.0	19
19	Nixdorf	Germany	2.8	2.8	18
20	Xerox	United States	2.8	17.6	20
21	Wang	United States	2.7	2.7	17
22	STC	United Kingdom	2.6	4.3	22
23	EDS	United States	2.5	5.5	27
24	NTT	Japan	2.3	2.3	32
25	Nihon Unisys	Japan	2.1	2.1	25
26	Amdahl	United States	2.1	2.1	28
27	Sun	United States	2.1	2.1	37
28	Memorex Telex	The Netherlands	2.1	2.1	23
29	Mitsubishi	Japan	2.0	21.0	44
30	Oki Electric	Japan	2.0	3.9	36

Information Systems Revenue is all the computer-related revenue for the company for the year. Total Revenue is the total revenue for the company for the year, including both Information Systems Revenue and noncomputer-related revenue. All revenue figures are stated in billions of U.S. dollars. As you can see, IBM is the dominant company in the computer industry with computer-related revenue of approximately $60,800,000,000. Incidentally, Lotus Development Corp. ranked 70 with revenue of $556 million. Microsoft ranked 50 with revenue of $953 million.

Enter this spreadsheet into the computer. Save the spreadsheet on your disk under the name CMPTR30. Please do *not* save another version of the spreadsheet under the same name later on during this exercise.

(a) Sort the the companies so the names appear in alphabetical order. Check to make sure that all of each company's data is moved with the company name.

(b) Sort the companies in descending order by Total Revenue.

(c) Sort the companies by Country. Within each Country, the company should appear in order of 1989 rank.

Restore the original spreadsheet from the disk. Set up a Criteria Range below the data.

(d) Find the companies from the United States.

(e) Find all the companies that had Total Revenue of over $10 billion.

(f) Find all the companies whose rank improved from 1988 to 1989.

Now set up an Output Range below the Criteria Range. After completing each of the following sections, erase the conditions in the Criteria Range and the data in the Output Range using / Range Erase.

(g) Extract the companies from Japan.

(h) Extract all the companies that had Total Revenue of over $10 billion.

(i) Extract all the companies whose IS Revenue account for at least 90% of their Total Revenue.

(j) Extract all of the companies from the United States whose rank either stayed the same or improved from 1988 to 1989.

(k) Extract all the companies that are from countries other than the United States or Japan.

(l) Extract all the companies from either the United States or Japan that had Total Revenue of over $25 billion.

(m) (*tricky*) Obtain a list of just the countries that have companies represented in the top 30. Each country should be listed only once. Write out the exact sequence of keystrokes needed to obtain this list.

15-3 Create a Lotus 1-2-3 database to keep track of all of the courses you have taken. For each course list the name of the course, the course number, the semester in which you took the course, the college or university at which you took the course, the grade you received, and your personal rating for the course from 1 through 4 (where 1 is a super course and 4 is a terrible course), and a brief comment on the course. For simplicity, drop any +'s or -'s in the grades you received. That is, record a B- as a B. Enter the data on the spreadsheet. (You may use fictional data if you prefer.) Save the spreadsheet on the disk.

(a) Sort the courses by course number.

(b) Sort the courses in chronological order by the semester in which you took the course and within each semester by the course number. Warning! Depending on how you encoded the semesters, they might not sort in chronological order, from earliest to latest. If they do not sort in the proper order, reenter the semester names in a way in which they will sort properly.

(c) Sort the courses in order by the grade you received in the course. The courses with highest grades should be listed first.

Restore the original spreadsheet from the disk. Set up a Criteria Range below the data.

(d) Find all the courses that you rated 2 or better.

(e) Find all the courses that you took last semester.

(f) Find all the courses in which you received a grade of B or better and that you rated 2 or better.

Now set up an Output Range below the Criteria Range. After completing each of the following sections, erase the conditions in the Criteria Range and the data in the Output Range using / Range Erase.

(g) Extract the courses that you rated 3 or below.

(h) Extract the courses not taken at your current college or university.

(i) Extract the courses that were taken last semester or the semester before that you rated 3 or better.

15-4 In the book *The 100* by Michael H. Hart (Galahad Books, New York, 1982) the author ranks "the most influential persons in history." Here is a list of his top 30:

Rank	Name	Current name of Country	Born	Died	What They Did
1	Muhammad	Saudi Arabia	570	632	Religious leader
2	Isaac Newton	England	1642	1727	Scientist
3	Jesus Christ	Israel	6 BC	30	Religious leader
4	Buddha	Nepal	563 BC	483 BC	Religious leader
5	Confucius	China	551 BC	479 BC	Religious leader
6	St. Paul	Turkey	4	64	Religious leader

7	Ts'ai Lun	China	c. 105		Inventor
8	Johann Gutenberg	Germany	1400	1468	Inventor
9	Christopher Columbus	Italy	1451	1506	Explorer
10	Albert Einstein	Germany	1879	1955	Scientist
11	Karl Marx	Germany	1818	1883	Philosopher
12	Louis Pasteur	France	1822	1895	Scientist
13	Galileo Galilei	Italy	1564	1642	Scientist
14	Aristotle	Greece	384 BC	322 BC	Philosopher
15	Lenin	Soviet Union	1870	1924	Political leader
16	Moses	Egypt	c. 1250 BC		Religious leader
17	Charles Darwin	England	1809	1882	Scientist
18	Shih Huang Ti	China	259 BC	210 BC	Political leader
19	Augustus Caesar	Italy	63 BC	14	Political leader
20	Mao Tse-Tung	China	1893	1976	Political leader
21	Genghis Khan	Mongolia	1162	1227	Political leader
22	Euclid	Egypt	c. 300 BC		Mathematician
23	Martin Luther	Germany	1483	1546	Religious leader
24	Nicolaus Copernicus	Poland	1473	1543	Scientist
25	James Watt	Scotland	1736	1819	Inventor
26	Constantine the Great	Italy	280	337	Political leader
27	George Washington	United States	1732	1799	Political leader
28	Michael Faraday	England	1791	1867	Scientist
29	James Clerk Maxwell	Scotland	1831	1879	Scientist
30	Orville Wright	United States	1871	1948	Inventor
30	Wilbur Wright	United States	1867	1912	Inventor

In a sense this is a more "realistic" database as the data is not quite as "clean" as we would like. For people whose birth and death years are not known, a single year near when they are thought to have lived is listed. For example, Moses is listed as having lived c. 1250 B.C. Here, "c." is short for circa which means "around." Listing years B.C. does not quite work in Lotus 1-2-3. For this exercise you will need to decide how to deal with these problems.

Enter this spreadsheet into the computer, somehow encoding all the dates. Save the spreadsheet on your disk under the name HUMAN30. Please do not save another version of this spreadsheet under the same name later on in the exercise.

(a) Sort the people so the names as entered appear in alphabetical order. Be sure that all of the data for each person are moved with the person's name.

(b) Sort the people in ascending order by birth date. All people born B.C. should precede all people born A.D.

(c) Sort the people by Country and within each country by rank.

Restore the original spreadsheet from the disk. Set up a Criteria Range below the data.

(d) Find the people from China.

(e) Find all the people born Before Christ.

(f) Find all the Scientists or Inventors who were alive after 1800.

Now set up the Output Range below the Criteria Range. After completing each of the following sections, erase the conditions in the Criteria Range and the data in the Output Range using / Range Erase. Be sure the Criteria Range is set to the correct size.

(g) Extract the people from Germany.

(h) Extract all people who were alive in 1500.

(i) Extract all people who lived to be over 70 years old.

(j) Extract all Religious leaders or Political leaders from China.

(k) Name five people on the list who have had religions named after them.

(l) Describe in a paragraph the accomplishments of each of the people from China.

(m) List five people who you think should be in the top 30 but are not. List five people who are on the list and you believe should not be. Justify your choices.

(n) Describe three ways to handle the birth dates and death dates in the spreadsheet and the advantages and disadvantages of each. Which did you choose? Why?

(o) Half the people who have lived were female. Why are no women listed in the top 30?

MORE ON DATA MANAGEMENT

16

The data management capabilities in Lotus 1-2-3 are rich and varied. In Chapter 15 we examined the / Data Sort and / Data Query commands. In this chapter we examine some of the other data management capabilities of Lotus 1-2-3. We look at how to transfer data from Lotus 1-2-3 to other programs. We also look at the / Data Table command, a hidden gem that greatly facilitates performing "What if" analysis by automatically applying formulas in a spreadsheet to a sequence of data values and recording the results.

FILL

The / Data Fill command is an easy way to put a sequence of numbers across a row or down a column. For example, suppose we want to put the years from 1985 through 2002 in B3..B20. An approach that we have used before in this book is to put the number 1985 in B3, the formula +B3+1 in B4 and then / Copy the formula from B4 to B5..B20. An alternative approach is to use the / Data Fill command.

After we select / Data Fill, Lotus 1-2-3 prompts us for four pieces of information: the "fill range," the "Start," the "Step," and the "Stop". The fill range is the section of the spreadsheet where we want the numbers to be placed. To put the years 1985 through 2002 in B3..B20 we would select B3..B20, as the fill range by either pointing or typing. The Start is the starting value for the sequence of numbers. Lotus 1-2-3 guesses 0 for the Start value. We enter 1985. The Step is the increment, the amount to add to each succeeding number. Lotus 1-2-3 guesses 1, which is fine. The Stop value is the last number in the sequence. Lotus 1-2-3 guesses 8191. We enter 2002, as in Figure 16-1. We press the Enter key and 1-2-3 proceeds to fill in the numbers 1985 through 2002 in B3..B20, as in Figure 16-2.

Lotus 1-2-3 fills in the range beginning with the Start number and incrementing by the Step number. 1-2-3 stops filling in numbers either when the last cell in the range is reached or the Stop number is reached. Thus, we could have left 8191 as the Stop number as the sequence would have stopped when it reached cell B20.

To fill in the sequence 20, 22, 24, 26 .. 40 we could set the Start to 20, the Step to 2, and the Stop to 40.

To fill in the sequence 10, 9, 8, 7, .. 1 we could set the Start to 10, the Step to -1, and the Stop to 1.

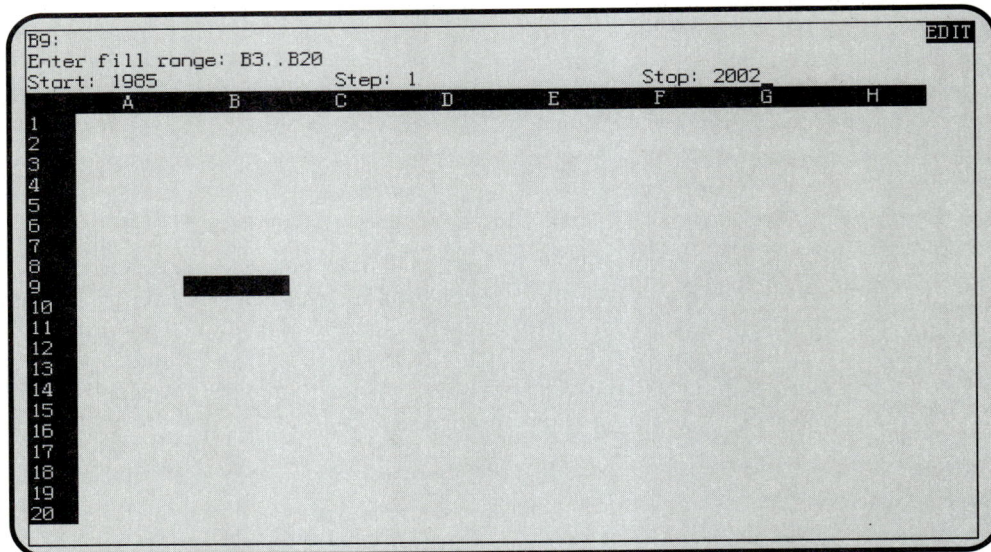

FIGURE 16-1 Entering the parameters for the / Data Fill command.

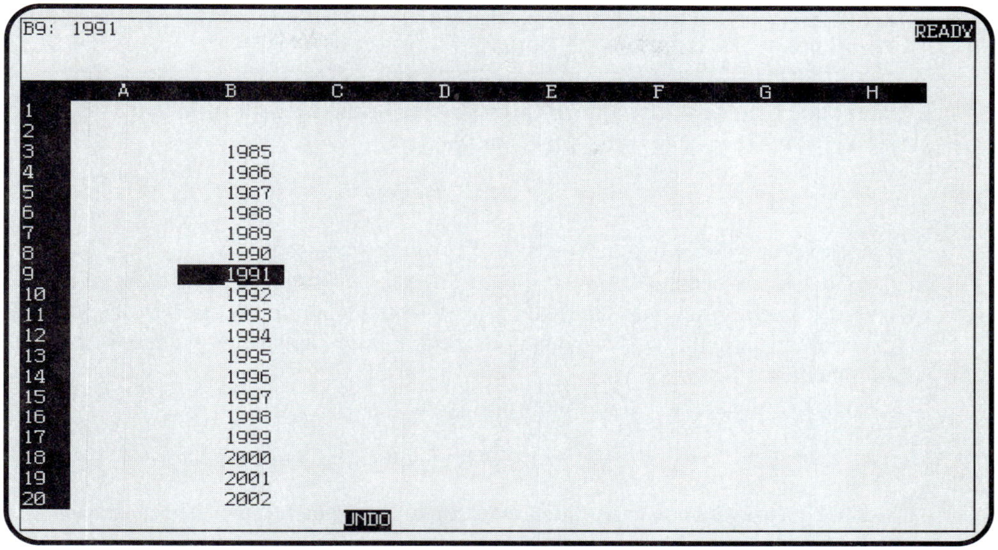

```
B9:  1991                                                        READY

         A          B          C          D      E      F      G      H
 1
 2
 3                 1985
 4                 1986
 5                 1987
 6                 1988
 7                 1989
 8                 1990
 9                 1991
10                 1992
11                 1993
12                 1994
13                 1995
14                 1996
15                 1997
16                 1998
17                 1999
18                 2000
19                 2001
20                 2002
                            UNDO
```

FIGURE 16-2 The result of the / Data Fill Command.

To fill the cells C4..K4 with the sequence 1991, 1992, ... we could set the fill range to C4..K4, the Start to 1991, the Step to 1, and leave the Stop at 8191. The sequence would stop automatically when it reached K4, the last cell in the fill range.

You might find the / Data Fill command easier to use to produce a sequence of numbers than entering and copying a formula.

DATABASE FUNCTIONS

The standard numerical functions @SUM, @COUNT, @AVG, @MAX, @MIN calculate simple statistics. Suppose that instead of finding, say, the average of all of the numbers in a range we want to find the average of only those numbers in rows meeting some criteria. For example, let's return to the real estate spreadsheet in Figure 15-1. To find the average price of all of the houses listed, we would use the @AVG function. Suppose we want to find out the average price of just the 4-bedroom houses. Now we would use the database average function @DAVG. Indeed, there are equivalent database functions @DSUM, @DCOUNT, @DAVG, @DMAX, @DMIN for each of the standard numerical functions listed. These functions selectively include numbers for calculation based on which rows fulfill stated conditions.

The database functions use several of the same concepts as the / Data Query commands discussed in Chapter 15. In particular, the database functions require an Input Range and a Criteria Range to be set up as described in Chapter 15. The top row of the Input Range must contain unique column headings. The rows below contain the data. The top row of the Criteria

Range must contain column headings that correspond to those in the top row of the Input Range. The row(s) below contains the conditions to be met.

To find the average price of houses with four bedrooms, we set up a spreadsheet with an Input Range and Criteria Range as in the previous chapter and Figure 16-3. In B24 in the spreadsheet in Figure 16-3 we have entered the condition

$$(B3=4)$$

to specify the criteria that the number of bedrooms equals 4.

While we do need to set up an Input Range and a Criteria Range in the spreadsheet, we do *not* go through the / Data Query command to establish the location of the Input Range and Criteria Range for the database functions. Rather, we establish these ranges in the arguments for the functions.

The @DAVG function has three arguments:

$$@DAVG(Input Range, Field, Criteria Range)$$

The first argument is the location of the Input Range in the spreadsheet. The column headings must be included as the top row of the Input Range. The second argument is the Field in the Input Range on which the average of selected cells is to be calculated. The Field is a number, the offset number of the column within the Input Range. The leftmost column in the Input Range is Field 0. The next column over from the left is Field 1. And so on. The third argument is the location of the Criteria Range in the spreadsheet. Again, the column headings must be included as the top row.

```
G27: (C0) [W11] @DAVG(A2..G19,6,A23..G24)                              READY

          A            B     C      D      E      F       G           H
14  19 Auburn St        4     2    0.35   Elec    22    $112,500
15  122 Stuyvesant Rd   3     2    1.25   Elec    14    $180,000
16  87 Newbury St       6     2    0.60   Gas     17    $120,000
17  1122 Bellevue       6     3    1.00   Gas      9    $140,000
18  19 Hill Rd          4     2    0.30   Oil     26    $110,000
19  1 Pond Rd           8     5    2.00   Gas     60    $245,000
20
21
22
23  ADDRESS          BDRMS BATHS   LOT    HEAT    AGE     COST
24                      0
25
26
27  AVERAGE COST OF A 4 BEDROOM HOUSE:                  $105,833
28
29
30
31
32
33
                         UNDO
```

FIGURE 16-3 Using the @DAVG function to calculate the average cost of a 4- bedroom house.

In the spreadsheet in Figure 16-3 cell G27 contains the formula

@DAVG(A2..G19,6,A23..G24)

The Input Range is A2..G19, as before. The second argument, the Field, is 6. So the values to be averaged are in the sixth column to the right of the leftmost column. This is column G, the cost of the properties. The Criteria Range is A23..G24. The function then calculates the average cost of the three houses with four bedrooms.

To find the most bedrooms in a house that costs under $100,000, we would set up the Criteria Range as follows:

	A	B	C	D	E	F	G	H
23	ADDRESS	BDRMS	BATHS	LOT	HEAT	AGE	COST	
24							(G4<100000)	

and use the formula

@DMAX(A2..G19,1,A23..G24)

This formula would find the maximum value in column B that is in a row in which the number in column G is under 100,000.

To count the number of homes that are on a lot of at least an acre and have Gas heat we would use the Criteria Range

	A	B	C	D	E	F	G	H
23	ADDRESS	BDRMS	BATHS	LOT	HEAT	AGE	COST	
24				(D4>=1)	(E4="Gas")			

and use the formula

@DCOUNT(A2..G19,1,A23..G24)

This formula would count how many cells in column B contain numbers and are in rows that have a number in column D that is greater than or equal to 1 and contain the word "Gas" in column E. In fact, the second argument in this formula could be 1, 2, 3, 5, or 6 as each of these corresponds to a column that contains numeric values.

As you may have noticed, an alternative to using the database functions is to first extract the rows that match the criteria using the / Data Query Extract command and then use the regular numeric functions on the extracted rows in the Output Range. In either case, statistics are being calculated on rows of data in the Input Range that fulfill the conditions in the Criteria Range.

FREQUENCY DISTRIBUTIONS

A frequency distribution is a tabulation of how many values in a data set fall in certain intervals. For example, if we are the Census Bureau we might want to know how many people in the country are under 5 years old, how many are between 5 and 15 years old, how many are between 15 and 25, and so on. Given the real estate data, we might want to know how many homes cost under $50,000, how many cost at least $50,000 but under $100,000, how many cost at least $100,000 but under $150,000, and so on.

The / Data Distribution command calculates a frequency distribution for a given range of values. The first step is to decide on the intervals ("bins") for the frequency distribution. You might want the dividing points for the bins for the frequency distribution for the real estate data to be $50,000, $100,000, $150,000, ..., or you might want the dividing points of the bins to be $100,000, $200,000, $300,000. You can have many narrow bins or a few broad bins. The bins need not be uniform. You could tabulate the frequency distribution for costs using bins of under $119,900, $119,900 to 133,500, and $133,500 or over. Thus the dividing points would be $119,900 and $133,500.

The second step is to decide on the location of the bin range and enter the dividing points of the bins in ascending order down a column. The cells to the right of the column must be blank.

The third step is to select / Data Distribution. Lotus 1-2-3 prompts you for the locations of the values range and the bin range, as in Figure 16-4. Note that the values range is not a full Input

```
A27: (C0) [W17] 250000                                                    POINT
Enter values range: G3..G19            Enter bin range: A23..A27

            A            B     C      D      E      F       G           H
14  19 Auburn St         4     2    0.35   Elec    22    $112,500
15  122 Stuyvesant Rd    3     2    1.25   Elec    14    $180,000
16  87 Newbury St        6     2    0.60   Gas     17    $120,000
17  1122 Bellevue        6     3    1.00   Gas      9    $140,000
18  19 Hill Rd           4     2    0.30   Oil     26    $110,000
19  1 Pond Rd            8     5    2.00   Gas     60    $245,000
20
21
22      PRICE RANGE    FREQUENCY
23         $50,000
24        $100,000
25        $150,000
26        $200,000
27        $250,000
28
29
30
31
32
33
```

FIGURE 16-4 Entering the parameters for the / Data Distribution command. The range A23..A27 is highlighted because it is being entered by pointing.

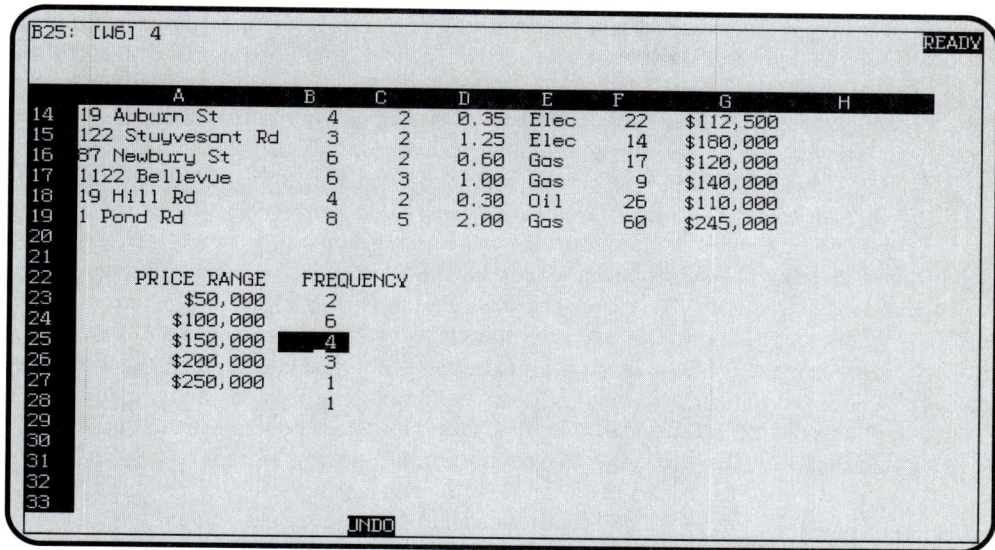

FIGURE 16-5 The resulting frequency distribution. There were four homes that cost over $100,000 but less than or equal to $150,000.

Range, but rather the range containing just the numbers to be tabulated. The bin range should contain just the numbers at the dividing points between the bins. The values range and the bin range can contain no labels or blank cells.

The result of the / Data Distribution command is shown in Figure 16-5. The frequency distribution has been tabulated in the column to the right of the bin range. The number 2 in B23 tells us that there are two numbers in G3..G19 that are less than or equal to 50,000. The number 6 in B24 tells us that there are six numbers in G3..G19 that are greater than 50,000 but less than or equal to 100,000. The number 1 in B28 tells us that there is one number in G3..G19 that is greater than or equal to 250,000.

EXCHANGING DATA WITH OTHER PROGRAMS

People do not use just Lotus 1-2-3 to solve problems. Rather, they use Lotus 1-2-3 as one of a set of powerful tools in their computer tool bag. Other commonly used software tools include word processing programs, database management programs, and accounting programs. It is important to be able to exchange data between Lotus 1-2-3 and other programs. If you have data that have been entered laboriously into another program, you would like to be able to bring it into Lotus 1-2-3 without retyping all the data. Similarly, you would like to be able to export 1000 rows of data from a 1-2-3 spreadsheet to another program without retyping everything.

It is easy to exchange data between two programs if you can find a file format that both programs can read and write. Basically, Lotus 1-2-3 Release 2.2 works with worksheet (.WK1) files and text (.PRN) files. Worksheet files contain the underlying formulas in the spreadsheet. Text files contain the values that appear in the spreadsheet. Any program that works with one of these types of files can exchange information with Lotus 1-2-3.

The .WK1 file format was developed by Lotus specifically for Lotus 1-2-3 Release 2. Lotus 1-2-3 can read .WK1 files from the disk using / File Retrieve and can write .WK1 files using / File Save. Lotus 1-2-3 is so popular that many different programs can read and write .WK1 files directly, also. Exchanging data with these programs is simple and direct. You write a .WK1 file to the disk in one program and read the file in the other program.

Text files can be read and written directly by word processing programs and by many other programs. A text file is simply a long sequence of typed characters that is saved on the disk.

To export data from Lotus 1-2-3 to a word processing program, and to many other programs we can save the data as a text file. In Chapter 6 we saw how to use the Print command to do this. Basically, the idea is to set up a report for printing but instead of sending it to the printer, we send it to a text file on the disk. This file then can be read by a word processing program. To export the data in the real estate database to a word processing program, we would select / Print File REALTY enter Range A1..G19 enter Go Quit. The result would be a text file named REALTY.PRN on the disk that would contain all the information that appears on the screen in the range A1..G19. We would then Quit out of Lotus 1-2-3, enter the word processing program, and read in the text file REALTY.PRN.

IMPORTING DATA FROM A WORD PROCESSING PROGRAM

To import data from a word processing program to Lotus 1-2-3, we can first save the information as a text file in the word processing program. We then quit out of the word processing program and enter Lotus 1-2-3. To bring the data in the text file into Lotus 1-2-3 we use the special command / File Import Text. We then might need to manipulate the data using the / Data Parse command.

For example, suppose that a list of employees, their job titles, salaries, and date of hire has been created using a word processing program and stored on the disk as a text file. A printout of a short version of the file appears in Figure 16-6. We would like to import the data into Lotus 1-2-3 so we can search through the database, sort the entries in various ways, tally up averages for different job titles, and so on. With a blank spreadsheet we select / File Import Text and enter the name of the text file. The information is read into Lotus 1-2-3. The resulting spreadsheet is shown in Figure 16-7.

The spreadsheet in Figure 16-7 may look all right at first glance, but a closer examination reveals a serious problem. The cursor in the screen display in Figure 16-7 is in A2. The top line of the screen reveals that A2 contains the full line of information! Cells B2, C2, D2, and E2 are blank! All the information in the first line has been placed in A2 as one long label. The / File Import Text command always places all information in column A, one line of text in each cell.

```
Jackson   Warren    Supervisor    47,000    08/24/88
Baker     Linda     Exec VP      167,000    11/15/85
Morris    John      Secretary     12,389    03/07/90
Rankin    Allen     Manager       83,700    04/12/78
Johnson   Tiffany   Clerk         10,466    08/22/88
Clark     Janet     Secretary     14,308    08/14/90
```

FIGURE 16-6 The data as it appears in the text file.

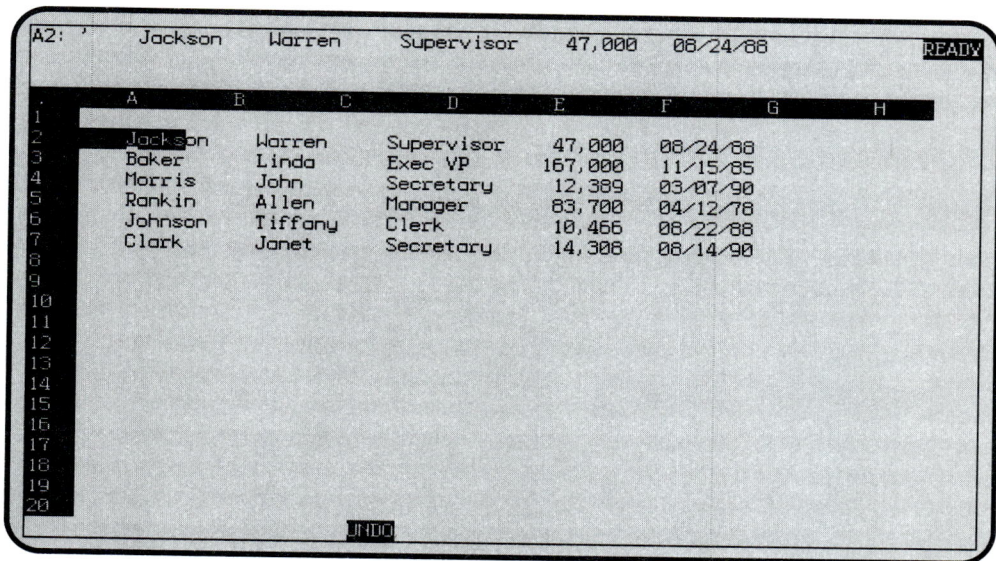

FIGURE 16-7 The spreadsheet that results from bringing in the data using / File Import Text.

The spreadsheet in Figure 16-7 is close to useless the way it is set up. For example, we could not total the salaries because the salaries do not appear as values in separate cells. Rather, the salaries are embedded in the middle of long labels in column A. To make the spreadsheet usable, we need to **parse** or break up the long labels in column A into separate entries.

THE / DATA PARSE COMMAND

The / Data Parse command is provided for the purpose of breaking up long labels into several cell entries. The / Data Parse command is another weird and wonderful Lotus 1-2-3 command with its own unique set of conventions.

In the example in Figure 16-7 we now select / Data Parse. The resulting screen is shown in Figure 16-8. The next step in parsing the labels is to create a format line by selecting Format-Line Create. The Format-Line Create command in the / Data Parse menu automatically inserts a new row above the cursor and places a newly created format line in the new cell in column A. A **format line** is a pattern for splitting up long labels into different entries. The format line created by this command for the label in A2 is shown in Figure 16-9.

A format line consists of a sequence of certain letters and other characters. The letters indicate the beginning position and the type of each entry or field. The meaning of each of the characters in a format line is as follows:

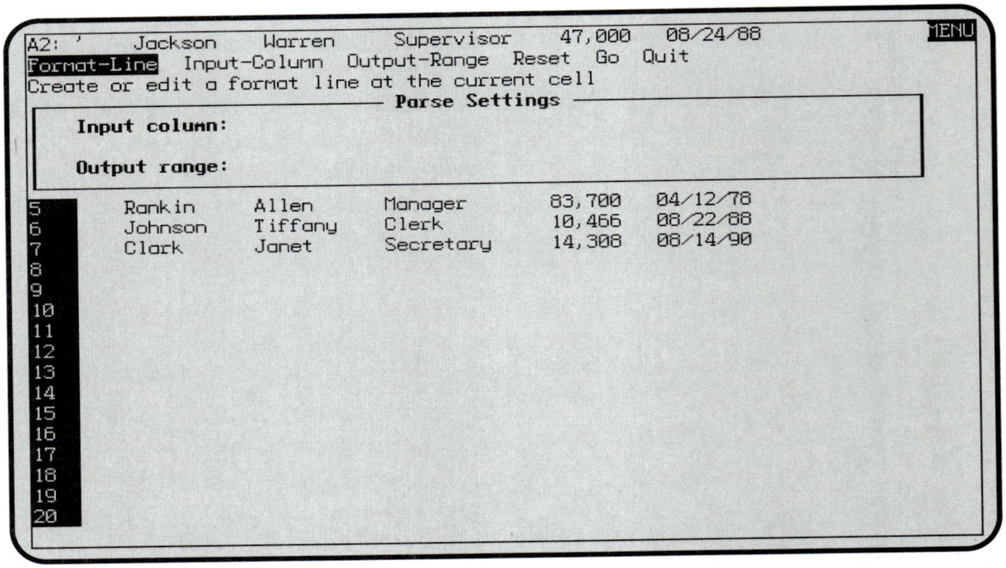

```
A2: '      Jackson    Warren    Supervisor    47,000    08/24/88              MENU
Format-Line  Input-Column  Output-Range  Reset  Go  Quit
Create or edit a format line at the current cell
                        ┌─── Parse Settings ───
    Input column:
    Output range:

5        Rankin     Allen     Manager     83,700    04/12/78
6        Johnson    Tiffany   Clerk       10,466    08/22/88
7        Clark      Janet     Secretary   14,308    08/14/90
8
9
10
...
20
```

FIGURE 16-8 The / Data Parse menu.

```
A2: |****L>>>>>>****L>>>>>*****L>>>>>>>>>****V>>>>>***D>>>>>>>                              READY

            A         B         C         D         E        F        G       H
1
2     ****L>>>>>>>*****L>>>>>*****L>>>>>>>>>****V>>>>>***D>>>>>>>
3     Jackson    Warren    Supervisor   47,000    08/24/88
4     Baker      Linda     Exec VP      167,000   11/15/85
5     Morris     John      Secretary    12,389    03/07/90
6     Rankin     Allen     Manager      83,700    04/12/78
7     Johnson    Tiffany   Clerk        10,466    08/22/88
8     Clark      Janet     Secretary    14,308    08/14/90
9
10
11
12
13
14
15
16
17
18
19
20
                            UNDO
```

FIGURE 16-9 The format line created by the / Data Parse command

L	Indicates the beginning of a Label field
V	Indicates the beginning of a Value field
D	Indicates the beginning of a Date field
T	Indicates the beginning of a Time field
S	Indicates the beginning of a Skip field
>	Indicates the continuation of a field
*	Indicates blank spaces that may be part of a field
|	The first character in a format line

Thus, the format line

|****L>>>>>>>****L>>>>>>*****L>>>>>>>>>>****V>>>>>>***D>>>>>>>>

indicates that the entry begins with four spaces (****), followed by a label of seven characters (L>>>>>>), followed by four spaces (****), followed a label of six characters (L>>>>>), followed by five spaces (*****), and so on. Note that the format line is wholly contained in A2.

If the format line created using the Format-Line Create command is not quite right, we can edit the format line using the Format-Line Edit command.

Once we are happy with the format line it is time to apply the format line to the column of labels. We need to specify the Input Column for the parsing process and the Output Range. The Input Column is simply the location of the labels to be parsed. The Output Range is the location in the spreadsheet where we want the entries to be placed.

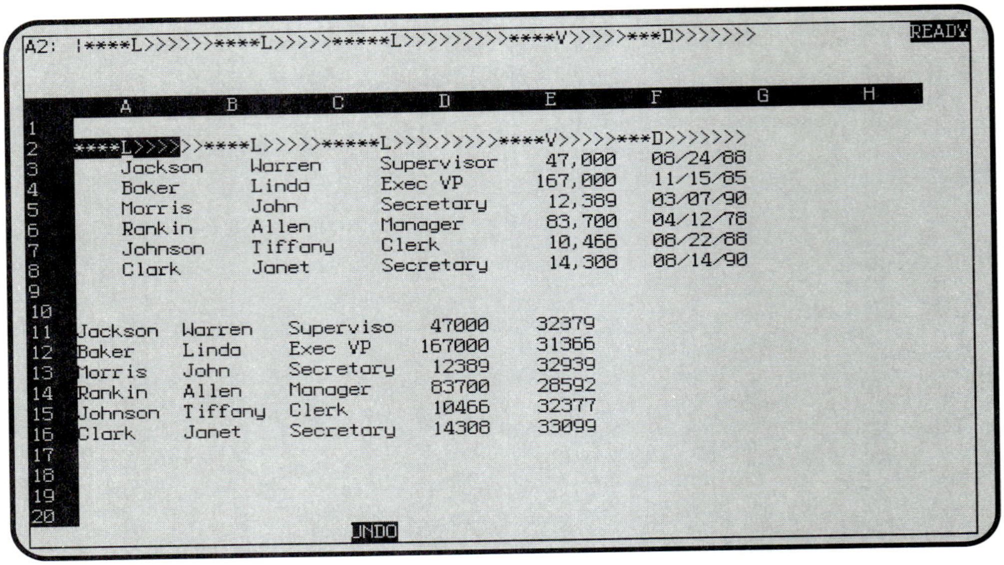

FIGURE 16-10 The result of the parsing process.

In the example, in the /Data Parse menu we select Input-Column A2..A8 enter. The top cell in the Input Column must be a format line. Then we select Output-Range A11 enter to indicate the top left corner of the range for the output of the parsing process. We next select Go. The resulting spreadsheet is shown in Figure 16-10.

In A11..E16 in Figure 16-10, the entries are each in different cells. The parsing process has broken apart the long labels in A3..A8 according to the format line in A2 and put the results in A11..E16. We could widen column C so that the full job titles show. The salary numbers were placed in D11..D16 without commas. We could format these cells as Comma with 0 decimal places. The dates were placed in E11..E16; the numbers in E11..E16 are the serial numbers for the dates. We could format the cells in E11..E16 as Date 4 so that the values would again appear as dates of the form MM/DD/YY.

The final step would be to erase the long labels in A2..A8 and then possibly move the data up toward the top of the worksheet. We now could work with the data just as we would the data in any other spreadsheet.

The / File Import command and / Data Parse command can be used to import the data in any text file.

THE TRANSLATE PROGRAM

Lotus does provide a program that translates Release 2.2 worksheet files into the file formats used by some other popular programs. The Translate program converts files between the .WK1 format, the format of Lotus 1-2-3 Release 2 worksheet files, and the file formats of

- 1-2-3 Release 1A
- dBASE II
- dBASE III (and dBASE III Plus)
- Multiplan
- Symphony

The Translate program is not part of 1-2-3 itself, but rather is a separate program, like PrintGraph. Translate can be entered through the Lotus 1-2-3 Access System by selecting Translate from the Access System menu (see Figure 2-5), or it can be run directly from the disk operating system by typing TRANS.

To move data from Lotus 1-2-3 Release 2.2 to another program using Translate, you would

1. save the data in Lotus 1-2-3 using / File Save or / File Xtract.
2. exit from 1-2-3.
3. run the Translate program, converting the file into the format for the program desired.
4. exit from the Translate program into DOS.
5. run the other program.
6. read in the data.

The / File Xtract command is like the / File Save command except it allows you to save only a portion of the current worksheet on the disk. Thus if you wanted to move only a portion of the current worksheet to another program, you would save just that portion on the disk using / File Xtract before running the Translate program.

The / File Xtract command is especially useful for moving Lotus 1-2-3 data to dBASE. The key to translating a worksheet file into a dBASE file is that the data in the worksheet file must be of the form of a Lotus 1-2-3 database Input Range, as described in the previous chapter. That is, the data that is translated must be a rectangular range that includes a top row of column headings. For example, to move the real estate data into dBASE you would first save the data values (with the column headings) by selecting / File Xtract Values HOUSES enter A2..G19 enter. You would then proceed with step 2. In the Translate program you would instruct the program to convert the HOUSES worksheet file into the appropriate dBASE format.

The Translate program is included with the commercial version of Lotus 1-2-3 Release 2.2 but is not included with many of the student versions.

DATA TABLES

The / Data Table command provides an outstanding tool for automating and recording "What if" analysis. The / Data Table command takes some work to understand but the effort is well worthwhile. The best way to explain what this powerful command does and how it works is with an example.

ARKANSAS CHICKEN WINGS

Everyone has always liked the Arkansas chicken wings you make using a time-honored recipe. People keep telling you that you ought to go into the chicken wing business. So you and your roommates decide to give it a try. You will make the wings in your kitchen. People will call up from 4 PM to midnight to order the wings by the pound, and you will deliver to their room or apartment. You figure it will cost $2.50 per pound to make the chicken wings, including chicken, sauce ingredients, packaging, and so on plus $200 per week to pay for advertising, promotions, automobile costs, and so on. You tentatively plan to charge $5.99 per pound for the wings. You and your roommates would like to know how much you would make financially.

Initially, you set up the spreadsheet in Figure 16-11. The spreadsheet shows that if you sell 100 pounds of chicken wings in a week at $5.99 per pound then you will show a profit of $149 for the week. To see the profits that would result from selling 150 pounds, you would change the number in cell D5 to 150.

Suppose you would like to know the profit that would result from selling 0 lb., 50 lb., 100 lb., ... 500 lb. of chicken wings each week. One approach would be to copy the formulas in column D across the spreadsheet and have each different column be the calculations for a different quantity of chicken wings sold. A second approach is to use the / Data Table command.

To use the / Data Table command we enter the different quantities that we might sell in column F, as in Figure 16-12. The / Data Table command will take each of the numbers in column F as "input" to the formulas in the spreadsheet and record the result of the calculations in column G. In

```
E5:                                                              READY

         A         B         C         D         E      F        G
1
2             ARKANSAS CHICKEN WINGS - WEEKLY PROFIT PROJECTIONS
3             ================================================
4
5    INPUTS     QTY SOLD IN LBS.        100
6               SELLING PRICE/LB.      $5.99
7
8               FIXED COST           $200.00
9               VARIABLE COST/LB.      $2.50
10
11   ---------------------------------------------------
12
13   RESULTS    TOTAL SALES          $599.00
14
15                 FIXED COST        $200.00
16                 VARIABLE COST     $250.00
17               TOTAL COST          $450.00
18
19               PROFIT              $149.00
20
                            UNDO
```

FIGURE 16-11 An initial spreadsheet for figuring your possible weekly profits from selling Arkansas chicken wings.

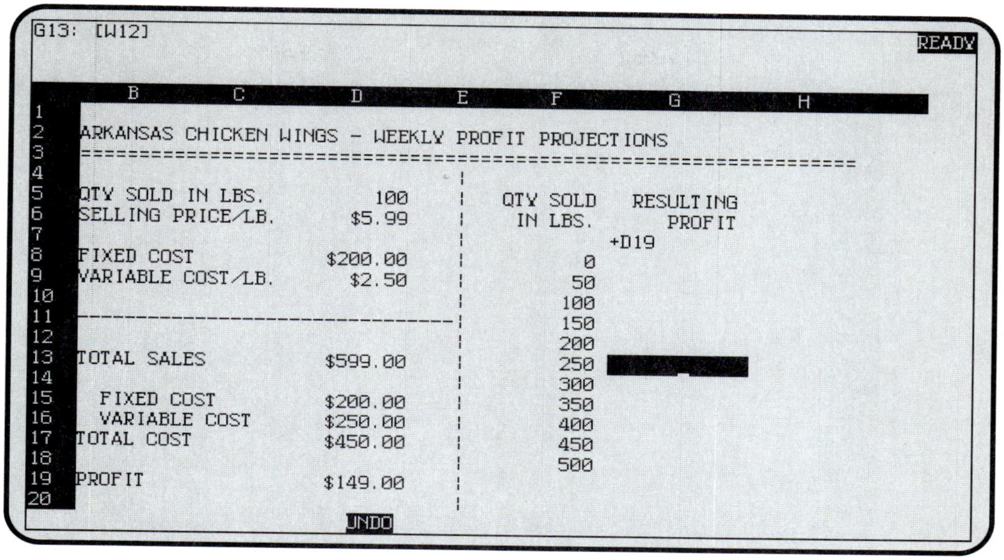

FIGURE 16-12 Setting up the spreadsheet for "What if" analysis using the / Data Table 1 command. The cell in G7 has been formatted using the / Range Format Text command. The cell contains the formula +D19 as D19 is the cell where the profit is to be found.

particular, we will inform Lotus 1-2-3 that each of the numbers in column F is to be used as input in cell D5. In cell G7 we put the formula +D19 so that Lotus 1-2-3 will know that the values to be put into column G are to be found in cell D19 after the calculations are complete. In the spreadsheet in Figure 16-12, we have formatted the cell in G7 as Text so that the formula is displayed.

After selecting / Data Table we are confronted with the choice of 1, 2, or Reset . There are two variations in the / Data Table command. Namely, we can create one-variable data tables or two-variable data tables. Here we will select 1 for one-variable data tables. In the next section we will create a two-variable data table. After selecting / Data Table 1 we are asked for the table range. We enter F7..G18.

The table range includes all of the input values to be tried plus blank cells to the right for the results of the calculations plus an extra row on top. The top left cell in the table range should be blank. The cell to the right in the top row must be a formula. The result of this formula will be the value that is entered in each of the cells below.

After entering the table range, we are asked for the input cell. We enter D5 as that is the cell where the numbers in column F are to be substituted. We press the Enter key. Lotus 1-2-3 fills in column G with the values that result after substituting each of the values in column F into D5. We then format the cells in G8..G18 as Currency with two places and widen column G so that the numbers all show. The spreadsheet in Figure 16-13 is the final result. We can see the profits that would result from different quantities sold.

Thus, the / Data Table command can be used to record the results of varying an input value in a spreadsheet. The basic idea is to set up a spreadsheet with all the formulas necessary to calculate

```
G13: (C2) [W12] 672.5                                              READY

        B        C        D        E    F       G          H
 1
 2  ARKANSAS CHICKEN WINGS - WEEKLY PROFIT PROJECTIONS
 3  =================================================================
 4                                      |
 5  QTY SOLD IN LBS.        100         |  QTY SOLD   RESULTING
 6  SELLING PRICE/LB.       $5.99       |   IN LBS.     PROFIT
 7                                      |             +D19
 8  FIXED COST              $200.00     |     0     ($200.00)
 9  VARIABLE COST/LB.       $2.50       |    50      ($25.50)
10                                      |   100       $149.00
11  -----------------------------------|   150       $323.50
12                                      |   200       $498.00
13  TOTAL SALES             $599.00     |   250       $672.50
14                                      |   300       $847.00
15     FIXED COST           $200.00     |   350     $1,021.50
16     VARIABLE COST        $250.00     |   400     $1,196.00
17  TOTAL COST              $450.00     |   450     $1,370.50
18                                      |   500     $1,545.00
19  PROFIT                  $149.00     |
20
                          UNDO
```

FIGURE 16-13 The spreadsheet after the completion of the / Data Table 1 command. The values in G8..G18 have been formatted as Currency.

```
K12: [W8]                                                          READY

        B       C      D   E F G    H      I      J      K      L
 1
 2  ARKANSAS CHICKEN WINGS - WEEKLY PROFIT PROJECTIONS
 3  =================================================================
 4                            |
 5  QTY SOLD IN LBS.     100  | PROFITS FOR VARIOUS QTY SOLD AND PRICE/LB
 6  SELLING PRICE/LB  $5.99   |
 7                            |               SELLING PRICE/LB.
 8  FIXED COST        $200.00 | +D19   2.99   3.99   4.99   5.99   6.99
 9  VARIABLE COST/LB  $2.50   |    0
10                            |   50
11  ------------------------- | Q 100
12                            | T 150
13  TOTAL SALES       $599.00 | Y 200
14                            |   250
15     FIXED COST     $200.00 | S 300
16     VARIABLE COST  $250.00 | O 350
17  TOTAL COST        $450.00 | L 400
18                            | D 450
19  PROFIT            $149.00 |   500
20                            |
                          UNDO
```

FIGURE 16-14 Setting up a two-variable data table.

the result for a given input value. We then set up a special table. The top left cell in the table is blank. The left column contains the different input values we would like to try. The top right cell contains a formula that yields the output value. The right column is blank and will be filled with the output values. We select / Data Table 1 and enter the table range and the location of the input cell for the formulas. Lotus 1-2-3 proceeds to repeat the calculations for each of the input values in the left column of the table and enter the resulting output in the cell to the right in the table.

TWO-VARIABLE DATA TABLES

We have seen how the profits from our chicken wing enterprise would change with different weekly sales volumes. Suppose we also would like to see the effect of different selling prices on the profits. That is, we wish to see the sensitivity of profits to different levels of both quantities sold and selling price. This is accomplished by creating a two-variable data table.

We return to the original spreadsheet of Figure 16-11. To the right we set up a table with various quantities down the left column and with various prices across the top row, as in Figure 16-14. In the top left cell, G8, of the table we put the output formula. The table has 5 columns of prices and 11 rows of quantity sold. Lotus 1-2-3 will run the formulas in the spreadsheet 55 times and fill in the profits that would result from each combination of prices and quantities in the appropriate cell of the table.

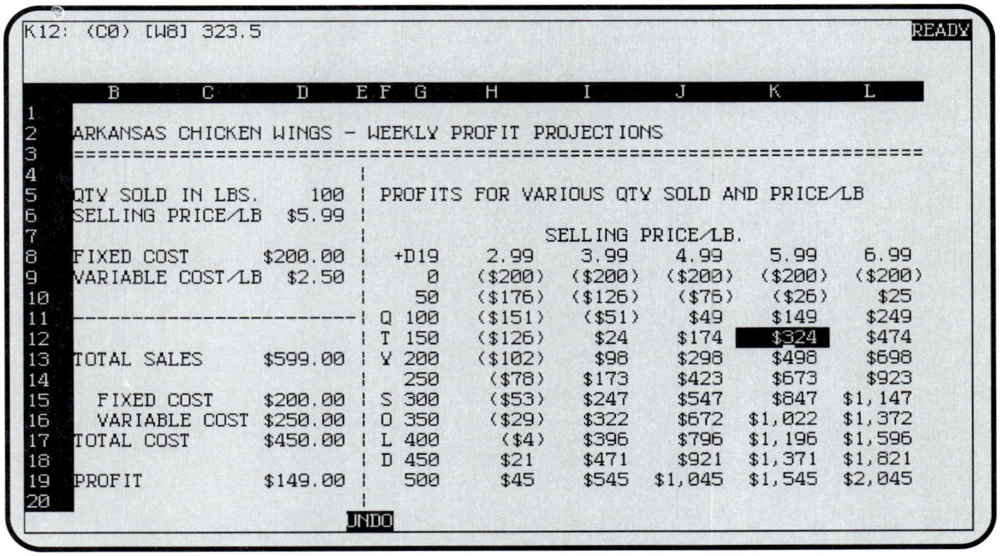

FIGURE 16-15 The two-variable data table with filled in values formatted as currency with no decimal places.

We select / Data Table 2 and then enter G8..L19 for the table range. It is vital that we include the top row of prices and the left column of quantities sold but not the labels above and to the left in the range of the table. The computer asks for "input cell 1." We enter D5, as D5 is the cell where the values in the left column should be substituted. The computer asks for "input cell 2." We enter D6, as D6 is the cell where the values in the top row should be substituted. That's it. The computer pauses a moment while it performs the 55 sets of calculations. We format the cells in H9..L19 as Currency with 0 decimal places. The spreadsheet in Figure 16-15 is the result. At a glance we can see the profits that would result from different levels of selling prices and quantities sold.

The / Data Table command works for any set of formulas and input values. This command really is one of the most powerful tools in Lotus 1-2-3.

PENCIL AND PAPER EXERCISES

16-1   Consider again the Used Car City database in Exercise 15-1. We would like to
       calculate some statistics on the cars listed in the database. For each of the following,
       please show (1) the formula and (2) the contents of the Criteria Range.
       (a) The number of Lincolns.
       (b) The year of the oldest Chevrolet.
       (c) The number of cars with over 100,000 miles.
       (d) The number of cars built before 1989 that have fewer than 50,000 miles.
       (e) The average mileage for 1988 models.
       (f) The lowest price of a car that is either a black Rolls Royce or a silver Mercedes-
           Benz.

16-2   We would like to create a table using the Used Car City database that lists each of the
       years from 1970 on and next to the year the number of cars on the lot from that year.
       Explain in detail how to create this table.

COMPUTER EXERCISES

16-3   Use the / Data Fill command to create columns containing the following:
       (a) The sequence of years from 1993 through 2010.
       (b) The sequence of years 1950, 1960, 1970, ..., 2100.
       (c) The sequence of numbers 24.3, 24.4, 24.5, ..., 26.6
       (d) The sequence of times 08:00 AM, 08:30 AM, 09:00 AM, ..., 06:00 PM.
       (e) The sequence of months Jul-92, Aug-92, Sep-92, ..., Jun-95.

16-4   Retrieve the spreadsheet from Exercise 15-2 with the list of the largest computer
       companies.
       (a) Use @DCOUNT to calculate the number of United States companies in the list.
           Hint: Count a numeric field.
       (b) Use @DMAX to find the highest Total Revenue of a Japanese company on the
           list.
       (c) Use a database function to find the best 1989 rank of a company that did not rank
           in the top 10 in 1988.
       (d) Use a database function to find the highest IS Revenue of a company that is not
           from the United States or Japan.

(e) Create a table that lists IS Revenue in increments of $1 billion and next to each amount the number of companies with IS Revenue of that amount.

16-5 Retrieve the spreadsheet from Exercise 15-3 with the list of courses you have taken.
   (a) Use @DMIN to find the best rating you gave a course you took last semester.
   (b) Use @DCOUNT to calculate the number of courses in which you received a B or better. *Hint: Count a numeric field.*
   (c) Use a database function to find the worst rating you gave a course in which you received a grade of B or better.
   (d) Use a database function to find the best rating you gave a course that you took at least a year ago.
   (e) Create a table that lists each of the ratings from 1 through 4 and next to each rating the number of courses given that rating. Use the / Data Distribution command.

16-6 Retrieve the spreadsheet from Exercise 15-4 with the list of the most influential persons in history.
   (a) Use @DAVG to find the average birth date of the religious leaders.
   (b) Use @DCOUNT to calculate the number of people from Germany in the list. *Hint: Count a numeric field.*
   (c) Use a database function to find the date of birth of the person on the list from China who was born the earliest.
   (d) Use a database function to find the best rank of a Political leader from China.
   (e) Find out how many of the people on the list lived in each 400-year period from 1400 B.C. through the present. That is, 1400 B.C. to 1000 B.C. is the first period, 1000 B.C. to 600 B.C. the next period, and so on through 1800 to 2200. Use the / Data Distribution command to create a table to answer this question.

16-7 Retrieve the spreadsheet from Exercise 15-2, 15-3, or 15-4.
   (a) Save the data portion of the spreadsheet as a text file using / Print File. Call the file EX16_7. Exit from Lotus 1-2-3.
   (b) Start up a word processing program. Read in the file. Add your name, the date, and Exercise 16-7b to the top of the page. Print the results. Exit from the word processing program.
   (c) Start up Lotus 1-2-3. With a blank worksheet on the screen, read the text file EX16_7 using the / File Import Text command. Look through the worksheet. Does all of the information appear in column A as long labels?
   (d) Use the / Data Parse command to create a format line for the data. You may need to Edit the format line to make it exactly right for all of the data. Print the format line and the top dozen lines of the data.
   (e) Use the format line and the / Data Parse command to break up the column of labels into separate entries.

(f) Just below the newly created database, add formulas to calculate the averages of the columns that contain numeric entries. For example, for the *Datamation* database in Exercise 15-2, you would add formulas to calculate the average IS Revenue of all the companies listed and the average Total Revenue. If you can successfully calculate the averages, then you have parsed the labels correctly. Print the bottom dozen rows of the database and the averages calculated.

16-8 For drawing up a will an attorney charges a base fee of $100 plus $75 per hour. Use the / Data Fill command and the / Data Table 1 command to create a table that shows the hours from 1 through 20 in one column and the resulting amount the attorney charges in the next column. Your spreadsheet should look as follows.

```
F15:                                                                    READY

          A          B          C          D          E          F          G          H
1
2                         FEES FOR DRAWING UP A WILL
3
4                    (At $100 base fee plus $75 per hour)
5
6
7               Hours       Fee
8                          +F11
9                 1        $175            Hours            3
10                2        $250
11                3        $325            Fee             $325
12                4        $400
13                5        $475
14                6        $550
15                7        $625
16                8        $700
17                9        $775
18               10        $850
19               11        $925
20               12      $1,000
                           UNDO
```

16-9 Use the / Data Table 2 command to create a multiplication table like the one shown in Figure 7-12.

16-10 Retrieve the spreadsheet on the Skopi Project from Exercise 13-7.

(a) To help determine the sensitivity of rate of return to annual revenues, add a one-dimensional data table to the spreadsheet. The left column in the table will show possible annual revenues (for years 5 through 13) of $0M, $1M, $2M, ..., $12M. The right column in the table will show the resulting internal rate of return for the project.

(b) Add a two-dimensional data table to the spreadsheet. The horizontal values at the top of the data table will be different possible Year 2 Construction Costs of $6M, $8M, $10M, ..., $18M. The vertical values to the left of the data table will be different possible annual revenues. The table will show the sensitivity of rate of return to different levels of initial construction costs and annual revenues.

ALLWAYS

17

Allways is a **spreadsheet publisher**, a separate program from Lotus 1-2-3 that can be used with 1-2-3 to print spreadsheets and graphs so they appear more professional. Allways is a great improvement over the / Print command. For example, with Allways text and numbers can be printed in different sizes, in different fonts, in bold or underlined. Graphs can be printed within spreadsheets. Areas of the spreadsheet can be printed shaded or with boxes drawn around them. Allways takes advantage of the capabilities of laser printers.

Allways is provided free with the standard edition of Lotus 1-2-3 Release 2.2, but not with the various student editions. Allways can be purchased as a separate product. To run Allways, your computer must have a hard disk and at least 512K of primary memory.

Allways has a setup procedure just like the installation procedure in Lotus 1-2-3. During the setup procedure, the relevant files are transferred under computer control to your hard disk. The setup procedure must be followed once, before you use Allways for the first time, but not again unless you change equipment. During the setup procedure you tell the program the printer(s) and type of display you use with your computer so that the proper drivers can be loaded with Allways. Drivers are low-level computer programs that directly control the printers and displays.

The screens and printouts produced by Allways look different on different computers. Higher-quality displays and printers produce much better-looking output with Allways.

ATTACHING AND INVOKING ADD-INS

Allways is an **add-in** program, a separate program that can be run with Lotus 1-2-3 to increase its power and capabilities. There are dozens of different add-in programs. There are add-in programs for auditing spreadsheets, annotating spreadsheets, producing three-dimensional graphs, and performing word processing tasks with spreadsheets. Add-in programs have been produced by Lotus Development and by other companies. Add-ins have become so popular that Release 2.2 of Lotus 1-2-3 includes commands for attaching and invoking add-in programs.

Attaching an add-in is the process of loading the program from the disk into the main memory along side of Lotus 1-2-3. Of course, add-in programs take up memory so you need to have some spare primary memory beyond what is required for the Lotus 1-2-3 program and your current spreadsheet. The amount of memory required for Allways varies depending on the display(s) and printer(s) you use on your system. On my system Allways requires 60K. You can check on the primary memory available at any time in Lotus 1-2-3 using the / Worksheet Status command.

To attach an add-in you can use / Add-In Attach. Lotus 1-2-3 then displays the names of the current add-in programs on the disk. You select Allways. (If Allways is not a choice then you have not run the Allways setup program properly. You must exit from 1-2-3 and set up Allways.) Next Lotus 1-2-3 displays the somewhat cryptic menu

```
No-Key 7 8 9 10
```

In this menu, Lotus 1-2-3 is asking you whether you wish to assign a special "speed key" for invoking the add-in program. For example, if you select 7 then you can invoke Allways at any time from Lotus 1-2-3 by pressing Alt-F7. If you select 8 then you can invoke Allways by pressing Alt-F8. After making your selection you should see the copyright notice for Allways and then be returned back to the / Add-In menu. At this point you can either Quit back into 1-2-3 or invoke Allways.

Invoking an add-in program means turning control of the computer over to the program. With add-in programs, your spreadsheet stays in primary memory all the time along with the Lotus 1-2-3 program and any add-ins that have been attached. There are two ways of invoking an add-in program from Lotus 1-2-3. You can either use the / Add-In Invoke command or you can use the "speed key" Alt-F7 if you established that shortcut when you attached the program.

Once you invoke an add-in program, control is turned over to the add-in program. Normally the spreadsheet still will be visible on the screen, but you will be communicating with the add-in program rather than Lotus 1-2-3. When you quit out of the add-in program, control is returned to Lotus 1-2-3.

USING ALLWAYS

Our company maintains regional headquarter offices in seven cities. Personnel assigned to these offices are paid different stipends depending on the cost of living in the cities. We have prepared the spreadsheet in Figure 17-1 showing the relative cost of living in each of the cities using the cost of living in New York as a base factor of 100. (This data is from the United Nations.) The spreadsheet will be used as an exhibit in a report and as part of a presentation, so we would like to print it out using Allways.

To invoke Allways, select / Add-In Invoke and then select Allways from the list of attached add-in programs (or press Alt-F7). Control is passed over to the Allways program. The details of the appearance of the screen will vary from computer to computer. Usually the screen is inverted in Allways; that is, black becomes white and white becomes black, as in Figure 17-2.

The cursor control keys work in Allways just as they do in Lotus 1-2-3, though the cursor moves more slowly in Allways. Allways uses a menu system just like that in Lotus 1-2-3, but of course with different commands. Allways contains a Help system that is accessed by pressing F1. To exit from Allways back to Lotus 1-2-3, either press the Escape key or select the Allways command / Quit.

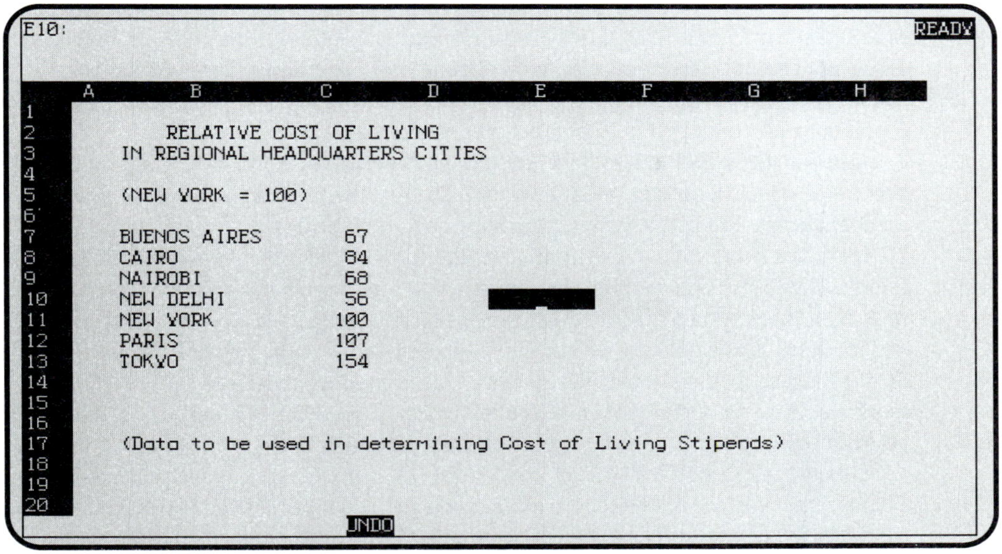

FIGURE 17-1 The original Lotus 1-2-3 spreadsheet.

FONT(1) Helvetica 10 pt
E10:

```
        A        B            C        D        E        F        G
1
2              RELATIVE COST OF LIVING
3              IN REGIONAL HEADQUARTERS CITIES
4
5              (NEW YORK = 100)
6
7              BUENOS AIRES        67
8              CAIRO               84
9              NAIROBI             68
10             NEW DELHI           56
11             NEW YORK           100
12             PARIS              107
13             TOKYO              154
14
15
16
17             (Data to be used in determining Cost of Living Stipends)
18
19
20
```

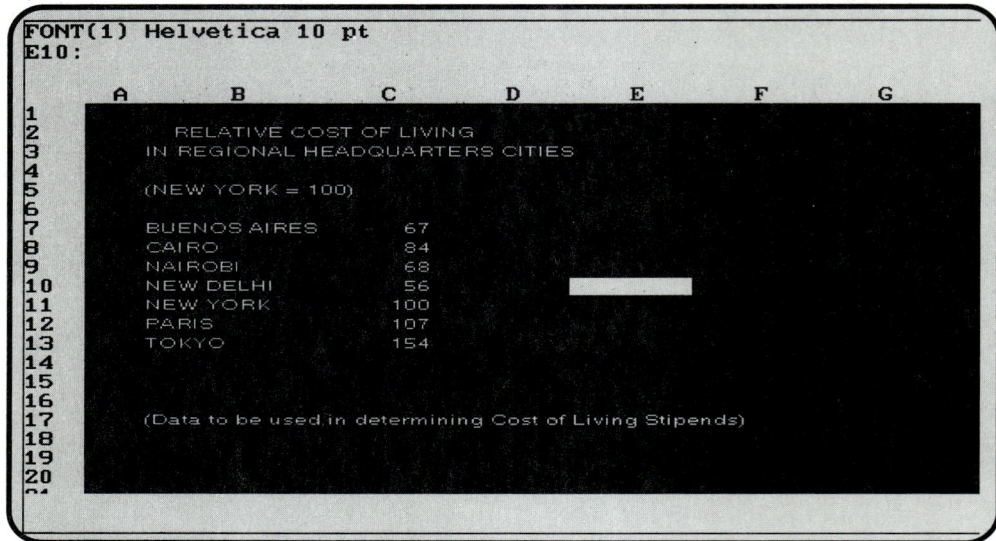

FIGURE 17-2 The screen after invoking Allways.

FONTS

Allways allows for characters to be displayed in different fonts and different styles. At the top of the screen in Figure 17-2 Allways is informing us that the current cell is displayed in Helvetica 10 point. The different fonts available depend on your printer. Some of the possible fonts are shown in Figure 17-3. The size of a character is stated in points. Allways offers type sizes of from 5 points to 24 points, with 10 points being standard.

Suppose we would like to have the top two lines of the spreadsheet appear in Helvetica 20 point. We select / Format Font in Allways. The resulting screen is shown in Figure 17-4. There are eight active fonts in Allways, which are shown in the box in the screen. To select Helvetica 20 point, we either type 4, the number of the font, or press the down arrow key three times to point to the font. Then we press the Enter key to inform Allways that we would like to Use this font. Next Allways asks us to "Enter range to format with font." We enter B2..B3. The result is that the entries in B2..B3 are written in Helvetica 20 point, as in Figure 17-5. Note that the heights of rows 2 and 3 have been increased to accommodate the larger type. Fewer rows of the worksheet now fit on the screen. We could have specified B2..H3 for the new font, but there was no need to, as the text actually is entered into B2 and B3.

Allways is a **WYSIWYG** program. WYSIWYG stands for What You See Is What You Get. That is, what you see on the screen is what you get on the printer. The screen display is the same as what will be printed. The top two lines are displayed in 20 point and will be printed in 20 point.

To show the next line in Helvetica Italic, we go through the same procedure. We select / Format Font, and then Helvetica Italic 10 point, and then select a range of B5.

This is Courier.
This is Helvetica.
This is Helvetica Italic.
This is Helvetica narrow.
This is New Century Schoolbook.
This is Palatino.
This is Times Roman.

FIGURE 17-3 Some of the fonts available in Allways. Font selection depends on your printer.

At any time there are eight active fonts in Allways. These are the fonts that show in the box when you select / Format Font. Many printers support dozens of fonts. To replace one of the eight active fonts with a different font, select / Format Font Replace. The program then displays all the fonts supported for your printer. You select the new font and font size you would like to use. Then you select the current active font you wish to replace. The new font now becomes one of the eight active fonts that you can use directly in your spreadsheet.

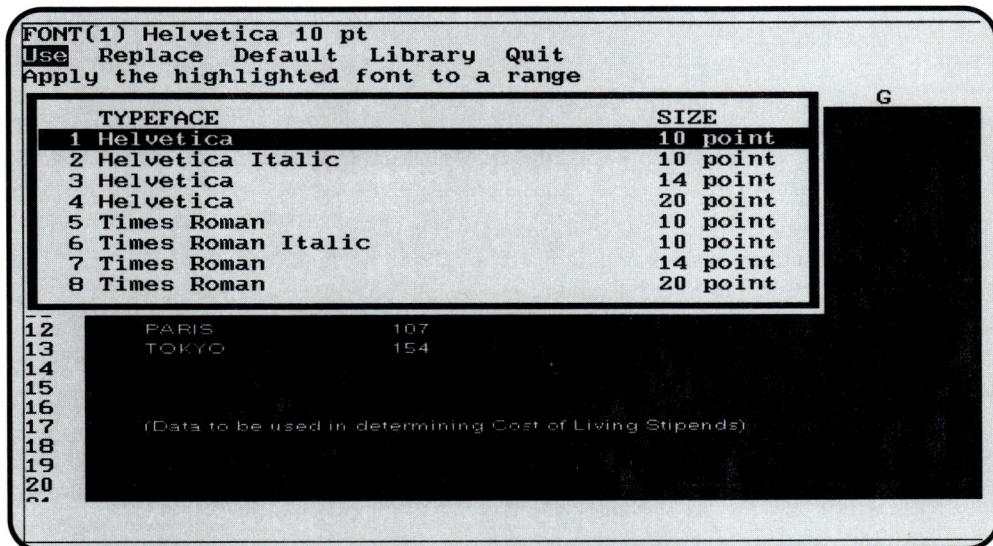

```
FONT(1) Helvetica 10 pt
Use  Replace  Default  Library  Quit
Apply the highlighted font to a range
                                                              G
     TYPEFACE                            SIZE
   1 Helvetica                           10 point
   2 Helvetica Italic                    10 point
   3 Helvetica                           14 point
   4 Helvetica                           20 point
   5 Times Roman                         10 point
   6 Times Roman Italic                  10 point
   7 Times Roman                         14 point
   8 Times Roman                         20 point

12      PARIS            107
13      TOKYO            154
14
15
16
17      (Data to be used in determining Cost of Living Stipends)
18
19
20
```

FIGURE 17-4 The / Format Font command is used to change the fonts with which the contents of cells are displayed and printed.

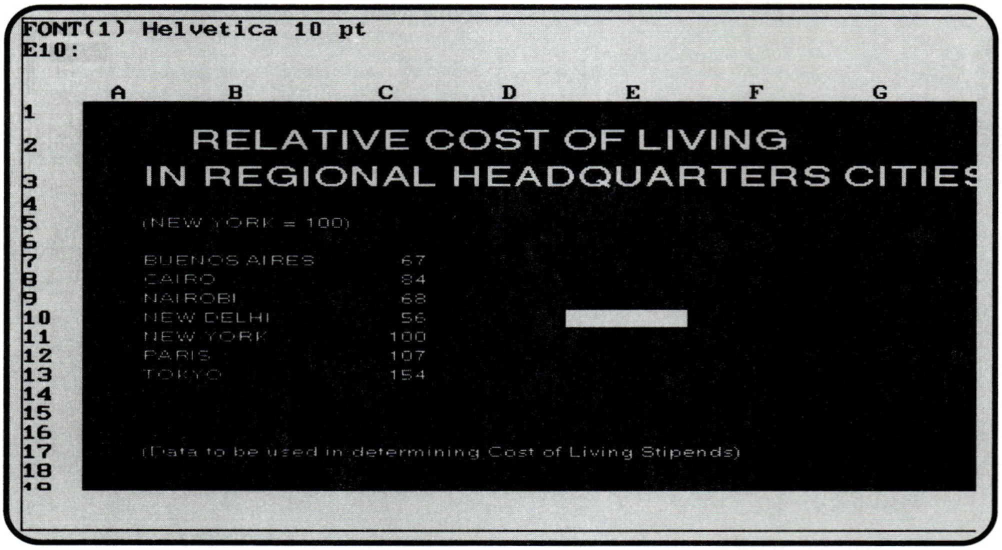

FIGURE 17-5 The top two lines are displayed in Helvetica 20 point.

LINES AND SHADES AND OTHER CELL FORMATS

In addition to different fonts, Allways allows cell entries to be displayed in bold, underlined, in different colors, with lines around all or part of the cells, and in shaded boxes. These options are accessed through the Allways / Format menu.

For example, suppose we would like to draw attention to the entry for Nairobi. We could "shade" the cells B9 and C9. We select / Format Shade Light B9..C9 . The result is that the background for the text in these cells will appear to be light gray rather than white when the spreadsheet is printed. The cells also appear to be shaded on the display, as in Figure 17-6.

We could put a box around B17..F17 by selecting / Format Lines Outline B17..F17. We also can put lines along the top, bottom, left, or right side of each cell in a range using the / Format Lines command.

Similarly, we could display the contents of cells in **boldface** using the / Format Bold command. We could underline the contents of cells using the / Format Underline command.

ADDING GRAPHS

With Allways, graphs created in Lotus 1-2-3 can be displayed and printed as part of the spreadsheet.

For example, suppose we created a simple bar graph in Lotus 1-2-3 for the spreadsheet in Figure 17-1. We used the / Graph Save command in Lotus 1-2-3 and saved the graph on the disk

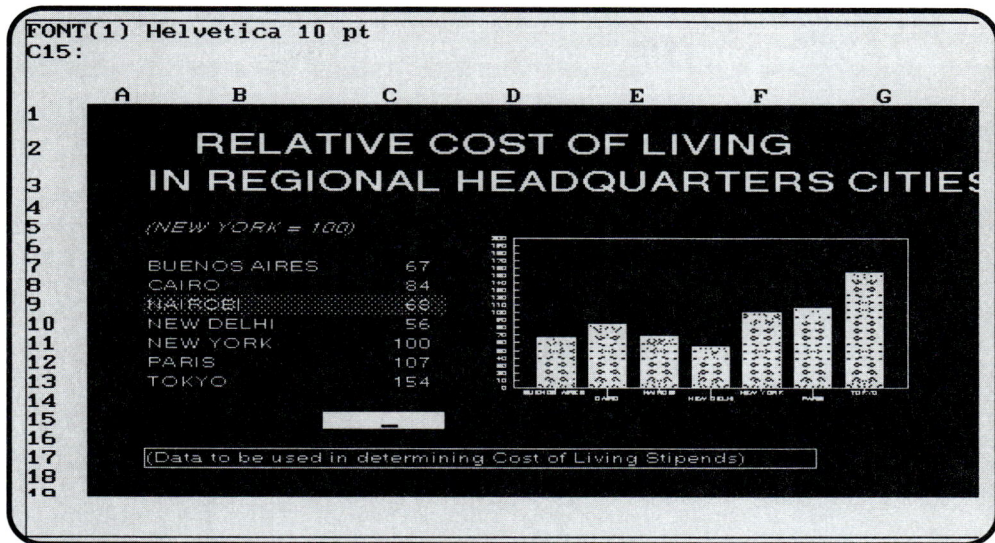

FIGURE 17-6 Illustrating some of the features of Allways.

under the name of, say, CITIES. In Allways, we select / Graph Add. We are shown a list of all the graphs saved on the disk. We select CITIES. Now we are asked to "Enter Range for Graph:". We enter D5..G14. Allways places the graph in D5..G14 in the Allways version of the spreadsheet. The result is shown in Figure 17-6. Allways automatically rescales the graph to fit exactly in the range specified.

Allways is a WYSIWYG program, so it attempts to show on the screen exactly what will be printed. However, it is common in personal computers for the screen display to be much coarser than the printer, especially if you are using a laser printer. This disparity between the resolution of the display and the resolution of the printer is apparent in the bars in the graph. The cross-hatchings in the original graph have been squeezed during the rescaling process so that they appear irregular in the display on the screen in Figure 17-6. The laser printer I use has much finer spatial resolution than does my display. The cross-hatchings in the graph appear fine in the final printout.

Displaying graphs in the spreadsheet is fun, but it slows down the operation of the program. You can speed up the operation of Allways by using the / Display Graphs No command. This command instructs the program to display a plain shaded box in the spreadsheet in place of the full graph. You can revert back to the display of the full graph by selecting / Display Graphs Yes. The very first time you start up Allways, you may see shaded rectangles on your screen instead of graphs. Selecting / Display Graphs Yes should remedy the situation.

An interesting feature of Allways is that graphs are "transparent." Any entries in cells in the underlying spreadsheet will show through a graph in Allways. This feature allows you to place comments or explanations within your graphs before they are printed by entering the text in the cells in Lotus 1-2-3. For example, we could move the cursor to E9, return to 1-2-3 by pressing the Escape key, enter in the label "WOW!, return to Allways by pressing Alt-F7, and move the cursor away to C15. The "WOW!" appears to be part of the graph, as illustrated in Figure 17-7.

SAVING THE ENHANCED SPREADSHEET

Allways spreadsheets are saved on the disk and retrieved from the disk using the / File commands in 1-2-3. Allways does not contain its own file commands for saving and retrieving worksheets. Instead, when Allways is attached, it modifies the / File commands in Lotus 1-2-3.

After you have prettified your spreadsheet in Allways, you should save the enhanced spreadsheet on the disk. To do this, return to Lotus 1-2-3 by pressing the Escape key or by selecting the Allways command / Quit. In Lotus 1-2-3 select / File Save. At the same time 1-2-3 saves your worksheet it also will save a special Allways file with all of your Allways settings and additions. The Allways file has the same first name you specify for the worksheet file and it is given the extension .ALL. Thus if your worksheet file is saved on your disk as COSTLIV.WK1, you also will have a file called COSTLIV.ALL that contains the Allways settings and additions.

To retrieve the enhanced spreadsheet, use the / File Retrieve command in Lotus 1-2-3 while Allways is attached. In Lotus 1-2-3 the spreadsheet will look as it always does in Lotus 1-2-3, with none of the enhancements made in Allways. However, if you now invoke Allways, your enhanced spreadsheet will appear on the screen.

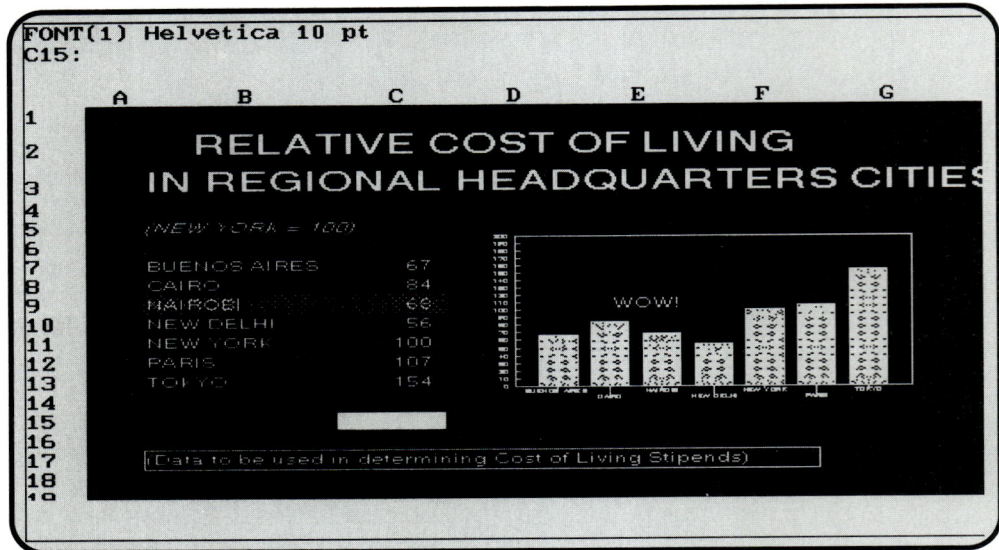

FIGURE 17-7 Adding a comment to the graph.

PRINTING

Allways contains its own print command. The first step in printing is to specify the range to be printed using the Allways / Print Range command. The spreadsheet is printed using the Go command in the Allways / Print menu. The result of printing the spreadsheet used as an example is shown in Figure 17-8.

   Thus, while file operations are done through 1-2-3, printing is done using a separate Allways Print command. You can print the spreadsheet using the Lotus 1-2-3 / Print command, but it will print as a plain 1-2-3 spreadsheet with no enhancements.

DISPLAY OPTIONS

Allways provides you with considerable control over the appearance of the worksheet on the screen.

   In the / Display command in Allways you can change the colors of background, foreground, and cell pointer using the Colors command.

   You can enlarge or shrink the display size of cells using the / Display Zoom command. Shrinking the display size of cells allows a larger portion of the spreadsheet to be displayed on the screen at the cost of making each individual cell entry more difficult to read. You also can enlarge the display size of cells using the speed-key Alt-F4 and shrink the display size of cells using the speed-key F4.

RELATIVE COST OF LIVING
IN REGIONAL HEADQUARTERS CITIES

(NEW YORK = 100)

BUENOS AIRES	67
CAIRO	84
NAIROBI	68
NEW DELHI	56
NEW YORK	100
PARIS	107
TOKYO	154

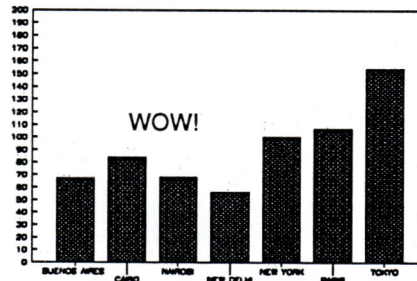

(Data to be used in determining Cost of Living Stipends)

FIGURE 17-8 Final printout of the spreadsheet.

The / Display Mode Text command reverts back to text display on the screen, the type of display we are used to in Lotus 1-2-3. In Text mode, Allways no longer is a WYSIWYG program. All characters are displayed in a single font. All characters are the same size. No shadings or boxes are displayed. The areas where graphs have been placed contain multiple "G"s. Text mode allows Allways to be used on computers that do not support graphic displays. Also, the Allways program operates much faster in Text mode. Even though the program is displaying the spreadsheet in Text mode, it remembers all of the additions and will print the enhanced spreadsheet out on the printer as before. To switch to the normal display mode, select / Display Mode Graphics.

PERMANENTLY ATTACHING ALLWAYS

Allways can become addictive. You might find that you are using Allways at every session. You can instruct Lotus 1-2-3 automatically to attach Allways each time you start up 1-2-3 using the / Worksheet Global Default Other Add-In Set command. You must then save your preference using / Worksheet Global Default Update. With these commands, each time you run Lotus 1-2-3 thereafter, Allways automatically will be loaded into memory.

COMPUTER EXERCISE

17-1 In this exercise you will practice some of the features of Allways.

(a) In Lotus 1-2-3, retrieve your favorite spreadsheet from the disk or enter one into the computer.

(b) Attach and then invoke Allways.

(c) Change the fonts in several of the cells. Use at least four different fonts, including large fonts and italic fonts, if available.

(d) Shade two of the cells.

(e) Draw a box around some of the cells.

(f) Change some of the cells to **boldface** and some to <u>underline</u>.

(g) Quit out of Allways and return into 1-2-3.

(h) Save the spreadsheet under a new name.

(i) Draw a graph using the data in the spreadsheet. Save the graph using / Graph Save.

(j) Invoke Allways.

(k) Add the graph you just created into the spreadsheet.

(l) Print the combined spreadsheet and graph.

(m) Quit out of Allways and return to 1-2-3.

(n) Save the spreadsheet again.

BEGINNING MACROS

Sometimes it seems that "macro" is the magic word in Lotus 1-2-3. Whenever anyone asks the local 1-2-3 guru how to use Lotus 1-2-3 to perform some particularly difficult task, the guru usually looks thoughtful for a while and then responds, "Well, you could write a macro for it." And the guru usually is right. Macros are very powerful tools, indeed.

In these final two chapters we will be learning how to make use of macros.

WHAT ARE MACROS?

At their simplest, macros are lists of keystrokes that are written down to save the user time. The keystrokes can be sequences of commands to Lotus 1-2-3 or they can be data or formulas to be entered. Suppose you have a spreadsheet that keeps track of sales in your division. Every week you need to print a sales report with the updated data. Each week you go through the same process: / Print Printer Range A1..K38 and so on. Wouldn't it be easier simply to write down the keystrokes (/PPRA1..K38 and so on) in a cell in the spreadsheet and then whenever you wanted to print out the report just tell Lotus 1-2-3 to follow the keystrokes in the cell? That's the basic idea behind macros.

There are two stages to using a macro: creating the macro and invoking the macro. When you create a macro, you write down the keystrokes that you want Lotus 1-2-3 to follow and you give the macro a name. When you invoke a macro, you tell Lotus 1-2-3 to go ahead and follow the keystrokes in the macro. You turn control of the program over to the macro. Once you have created a macro, you can store it on the disk with the rest of the spreadsheet and use that macro many times in the future.

A SIMPLE EXAMPLE OF A MACRO

Suppose we work for Allied Electronics, Inc. We constantly find ourselves writing "Allied Electronics, Inc." in our spreadsheets. We would like to save ourselves the trouble of typing out "Allied Electronics, Inc." each time by creating a macro that will type this phrase for us. We move the cursor to an empty cell, and in the cell we type

```
Allied Electronics, Inc.
```

Now we give the cell a name by selecting / Range Name Create. When the computer asks us for the name we enter \A (backslash A). A backslash before a one-letter name means that this is a macro name. When the computer asks us the range, we enter the address of the cell. We now have created a simple macro named \A.

To invoke the macro at any time, we type Alt-A. That is, we hold down the Alt key and while it is held down we type an A. Whenever we type Alt-A the computer will put Allied Electronics, Inc. in its place. For example, if we move the cursor to a blank cell and type `Revenue Projections for` and press Alt-A and then type `for Ten Years`, on the screen will be `Revenue Projections for Allied Electronics, Inc. for Ten Years`

CREATING MACROS

A spreadsheet can have dozens of macros. Before creating these macros, we set aside a separate area of the spreadsheet for the macros, away from the rest of the spreadsheet. The best plan is to place the macros well below and to the right of the spreadsheet. Otherwise, if you insert or delete rows or columns in the formula area of the spreadsheet, you can unintentionally affect the macro area. In Figure 18-1 the macros have been placed in a section of the worksheet beginning at AA1000.

```
AC1012:  [W30] ' {D 4}                                          READY

        AA      AB                   AC                            AD
998
999
1000
1001                    MACRO DEFINITION AREA
1002
1003    NAME        MACRO                      DESCRIPTION
1004    ----        ------------------------   -------------------
1005
1006    \A          Allied Electronics, Inc.   Type the text
1007
1008    \B          Budget Report              Type the text
1009
1010    \C          {DOWN}{DOWN}{DOWN}{DOWN}    Move the cursor down 4 cells
1011
1012    \D          {D 4}.                     Move the cursor down 4 cells
1013
1014    \G          {HOME}{R 4}{D}             Move the cursor to cell E2
1015
1016    \H          {GOTO}E2~                  Move the cursor to cell E2
1017
                            UNDO
```

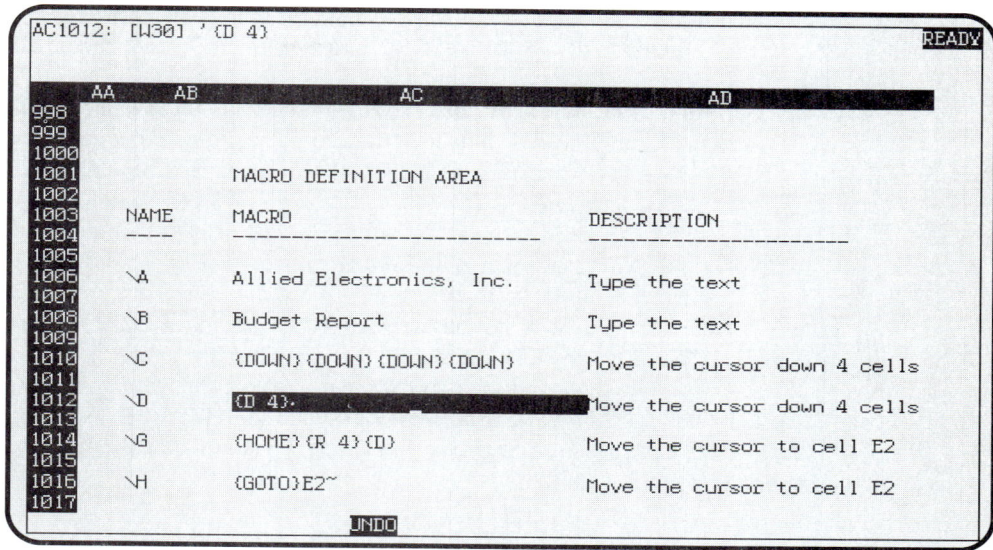

FIGURE 18-1   Some sample macros.

Incidentally, in early versions of Lotus 1-2-3, placing entries in cells far away from A1 would cause spreadsheets to use great amounts of the internal memory of the computer. However, in Release 2.2 Lotus uses a memory management scheme where the location of the macros is irrelevant to the amount of memory required. Placing macros beginning in AA1000 uses no more internal memory than placing the macros beginning in B2.

A range at least three columns wide should be left for the macros. The left column should have the names of the macros, for reference. The middle column will contain the macros themselves. The right column should contain English descriptions of the macros, documentation for users. This is illustrated in Figure 18-1. Only the middle column is required by Lotus 1-2-3, but it is important to document macros so that users can understand what they do.

When we create a macro, we need to specify the contents of the macro. We need to enter the keystrokes that the program is going to follow when the macro is invoked. In the foregoing example, we enter

            Allied Electronics, Inc.

into AC1006 for macro \A, as in Figure 18-1. We might enter

            Budget Report

into AC1008 for macro \B.

After we have entered the contents of a macro, we name the macro. Move the cursor to the cell of the macro, for example, to AC1008. Select / Range Name Create and enter the name of the macro.

There are two choices for macro names. The first choice is to enter a backslash followed by a single letter, for example, \B. This is the "traditional" approach to naming macros, the only approach allowed in Releases 1, 1A, 2, and 2.01 of Lotus 1-2-3. With Release 2.2, a second approach to naming macros was introduced. Macros now can be more than one letter long, but they then need to be invoked differently. We will discuss using extended macro names shortly. Here, we will cover macro names consisting of a backslash followed by a single letter.

After the name has been created, it is a good idea to type the macro name in the cell to the left of the macro. The program does not require this step, but it makes life much easier for people who are trying to understand your spreadsheet. Do note that if you just enter \B into a cell, Lotus 1-2-3 will take this to be a repeating label, and so BBBBBBBB will appear in the cell. To enter literally \B, you must begin the entry with a space or apostrophe to indicate that you are entering a regular label. So we type ' \B into AB1008.

ENTERING THE NAMES OF KEYSTROKES

We would like to create a macro that moves the cursor down four cells. The down arrow key moves the cursor down one cell. The PgDn key moves the cursor down 20 cells. We would like to be able to type Alt-C and have the cursor move down four cells.

We will enter the macro for moving the cursor down four cells into cell AC1010. Normally, to move the cursor down four cells we press the down arrow key four times. What are we going to enter into cell AC1010? If we move the cursor to cell AC1010 and then literally press the down arrow key four times, the cursor simply will move down to AC1014. Instead, what we can enter into cell AC1010 is the following:

```
{DOWN}{DOWN}{DOWN}{DOWN}
```

In a macro, the word {DOWN} in curly braces stands for the down arrow key. We type the word {DOWN} into the cell four times. Later, when we invoke the macro by typing Alt-C, Lotus 1-2-3 interprets the word {DOWN} as meaning the down arrow key and performs the action specified, namely, moving the cursor down four cells. The word {DOWN} is the "macro key name" for the down arrow key.

Lotus 1-2-3 has special names for many keys that can be used in macros. For example, the macro key name for the PgDn key is {PGDN}. The macro key name for the Home key is {HOME}. The complete list of macro key names is given in Appendix H.

In Lotus 1-2-3, the name for the down arrow key can be abbreviated as {D}. So the macro could be written

```
{D}{D}{D}{D}
```

There are four {D}'s in a row. This statement can be further abbreviated as

$$\{D\ 4\}$$

Thus macro \C in Figure 18-1 is the same as macro \D. Both macros instruct Lotus 1-2-3 to type the down arrow key four times, which moves the cursor down four cells.

As another example, if we would like a macro that always moves the cursor to cell E2 we could create a macro consisting of

$$\{HOME\}\{R\ 4\}\{D\}$$

This is macro \G in Figure 18-1. When invoked, this macro tells Lotus 1-2-3 to press the Home key, which moves the cursor to A1, and then to press the right arrow key four times and the down arrow key once, thus moving the cursor to E2.

Alternatively, we could create a macro that moves the cursor to E2 using function key F5, the GoTo key. The macro name for the GoTo key is {GOTO}. The macro for moving the cursor to E2 would be

$$\{GOTO\}E2\sim$$

The character at the end of the macro is ~, which is called a **tilde** (pronounced as in "Matilda"). The tilde is the macro name for the Enter key. That is, when a macro is invoked and the macro

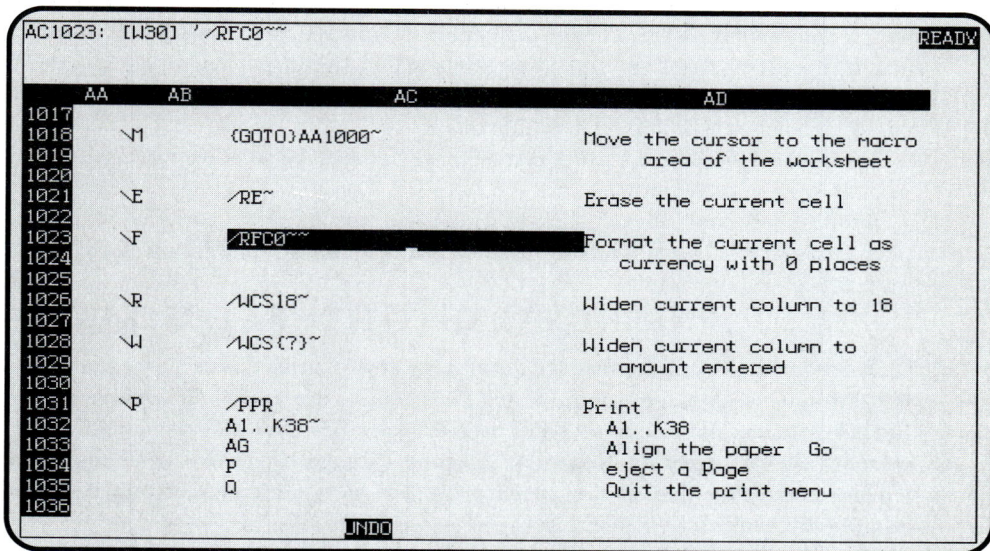

FIGURE 18-2 More macros.

contains a tilde, Lotus 1-2-3 interprets the tilde as meaning the Enter key. Thus invoking the above macro is equivalent to typing four keys: function key F5 (the GOTO key), the E key, the 2 key, and the Enter key.

It is convenient to create a macro to move the cursor to the macro area of the spreadsheet. Macro \M in Figure 18-2 is

```
{GOTO}AA1000~
```

When we type Alt-M we invoke macro \M, which moves the cursor to AA1000.

MACROS FOR COMMANDS

Lotus 1-2-3 has no single key to press to erase a cell. This seems like a strange oversight as this operation is performed fairly frequently. Suppose we would like to create a macro \E to erase the current cell. The command for erasing the current cell is / Range Erase and press the Enter key. Thus, the macro for erasing the current cell is

```
/RE~
```

To place /RE~ in a cell we must first type an apostrophe so that Lotus 1-2-3 knows that we are entering a label. Otherwise, if we move the cursor to AC1021 and just type /RE~ the computer will think that we are invoking a command. Thus, we move the cursor to AC1021 and then type ′/RE~ and press the Enter key to enter the text into the cell. We name the cell by selecting / Range Name Create \E enter enter. Now we can erase any cell we would like by placing the cursor on the cell and typing Alt-E to invoke our new macro. The cell will be erased automatically. At the top of the screen you will see the computer stepping through the command menus as if you were typing the keys.

The apostrophes and the tildes and the backslashes take some getting used to. Let's work through some more examples.

Suppose we would like a macro to format the current cell as currency with zero decimal places. We move the cursor to AC1023. We type an apostrophe followed by

```
/RFC0~~
```

These are the keystrokes needed to select / Range Format Currency 0 enter enter. The "0" is a zero and indicates the number of decimal places to the right of the decimal point. The first Enter key enters the 0. The second Enter key specifies that this format applies only to the current cell. We name the macro by selecting / Range Name Create \F enter enter. Now, whenever we press Alt-F we invoke the macro \F, which automatically formats the current cell as currency with zero decimal places.

Macro \R in cell AC1026 in Figure 18-2 is

```
/WCS18~
```

This macro automatically widens the current column to 18 places by selecting / Worksheet Column Set-Width 18 enter.

Suppose we would like a macro that changes the width of the current column to some number that the user enters. We do not want to fix the width of the column as in macro \R. Rather we want to provide the user with the opportunity to enter the number in the middle of the macro.

The text {?} in the middle of a macro allows the user to enter data in to the macro. In particular, the {?} instructs Lotus 1-2-3 to temporarily suspend the operation of the macro so that the user can enter data or press the arrow keys or whatever. When the user presses the Enter key then control is returned to the macro.

Thus, the macro

```
/WCS{?}~
```

in cell AC1028 in Figure 18-2 instructs Lotus 1-2-3 to select / Worksheet Column Set-Width and then allows the user to type a number which is entered as the column width.

Note the need to include the tilde, the macro key name for the Enter key, at the end of the macro in AC1028. The user will type in the column width followed by the Enter key. But this Enter will only serve to terminate input and pass control back to the macro. Yet another Enter must be supplied via the tilde to enter the number in as the column width. This can get confusing. Macros often require trial and error to get them working right.

MULTI-LINE MACROS

Macros can be quite long and involved. Often it is easier to create and understand macros if they are broken up into several cells. As illustrated in Figure 18-2 and Figure 18-3, macros can extend beyond one cell into the cells directly below.

When a macro is invoked, Lotus 1-2-3 steps through the keystrokes in the named cell. Lotus 1-2-3 then looks at the next cell below. If the cell is blank the macro is terminated. If the cell below is not blank then the contents of that cell are treated as the next part of the macro. The computer proceeds down the cells in the column until it reaches a blank cell.

Hence, it is critical that the cell below each unrelated macro is blank. If you forget to leave a blank cell between macros, the computer will run into the second macro upon completing execution of the first. On occasion this is desirable, but here we will assume that each macro is distinct, so we will leave a blank cell between each macro.

We began the chapter with the example of automating the printing of a weekly report. A macro for printing a report is shown in AC1031..AC1035 in Figure 18-2. The macro instructs the computer to select / Print Printer Range A1..K38 enter Align Go Page Quit . We could make the macro more elaborate and include a header, a footer, a setup string, and so on.

With a multi-line macro, either you can assign the name of the macro just to the top cell in the macro, or you can assign the name of the macro to the entire range of the macro. After entering the print macro in AC1031..AC1035, we could select either / Range Name Create \P enter AC1031 enter or / Range Name Create \P enter AC1031..AC1035 enter .

```
AC1043: [W30] '@NOW~                                              READY

        AA      AB              AC                      AD
 1037
 1038                                         Date and Time Stamp
 1039       \S        /WCS10~                     widen column
 1040                 @NOW~                        enter @NOW into cell
 1041                 /RFD1~                       format cell as DD-MMM-YY
 1042                 {DOWN}                        move cursor down
 1043                 @NOW~                         enter @NOW into cell
 1044                 /RFDT2~                       format cell HH:MM AM/PM
 1045
 1046                                         Adjust the screen so the
 1047       \T        {D 21}                    current cell is at the
 1048                 {U 21}                     top of the screen
 1049
 1050
 1051
 1052
 1053
 1054
 1055
 1056
                              UNDO
```

FIGURE 18-3   More multi-line macros.

Macro \S in AC1039..AC1044 in Figure 18-3 date and time stamps the spreadsheet by putting the current date in the current cell and the current time in the cell below. The first cell in the macro widens the current column to 10 so the date can be displayed. The portion of the macro in cell AC1040 enters the formula @NOW in the current cell. The portion of the macro in AC1041 formats the current cell so it displays in date format 1, for example, as 04-Jul-92. Under macro control the cursor moves down one cell. The formula @NOW is entered in the cell below the date. This cell is then formatted in time format 2, for example, as 09:45 AM. When the computer encounters the blank cell in AC1045, it stops the macro execution and returns to Ready mode.

Macro \T in AC1047..AC1048 in Figure 18-3 adjusts the screen so that the row of the current cell becomes the top row on the screen. The macro works by first driving the cursor down 21 cells. At this point the original cell is off the top of the screen. The second part of the macro moves the cursor back up 21 cells to where it started. However, now, because of the way scrolling works in Lotus 1-2-3, the cursor is located in the top row of the screen.

EXTENDED MACRO NAMES

In the spreadsheet in Figures 18-1, 18-2, and 18-3 each macro was assigned a name consisting of a backslash followed by a letter. An attempt was made to select a letter that stands for the function of the macro. For example, the macro that erases the current cell was named \E. The print macro was named \P, and so on. Some of the names are a bit stretched. For example, the macro that widens the cell to 18 characters was named \R (since R is the eighteenth character in the alphabet!). The idea is to select names for the macros that will be remembered a month from now when you are using the spreadsheet. Comments are included next to the macros so that if you cannot remember the macros in the spreadsheet, you can look in the macro area and see at a glance what macros exist and what they do.

Limiting macro names to a backslash followed by a single letter is a serious restriction. This naming convention makes it difficult to remember macro names. The naming convention also means that you cannot have more than 26 different macros in a spreadsheet.

With Release 2.2 of 1-2-3, Lotus opened up the naming of macros by allowing **extended macro names**. Now any name that is legitimate for a range is legitimate for a macro. A macro name can be up to 15 characters, with a few restrictions. Macro names should not be cell addresses. That is you should not use C4 for a macro name. You may not use any of the macro key names in Appendix H or any of the macro commands in Appendix I as the name of a macro. You may not include spaces, commas, semicolons, or periods in a macro name. Instead of \R for a macro name, you can use WIDEN18 or, better, \WIDEN18.

The price that is paid for extended macro names is that there is an extra step in invoking the macros. With single-letter names a macro can be invoked by holding down the Alt key and typing the letter. With extended macro names to invoke a macro you first press the **Run key**, which is **Alt-F3.** After you type Alt-F3, Lotus 1-2-3 displays a list of all the named ranges. You invoke the macro by selecting the name of the macro you wish to run. As usual, you can select the macro either by typing its name or by pointing to it and pressing the Enter key.

When you type Alt-F3, all the range names that have been defined are displayed. Lotus 1-2-3 does not distinguish between named ranges that contain data or formulas and named ranges that contain macros. All the range names are displayed in alphabetical order. If you select the name of a range that contains data or formulas, Lotus 1-2-3 still will attempt to follow the contents of the cells as if they were keystrokes for a macro. This can lead to problems.

When using extended macro names, it is good practice to begin each name with a backslash. The initial backslash allows the user to distinguish between macros and other types of named ranges.

THE LEARN FEATURE

It is critical when creating a macro to enter all of the keystrokes exactly as they are required. A tilde must be written down for the Enter key. The appropriate names in curly brackets must be written down for the cursor control keys. People using early versions of Lotus 1-2-3 who wanted to create a macro often would find themselves with a pad and pencil writing down each of the keystrokes on paper as they made their way through the printing of a report or some other procedure in Lotus 1-2-3. Then they would carefully read the keystrokes off the paper and enter each of the keystrokes into the cells for the macro. Writing down keystrokes on paper and then typing them into Lotus 1-2-3 cells is a time-consuming and error-prone process.

The developers of Release 2.2 of Lotus 1-2-3 came to the rescue with the **Learn** feature. The Learn feature allows us to instruct the computer to record our keystrokes. We then work our way through the procedure. As we perform the task, the computer writes down the keystrokes. When we are finished, we then can name those cells and use them as a macro.

The steps in using the Learn feature are as follows:

1. Select and specify the **learn range**. The learn range is the location where the recorded keystrokes are to be written. The learn range should be a single column range, a range one cell wide and long enough to hold all of the keystrokes. Be sure the learn range does not intersect the rest of your spreadsheet. The learn range is specified using the / Worksheet Learn Range command.

2. Record the keystrokes. To start recording keystrokes press the **Learn** key, which is **Alt-F5**. The word LEARN appears next to the word UNDO as a Status Indicator at the bottom of the screen. Perform the task you want to record. After each cell entry or command, Lotus 1-2-3 records your previous keystrokes in the learn range. For example, if you press the left arrow key, Lotus 1-2-3 will place {L} in the next cell in the learn range. Each cursor control key and cell entry is recorded in a different cell, so you need to have allocated plenty of cells in the Learn range. Press Learn (Alt-F5) again to have Lotus 1-2-3 stop recording keystrokes. You then need to press the Enter key one more time to record the final cell entry.

3. Name the macro. Use / Range Name Create to assign a name either to the entire range or to the top cell in the range.

4. Enter the name of the macro to the left of the macro for future reference.

5. Enter descriptive comments to the right of the macro for documentation.

The Learn feature is very useful for creating macros. Exercise 18-3 takes you through the process of using the Learn feature to create a macro that places your name and the exercise number on a spreadsheet.

DEBUGGING MACROS

Macros can become quite complicated. Even with the Learn feature, macros do not always work the way we would like them to, especially the first time we try them. A small error in a macro (or in a spreadsheet or in a computer program) is called a **bug**. The process of finding and eliminating bugs is called **debugging**. Lotus 1-2-3 has a special feature for debugging macros.

Trying to find the errors in a macro by running it can be difficult because the macro goes by so fast. The macro debug feature allows you to step through a macro one keystroke at a time.

To initiate the debug feature, press Alt-F2. The word STEP appears as a Status Indicator at the bottom of the screen. Now when you invoke a macro, 1-2-3 will stop right at the beginning of the macro. Each time you press the space bar (or any other key) Lotus 1-2-3 will follow the next keystroke in the macro. You step through the macro by continuing to press the space bar. If you find an error, a place where the macro is not doing what it should, you can stop the process by pressing Ctrl-Break. Then you would correct the error in the macro and try the macro again. You would repeat the process until all of the bugs in the macro have been corrected and the macro seems to work perfectly. Press Alt-F2 again to turn off the debug feature.

Some types of macro bugs are very common. These include:

- Spelling errors
- Inserting extra spaces
- Missing tildes in a command sequence
- Using square brackets or parentheses instead of curly braces { }
- Incorrect cell or range references
- Using a macro key name or macro command name as an extended name for a macro

Watch out for these when you are creating your macros.

PENCIL AND PAPER EXERCISE

18-1 Give a full description in English of the effect of invoking each of the following macros.

(a)   `Marketing Department`

(b)   `Marketing Department~`

(c)   `Marketing Department`
       `{D}`
       `(1900+@YEAR(@NOW))`
       `{D}`

(d)   `/RLR~`

(e)   `/M~{R}~`

(f)   `/WIR~`

(g)   `/FSTEMP~~`

(h)   `/WDR{D 15}~`

(i)   When would you use the macro in (b) as opposed to the macro in (a)?

COMPUTER EXERCISES

18-2 This exercise is designed to take you step by step through the process of creating a macro by directly entering the keystrokes into the cells. The macro will place your name and the exercise number in successive cells. You should start with a fresh spreadsheet.

(a) Enter the macro as follows:

C10	your name	
C11	`{D}`	
C12	`Exercise {?}~`	
C13	`'/WCS15~`	note: type the initial apostrophe but it won't show on the screen
B10	`'\N`	note: apostrophe backslash N

(b) Now name the macro by selecting / Range Name Create . For the name, type \N (backslash N) Enter. For the range, select C10..C13.

(c) Move the cursor to B2. Invoke the macro by pressing the Alt key and while it is held down type an N. Your name should appear in B2. The computer will type out the word `Exercise` and then wait for you to type. You should type `18-2` and press the Enter key. The computer will enter `Exercise 18-2` into B3. Next the macro will widen column B to 15 characters. Finally the macro will terminate and control will be returned to Lotus 1-2-3.

(d)   Move the cursor to E17. Try the macro again by typing Alt-N.

(e)   Try the debugging feature. Press Alt-F2. The word STEP should appear at the bottom of the screen. Move the cursor to A7. Invoke the macro by pressing Alt-N. The first cell of the macro should appear in the bottom left of the screen. Step through the macro by pressing the space bar. Each time you press the space bar the next character will be "typed" at the top of the screen. At the same time the highlighter on the cell entry at the bottom of the screen should progress to the next character. When you reach the exercise number, the word SST will appear at the bottom of the screen. SST indicates that a macro in Step mode is waiting for input. Type 18-2 Enter. Continue pressing the space bar until the macro is complete. Press Alt-F2 to turn off the debugging feature.

(f)   Give the macro an extended name by selecting / Range Name Create \MYNAME enter C10..C13 enter. Move the cursor to D15. Invoke the macro by pressing the Run key Alt-F3 and then selecting \MYNAME as the macro to run.

18-3   This exercise is designed to take you through the process of using Learn mode to have Lotus 1-2-3 record a macro. Start with a fresh worksheet and the cursor in A1.

(a)   Specify the learn range by selecting / Worksheet Learn Range C10..C20 enter.

(b)   Press Alt-F5 to instruct Lotus 1-2-3 to begin recording the keystrokes. The word LEARN should appear at the bottom of the screen to indicate that the program is in Learn mode.

(c)   Press the following keys, exactly as shown, substituting your name for mine and pressing the Enter key where it says Enter. The ↓ is the down arrow.

> `Jim Gips`↓`Exercise {?}` Enter `/WCS15` Enter

Press Alt-F5 to turn off Learn mode. The word LEARN should no longer appear at the bottom of the screen. Press the Enter key one more time to record the final cell entry.

You should see your name in A1 and the phrase `Exercise {?}` in A2. Column A should be set to a width of 15 characters. At the same time, your keystrokes were recorded as a macro in the Learn Range. After you pressed the first Enter key, the key strokes for your name should have been written down in cell C10. Similarly, after the second and third Enter keys the keystrokes should have appeared in C11 and C12.

(d)   Select / Range Name Create to name cell C10 as \N.

(e)   For documentation, enter ' \N in cell B10.

(f)   For documentation enter `MACRO TO ENTER MY NAME AND THE EXER-CISE NUMBER` in E10.

(g)   Move the cursor to D14. Invoke the macro by typing Alt-N. Your name and the word `Exercise` should appear. Type 18-3 Enter. The column should be widened to 15 characters.

(h)   Teach Lotus 1-2-3 another macro. Select / Range Erase C10..C15. Enter Learn mode by typing Alt-F5. Press the right arrow key three times. Type the word HELLO. Press the down arrow key two times and the PgDn key. Type the word GOODBYE. Press the left arrow key twice, the PgUp key. Exit Learn mode by typing Alt-F5 again. Press the Enter key once. Name the macro by selecting / Range Name Create \D enter enter. Move the cursor to D5. Invoke the macro by typing Alt-D.

18-4 Implement macros on the computer to perform the following tasks. Type the name of the macro on the left, the macro itself in the center of the spreadsheet, and a description of the macro on the right. During the course of the exercise try both typing the macro explicitly and using the Learn feature. Be sure to leave a blank cell between macros.

(a) A macro that places the word TOTAL in the current cell and moves the cursor down to the next cell.

(b) An encouragement macro that enters the message GREAT JOB in the current cell, causes the cursor to move down 8 cells, up 8 cells, and then erases the current cell.

(c) A macro that causes the current time to appear in the current cell briefly but legibly and then erases the cell.

(d) A macro that formats the current cell as currency with two places.

(e) A macro that inserts a row at the top of the spreadsheet.

(f) A macro that saves the current spreadsheet under the current file name.

(g) A macro that causes a label in the current cell to be indented three spaces. Use intraline editing in the macro.

(h) A macro that places the three letter abbreviation of the names of the 12 months JAN, FEB, MAR, and so on in separate cells across the spreadsheet beginning at the current cell. The names should then be centered in their cells.

(i) A copy macro that copies the current cell but leaves the TO range up to you to enter.

(j) An underline macro that places dashes in 12 cells across the spreadsheet beginning with the current cell.

(k) A vertical line macro that places the vertical line character in the center of the current cell and then copies it down the worksheet as far as you indicate.

(l) A macro that establishes a print header of your name and the current date.

(m) A macro that uses the / Print command to print out the range A1..D8 and then the range D12..H18.

(n) A macro that (1) prints a range specified by the user, (2) prints the formulas in that range (using /PPOOC), (3) resets the print settings so that future printouts will be of the values rather than the formulas, and (4) returns to Ready mode.

(o) A macro that (1) saves the worksheet under the name PREPRINT, (2) prints a range specified by the user, (3) resets the format of all of the cells to the global format (/ Range Format Reset), (4) sets the global format to Text, (5) widens all the columns, (6) prints the range with the formulas showing, (7) retrieves the file PREPRINT.

MORE ON MACROS

19

We have seen how macros can be used to save time by automating the typing of common text and commands. Macros can be used as well for customizing spreadsheets for specific users and applications. In this chapter we will look at some of the more advanced macro capabilities in Lotus 1-2-3.

MACRO LOOPS USING {BRANCH}

As described in the Chapter 18, macro execution normally proceeds from the top cell in the macro range down through each successive cell in the column until a blank cell is encountered. It is possible to alter the path of macro execution using the {BRANCH} macro command.

Consider the macro called \DS in AC1055..AC1057 in Figure 19-1. Sometimes when you are printing out the results of a spreadsheet you would like the printout to appear double-spaced. This macro will double-space an existing spreadsheet by inserting a blank row between each row in the spreadsheet.

When the macro \DS is invoked using the Run key Alt-F3, the computer begins following instructions at AC1055. The keystrokes in AC1055 instruct the computer to insert a new blank row at the cursor. The cursor is left in the new blank row. Control then passes to AC1056. The command in AC1056 causes the cursor to move down two rows in the spreadsheet to the row below the original location of the cursor. Control then passes to cell AC1057. This cell contains the macro command

{BRANCH \DS}

The {BRANCH} macro command instructs the computer to take its next instructions from the cell address indicated. Thus control passes to cell AC1055, which has been named \DS. Cell AC1055 instructs the computer to insert a new blank row. Control then proceeds to AC1056. And so on. The cursor travels down through the spreadsheet inserting blank rows as it goes, while macro control loops through the three cells AC1055, AC1056, AC1057.

When does this macro stop? Never. When you invoke the macro \DS the computer goes into an **infinite loop**. The computer is in a loop because it repeats the instructions in AC1055, AC1056, and AC1057. The computer is in an infinite loop because the repetition goes on forever. Eventually, the cursor will reach row 8192 at the bottom of the spreadsheet. The cursor is halted

```
AB1054:                                                              READY
        AA        AB            AC                        AD
1051 *********************************************************************
1052
1053 Macro to double space rows until CTRL-BRK is pressed
1054 ████████  ▄
1055    \DS       /WIR~                         Insert a row
1056              {D 2}                         Move cursor down two cells
1057              {BRANCH \DS}                  Do it again
1058
1059 *********************************************************************
1060
1061 Macro to double space 8 rows
1062
1063    \DS8      {FOR CTR,1,8,1,\INSROW}       Do \INSROW  8 times
1064
1065    \INSROW   /WIR~                         Insert a row
1066              {D 2}                         Move cursor down 2 cells
1067
1068    CTR                                     AC1068 will contain a number
1069
1070 *********************************************************************
                              UNDO
```

FIGURE 19-1 Two macros for double-spacing a spreadsheet by inserting rows.

here, but the macro is not. Rather, the computer keeps beeping an error message as it tries to move the cursor below the bottom row and insert a new row at the bottom.

The only way to stop the macro \DS is to press Ctrl-Break. That is, while holding down the Ctrl key, press the Break key. The Break key often is hidden on keyboards. Usually, "BREAK" is written on the side of the Pause key or under the Scroll Lock key. So in effect, you type Ctrl-Pause or Ctrl-Scroll Lock. In an emergency you always can turn off the computer!

The macro \DS would be used as follows. First, save the spreadsheet, in case anything goes wrong. Place the cursor at the top of the spreadsheet. Invoke the macro. When the cursor reaches the bottom of the portion of the worksheet to be printed press Ctrl-Break. Print the spreadsheet. Retrieve the original spreadsheet from the disk. Alternatively, one could write a macro to convert the double-spaced spreadsheet into a single-spaced spreadsheet by deleting every other row.

MACRO LOOPS USING {FOR}

Using a {BRANCH} command to create an infinite loop in a macro is, shall we say, a bit inelegant. An alternative control structure for the macro is the {FOR} command. The {FOR} command causes a macro to be invoked some fixed number of times.

For example, the macro \DS8 in AC1063 of Figure 19-1 uses a {FOR} command to cause exactly eight rows of a spreadsheet to be double spaced. The macro consists of the command

```
{FOR CTR,1,8,1,\INSROW}
```

which causes the macro called \INSROW to be invoked exactly eight times. Here we have one macro invoking another.

The general form of the {FOR} macro command is

{FOR counter,start-number,stop-number,step-number,macro}

The word FOR is followed by a space and then five arguments. The first argument is the address or name of a cell in the spreadsheet which will be used to keep track of the number of times the FOR command calls the macro subroutine. Thus in Figure 19-1, the cell named CTR, which is cell AC1068, will be used by the macro to count up the number of times the FOR command calls the macro called \INSROW. The second argument is the start-number, the initial value to be placed in the counter. In the macro \DS8 the start-value is 1. The third argument is the stop-number, the value in the counter which is to trigger the termination of the {FOR} command. In the example the stop-number is 8. The fourth argument is the step-number, the value with which the counter is to be incremented each time. In the example, the step-number is 1. The fifth argument is the name of the macro to be invoked each time.

Thus when we invoke the macro \DS8, the macro initially sets CTR to 1. The macro \INSROW is called. When that macro is finished, control returns to the {FOR} command in \DS8. The cell named CTR is incremented by 1, which is the step-value. The macro \INSROW is called again. This continues until the number in CTR exceeds the stop-value of 8. Thus, the macro \INSROW is called 8 times. The macro \INSROW causes a new row to be inserted and the cursor to be moved down to the next row. The result of invoking \DS8 is to double-space eight rows.

The {FOR} macro command takes some getting used to. The {FOR} command can be used only within a macro. The {FOR} command causes another macro to be invoked some fixed number of times in succession.

THE {IF} MACRO COMMAND

The {IF} command is the macro command equivalent of the @IF function. The general form of the {IF} command is

{IF condition}

The condition is an expression that evaluates to *True* or *False*, just as in the @IF function described in Chapter 11. The {IF} command works as follows. When the computer encounters the {IF} command it first evaluates the condition. If the condition is *True*, then the computer continues with the macro commands that follow the {IF} command in the same cell. If the condition is *False*, then the computer skips over the remainder of the cell and continues on to the next cell below. The macro commands in the same cell can contain a {BRANCH} command to redirect control if the condition is *True* or there can be a {QUIT} command in the cell. A **{QUIT}** command causes all macros to terminate and control to return to the user.

The macro \DSKEY in Figure 19-2 double-spaces a spreadsheet until any key is struck. The macro makes use of the {BLANK} command and the {LOOK} command as well as the {IF} command.

SOME OTHER MACRO COMMANDS

The **{BLANK}** command erases the indicated cell or range of cells. In the macro \DSKEY the {BLANK} command erases the contents of the cell named nkey, which is cell AC1081. This cell will be used to hold the first keystroke made by the user.

The **{LOOK}** command checks to see if the user has typed a key. If the user has typed a key, the keystroke is placed into the indicated cell. If the user has not struck a key then the indicated cell remains unchanged. The {LOOK} command in the macro \DSKEY places a keystroke, if any, into the cell named nkey.

The macro \DSKEY first blanks AC1081. Then it loops through AC1075, AC1076, AC1077, and AC1078, inserting rows in the spreadsheet and moving the cursor down the spreadsheet until the user types a key. As soon as the key is typed, the macro quits. Cell AC1078 contains

```
{IF nkey=""}{BRANCH LOOP}
```

This command instructs the computer to take its next command from AC1075 if the cell nkey is blank as LOOP is the name that has been assigned to AC1075. If nkey is not blank, the next command is taken from AC1079, the next cell down, which contains the {QUIT} command.

Strictly speaking, the {QUIT} command in AC1079 is not necessary, as the macro would quit anyway when a blank cell is encountered. With longer macros it is good practice to use the {QUIT} command as the {QUIT} command makes the macro easier to understand.

The macro \DSBLNK in Figure 19-2 performs a similar function. When \DSBLNK is invoked, new blank rows are inserted between each row down the spreadsheet until a blank cell is encountered in the column.

In the macro \DSBLNK the built-in function **@CELLPOINTER** is used. This function is designed specifically for use in macros. The @CELLPOINTER function provides information about the current cell, the cell with the cursor. The @CELLPOINTER function takes a single argument, a label, which indicates the particular type of information about the cell to be returned. For example, @CELLPOINTER("type") indicates the type of the current cell. If the current cell is blank, the result of @CELLPOINTER("type") is "b". If the current cell contains a numeric value or formula, the result of @CELLPOINTER("type") is "v". If the current cell contains a label, the result of @CELLPOINTER("type") is "l". @CELLPOINTER("contents") returns the contents of the current cell. @CELLPOINTER("address") returns the address of the current cell.

The macro \DSBLNK also makes use of the macro command **{BEEP}**. The command {BEEP 1} uses the tone generator in the computer to produce a tone. The number following the word

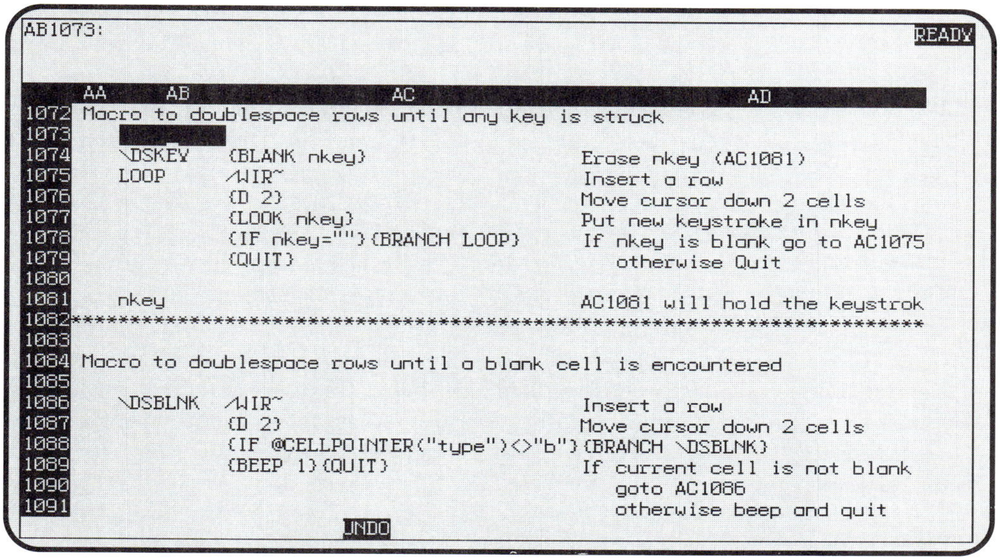

```
AB1073:                                                              READY

      AA      AB               AC                          AD
1072 Macro to doublespace rows until any key is struck
1073
1074    \DSKEY    {BLANK nkey}                     Erase nkey (AC1081)
1075    LOOP      /WIR~                            Insert a row
1076              {D 2}                            Move cursor down 2 cells
1077              {LOOK nkey}                      Put new keystroke in nkey
1078              {IF nkey=""}{BRANCH LOOP}        If nkey is blank go to AC1075
1079              {QUIT}                              otherwise Quit
1080
1081    nkey                                       AC1081 will hold the keystrok
1082*****************************************************************
1083
1084 Macro to doublespace rows until a blank cell is encountered
1085
1086    \DSBLNK   /WIR~                            Insert a row
1087              {D 2}                            Move cursor down 2 cells
1088              {IF @CELLPOINTER("type")<>"b"}{BRANCH \DSBLNK}
1089              {BEEP 1}{QUIT}                   If current cell is not blank
1090                                                  goto AC1086
1091                                                  otherwise beep and quit
                        UNDO
```

FIGURE 19-2 Two macros that use the {IF} command to double-space a spreadsheet by inserting rows.

BEEP is called the tone number and indicates the frequency of the tone to be played. The tone number can be 1, 2, 3, or 4. The {BEEP} command often is used to wake up the user when an input is required or when an operation is completed. The command {BEEP 1} sounds the same tone that is used as an error indicator in Lotus 1-2-3.

The macro \DSBLNK keeps looping through AC1086, AC1087, and AC1088 until a blank cell is encountered. Each time control passes to AC1086, a blank row is inserted at the cursor. At AC1087, the cursor is moved down two cells. At AC1088, the computer checks the current cell to see if it is blank. If the cursor is not in a blank cell, then the macro loops back to AC1086 and continues. If the cursor has reached a blank cell, then the macro sounds a tone and quits, returning control to the user.

MACRO COMMANDS FOR SCREEN CONTROL

Several macro commands control the appearance of the screen.

The **{PANELOFF}** command freezes the appearance of the control panel in its current state. The control panel is the top three lines of the screen, above the spreadsheet. This command prevents the various menus from appearing at the top of the screen as the computer makes its way through commands in the macro. The {PANELOFF} command also prevents the cell addresses and cell contents from appearing at the top of the screen as the cursor is moved.

A variant on the {PANELOFF} command is the **{PANELOFF CLEAR}** command. The {PANELOFF CLEAR} command first erases the top three lines of the screen before freezing them.

The {PANELOFF} command holds until either the macro ends or the computer encounters a {PANELON} command in the macro. The **{PANELON}** command unfreezes the top three lines.

The **{BORDERSOFF}** command erases the row numbers and column letters on the screen. The **{BORDERSON}** command restores the row numbers and column letters to the screen. The **{FRAMEOFF}** command is identical to the {BORDERSOFF} command. The **{FRAMEON}** command is identical to the {BORDERSON} command.

The **{WINDOWSOFF}** command freezes the worksheet area of the screen. The **{WINDOWSON}** command unfreezes the worksheet area of the screen.

The **{INDICATE}** command allows you to set the mode indicator at the top right of the screen to whatever you would like. For example {INDICATE HELLO} would place the word HELLO in the top right of the screen instead of READY or EDIT or whatever. The {INDICATE message} command is quite sticky. If you place the command {INDICATE BUDGET} in a macro, the word BUDGET will stay as the mode indicator even after the macro is finished. The command {INDICATE} with no arguments restores the mode indicator to its normal operation.

The **{WAIT}** command suspends the operation of the macro and causes the computer to wait until the time indicated. The general format for the wait command is

{WAIT time-serial-number}

where the argument is the serial number of the time at which the computer is to resume operation. For example, {WAIT @NOW+@TIME(0,1,0)} causes the computer to wait for a minute before resuming operation. The command {WAIT @TIME(10,30,0)} would cause the computer to suspend operation until the system clock reaches 10:30 AM.

AUTOEXECUTE MACRO

An **autoexecute macro** is a macro that automatically is invoked when the spreadsheet is read from the disk. The name **\0** (backslash zero) is reserved for the autoexecute macro (also called the **start-up macro**). That is, if a spreadsheet has a macro named \0 then that macro automatically will be started up when the spreadsheet is retrieved from the disk.

An example of a start-up macro is shown in Figures 19-3 and 19-4. This macro will clear the screen, play some tones, and slowly print a welcoming message on the screen. Then the macro moves the cursor to A1, restores the screen, and quits.

The macro begins in AC1105. In AC1105 and AC1106 the top of the screen and the row numbers and column letters are cleared off the screen. The message that will be printed on the screen actually will be placed into BA2000..BA2010. The commands in AC1107 erase that portion of the screen using the / Range Erase command. The command in AC1108 moves the cursor to BA2000 in two steps. First, the cursor is moved to AX2000 by using F5, the GoTo key. When the cursor is moved to AX2000, the screen is positioned so that column AX is the left column on the screen. The cursor then is moved right three cells to BA2000. The cursor

```
AB1104:                                                              READY

        AA      AB               AC                        AD
1100
1101 ***********************************************************************
1102
1103 Start-up macro -- Sound a flourish and display the opening message
1104
1105     \0          {PANELOFF CLEAR}              Erase the top of the screen
1106                 {BORDERSOFF}                  Erase row and col. names
1107                 /REBA2000..BA2010~            Erase BA2000..BA2010
1108                 {GOTO}AX2000~{R 3}            Move cursor to BA2000
1109                 {BEEP 4}                      Play the trumpets
1110                 {WAIT @NOW+@TIME(0,0,0.4)}         "
1111                 {BEEP 1}                           "
1112                 {WAIT @NOW+@TIME(0,0,0.4)}         "
1113                 {BEEP 4}                           "
1114                 {WAIT @NOW+@TIME(0,0,0.4)}         "
1115                 {BEEP 1}                           "
1116                 {WAIT @NOW+@TIME(0,0,1)}           "
1117            THE WIDGET DIVISION~               Type first line
1118                 {D 2}                         Move cursor down 2 cells
1119                 {WAIT @NOW+@TIME(0,0,2)}      Wait 2 seconds
                                    UNDO
```

FIGURE 19-3 The first half of an autoexecute macro.

```
AB1124:                                                              READY

        AA        AB                  AC                      AD
1120                        PRESENTS~                Type second line
1121              {D 2}                               Move cursor down 2 cells
1122              {WAIT @NOW+@TIME(0,0,2)}            Wait 2 seconds
1123              A FIVE YEAR PROJECTION~             Type third line
1124     [      ] {D 2}                               Move cursor down 2 cells
1125              {WAIT @NOW+@TIME(0,0,2)}            Wait 2 seconds
1126                  FOR WIDGET SALES~               Type fourth line
1127              {D 2}                               Move cursor down 2 cells
1128              {WAIT @NOW+@TIME(0,0,2)}            Wait 2 seconds
1129              /REBA2000..BA2010~                  Erase message
1130              {HOME}                              Move the cursor to A1
1131              {BORDERSON}                         Restore row and col. names
1132              {PANELON}                           Restore top of screen
1133              {BEEP 1}                            Sound a tone
1134              {QUIT}                              Quit the macro
1135
1136 *****************************************************************
1137
1138
1139
                                UNDO
```

FIGURE 19-4   The second half of the autoexecute macro.

now is in the center of the screen at the top of where the worksheet area would be on the screen. Remember, the top panel and the row and column names have been erased.

The commands in AC1109..AC1116 play a flourish on the computer, a poor imitation of a trumpet call before the royal announcement. Four notes are sounded with a 0.4-second delay between the notes.

In AC1117..AC1128 a four-line introductory message is displayed on the screen. After each line is displayed, the cursor moves down two rows and the computer delays for 2 seconds to give the user time to read the text. The view on the screen during the delay in AC1128 is shown in Figure 19-5.

The commands in AC1129..AC1134 restore the spreadsheet and screen and terminate the macro. In AC1129 the message is erased from the spreadsheet and screen. In AC1130 the cursor is moved back to A1. In AC1131 and AC1132 the row numbers, the column letters, and the top panel are restored to the screen. In AC1133 the macro sounds a tone to notify the user that the macro is finished. In AC1134 the macro terminates and control is turned over to the user.

Note that the autoexecute macro can be suppressed using the / Worksheet Global Default Autoexecute No command. With this command, the computer will not automatically invoke a macro named \0 if one exists on a spreadsheet that is retrieved from the disk.

MACRO SUBROUTINES

A macro subroutine is a sequence of macro commands that acts as a unit. Subroutines have some important advantages. First, the use of subroutines can make complicated macros easier

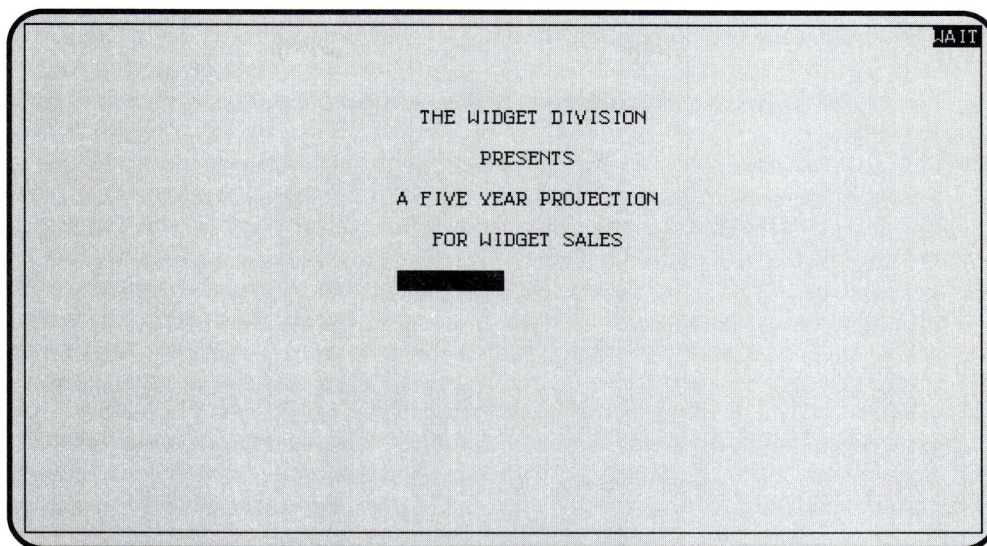

FIGURE 19-5 The final screen presented by the autoexecute macro.

to understand. Second, subroutines make macros easier to construct. Subroutines act as building blocks in creating macros. You can use the same subroutine in several macros without writing out the commands each time.

For example, we could take the eight commands for sounding the flourish in the autoexecute macro of Figures 19-3 and 19-4 and make them into a separate subroutine. The resulting macros are shown in Figures 19-6 and 19-7.

In the main macro \0, the eight commands that sounded the tones have been replaced by the command {\FLOURISH} in cell AC1109. The {\FLOURISH} command is *not* built into Lotus 1-2-3. Rather we have created a macro subroutine and named it \FLOURISH. By putting the name of the macro subroutine in curly braces we are instructing Lotus 1-2-3 to "call" the subroutine, to take an excursion to the subroutine, perform the commands contained in the subroutine, and then when the subroutine is completed to resume the commands in the main macro right where the computer left off.

The macro subroutine named \FLOURISH is in AC1130..AC1138. The cell AC1130, the first cell of the subroutine, has been named \FLOURISH using / Range Name Create.

All subroutines end with a {RETURN} command. The **{RETURN}** command indicates that a macro subroutine is finished and that control should be returned to the main macro right after the place where the subroutine was called.

When the autoexecute macro \0 in Figure 19-6 is invoked, the computer takes its first command from AC1105. The computer then follows the commands in AC1106, AC1107, and AC1108. When the computer encounters the {\FLOURISH} command in AC1109, it looks up the location of the cell named \FLOURISH. Cell AC1130 has been named \FLOURISH so

```
AB1106:                                                              READY

        AA        AB                  AC                        AD
1101 ***********************************************************************
1102
1103 Start-up macro -- Sound a flourish and display the opening message
1104
1105     \0          {PANELOFF CLEAR}              Erase the top of the screen
1106                 {BORDERSOFF}                  Erase row and col. names
1107                 /REBA2000..BA2010~            Erase BA2000..BA2010
1108                 {GOTO}AX2000~{R 3}            Move cursor to BA2000
1109                 {\FLOURISH}                   Call the \FLOURISH subroutine
1110                   THE WIDGET DIVISION~         Type first line
1111                 {D 2}                          Move cursor down 2 cells
1112                 {WAIT @NOW+@TIME(0,0,2)}       Wait 2 seconds
1113                     PRESENTS~                  Type second line
1114                 {D 2}                          Move cursor down 2 cells
1115                 {WAIT @NOW+@TIME(0,0,2)}       Wait 2 seconds
1116                 A FIVE YEAR PROJECTION~        Type third line
1117                 {D 2}                          Move cursor down 2 cells
1118                 {WAIT @NOW+@TIME(0,0,2)}       Wait 2 seconds
1119                     FOR WIDGET SALES~          Type fourth line
1120                 {D 2}                          Move cursor down 2 cells
                                 UNDO
```

FIGURE 19-6 The autoexecute macro with a \Flourish subroutine (first half).

```
AB1126:                                                              READY

        AA        AB                  AC                        AD
1121                 {WAIT @NOW+@TIME(0,0,2)}       Wait 2 seconds
1122                 /REBA2000..BA2010~            Erase message
1123                 {HOME}                         Move the cursor to A1
1124                 {BORDERSON}                    Restore row and col. names
1125                 {PANELON}                      Restore top of screen
1126                 {BEEP 1}                       Sound a tone
1127                 {QUIT}                         Quit the macro
1128
1129 Subroutine to sound a flourish on the "trumpet"
1130     \FLOURISH{BEEP 4}                          Sound tone 4
1131                 {WAIT @NOW+@TIME(0,0,0.4)}     Wait 0.4 seconds
1132                 {BEEP 1}                       Sound tone 1
1133                 {WAIT @NOW+@TIME(0,0,0.4)}     Wait 0.4 seconds
1134                 {BEEP 4}                       Sound tone 4
1135                 {WAIT @NOW+@TIME(0,0,0.4)}     Wait 0.4 seconds
1136                 {BEEP 1}                       Sound tone 1
1137                 {WAIT @NOW+@TIME(0,0,1)}       Wait 1 second
1138                 {RETURN}                       Return to the main macro
1139
1140 ***********************************************************************
                                 UNDO
```

FIGURE 19-7 The second half of the improved autoexecute macro.

the computer proceeds to take its next command from AC1130. However, before control passes to AC1130, the computer notes to itself that the subroutine call was in cell AC1109. The computer follows the instructions in AC1130, AC1131, and so on through AC1137. When the computer encounters the {RETURN} command in AC1138 it looks up in its memory the location of the latest subroutine call, which was AC1109. The computer then returns to that point and takes its next instruction from AC1110. The computer proceeds to follow the commands in AC1111, AC1112, and so on until it hits the {QUIT} command in AC1127. At that point, control is passed from the macro to the user and the program enters READY mode.

Note that any macro can be called as a subroutine by placing its name in curly braces. However, if the macro does not end with a {RETURN} command, then control will never be returned to the main macro. The difference between the command {BRANCH \FLOURISH} and {\FLOURISH} is that in the latter case the computer remembers the location of the command and when a {RETURN} is encountered the computer returns to the following command in the original macro.

A macro can call many subroutines. It is possible to have a macro call a subroutine and then have that macro call another subroutine, and so on.

SETTING UP CUSTOM MENUS USING {MENUBRANCH}

The {MENUBRANCH} command allows you to set up your own custom menu system. An example is shown in Figure 19-8. The cell AF1204 is named \N. When the user invokes the

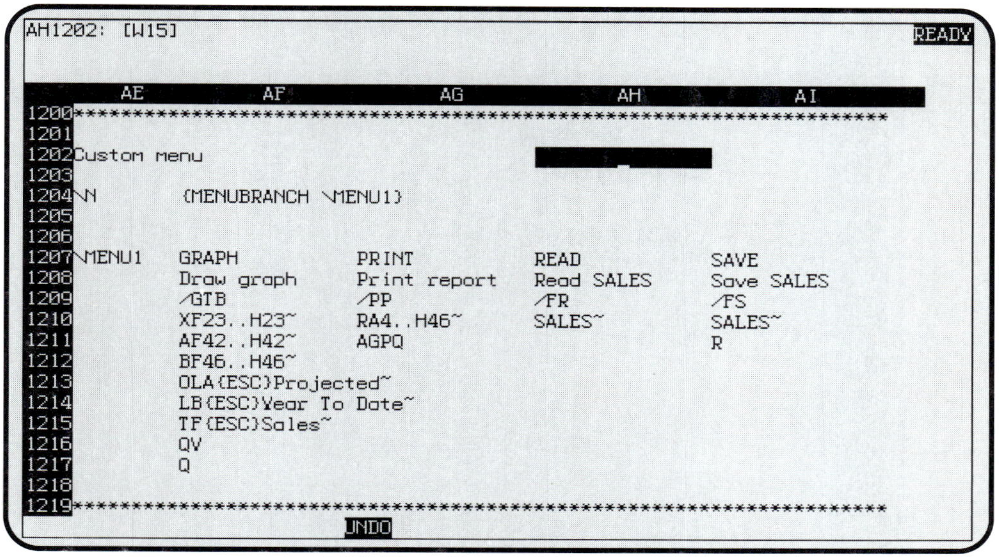

```
AH1202:  [W15]                                                          READY
          AE          AF          AG          AH          AI
1200 ************************************************************************
1201
1202 Custom menu
1203
1204 \N        {MENUBRANCH \MENU1}
1205
1206
1207 \MENU1    GRAPH         PRINT         READ          SAVE
1208          Draw graph    Print report  Read SALES    Save SALES
1209          /GTB          /PP           /FR           /FS
1210          XF23..H23~    RA4..H46~     SALES~         SALES~
1211          AF42..H42~    AGPQ                          R
1212          BF46..H46~
1213          OLA{ESC}Projected~
1214          LB{ESC}Year To Date~
1215          TF{ESC}Sales~
1216          QV
1217          Q
1218
1219 ************************************************************************
                              UNDO
```

FIGURE 19-8 Setting up a custom menu using {MENUBRANCH}.

macro by typing Alt-N, control is passed to AF1204. The command in AF1204 is

$$\{MENUBRANCH \ \backslash MENU1\}$$

which informs the computer that it is to set up a macro menu using the information that begins in the cell named \MENU1, which is cell AF1207. (Note that it is cell AF1207 that is named \MENU1. As usual, the name of the cell appears to the left in cell AE1207 for human reference.)

The menu information for a {MENUBRANCH} must be entered in a special format. Up to eight menu items are entered in successive columns beginning at the address indicated in the {MENUBRANCH} command. The first row of entries are the actual menu items. These menu items must be labels. Each menu item must begin with a different letter. The second row contains the description of the menu item that is to appear in the second line of the menu when the menu item is highlighted. The third and successive rows contain the macro commands that are to be followed when the user selects that item.

In the example in Figure 19-8, there are four menu items: GRAPH PRINT READ SAVE. When the macro is invoked, as in Figure 19-9, these four menu items appear at the top of the screen. When GRAPH is highlighted, as in Figure 19-9, the text that is entered in AF1208 in Figure 19-8 appears as the description for the menu item. When the user selects one of the items either by typing the first letter of the item or by highlighting the item and pressing the Enter key, the computer then proceeds to follow the macro commands entered below the item in row 1209 and below in the spreadsheet. Lotus 1-2-3 handles all of the mechanics of menu display and selection.

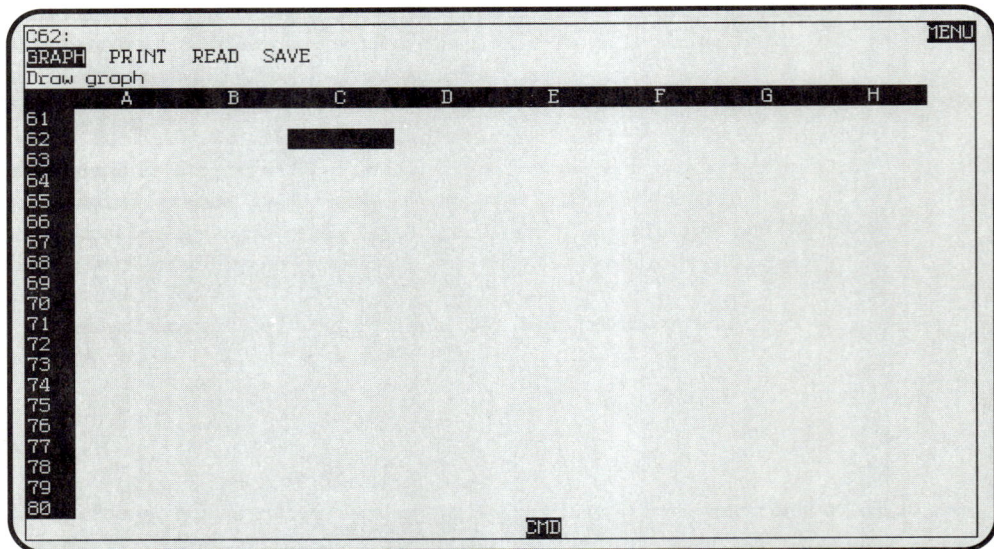

FIGURE 19-9 The custom menu appears when the user types Alt-N.

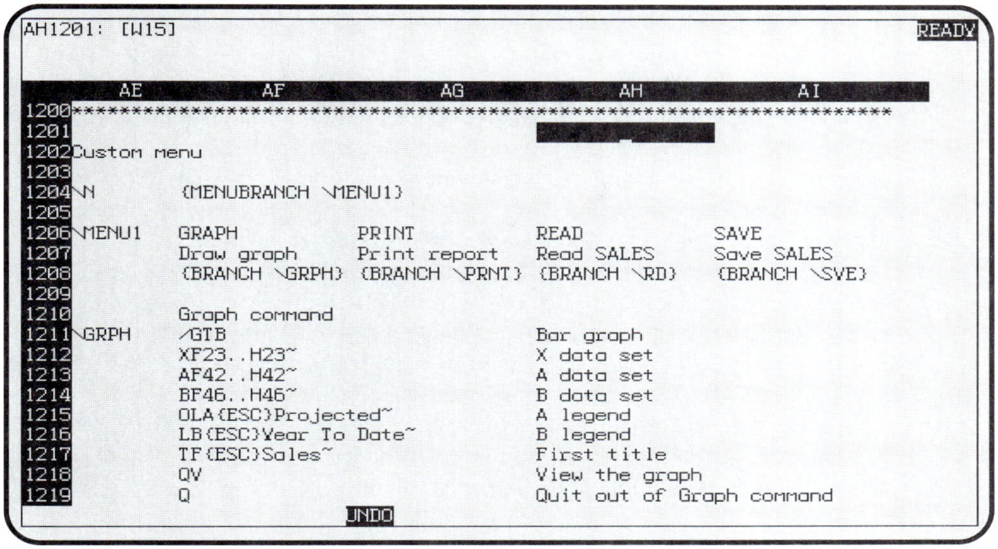

```
AH1201: [W15]                                                        READY

          AE          AF          AG          AH          AI
1200*******************************************************************
1201
1202Custom menu
1203
1204\N         {MENUBRANCH \MENU1}
1205
1206\MENU1     GRAPH          PRINT          READ           SAVE
1207          Draw graph     Print report   Read SALES     Save SALES
1208          {BRANCH \GRPH} {BRANCH \PRNT} {BRANCH \RD}    {BRANCH \SVE}
1209
1210          Graph command
1211\GRPH     /GTB                          Bar graph
1212          XF23..H23~                    X data set
1213          AF42..H42~                    A data set
1214          BF46..H46~                    B data set
1215          OLA{ESC}Projected~            A legend
1216          LB{ESC}Year To Date~          B legend
1217          TF{ESC}Sales~                 First title
1218          QV                            View the graph
1219          Q                             Quit out of Graph command
                              UNDO
```

FIGURE 19-10 A better organization for the customized menu macro (first half).

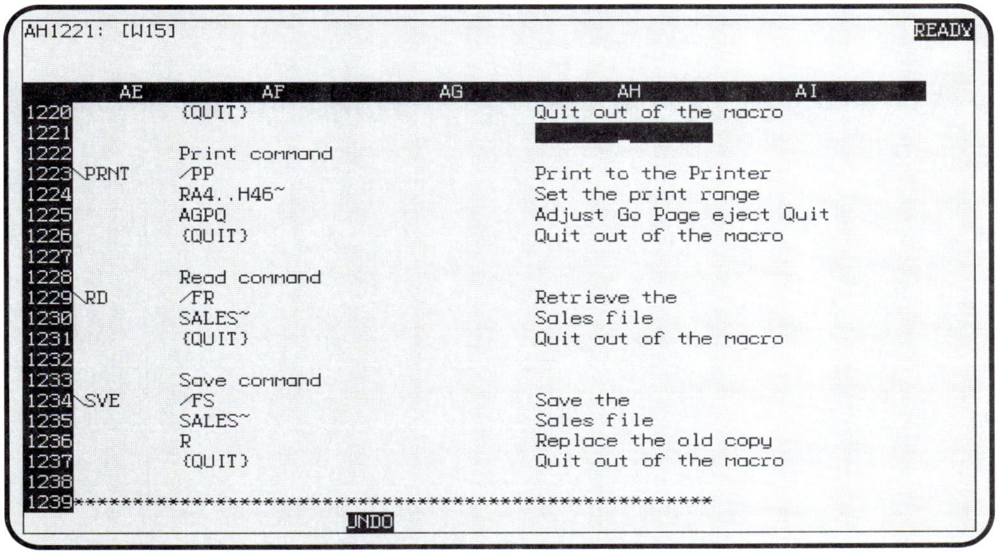

```
AH1221: [W15]                                                        READY

          AE          AF          AG          AH          AI
1220          {QUIT}                        Quit out of the macro
1221
1222          Print command
1223\PRNT     /PP                           Print to the Printer
1224          RA4..H46~                     Set the print range
1225          AGPQ                          Adjust Go Page eject Quit
1226          {QUIT}                        Quit out of the macro
1227
1228          Read command
1229\RD       /FR                           Retrieve the
1230          SALES~                        Sales file
1231          {QUIT}                        Quit out of the macro
1232
1233          Save command
1234\SVE      /FS                           Save the
1235          SALES~                        Sales file
1236          R                             Replace the old copy
1237          {QUIT}                        Quit out of the macro
1238
1239******************************************************************
                              UNDO
```

FIGURE 19-11 The second half of the improved customized menu macro.

A better approach to organizing custom menus is shown in Figures 19-10 and 19-11. Here we have created separate macro modules for each of the commands in the custom menu. This makes the macro easier to understand. If the user types Alt-N and then selects the GRAPH command in the custom menu, Lotus 1-2-3 branches to the cell named \GRPH, which is cell AF1211, for its next macro command. When the graph has been displayed and the macro is completed, Lotus 1-2-3 quits out of the macro and returns control to the user. The macro in Figure 19-8 and the macro in Figures 19-10 and 19-11 perform identically when invoked. They simply have been written out in the spreadsheet in different styles.

If we wanted, instead of the {QUIT} command in AF1220, AF1226, AF1231, and AF1237, we could place the command {BRANCH \N}. This would set up a loop where whenever one of the customized menu commands was completed the customized menu automatically would be reentered. The user would exit from the menu by pressing the Escape key. Alternatively, we could add a QUIT command to the customized menu.

You can create as many macros with custom menus as you wish. The {MENUBRANCH} command can be embedded in long macros. You can create a submenu by placing another {MENUBRANCH} command under a menu item.

COMPUTER EXERCISES

19-1 Design, implement, and test macros that set column widths, as follows.

    (a) A macro that enters an infinite loop and moves right setting column widths to 15 until you press Ctrl-Break.

    (b) A macro that uses a {FOR} command to set the 12 columns to the right to a width of 15 characters.

    (c) A macro that uses an {IF} command to set columns to the right to width 15 until any key is typed.

    (d) A macro that uses an {IF} command to set columns to the right to width 15 as long as they contain numbers.

    (e) A macro that moves to the right, setting cells that contain labels to width 18 and cells that contain numbers to width 10. The macro should halt when it encounters a blank cell.

19-2 Design, implement, and test an underline macro that moves to the right placing repeating dashes \- in cells below the current row as long as the cell in the current row is not blank. The macro should halt as soon as a blank cell is encountered in the current row.

19-3 Working on the computer can be tiring.

    (a) Set up a macro that acts as an alarm clock so you can take a catnap. The macro should wait for 10 minutes and then sound tones until a key is pressed.

    (b) While the macro is waiting, have it show the number of minutes and seconds until wakeup. This display should be updated continuously.

19-4 Design, implement, and test an alarm macro that blanks the entire screen and then puts the message THINKING. PLEASE DO NOT DISTURB on the screen. If anyone does press a key, the computer should sound 20 beeps and then revert to its previous status. The only way out of the macro should be by pressing Ctrl-Break.

19-5 Design, implement, and test a macro that plays a recognizable tune.

19-6 We would like to be able to put a box of asterisks (*'s) around a portion of a spreadsheet to distinguish it from the rest of the spreadsheet. Horizontal portions of the box should contain repeating asterisks created using *. Vertical portions of the box should contain a single asterisk. Design a macro that enables a user interactively to place asterisks around any portion of the spreadsheet. Full instructions for the user should be contained in the spreadsheet. There are many possible solutions to this problem. Be creative. You may want to consult the Appendices for additional functions and macro commands.

19-7 Create a start-up macro for your assignments. The macro should at least place your name, the date the assignment was completed (*not* the current date), and the exercise number on the screen before moving the cursor to A1 and relinquishing control. Have the macro also play a welcoming tune or tell a joke or whatever. Be creative.

19-8 Select one of your favorite spreadsheets. Create a customized menu that allows the user to perform four useful operations on the spreadsheet.

MODE
INDICATORS*

The Mode Indicator in the top right of the screen tells you the current state of Lotus 1-2-3. Some keys work differently depending on the mode.

The possible Mode Indicators are as follows:

EDIT	You can edit the cell entry displayed in the control panel.
ERROR	An error has occurred—press the Help, Esc, or Enter key.
FILES	1-2-3 is displaying a menu of file names.
FIND	A / Data Query Find operation is in progress.
FRMT	You selected / Data Parse Format-Line to edit a format line.

*Based on the Lotus 1-2-3 Help screens. Copyright © 1990 Lotus Development Corporation. Used with permission.

HELP   You are using the on-line Help system.
LABEL   You are entering a label.
MENU   1-2-3 is displaying a menu of commands in the control panel.
NAMES   1-2-3 is displaying a menu of range, graph, or add-in names.
POINT   1-2-3 is prompting you to specify a range by highlighting it.
READY   1-2-3 is waiting for your next command.
STAT   You selected /Worksheet Status or /Worksheet Global Default Status.
VALUE   You are entering a value (a number or a formula).
WAIT   1-2-3 is completing a command or process.

STATUS INDICATORS*

The Status Indicators at the bottom of the screen tell you when certain keys have been **pressed** or when a particular program condition exists.

The possible Status Indicators are as follows:

CALC	Formulas in the worksheet need to be recalculated.
CAPS	The Caps Lock key is on.
CIRC	The worksheet contains a formula that refers to itself.
CMD	1-2-3 is pausing during a macro.
END	The End key is on.

*Based on the Lotus 1-2-3 Help screens. Copyright © 1990 Lotus Development Corporation. Used with **permission**.

LEARN — Keystrokes are being recorded in the Learn range. The Learn key (Alt-F5) is pressed to turn on and turn off keystroke recording.

MEM — Memory available for new cells has been reduced to 4000 bytes. Continuing to add data will result in a "Memory-Full" error.

NUM — The Num Lock key is on.

OVR — The Ins key is on.

RO — The current file has read-only status (networks only).

SCROLL — The Scroll Lock key is on.

SST — A macro in single-step mode is waiting for input.

STEP — Single-step mode for debugging macros has been turned on. The Step key (Alt-F2) is pressed to turn on and turn off Step mode.

UNDO — You can press Undo (Alt-F4) to cancel changes made to the worksheet since 1-2-3 was last in Ready mode.

FUNCTION KEYS*

APPENDIX C

Each function key, except F6, performs two operations: one when you press the function key by itself and another when you hold down the Alt or Shift key and press the function key.

The function keys pressed by themselves perform the following actions.

F1 Help   Displays a 1-2-3 Help screen.
F2 Edit   Puts 1-2-3 in Edit mode and displays the contents of the current cell in the control panel.
F3 Name   Displays a menu of range names.
F4 Abs   Cycles a cell or range address between relative, absolute, and mixed.

*Based on the Lotus 1-2-3 Help screens. Copyright © 1990 Lotus Development Corporation. Used with permission.

F5	GoTo	Moves cell pointer directly to a particular cell.
F6	Window	Moves cell pointer between two windows. Turns off the display of setting sheets (Menu mode only).
F7	Query	Repeats most recent / Data Query operation.
F8	Table	Repeats most recent / Data Table operation.
F9	Calc	Recalculates all formulas (Ready mode only). Converts formula to its value (Value and Edit modes).
F10	Graph	Draws a graph using current graph settings.

To use one of the following 1-2-3 keys, hold down the Alt key, press the function key, and then release both keys.

Alt-F1	Compose	When used with alphanumeric keys, creates characters you cannot enter directly from the keyboard.
Alt-F2	Step	Turns on Step mode, which executes macros one step at a time for the purposes of debugging.
Alt-F3	Run	Displays a menu of named ranges in the worksheet so you can select the name of a macro to run.
Alt-F4	Undo	Cancels any changes made to worksheet since 1-2-3 was last in Ready mode. Press again to redo changes.
Alt-F5	Learn	Turns learn feature on and records keystrokes in the learn range. Press again to turn off the learn feature.
Alt-F7	App1	Activates add-in program assigned to key, if any.
Alt-F8	App2	Activates add-in program assigned to key, if any.
Alt-F9	App3	Activates add-in program assigned to key, if any.
Alt-F10	App4	Activates add-in program assigned to key, or displays / Add-In menu, if there is no add-in assigned to key.

APPENDIX D

THE PRECEDENCE OF OPERATORS

Formulas are evaluated as follows:

1. Operations in parentheses are evaluated first.
2. Operators within parentheses or outside of parentheses are evaluated in order of the precedence numbers listed below.
3. Operators with the same precedence number are evaluated from left to right.

The following table shows the operators that can be used in formulas in Lotus 1-2-3 and their order of precedence. Operators with lower precedence numbers are performed first.

Operator	Precedence Number	Definition	Number of Operands
^	1	Exponentiation	2
- +	2	Negative and positive values	1
* /	3	Multiplication and division	2
+ -	4	Addition and subtraction	2
= <> < > >= <=	5	Comparison operators	2
#NOT#	6	Logical-NOT	1
#AND# #OR#	7	Logical-AND and Logical-OR	2
&	7	String concatenation	2

The - and + of Precedence 2 refer to the use of the - sign and + sign that indicate whether a value is negative or positive. For example in the formula +6*-5 the + sign and - sign do not indicate addition and subtraction but rather indicate that the values are positive and negative. These operators have one operand. The operand for the + sign is 6. The operand for the - sign is 5. In the formula (6+11) the + sign indicates addition and has two operands, 6 and 11.

The formula -3*4 would be the same as (-3)*4 because the negative sign has a lower precedence number than does multiplication, and, hence, the negative sign would be evaluated first. The formula would evaluate to -12.

The formula -3^4 would be the same as -(3^4) because the exponentiation operator has a lower precedence number than does the negative sign and, hence, the exponentiation would be evaluated first. This formula would evaluate to -81.

The formula -3+4 would be the same as -(3)+4 because the negative sign has a lower precedence number than does the addition operator and, hence, the negation would be evaluated first. This formula would evaluate to 1.

For further discussion, see Chapter 2. The comparison operators and logical operators are discussed in Chapter 11.

BUILT-IN FUNCTIONS*

A
P
P
E
N
D
I
X

@@(location)

Is an indirect cell reference that returns the contents of the cell location referred to.

@ABS(x)

Calculates the absolute (positive) value of x. For example, the value of @ABS(-3.6) is 3.6. @ABS(3.6) is 3.6.

@ACOS(x)

Calculates the arc cosine of value x. The value returned is in radians.

*Based on the Lotus 1-2-3 Help screens. Copyright © 1990 Lotus Development Corporation. Used with permission.

@ASIN(x) Calculates the arc sine of value x. The value returned is in radians.

@ATAN(x) Calculates the arc tangent of value x. The value returned is in radians.

@ATAN2(x,y) Calculates the four-quadrant arc tangent of two values.

@AVG(list) Finds the arithmetic mean, or average, of a list of values.

@CELL(attribute,range) Returns information about a cell. For example, @CELL("type",B5) returns "v" if B5 contains a value, "b" if B5 is blank, and "l" if B5 contains a label.

@CELLPOINTER(attribute) Returns information about the current cell. For example, @CELLPOINTER("type") returns "v" if the current cell contains a value, "b" if the current cell is blank, and "l" if the current cell contains a label.

@CHAR(x) Returns the character that a Lotus International Character Set (LICS) code produces.

@CHOOSE(offset,list) Finds a specified value or string in a list of values and/or strings.

@CLEAN(string) Removes control characters from a string.

@CODE(string) Returns the LICS code that corresponds to the first character in a string.

@COLS(range) Counts the columns in a range.

@COS(x) Calculates the cosine of an angle (x) measured in radians.

@COUNT(list) Counts the nonblank cells in list of values.

@CTERM(interest,future-value,present-value) Calculates the number of compounding periods necessary for an investment to grow to a future value.

@DATE(year,month,day) Calculates the serial number for a set of year, month, and day values.

@DATEVALUE(string) Converts a string that looks like a date into its equivalent serial number.

@DAVG(input,field,criteria)

Averages values in a field of the input range that meet criteria in the criteria range.

@DAY(serial-number)

Calculates the day of the month (an integer from 1 to 31) of the date corresponding to serial-number.

@DCOUNT(input,field,criteria)

Counts nonblank cells in a field of the input range that meet criteria in the criteria range.

@DDB(cost,salvage,life,period)

Calculates the depreciation allowance of an asset for a specified period, using double-declining-balance method.

@DMAX(input,field,criteria)

Finds the largest value in a field of the input range that meets the criteria in the criteria range.

@DMIN(input,field,criteria)

Finds the smallest value in a field of the input range that meets the criteria in the criteria range.

@DSTD(input,field,criteria)

Calculates the population standard deviation of the values in a field of an input range that meet the criteria in the criteria range.

@DSUM(input,field,criteria)

Sums the values in a field of an input range that meet the criteria in the criteria range.

@DVAR(input,field,criteria)

Calculates the population variance of the values in a field of an input range that meet the criteria in the criteria range.

@ERR

Returns the value ERR (error). ERR is a special value in 1-2-3 that indicates an error in a formula. ERR has a ripple-through effect on formulas. @ERR is seldom used by itself, but is often used with @IF to indicate an ERR value only under certain conditions.

@EXACT(string1,string2)

Tests whether string1 and string2 are the same. If the two strings match exactly, @EXACT returns 1 (*True*); if the two strings are not the same. @EXACT returns 0 (*False*).

@EXP(x)	Calculates the value of *e* (approximately 2.718282) raised to the power x.
@FALSE	Returns the logical value 0 (*False*).
@FIND(search-string,string,start-number)	Calculates the position in string at which 1-2-3 finds the first occurrence of search-string.
@FV(payments,interest,term)	Calculates the future value of an invest ment, based on a series of equal payments, earning a periodic interest rate, over the number of payment periods in term.
@HLOOKUP(x,range,row)	Finds the contents of the cell in a specified row of a horizontal lookup table. A horizon tal lookup table is a range with value in-formation in ascending order in the top row.
@HOUR(serial-number)	Calculates the hour, an integer from 0 (midnight) to 23 (11:00 PM), in the frac-tional part of a serial-number.
@IF(condition,x,y)	Evaluates condition and takes one of two actions, depending on the result of the evaluation. If condition is true, @IF returns x; if condition is false, @IF returns y. Condition is usually a logical formula or a reference to a cell that contains a logical formula. The arguments x and y can be values or strings. A logical formula can contain one or more logical operators and can contain nested @IF functions.
@INDEX(range,column-offset,row-offset)	Finds the value in the cell located at a specified column-offset and row-offset of range.
@INT(x)	Returns the integer portion of x, without rounding the value. For example @INT(23.89) is 23.
@IRR(guess,range)	Calculates the internal rate of return ex-pected from a series of cash flows generated by an investment. 1-2-3 assumes cash flows are received at regular, equal intervals.
@ISAAF(name)	Tests name for a defined add-in @function.

@ISAAP(name) — Tests name for an attached add-in.

@ISERR(x) — Tests x for the value ERR. If x is the value ERR, @ISERR returns 1 (*True*); if x is not the value ERR, @ISERR returns 0 (*False*).

@ISNA(x) — Tests x for the value NA. If x is the value NA, @ISNA returns 1 (*True*); if x is not the value NA, @ISNA returns 0 (*False*).

@ISNUMBER(x) — Tests x for a value. If x a value or a blank cell, @ISNUMBER returns 1 (*True*); if x is a string, @ISNUMBER returns 0 (*False*).

@ISSTRING(x) — Tests x for a string. If x is a literal string or cell that contains a label or string formula, @ISSTRING returns 1 (*True*); if x is a value or a blank cell, @ISSTRING returns 0(*False*).

@LEFT(string,n) — Returns the first n characters in string.

@LENGTH(string) — Counts the number of characters in string.

@LN(x) — Calculates the natural logarithm (base *e*) of x.

@LOG(x) — Calculates the common logarithm (base 10) of x.

@LOWER(string) — Converts all the letters in string to lower case.

@MAX(list) — Finds the largest value in list.

@MID(string,start-number,n) — Returns n characters from string (including spaces and punctuation) beginning with the character at the start-number.

@MIN(list) — Finds the smallest value in list.

@MINUTE(serial-number) — Calculates the minute, an integer from 0 to 59, in the fractional part of a serial-number.

@MOD(x,y) — Calculates the remainder (modulus) of x/y. For example, @MOD(63,5) is 3.

@MONTH(serial-number) — Calculates the month, an integer from 1 (January) to 12 (December), of the month of the date corresponding to serial-number.

@N(range) — Returns the entry in the first cell in a range as a value. If the cell contains a label, @N returns the value 0.

@NA	Returns the value NA (not available).
@NOW	Calculates the serial number that corresponds to the current date and time. This includes both a date number (integer portion) and a time number (decimal portion).
@NPV(interest,range)	Calculates the present value of a series of future cash flows discounted at a fixed, periodic interest rate. 1-2-3 assumes that the cash flows occur at equal time intervals, that the first cash flow occurs at the end of the first period, and subsequent cash flows occur at the end of subsequent periods.
@PI	Returns the value pi (calculated at 3.1415926536).
@PMT(principal,interest,term)	Calculates the amount of the periodic payment needed to pay off a loan (the principal), given a specified periodic interest rate and number of payment periods (the term). 1-2-3 assumes your calculations are for payments you make at the end of each payment period (an ordinary annuity).
@PROPER(string)	Converts the letters in string to proper capitalization; the first letter of each word in uppercase and the remaining letters in lowercase.
@PV(payments,interest,term)	Calculates the present value of an investment, based on a series of equal payments discounted at a periodic interest rate over a number of payment periods (term).
@RAND	Generates a random value between 0 and 1. Each time 1-2-3 recalculates your work, @RAND generates a new random value.
@RATE(future-value,present-value,term)	Calculates the periodic interest rate necessary for an investment (present-value) to grow to a future-value over the number of compounding periods in term.
@REPEAT(string,n)	Duplicates a string the number of times specified by n.

@REPLACE(original-string,start,n,new-string)   Replaces n characters in original-string with the new-string, beginning at the start number.

@RIGHT(string,n)   Returns the last n characters in string.

@ROUND(x,n)   Rounds the value x to n places.

@ROWS(range)   Counts the number of rows in range.

@S(range)   Returns the entry in the first cell in range as a label if the cell contains a label. If the cell contains a value or is blank, @S returns a blank cell.

@SECOND(serial-number)   Calculates the seconds, an integer from 0 to 59, in the fractional part of serial-number.

@SIN(x)   Calculates the sine of an angle (x) measured in radians.

@SLN(cost,salvage,life)   Calculates the straight-line depreciation allowance of an asset for one period, given the cost, the predicted salvage value, and the life of the asset.

@SQRT(x)   Calculates the positive square root of x.

@STD(list)   Calculates the population standard deviation of the values in list.

@STRING(x,n)   Converts value x into a string with n decimal places.

@SUM(list)   Adds the values in list.

@SYD(cost,salvage,life,period)   Calculates the sum-of-the-years'-digits depreciation allowance of an asset for a specified period, given the cost, the predicted salvage value, and the life of the asset.

@TAN(x)   Calculates the tangent of an angle (x) measured in radians.

@TERM(payments,interest,future-value)   Calculates the number of payment periods in the term of an investment necessary to accumulate a future-value, assuming equal payments, when the investment earns a periodic interest rate.

@TIME(hour,minutes,seconds)	Calculates the serial number for the specified hour, minutes, and seconds.
@TIMEVALUE(string)	Calculates the serial number for a string that looks like a time.
@TRIM(string)	Removes leading, trailing, and consecutive spaces from string.
@TRUE	Returns the logical value 1 (*True*).
@UPPER(string)	Converts all the letters in string to upper case.
@VALUE(string)	Converts a string that looks like a value into that value.
@VAR(list)	Calculates the population variance of the values in list.
@VLOOKUP(x,range,column)	Finds the contents of the cell in a specified column of a vertical lookup table, a range with value information in ascending order in the first column.
@YEAR(serial-number)	Calculates the year, an integer from 0 (1900) to 199 (2099), of the date corresponding to serial-number.

COMMAND
SUMMARY

Starting Up

Ch. 2

With no built-in hard disk, at the A> prompt,
   insert the Lotus System disk, type   LOTUS Enter
    At the 1-2-3 Access System, press   Enter

With a built-in hard disk, if 1-2-3 is in a subdirectory,
   at the C> prompt type   CD *subdirectory* Enter
    Then type   LOTUS Enter
    At the 1-2-3 Access System, press   Enter

With a built-in hard disk, if 1-2-3 is not in a subdirectory,
    at the C> prompt type   LOTUS Enter
    At the 1-2-3 Access System, press   Enter

Ending 1-2-3   Ch. 2

To return from 1-2-3 to the 1-2-3 Access System	/QY	
To return from the 1-2-3 Access System to DOS	E	

File Commands

Retrieve a spreadsheet from the disk	/FR	Ch. 3
Retrieve part of a spreadsheet from the disk	/FCCN	Ch. 8
Save the current spreadsheet on the disk	/FS	Ch. 3
Save part of the current spreadsheet on the disk	/FXF	
Save the values only from part of the current spreadsheet	/FXV	Ch.16
Add the values from another spreadsheet on the disk	/FCA	Ch. 8
Subtract the values from another spreadsheet on the disk	/FCS	Ch. 8
Copy the values from another spreadsheet on the disk	/FCC	Ch. 8
Erase a file from the disk	/FE	
Display a list of the spreadsheets on the disk	/FLW	Ch. 3
Display a list of the graph files on the disk	/FLG	
Display a list of the .PRN (print) files on the disk	/FLP	
Display a list of the files linked by the current spreadsheet	/FLL	
Change the default directory for this session	/FD	Ch. 3
Change the default directory for future sessions	/WGDD	
Enter *directory* and then	UQ	
Create a new directory: enter DOS by	/S	
in DOS	MD *new-directory* Enter	
Return to 1-2-3 by	EXIT Enter	
Import a text file one line per cell	/FIT	Ch.16
Break up the text into separate cells	/DP	Ch.16

Erase

Erase the current cell	/RE Enter	Ch. 3
Erase a range	/RE	
Erase the entire worksheet	/WEY	Ch. 2

Undo

Disable Undo (to save memory)	/WGDOUDQ
Enable Undo	/WGDOUEQ
(Press Alt-F4 to Undo)	

Formatting Cells   Ch. 5

Display formulas on screen	/RFT
Format numbers globally	/WGF
Format range of numbers	/RF

Numeric formats:

Fixed	xxxx.xx
Scientific	x.xxE+xx
Currency	$x,xxx.xx
, (Comma)	x,xxx.xx
General	as calculated or entered
Percent	x.xx%
Hidden	
Text	formula

Date 1	DD-MMM-YY	Ch.12
2	DD-MMM	
3	MMM-YY	
4	MM/DD/YY	
5	MM/DD	
6	HH:MM:SS AM/PM	
7	HH:MM AM/PM	
8	HH:MM:SS (24 Hour)	
9	HH:MM (24 Hour)	

Change the currency sign from a $ to another symbol	/WGDOIC	
Change the international date formats (D4 and D5)	/WGDOID	Ch.12
Change the international time formats (D8 and D9)	/WGDOIT	Ch.12
Align all future labels entered	/WGL	Ch. 5
Align labels in range of cells	/RL	

Insert and Delete   Ch. 5

| Insert row(s) | /WIR |
| Insert column(s) | /WIC |

Delete row(s)	/WDR	
Delete column(s)	/WDC	

Column Widths
Ch. 5

Change width of current column	/WCS	
Change global column width	/WGC	

Titles
Ch. 8

Freeze the rows above the cursor	/WTH	
Freeze the columns to the left of cursor	/WTV	
Freeze both row and columns	/WTB	
Clear frozen titles	/WTC	

Windows
Ch. 7

Create horizontal windows	/WWH	
Create vertical windows	/WWV	
Clear windows	/WWC	
(Press F6 to jump between windows)		

Cell Protection
Ch. 8

Unprotect cells you wish to enter data into	/RU	
Enable protection	/WGPE	
Protect some cells you unprotected	/RP	
Disable protection	/WGPD	

Copy and Move

Copy a cell or range of cells	/C	Ch. 4
Enter the FROM range and the TO range		
Be sure to enter a full range for the TO range		
Be sure that addresses that should not be adjusted are written with $ signs, as in $G$23		Ch. 7
Move a cell or range of cells	/M	Ch. 5
Enter the FROM range		
and the top left address of TO range		

Recalculation
Ch. 8

Manual		
(Press F9 to recalculate)	/WGRM	
Automatic	/WGRA	

Display at Bottom Left of Screen   Ch.12

Display the current time and date	/WGDOCCQ
Display the name of the current file	/WGDOCFQ
No display at bottom left of screen	/WGDOCNQ

Range Names   Ch. 5

Create a name for a range	/RNC
List all names and their ranges	/RNT
and specify a range 2 cells across and n cells down	
Delete a range name	/RND
Delete all range names	/RNR

Printing   Ch. 6

Specify range to print	/PPR
Advance one line at printer	/PPL
Advance to top of page	/PPP
Specify that printer is at top of page	/PPA
Begin printing	/PPG
Print listing of formulas one cell per line	/PPOOCQ
Print normally, as displayed on screen	/PPOOAQ
Set margins	
Top—normally 2 lines	/PPOMT
Bottom—normally 2 lines	/PPOMB
Left—normally 4 from left edge	/PPOML
Right—normally 76 from left edge	/PPOMR
Set page length—normally 66 lines	/PPOP
Permanently change default printer settings	/WGDP
Make change(s) and then	QUQ
Set header	/PPOH
Set footer	/PPOF
Use @ to print current date	
Use # to print page number	
Use | to separate left | center | right fields	
Print to file	/PF

Graphing

Select graph type	
Line	/GTL
Bar	/GTB
XY	/GTX
Stack-Bar	/GTS
Pie	/GTP
Select X data range to graph	/GX
A	/GA
B	/GB
etc.	
View the graph	/GV
(or press F10)	
Enter graph legends	/GOL
Enter graph titles	/GOT
Draw lines between data points in Line or XY graph	/GOFGLQ
Draw symbols at data points but no lines in Line or XY graph	/GOFGSQ
Draw symbols at data points and lines between points	/GOFGBQ
Set horizontal or vertical grid lines	/GOG
Change the scale of the X axis or Y axis	/GOS
Select X axis or Y axis	
Select Lower bound and/or Upper bound	
Implement your manual selection by	MQ
Return to automatic scaling of X axis or Y axis	/GOS
Select X axis or Y axis	
And then	AQ
Format the X axis or Y axis scale numbers	/GOS
Select X axis or Y axis	
And then	F
And select format desired and	Q
Label the data points on the graph	/GOD
Display the graph in color	/GOC
Display the graph in black and white	/GOB

Save the graph for later printing in PrintGraph or Allways	/GS	

Data Management

Fill in a range with a sequence of numbers	/DF	Ch.16
Sort	/DS	Ch.15
Specify data range to be sorted	/DSD	
(Do not include column headings)		
Select primary column to determine the order of rows	/DSP	
Select secondary (tie-breaker) column	/DSS	
Go ahead and sort	/DSG	
Querying		Ch.15
Specify location of input data range	/DQI	
(Include column headings)		
Specify location of criteria	/DQC	
(Include column headings)		
Specify location for output range	/DQO	
(Include column headings)		
Highlight each record that meets criteria (Find)	/DQF	
Copy all records that meet the criteria (Extract)	/DQE	
Copy records that meet criteria eliminating duplicates (Unique)	/DQU	
Delete all records that meet criteria (Delete)	/DQD	
(To repeat most recent /DQ operation from Ready mode press F7)		
Create a frequency table	/DD	Ch.16
Enter the location of the values to be tabulated		
Enter the location of the output bins		

Add-Ins (Such as Allways)   Ch.17

Attach an add-in program	/AA	
Detach an add-in prgram	/AD	
Invoke an already attached add-in program	/AI	
Permanently attach an add-in program	/WGDOAS	
Select an add-in number, the program,		
And a speed-key and then	NQU	

Allways Commands   Ch.17

Change the font of a range	/FF	

Draw a box around a range	/FLO
Draw boxes around each cell in a range	/FLA
Draw a horizontal line below a range	/FLB
Draw a vertical line to the right of a range	/FLR
Display a range in **boldface**	/FB
Display a range in <u>underline</u>	/FU
Shade a range of cells	/FS
Specify a color for a range	/FC
Specify the width of columns	/WCS
Specify the height of rows	/WRS
Draw a thick horizontal line in an empty row	/WRS
And then select a height and	/FSS
Insert or remove a page break	/WP
Add a graph to the spreadsheet	/GA
Display the graphs in the spreadsheet	/DGY
Display a shaded box instead of the graphs	/DGN
Print in Allways	/PRS
Select range and then	G
Specify the page size	/LP
Set left, right, top, or bottom margins	/LM
Specify or remove a header or footer	/LT
Print border column and/or rows	/LOB
Set the thickness of lines that are drawn	/LOL
Turn printing of gridlines on or off	/LOG
Display screen in graphics mode (high quality but slow)	/DMG
Display screen in text mode (low quality but fast)	/DMT
Enlarge or reduce the display size of cells	/DZ
Change colors of screen elements	/DC
Exit from Allways to 1-2-3	/Q
(or press the Escape key)	

(To save Allways settings, return to 1-2-3 and /FS)

To Enter PrintGraph   Ch.10

From 1-2-3, first create a graph and save it using	/GS
Quit out of the Graph command	Q
Quit out of 1-2-3 into the 1-2-3 Access System	/QY
In the 1-2-3 Access System select PrintGraph	P

From DOS	PGRAPH Enter

PrintGraph Commands   Ch.10

Select a graph to be printed	I
Inform the computer that the paper is at the top of the page	A
Print the graph with the current settings	G
Advance paper to top of next page	P

Change the size of the printout of the graph	SIS
Change the font of characters printed in graph	SIF
Change the directory to find the graph files	SHG
Change the directory to find the fonts files	SHF
Change printer or plotter type	SHP
(Note: Choice is dependent on selections made in Install program)	
Change printer or plotter interface port	SHI
Change the paper size	SHS

Exit from PrintGraph	EY

COMMAND TREES

Lotus 1-2-3 Command Tree

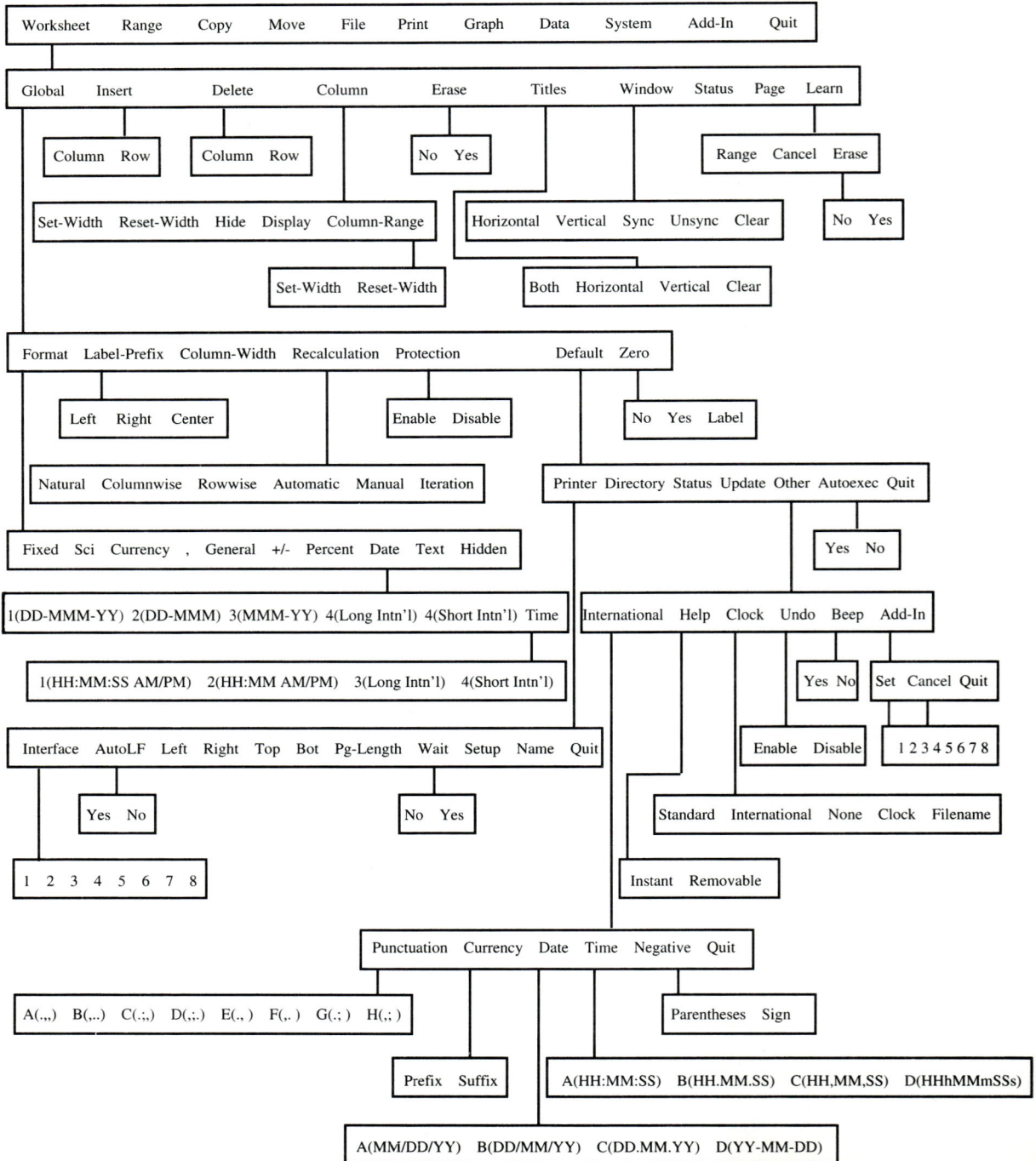

Worksheet   Range   Copy   Move   File   Print   Graph   Data   System   Add-In   Quit

Global   Insert   Delete   Column   Erase   Titles   Window   Status   Page   Learn

Column   Row

Column   Row

No   Yes

Range   Cancel   Erase

Set-Width   Reset-Width   Hide   Display   Column-Range

Horizontal   Vertical   Sync   Unsync   Clear

No   Yes

Set-Width   Reset-Width

Both   Horizontal   Vertical   Clear

Format   Label-Prefix   Column-Width   Recalculation   Protection   Default   Zero

Left   Right   Center

Enable   Disable

No   Yes   Label

Natural   Columnwise   Rowwise   Automatic   Manual   Iteration

Printer   Directory   Status   Update   Other   Autoexec   Quit

Yes   No

Fixed   Sci   Currency   ,   General   +/-   Percent   Date   Text   Hidden

International   Help   Clock   Undo   Beep   Add-In

1(DD-MMM-YY)   2(DD-MMM)   3(MMM-YY)   4(Long Intn'l)   4(Short Intn'l)   Time

Yes   No

Set   Cancel   Quit

1(HH:MM:SS AM/PM)   2(HH:MM AM/PM)   3(Long Intn'l)   4(Short Intn'l)

Enable   Disable

1 2 3 4 5 6 7 8

Interface   AutoLF   Left   Right   Top   Bot   Pg-Length   Wait   Setup   Name   Quit

Yes   No

No   Yes

Standard   International   None   Clock   Filename

1   2   3   4   5   6   7   8

Instant   Removable

Punctuation   Currency   Date   Time   Negative   Quit

A(.,,)   B(,..)   C(.;,)   D(;.)   E(.,)   F(,.)   G(.;)   H(,;)

Parentheses   Sign

Prefix   Suffix

A(HH:MM:SS)   B(HH.MM.SS)   C(HH,MM,SS)   D(HHhMMmSSs)

A(MM/DD/YY)   B(DD/MM/YY)   C(DD.MM.YY)   D(YY-MM-DD)

Lotus 1-2-3 Command Tree (continued)

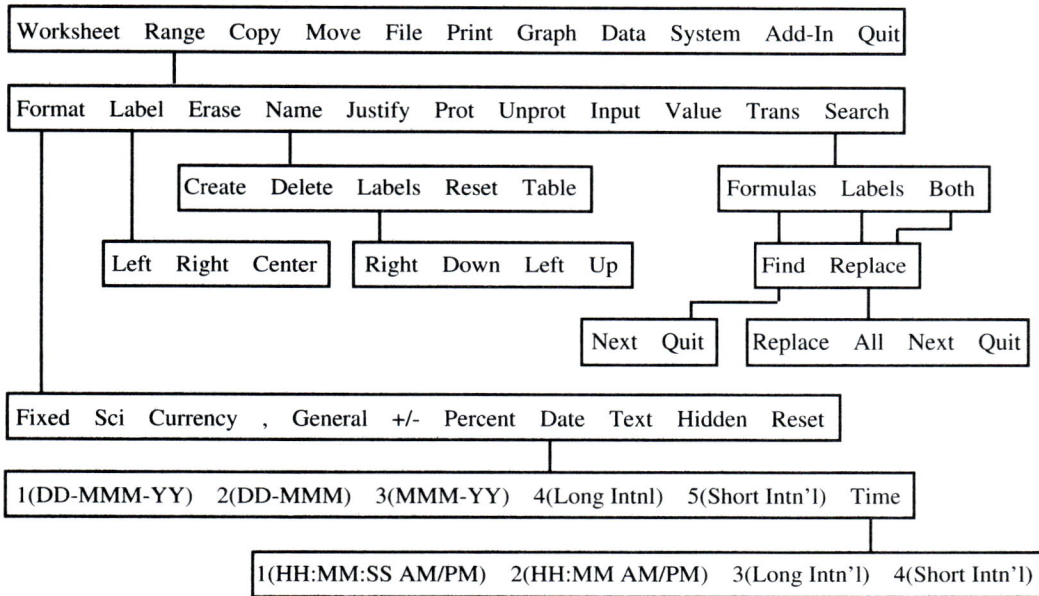

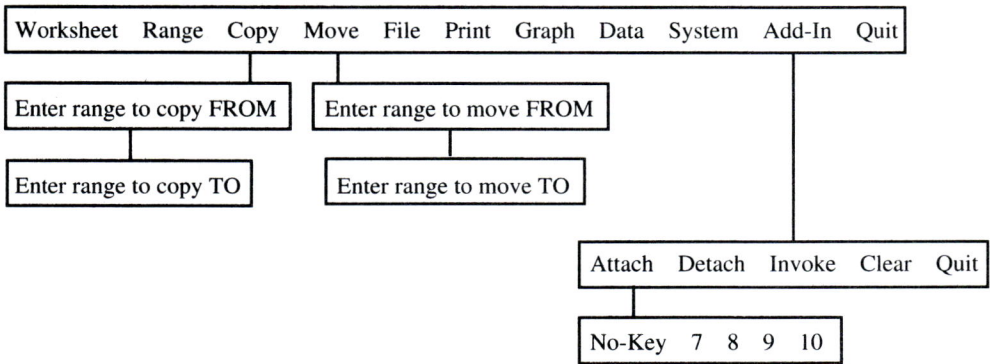

| Worksheet | Range | Copy | Move | File | Print | Graph | Data | System | Add-In | Quit |

| Format | Label | Erase | Name | Justify | Prot | Unprot | Input | Value | Trans | Search |

| Create | Delete | Labels | Reset | Table |

| Formulas | Labels | Both |

| Left | Right | Center |

| Right | Down | Left | Up |

| Find | Replace |

| Next | Quit |

| Replace | All | Next | Quit |

| Fixed | Sci | Currency | , | General | +/- | Percent | Date | Text | Hidden | Reset |

| 1(DD-MMM-YY) | 2(DD-MMM) | 3(MMM-YY) | 4(Long Intnl) | 5(Short Intn'l) | Time |

| 1(HH:MM:SS AM/PM) | 2(HH:MM AM/PM) | 3(Long Intn'l) | 4(Short Intn'l) |

| Worksheet | Range | Copy | Move | File | Print | Graph | Data | System | Add-In | Quit |

| Enter range to copy FROM |

| Enter range to move FROM |

| Enter range to copy TO |

| Enter range to move TO |

| Attach | Detach | Invoke | Clear | Quit |

| No-Key | 7 | 8 | 9 | 10 |

Lotus 1-2-3 Command Tree (continued)

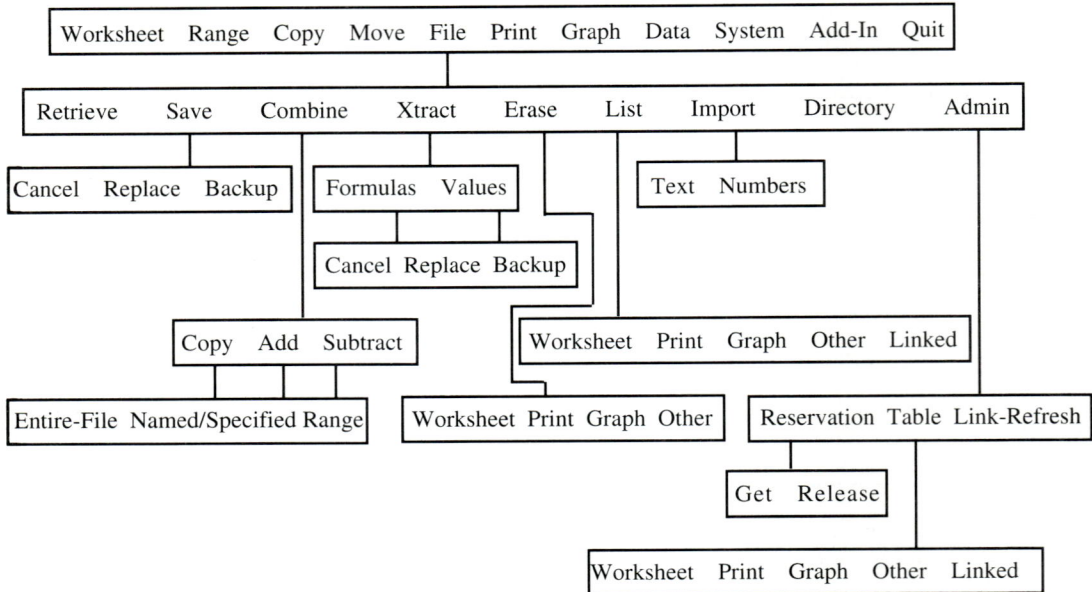

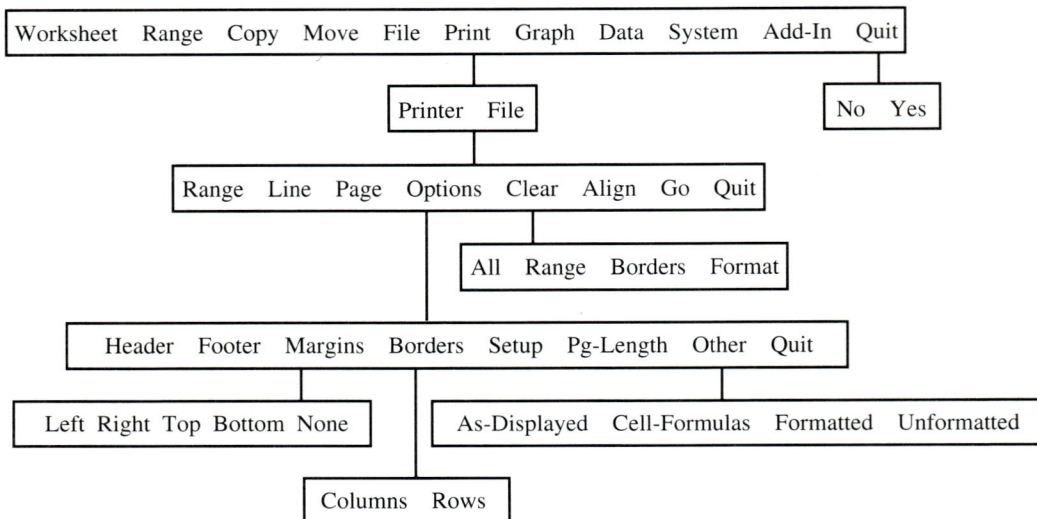

| Worksheet | Range | Copy | Move | File | Print | Graph | Data | System | Add-In | Quit |

| Retrieve | Save | Combine | Xtract | Erase | List | Import | Directory | Admin |

| Cancel | Replace | Backup |

| Formulas | Values |

| Text | Numbers |

| Cancel | Replace | Backup |

| Copy | Add | Subtract |

| Worksheet | Print | Graph | Other | Linked |

| Entire-File | Named/Specified Range |

| Worksheet | Print | Graph | Other |

| Reservation | Table | Link-Refresh |

| Get | Release |

| Worksheet | Print | Graph | Other | Linked |

| Worksheet | Range | Copy | Move | File | Print | Graph | Data | System | Add-In | Quit |

| Printer | File |

| No | Yes |

| Range | Line | Page | Options | Clear | Align | Go | Quit |

| All | Range | Borders | Format |

| Header | Footer | Margins | Borders | Setup | Pg-Length | Other | Quit |

| Left | Right | Top | Bottom | None |

| As-Displayed | Cell-Formulas | Formatted | Unformatted |

| Columns | Rows |

Lotus 1-2-3 Command Tree (continued)

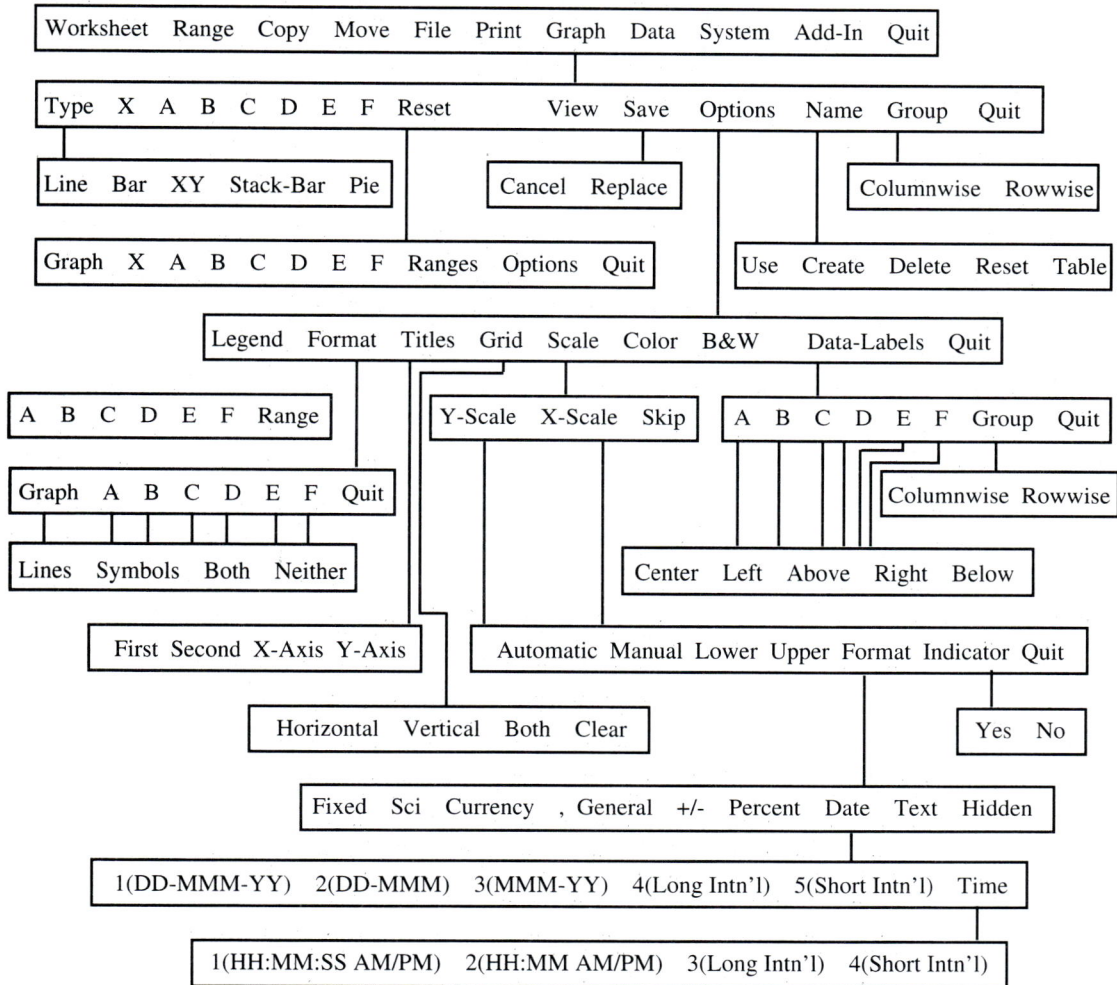

Worksheet Range Copy Move File Print Graph Data System Add-In Quit

Type X A B C D E F Reset   View Save   Options Name Group Quit

Line Bar XY Stack-Bar Pie   Cancel Replace   Columnwise Rowwise

Graph X A B C D E F Ranges Options Quit   Use Create Delete Reset Table

Legend Format Titles Grid Scale Color B&W   Data-Labels Quit

A B C D E F Range   Y-Scale X-Scale Skip   A B C D E F Group Quit

Graph A B C D E F Quit   Columnwise Rowwise

Lines Symbols Both Neither   Center Left Above Right Below

First Second X-Axis Y-Axis   Automatic Manual Lower Upper Format Indicator Quit

Horizontal Vertical Both Clear   Yes No

Fixed Sci Currency , General +/- Percent Date Text Hidden

1(DD-MMM-YY) 2(DD-MMM) 3(MMM-YY) 4(Long Intn'l) 5(Short Intn'l) Time

1(HH:MM:SS AM/PM) 2(HH:MM AM/PM) 3(Long Intn'l) 4(Short Intn'l)

Lotus 1-2-3 Command Tree (continued)

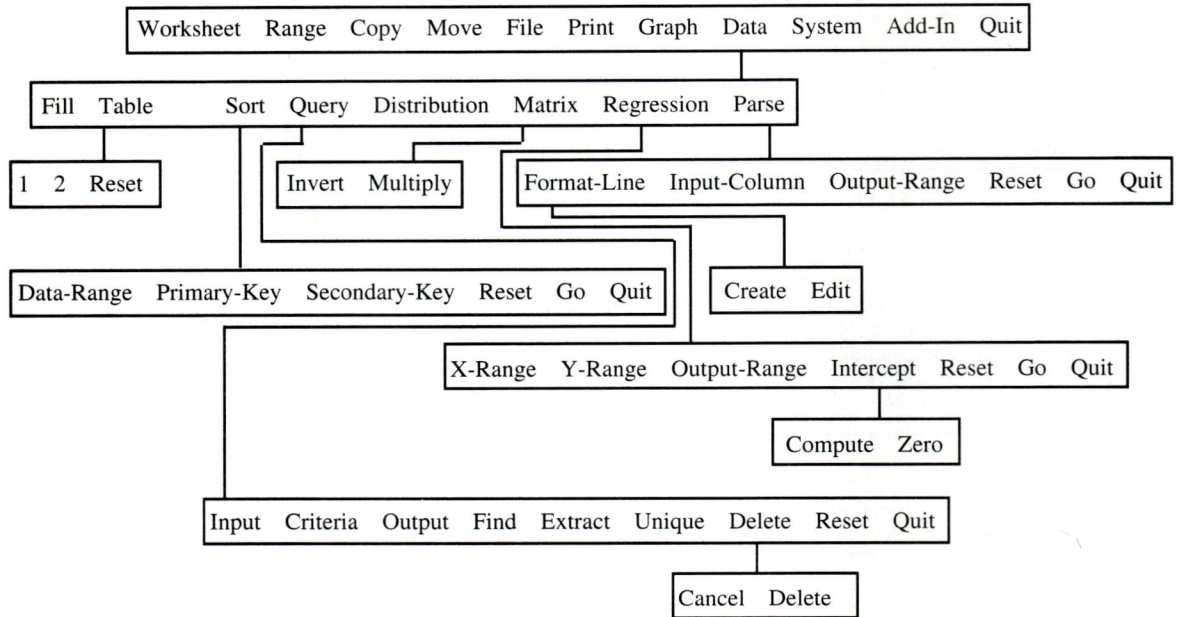

Worksheet	Range	Copy	Move	File	Print	Graph	Data	System	Add-In	Quit

Fill	Table		Sort	Query	Distribution	Matrix	Regression	Parse

1	2	Reset

Invert	Multiply

Format-Line	Input-Column	Output-Range	Reset	Go	Quit

Data-Range	Primary-Key	Secondary-Key	Reset	Go	Quit

Create	Edit

X-Range	Y-Range	Output-Range	Intercept	Reset	Go	Quit

Compute	Zero

Input	Criteria	Output	Find	Extract	Unique	Delete	Reset	Quit

Cancel	Delete

Allways Command Tree

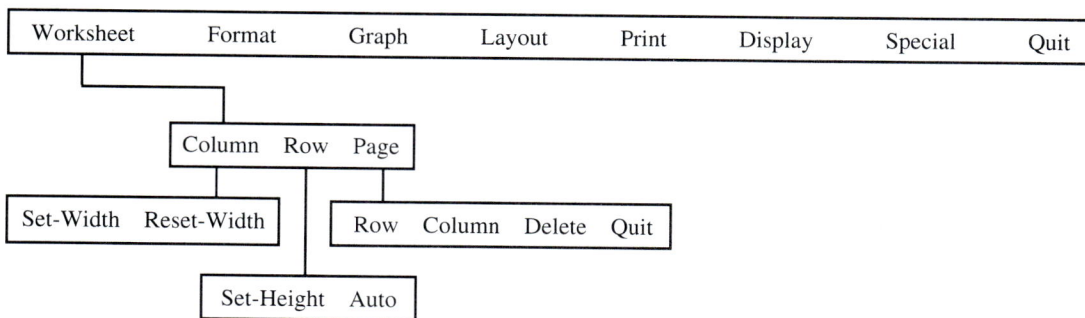

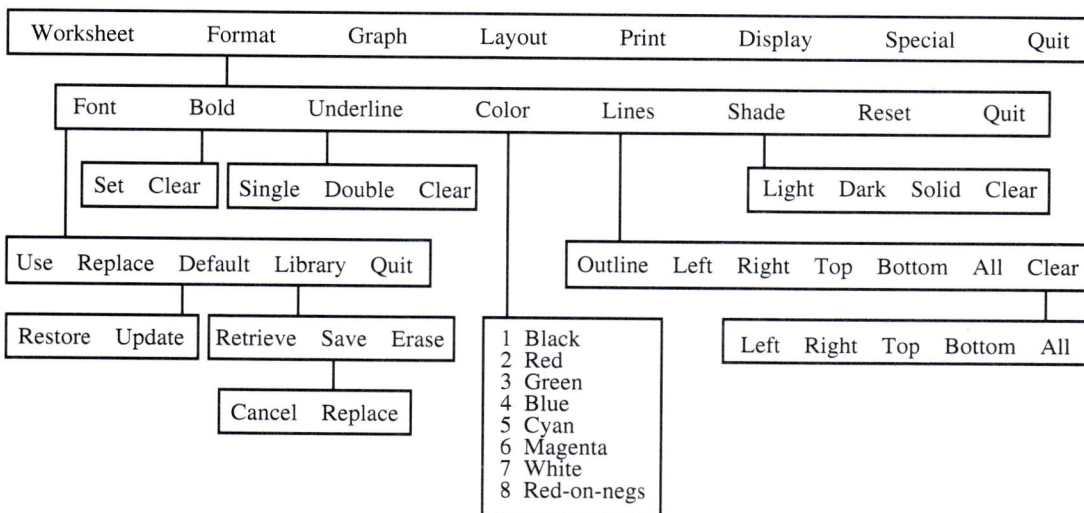

Worksheet	Format	Graph	Layout	Print	Display	Special	Quit

Column	Row	Page

Set-Width	Reset-Width

Row	Column	Delete	Quit

Set-Height	Auto

Worksheet	Format	Graph	Layout	Print	Display	Special	Quit

Font	Bold	Underline	Color	Lines	Shade	Reset	Quit

Set	Clear

Single	Double	Clear

Light	Dark	Solid	Clear

Use	Replace	Default	Library	Quit

Outline	Left	Right	Top	Bottom	All	Clear

Restore	Update

Retrieve	Save	Erase

Left	Right	Top	Bottom	All

1 Black
2 Red
3 Green
4 Blue
5 Cyan
6 Magenta
7 White
8 Red-on-negs

Cancel	Replace

Allways Command Tree (continued)

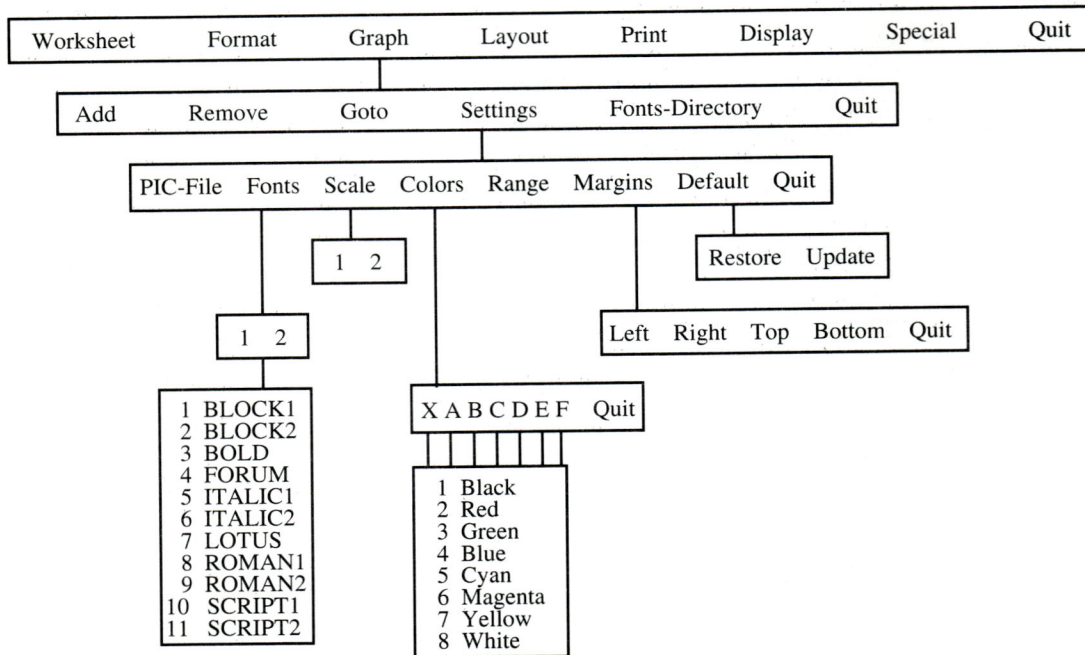

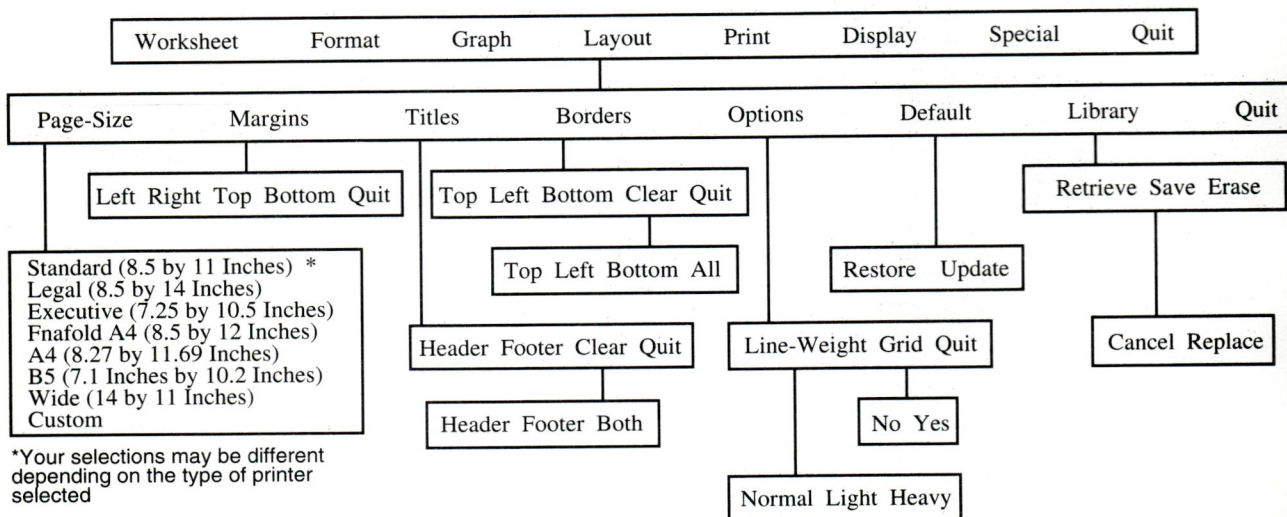

Worksheet	Format	Graph	Layout	Print	Display	Special	Quit

Add	Remove	Goto	Settings	Fonts-Directory	Quit

PIC-File	Fonts	Scale	Colors	Range	Margins	Default	Quit

1	2

Restore	Update

1	2

Left	Right	Top	Bottom	Quit

X A B C D E F	Quit

Fonts:
1	BLOCK1
2	BLOCK2
3	BOLD
4	FORUM
5	ITALIC1
6	ITALIC2
7	LOTUS
8	ROMAN1
9	ROMAN2
10	SCRIPT1
11	SCRIPT2

Colors:
1	Black
2	Red
3	Green
4	Blue
5	Cyan
6	Magenta
7	Yellow
8	White

Worksheet	Format	Graph	Layout	Print	Display	Special	Quit

Page-Size	Margins	Titles	Borders	Options	Default	Library	**Quit**

Left	Right	Top	Bottom	Quit

Top	Left	Bottom	Clear	Quit

Restore	Update

Retrieve	Save	Erase

Top	Left	Bottom	All

Cancel	Replace

Page-Size:
```
Standard (8.5 by 11 Inches)  *
Legal (8.5 by 14 Inches)
Executive (7.25 by 10.5 Inches)
Fnafold A4 (8.5 by 12 Inches)
A4 (8.27 by 11.69 Inches)
B5 (7.1 Inches by 10.2 Inches)
Wide (14 by 11 Inches)
Custom
```

Header	Footer	Clear	Quit

Line-Weight	Grid	Quit

*Your selections may be different
depending on the type of printer
selected

Header	Footer	Both

No	Yes

Normal	Light	Heavy

Allways Command Tree (continued)

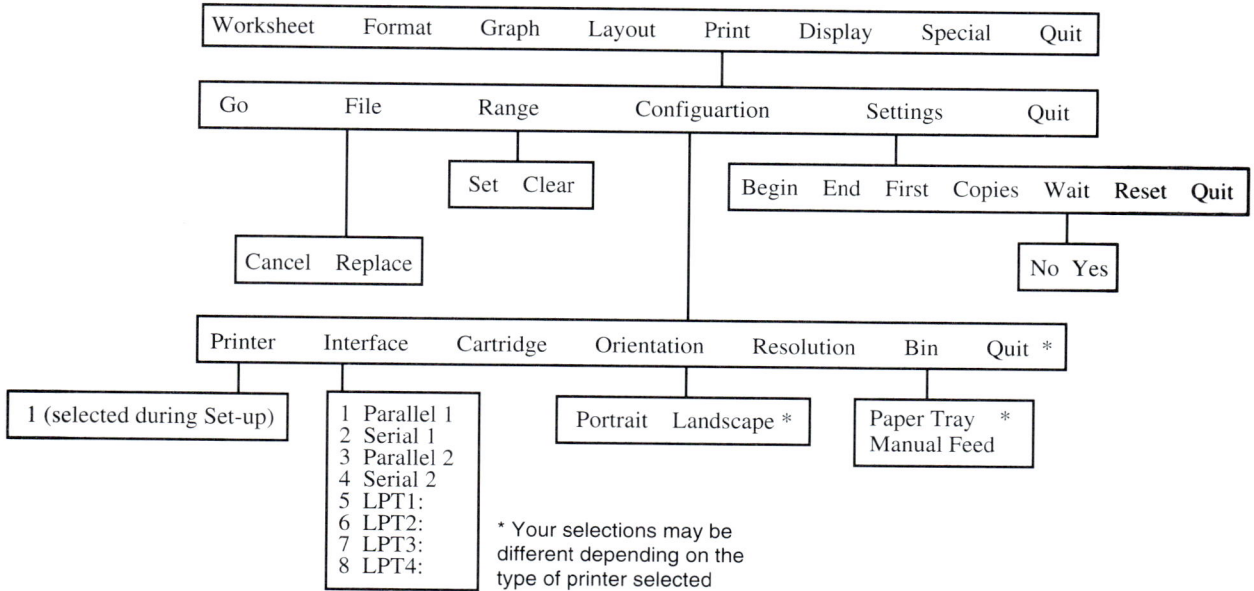

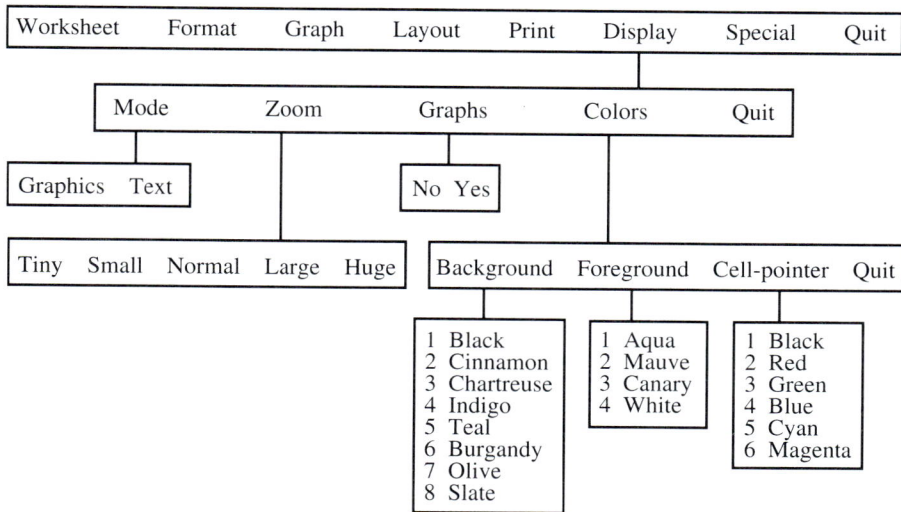

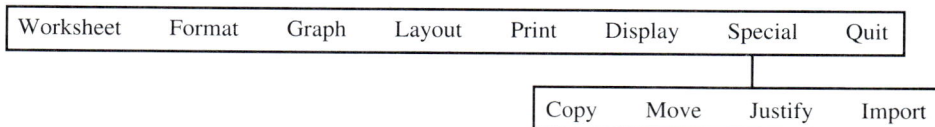

Worksheet	Format	Graph	Layout	Print	Display	Special	Quit

Go	File	Range	Configuartion	Settings	Quit

Set	Clear

Begin	End	First	Copies	Wait	**Reset**	**Quit**

Cancel	Replace

No	Yes

Printer	Interface	Cartridge	Orientation	Resolution	Bin	Quit *

1 (selected during Set-up)

Portrait	Landscape *

| Paper Tray * |
| Manual Feed |

1 Parallel 1
2 Serial 1
3 Parallel 2
4 Serial 2
5 LPT1:
6 LPT2:
7 LPT3:
8 LPT4:

* Your selections may be
different depending on the
type of printer selected

Worksheet	Format	Graph	Layout	Print	Display	Special	Quit

Mode	Zoom	Graphs	Colors	Quit

Graphics	Text

No	Yes

Tiny	Small	Normal	Large	Huge

Background	Foreground	Cell-pointer	Quit

Background	Foreground	Cell-pointer
1 Black	1 Aqua	1 Black
2 Cinnamon	2 Mauve	2 Red
3 Chartreuse	3 Canary	3 Green
4 Indigo	4 White	4 Blue
5 Teal		5 Cyan
6 Burgandy		6 Magenta
7 Olive		
8 Slate		

Worksheet	Format	Graph	Layout	Print	Display	Special	Quit

Copy	Move	Justify	Import

Lotus PrintGraph Command Tree

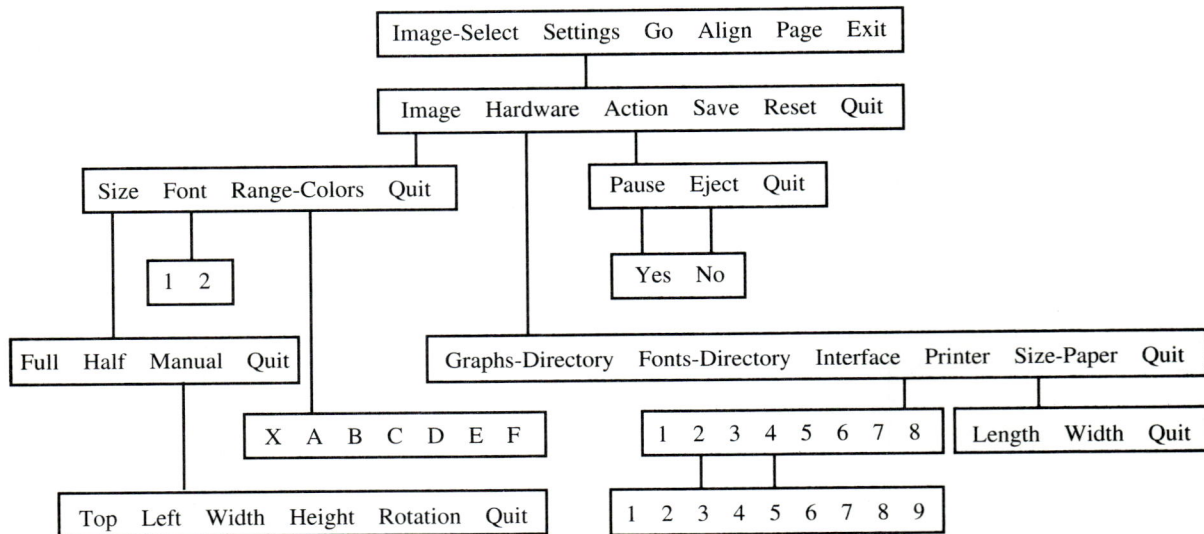

```
┌──────────────────────────────────────────────────────────────┐
│  Image-Select   Settings   Go   Align   Page   Exit           │
└──────────────────────────────────────────────────────────────┘
              ┌──────────────────────────────────────────┐
              │  Image   Hardware   Action   Save   Reset   Quit  │
              └──────────────────────────────────────────┘
      ┌───────────────────────────────┐        ┌──────────────────────┐
      │  Size   Font   Range-Colors   Quit  │   │  Pause   Eject   Quit  │
      └───────────────────────────────┘        └──────────────────────┘
                   ┌─────┐                              ┌──────────┐
                   │ 1  2 │                             │  Yes   No │
                   └─────┘                              └──────────┘
   ┌───────────────────────────┐   ┌─────────────────────────────────────────────────────────────────────┐
   │  Full   Half   Manual   Quit │ │  Graphs-Directory   Fonts-Directory   Interface   Printer   Size-Paper   Quit │
   └───────────────────────────┘   └─────────────────────────────────────────────────────────────────────┘
                 ┌─────────────────────┐     ┌──────────────────────────┐   ┌─────────────────────────┐
                 │  X  A  B  C  D  E  F │     │  1  2  3  4  5  6  7  8   │   │  Length   Width   Quit   │
                 └─────────────────────┘     └──────────────────────────┘   └─────────────────────────┘
   ┌──────────────────────────────────────────────┐   ┌────────────────────────────┐
   │  Top   Left   Width   Height   Rotation   Quit │   │  1  2  3  4  5  6  7  8  9   │
   └──────────────────────────────────────────────┘   └────────────────────────────┘
```

Macro
Key Names*

1-2-3 key	Macro key name
↓	{DOWN} or {D}
↑	{UP} or {U}
←	{LEFT} or {L}
→	{RIGHT} or {R}
Abs (F4)	{ABS}
App1 (Alt-F7)	{APP1}
App2 (Alt-F8)	{APP2}

*Based on the Lotus 1-2-3 Help screens. Copyright © 1990 Lotus Development Corporation. Used with permission.

App3 (Alt-F9)	{APP3}
App4 (Alt-F10)	{APP4}
Backspace	{BACKSPACE} or {BS}
Big Left (Ctrl-↔) or Backtab (Shift-Tab)	{BIGLEFT}
Big Right (Ctrl-→) or Tab	{BIGRIGHT}
Calc (F9)	{CALC}
Del	{DELETE} or {DEL}
Edit (F2)	{EDIT}
End	{END}
Enter	~
Esc	{ESCAPE} or {ESC}
GoTo (F5)	{GOTO}
Graph (F10)	{GRAPH}
Help (F1)	{HELP}
Home	{HOME}
Ins	{INSERT} or {INS}
Name (F3)	{NAME}
PgDn	{PGDN}
PgUp	{PGUP}
Query (F7)	{QUERY}
Table (F8)	{TABLE}
Window (F6)	{WINDOW}
/ (slash) or < (less than symbol)	{MENU}
~ (tilde)	{~}
{ (open brace)	{{}
} (close brace)	{}}

MACRO COMMANDS*

{subroutine [arg1],[arg2],...[argn]}

Calls a subroutine, which is a discrete unit of macro instructions. When 1-2-3 encounters a {subroutine} command, it

1. Shifts macro control from the current macro to the subroutine whose name or address is in the braces.
2. Passes any included arguments to the {DEFINE} command in the subroutine for evaluation and storage.

*Based on the Lotus 1-2-3 Help screens. Copyright © 1990 Lotus Development Corporation. Used with permission.

3. Executes the instructions in the subroutine.

4. When it reaches a {RETURN} command or a blank or numeric cell in the subroutine, returns macro control to the original macro location and continues the macro at the instruction immediately following the {subroutine} command.

{?}   Suspends macro execution to let you move the cell pointer, complete part of a command, or enter data. When you press Enter, the macro continues. To have the macro enter what you typed while the macro was suspended, follow {?} with a ~ (tilde).

{BEEP [tone-number]}   Sounds your computer's bell. The optional tone-number argument (1, 2, 3, or 4) determines the tone. Use {BEEP} to signal the end of a macro or to alert a user to an on-screen message.

{BLANK location}   Erases the contents of location.

{BORDERSOFF} and {BORDERSON}   {BORDERSOFF} suppresses display of the worksheet frame (column letters and row numbers). The command remains in effect until 1-2-3 reaches {BORDERSON} command or the macro ends. {BORDERSOFF} and {BORDERSON} are identical to {FRAMEOFF} and {FRAMEON}.

{BRANCH location}   Transfers macro control from the current column of macro instructions to the macro instructions in location. Use {BRANCH} in conjunction with {IF} to have the macro do different things depending on the current data. You can also use {BRANCH} to create a looping (repeating) macro.

{BREAK}

During data entry or selection of a 1-2-3 command, returns 1-2-3 to Ready mode. {BREAK} will not interrupt a macro.

{BREAKOFF}

Disables Ctrl-Break, preventing interruption of a macro until the macro ends or reaches {BREAKON}.

{BREAKON}

Restores use of Ctrl-Break while a macro is running, undoing a {BREAKOFF} command.

{CLOSE}

Closes the open text file, if one is open. After executing a {CLOSE} command, 1-2-3 goes directly to the next cell in the macro. Do not enter macro instructions on the same line after the {CLOSE} command because 1-2-3 will not execute them.

{CONTENTS target-location,source-location, [width],[cell-format]}

Copies the contents of source-location to target-location as a label. Use {CONTENTS} to store a numeric value as a string in order to use it in a string formula.

Code numbers for [cell-format]:

0..15	Fixed, 0-15 decimals	117	Text
16..31	Scientific, 0-15 decimals	118	Hidden
32..47	Currency, 0-15 decimals	119	D6 (HH:MM:SS AM/PM)
48..63	Percent, 0-15 decimals	120	D7 (HH:MM AM/PM)
64..79	Comma, 0-15 decimals	121	D4 (Long Intn'l Date)
112	+/-	122	D5 (Short Intn'l Date)
113	General	123	D8 (Long Intn'l Time)
114	D1 (DD-MMM-YY)	124	D9 (Short Intn'l Time)
115	D2 (DD-MMM)	127	Worksheet's global cell format
116	D3 (MMM-YY)		

{DEFINE location1,location2,...,locationN}

Stores arguments passed to a subroutine in a {subroutine} command so those arguments can be used later in the subroutine. {DEFINE} must have the same number of arguments as the corresponding {subroutine}. By default, {DEFINE} stores {subroutine} arguments as labels. To have {DEFINE} store a {subroutine} argument as a number, formula, or cell reference, add the suffix, :value (:v) to the argument.

{DISPATCH location}

Performs an indirect branch by transferring macro control to the cell whose name or address is entered in location. Location must be a single cell.

{FILESIZE location}

Enters in location the number of bytes in the open text file.

{FOR counter,start-number,stop-number, step-number,subroutine}

Creates a for loop that repeats the specified subroutine. The start, stop, and step (increment) numbers determine the total number of repetitions. The counter cell keeps track of the repetitions performed so far.

{FORBREAK}

Immediately ends a for loop created by a {FOR} command. Macro execution continues at the macro instruction that immediately follows the {FOR} command. Caution: Use {FORBREAK} only within a for loop. Using it anywhere else causes the macro to terminate with an error.

{FRAMEOFF} and {FRAMEON}

{FRAMEOFF} suppresses display of the worksheet frame (column letters and row numbers). The command remains in effect until 1-2-3 reaches a {FRAMEON} command or the macro end {FRAMEOFF} and {FRAMEON} are identical to {BORDERSOFF} and {BORDERSON}.

{GET location}

Suspends macro execution until you press a key, records your keystroke as a label in location, and continues the macro. You can press any key except Ctrl-Break.

{GETLABEL prompt-string,location}

Displays prompt in the control panel and suspends macro execution while you type a response. When you press Enter, 1-2-3 stores whatever you typed as a left-aligned label in location and continues the macro.

{GETNUMBER prompt-string,location}

Displays prompt in the control panel and suspends macro execution while you type a response. The response must be a number or a numeric formula. When you press Enter, 1-2-3 stores the number in location and continues the macro.

{GETPOS location}

Enters a number in location. This number reports the current byte pointer position (the position at which data is read from or written to) in the open text file. After executing a {GETPOS} command, 1-2-3 skips any further macro instructions in the same cell and goes directly to the next cell in the macro. If no file is open, 1-2-3 ignores {GETPOS} and executes the instructions that follow it in the same cell.

{GRAPHOFF}

Removes a graph displayed by a {GRAPHON} command and redisplays the worksheet.

{GRAPHON [named-graph],[nodisplay]}

Has three possible results, depending on the arguments you use. In all cases, the macro continues to run while {GRAPHON} is in effect.

1. {GRAPHON} with no arguments displays the current graph.
2. {GRAPHON named-graph} makes the named-graph settings current and displays the graph.

3. {GRAPHON named-graph,nodisplay} makes the named-graph settings current but does not display the graph.

{GRAPHON} ends when 1-2-3 reaches {GRAPHOFF}, another {GRAPHON}, or the end of the macro. In addition, if {GRAPHON} is displaying a graph, it ends when the macro reaches any advanced macro command that displays a prompt or menu in the control panel, a {?} command, or an {INDICATE} command.

{IF condition}	Evaluates condition as true or false. If condition is true, 1-2-3 executes the macro instructions that follow the {IF} command in the same cell. If condition is false, 1-2-3 skips to the cell below the {IF} command and executes the macro instructions there. Condition is typically a logical formula (a formula that uses one of the logical operators < > = <> >= <= #NOT# #AND# #OR#) or a reference to a cell that contains a logical formula.
{INDICATE [string]}	Changes the mode indicator (in the upper right corner of the screen) to string. {INDICATE} with no argument restores standard operation of the mode indicator.
{LET location,entry}	Enters a number or label in location. Entry can be a number, literal string, formula, or reference to a cell that contains a number, string, or formula. You can add the suffix :string (:s) or :value (:v) to entry to tell 1-2-3 whether to treat the argument as a literal string or to evaluate the argument before entering it.
{LOOK location}	Records in location the first keystroke in the keyboard buffer. If the buffer is empty, enters an apostrophe in location.

INDEX